A History of Central Banking in Great Britain and the United States

Central banks in Great Britain and the United States arose early in the financial revolution. The Bank of England was created in 1694, whereas the first banks of the United States appeared during 1791–1811 and 1816–36 and were followed by the Independent Treasury, formed from 1846 to 1914. These institutions, together with the Suffolk Bank and the New York Clearing House, exercised important central banking functions before the creation of the Federal Reserve System in 1913. Significant monetary changes in the lives of these British and American institutions are examined within a framework that deals with the knowledge and behavior of central bankers and their interactions with economists and politicians. Central bankers' behavior has shown considerable continuity in the influence of incentives and their interest in the stability of the financial markets. For example, the Federal Reserve's behavior during the Great Depression and the periods of low inflation of the 1990s and its resurgence the next decade follow from its structure and from government pressures rather than from accidents of personnel.

John H. Wood is R. J. Reynolds Professor of Economics at Wake Forest University, Winston-Salem, North Carolina. He has also taught at the Universities of Birmingham, Pennsylvania, and Singapore and at Northwestern University. A Life Fellow of Clare Hall, Cambridge, and a Visiting Fellow of the American Institute for Economic Research, Professor Wood has also been a full-time or visiting economist at the Federal Reserve Board and the Federal Reserve Banks of Chicago, Dallas, and Philadelphia. His earlier studies of central banking include in 1967 the first application of the theory of economic policy to Federal Reserve behavior. Professor Wood's research has appeared in leading journals such as the *American Economic Review*, *Journal of Political Economy*, *Quarterly Journal of Economics*, *Journal of Finance*, and *Journal of Monetary Economics*.

STUDIES IN MACROECONOMIC HISTORY

SERIES EDITOR: Michael D. Bordo, *Rutgers University*

EDITORS: Forrest Capie, *City University Business School, London*
Barry Eichengreen, *University of California, Berkeley*
Nick Crafts, *London School of Economics*
Angela Redish, *University of British Columbia*

The titles in this series investigate themes of interest to economists and economic historians in the rapidly developing field of macroeconomic history. The four areas covered include the application of monetary and finance theory, international economics, and quantitative methods to historical problems; the historical application of growth and development theory and theories of business fluctuations; the history of domestic and international monetary, financial, and other macroeconomic institutions; and the history of international monetary and financial systems. The series amalgamates the former Cambridge University Press series *Studies in Monetary and Financial History* and *Studies in Quantitative Economic History*.

Other books in the series:

Norio Tamaki
Japanese Banking
0-521-49676-4

*Competition and Monopoly
in the Federal Reserve System,
1914–1951*
Mark Toma
0-521-56258-9

*The Strategy and Consistency of
Federal Reserve Monetary Policy,
1924–1933*
David C. Wheelock
0-521-39155-5

*Banking Panics of the Great
Depression*
Elmus Wicker
0-521-66346-6

Monetary Regimes in Transition
Michael D. Bordo and Forrest
Capie, editors
0-521-41906-9

Canada and the Gold Standard
Trevor J. O. Dick and John E.
Floyd
0-521-40408-8

Elusive Stability
Barry Eichengreen
0-521-44847-6

Europe's Postwar Recovery
Barry Eichengreen, editor
0-521-48279-8

A History of Central Banking in Great Britain and the United States

JOHN H. WOOD

Wake Forest University

CAMBRIDGE
UNIVERSITY PRESS

CAMBRIDGE UNIVERSITY PRESS
Cambridge, New York, Melbourne, Madrid, Cape Town, Singapore, São Paulo

Cambridge University Press
40 West 20th Street, New York, NY 10011-4211, USA

www.cambridge.org
Information on this title: www.cambridge.org/9780521850131

First published 2005

Printed in the United States of America

A catalog record for this book is available from the British Library.

Library of Congress Cataloging in Publication Data

Wood, John H. (John Harold)
A history of central banking in Great Britain and the United States / John H. Wood.
p.   cm. – (Studies in macroeconomic history)
Includes bibliographical references and index.
ISBN 0-521-85013-4 (hardcover)
1. Banks and banking, Central – Great Britain – History.   2. Bank of England – History.
3. Monetary policy – Great Britain – History.   4. Banks and banking, Central – United
States – History.   5. Board of Governors of the Federal Reserve System (U.S.) – History.
6. Monetary policy – United States – History.   I. Title.   II. Series.
HG2994.W66   2005
332.1′1′0941–dc22   2004024984

ISBN-13   978-0-521-85013-1 hardback
ISBN-10   0-521-85013-4 hardback

To Norma, as always

Whoever, then, possessed the power of regulating the quantity of money could always govern its value. But the currency . . . was left entirely under the management and control of a company of merchants – individuals, he was most ready to admit, of the best character, and actuated by the best intentions; but who, nevertheless, . . . did not acknowledge the true principles of the currency, and who, in fact, in his opinion, did not know anything about it.

David Ricardo, House of Commons, June 12, 1822

[N]o semblance of acquisitiveness prompts [the Federal Reserve Board's] operations; no banking interest is behind, and no financial interest can pervert or control it. It is an altruistic institution, a part of the Government itself, representing the American people, with powers such as no man would dare misuse.

Carter Glass, House of Representatives, September 10, 1913

Contents

Figures

Plates

Tables

Preface

I have been involved in monetary policy only remotely in groups briefing Federal Reserve Bank presidents for Federal Open Market Committee meetings, but I have had numerous opportunities to observe policymakers and their close advisors: as a graduate student at the Federal Reserve Bank of Chicago, an economist at the Federal Reserve Board, and visitor at the Federal Reserve Banks of Philadelphia, Dallas, and Chicago. It has always been clear to me – at first very disapprovingly, then less so – that central bankers do not see the world like economists. Examinations of the statements and actions of earlier central bankers in Great Britain as well as the United States convinced me that this has always been so.

I do not touch on the questions of whether central banks have been more harmful than beneficial or whether they ought to exist, but rather on understanding them. I hope the study will come across as a sympathetic inquiry by an economist into the knowledge and behavior of central bankers – into what makes them tick. I give them no grades, but I hope that a better understanding of the continuity of their behavior, while at the same time recognizing that they are not immune to ideas, may promote a more useful interaction between them and economists.

Much of the research and writing of this book took place at Clare Hall, Cambridge, with its access to the University and Marshall Libraries, and at the American Institute for Economic Research, Great Barrington, Massachusetts. I am grateful to these institutions and to the above-the-call-of-duty editorial guidance and advice of Michael Bordo, Robert Hetzel, and Anna Schwartz. Most of my other debts are revealed in the citations to the many excellent studies of central banking of which I am one of the fortunate inheritors.

ONE

Understanding Central Bankers and Monetary Policy

Our monetary system is unprecedented. After decades of instability, central bankers, governments, and economists have reached a consensus that the appropriate role of a central bank in the prevailing fiat-money regime includes: (1) the clear assignment of the responsibility for inflation to the central bank; (2) agreement that inflation should be low and stable; (3) rejection of price controls as a means of controlling inflation; and (4) acceptance of whatever degree of fluctuation is required in interest rates to achieve the inflation objective. This is at once more ambitious and more modest (realistic) than earlier systems. The gold standard was a way to price stability in the long run, and Keynesian monetary and fiscal policies aspired to multiple (if inconsistent) price and quantity goals.

The system is not accidental. This book traces its development through successive interactions of central bankers, economic ideas, and governments, all affected in greater or lesser degrees by the experiences of earlier systems. There are several excellent histories of central banking for particular periods.[1] However, this is the first attempt to tie the threads across

---

[1] Standouts include the authorized histories of the Bank of England by John Clapham (for 1797–1914), Ralph Sayers (1890–1944), and John Fforde (1941–58) and, for the United States, Richard Timberlake's history of monetary policy from Alexander Hamilton to Alan Greenspan and Milton Friedman and Anna Schwartz's *Monetary History of the United States from 1867 to 1960*. Further useful studies of British experiences are those of T. Fortune, *A Concise and Authentic History of the Bank of England*, Thorold Rogers, *The First Nine Years of the Bank of England*, A. Andreades, *History of the Bank of England*, A. E. Feavearyear, *The Pound Sterling*, Marston Acres, *The Bank of England from Within*, P. G. M. Dickson, *The Financial Revolution in England: A Study in the Development of Public Credit, 1688–1756*, R. G. Hawtrey, *A Century of Bank Rate*, and Richard Roberts and David Kynaston, *The Bank of England: Money, Power and Influence, 1694–1994*. An

three centuries within a unified framework that is made up not only of monetary theory but of the situations of central bankers in the financial markets. The story is told from the standpoints of central bankers in two countries, from the establishments of the Bank of England in 1694 and the Bank of the United States in 1791, although similar policy regimes in Europe and elsewhere suggest that it has wider applicability (which will be examined in the last chapter).

The focus on central bankers has several advantages for understanding the monetary system. Their position at the center provides a unique perspective on the progress of events, and their responsibility for day-to-day policy gives their exchanges with governments insight into policy in practice. The views of policymakers as revealed in the statements of Governors Whitmore, Harman, and Palmer before parliamentary inquiries in 1810, 1832, and 1848 are not found elsewhere; nor are Governor Hankey's quarrel with the *Economist's* Walter Bagehot, Governor Lidderdale's reactions to the Crisis of 1890, Governor Norman's defenses of resumption in the 1920s, the resistance of Governors Cobbold and Cromer to government pressures in the 1950s and 1960s, or Governor George's exposition of the new consensus in 1998.[2] The institutions of American monetary policy have been more changeable, but Nicholas Biddle's defense against Andrew Jackson's war on the Second Bank of the United States and the explanations of Treasury monetary policies by Secretaries Guthrie, Sherman, and Shaw and of Federal Reserve policies by Governors Strong, Harrison, Eccles, Martin, Maisel, Burns, Volcker, and Greenspan are equally valuable. Heads of Federal Reserve Banks were called governors before the Banking Act of 1935 (for example, New York's Benjamin Strong and George Harrison); they were called presidents thereafter.

Finally, their common situation in the financial markets provides a strong element of continuity to the development of central banks. We

---

American sample is provided by Parker Willis, *The Federal Reserve System*, Paul Warburg, *The Federal Reserve System: Its Origin and Growth*, Randolph Burgess, *The Reserve Banks and the Money Market*, Seymour Harris, *Twenty Years of Federal Reserve Policy*, E. A. Goldenweiser, *Federal Reserve System in Operation*, Lester Chandler, *Benjamin Strong, Central Banker* and *American Monetary Policy, 1928–41*, Elmus Wicker, *Federal Reserve Monetary Policy, 1917–33*, and David Wheelock, *The Strategy and Consistency of Federal Reserve Monetary Policy, 1924–33*. Although Alan Meltzer's history of the Federal Reserve from 1913 to 1951 did not appear until 2003, many of its previously published components are used.

[2] Jeremiah Harman, Horsley Palmer, and Thomson Hankey were past governors on these occasions (Richard Roberts and David Kynaston, eds., *The Bank of England, 1694–1994*, app. 2)

will see how central bankers' concern for financial stability has become reconciled with monetary policy. Technology has developed, but the fundamental characters of money and the credit markets, as well as of reputation and speculation, persist. Central bankers' earliest and longest experiences were within the framework of the gold standard, but their intellectual positions have been similar under paper standards.

Instead of treating monetary episodes as distinct, I examine policy as a sequence of actions by durable groups with shared experiences and environments. In the 18th century, the Bank of England – the model central bank (although its directors had to be told at the end of the century that this is what they had become) – focused on profits and survival, the latter requiring the payment of gold on demand for its notes. The long 19th century – until 1914 – saw the progress of the Bank's acceptance of a wider responsibility for financial stability, although convertibility remained in ascendance. The United States had no institution that could be called a central bank – except two short-lived Banks of the United States between 1791 and 1836 – before the establishment of the Federal Reserve in 1913. Nevertheless, the federal Treasury Department, central money markets, and clearinghouses performed central banking functions that were governed by the same ideas that prevailed across the Atlantic, that is, profits for private institutions and seigniorage for the government, subject to currency convertibility and with attention to financial stability.

Central bankers failed to cope with the disruptions of World War I and the Great Depression of the 1930s and tended to make matters worse as the old system collapsed. Monetary theory and practice since that time have to a large extent been quests for an adequate replacement of the pre-1914 system. The dollar-exchange system that was agreed at Bretton Woods in 1944 to achieve the solidity of the gold standard without its rigidity proved inconsistent with concurrent monetary stimulations, and its breakdown in the 1970s presaged an agonizing period of accelerating inflation and unemployment.

The anti-inflationary monetarist policies associated with Federal Reserve Chairman Paul Volcker and Prime Minister Margaret Thatcher may be understood as reactions to inflations that had failed to bring the promised benefits, and monetary debates since 1979 have led to the consensus just described. Commitments to the new policy were legalized in the Bank of England Act of 1998 and, less formally in the United States, by the statement of Chairmen Volcker that "price stability . . . is to be treasured and enshrined as the prime policy priority; that objective is inextricably part of a broader concern about the basic stability of the financial and economic system" and that of Chairman Greenspan, who stipulates, "Monetary policy basically is a single tool and you can only implement one goal consistently."[3]

Nonetheless, we must pay attention to Greenspan's warnings of "irrational exuberance in the stock market," as well as his worries of a shift in bankers' attitudes toward risk during the 1998 Asian financial crisis: "If there was a dime to turn on," they did, he said. A "fear-induced psychological response is provoking a sudden rush to liquidity that poses a threat to world economic growth.... When human beings are confronted with uncertainty ... they disengage." Comparing investors to a pedestrian crossing the street, he observed, "When ... you're uncertain as to whether a car is coming, you stop."[4]

Economists have been critical of central bankers' attention to the financial markets at the expense of their macroeconomic responsibilities. Allan Meltzer was in the tradition of David Ricardo when he told a congressional committee in 1964 that the Federal Reserve's "knowledge of the monetary process is woefully inadequate, ... dominated by extremely short-run week-to-week, day-to-day, or hour-to-hour events in the money and credit markets. [T]heir viewpoint is frequently that of a banker rather than that of a regulating authority for the monetary system and the economy."[5]

Notwithstanding these criticisms, we will learn how central bankers' understanding of their role in monetary policy has grown. The stage for the intellectual gap between the two groups is set in Chapter 2, which examines the Bank of England's denial of the Bullion Committee's charge of economy-wide effects of what the Bank saw as normal lending practices. Its rejection of the risks and responsibilities of managing the currency was the occasion of Ricardo's censure that opens the book. We will encounter more instances of this difference in viewpoint, but jumping ahead to 1998, we see that the conflict between the career central bankers and economists on the Bank's Monetary Policy Committee (MPC) was similar to that between the Bank and the economists on the 1810 Bullion Committee.

According to the Monetary Policy Committee's minutes, although the staff's economic model recommended a rise in the Bank's interest rate, Bank careerists favored "delaying any rise in interest rates, even if a rise

---

[3] Forrest Capie et al., eds., *The Future of Central Banking*, pp. 258, 343.

[4] *Wall Street Journal*, Dec. 9, 1996, p. C1, and Oct. 8, 1998, p. A2.

[5] *The Federal Reserve System after Fifty Years*, Hearings before the Subcommittee on Domestic Finance of the Committee on Banking and Currency, 88th Cong., 2nd sess., Feb. 11, 1964, pp. 927, 932.

were necessary."[6] They referred to "unusually large" near-term uncertainties and did not "feel very confident about the outlook and it would not necessarily be right to draw policy conclusions mechanically from the [staff's] projection. In these circumstances there was a case for delay so as to allow judgment to be made later in the light of more information." If the downturn proved sharper than expected, an increase in interest rates might have a severe negative effect on output, "and would have to be quickly reversed. Such a reversal could impair confidence in the economy" and create "confusion about monetary policy.... There was thus a strong case for waiting to get a clearer impression of the extent of the slowdown in the economy before taking policy action."[7]

This thinking was like that of the Bank directors in 1819, who protested Ricardo's money rule as "fraught with very great uncertainty and risk" in which "discretionary power is to be taken away from the Bank," and might, because of the impossibility of deciding "beforehand what shall be the course of events," impose "an unrelenting continuance of pecuniary pressures upon the commercial world of which it is impossible for them either to foresee or estimate the consequences."

The 1998 Committee's academic economists opposed this position by arguing that "policy should reflect the latest news and that uncertainty in itself was no reason for delay." They believed that to delay decisions to reduce the risks of reversal was "irrational." "So long as any policy reversals could be properly explained by new developments or improved analysis of the outlook, they need not create confusion about policy.... [T]he desire to minimise the risk of policy reversals was likely to mean that interest rate changes would, on average, be made too late." The tie vote was broken by Governor George in favor of waiting.

Economists have found it "difficult to rationalize" central bankers' concern for smooth interest rates and short-term stability in the financial markets.[8] Nonetheless, they must take it into account. Central bankers cannot help behaving like bankers at least part of the time. Rules are incomplete, and if economists hope to explain and influence the conduct

---

[6] Those with histories as primarily academic economists on the Monetary Policy Committee were Sir Alan Budd, Professors Willem Buiter and Charles Goodhart, and Deputy Governor Mervyn King; those with careers at the Bank or in industry were Governor Edward George, Deputy Governor Ian Plenderleith, David Clementi, and DeAnne Julius.

[7] This and the next paragraph are from MPC minutes for February and May 1998, Bank of England, *Inflation Report*, May and August 1998.

[8] Lars Svensson, "What Is Wrong with Taylor Rules? Using Judgment in Monetary Policy through Targeting Rules."

of monetary policy, they need to try to understand central bankers on their own ground. Central bankers are informed parties to the new consensus, but monetary policy results from the interplay of central bankers' pragmatism with economists' ideas and the wishes of governments.

The latter – the ultimate authority – cannot be ignored. The freedoms that central banks have been given can be taken away. Past government attitudes toward central banks have depended on their need for them. The end of war (and government pressure for cheap finance) brought an increase in the Bank of England's independence in 1833 similar to that given in 1998. President Jackson's veto of the renewal of the charter of the Bank of the United States in 1832 was influenced by the approaching end of the national debt. Senator Thomas Hart Benton declared, "The war made the Bank; peace will unmake it."[9]

The greater independence of the Federal Reserve after the collapse of the Soviet Union might have reflected the government's diminished need for finance as much as the public's revulsion to inflation and disillusionment with the Phillips Curve. By the same token, the deficits arising from the War on Terror will bring pressure for monetization. In any case, monetary policy is at bottom a political decision.

Legislatures have also paid attention to central banks in peacetime, especially during the periods of price instability following wars, during the Great Depression, and in the 1970s. Monetary standards are decided by governments. The creation of the International Monetary Fund in 1944 and its rejection by President Nixon in 1971 were not unusual in the minimal roles played by the central bank. Wartime suspensions, devaluations, gold standard acts, and the creation of the Federal Reserve were political decisions. The task of central bankers even at the height of "independence" is the daily conduct of policy within the framework set by government.

Governments have taken direct control of monetary policy when they lost confidence in central banks. Their institutional shells remained, but monetary control was transferred in the early 1930s to the Treasury in both countries. The Federal Reserve regained control in 1951 when public opinion and Congress determined that the president had abused his monetary powers, a victory that had to be won again in 1979. The Bank of England, although possessing advisory influence, did not approach its former powers until the 1990s.

---

[9] U.S. Senate, February 2, 1831; Herman Krooss, *Documentary History of Banking and Currency in the United States*, p. 736.

The last chapter surveys the present and speculates about the future of central banking. The current consensus rests on an understanding, developed over many years of hard experience, of what monetary policy can do. Central bankers apparently understand their assignment, although history shows that they also take the financial markets and political pressures seriously. Nevertheless, if we accept the goal of low inflation in free markets, with the understanding that this is the best that monetary policy can do, central bankers will be able to adjust to unusual events in ways that substantially deliver the goal while smoothing the financial markets – such as when the Federal Reserve supplied liquidity after the 1987 stock market crash, during the run-up to the millennium, and after 9/11, and also when it tries to soften the impact of monetary policy on the money markets by improving its transparency.[10]

---

[10] Such cases include the asymmetric directive and the promise in August 2003 of low interest rates "for a considerable period"; Daniel Thornton and David Wheelock, "A History of the Asymmetric Policy Directive," and Richard Anderson and Daniel Thornton, "The FOMC's 'Considerable Period'."

TWO

An Introduction to Central Bankers

Do you consider the amount of Bank of England notes during the last year to have borne nearly the same proportion to the occasions of the public as in former times? – The same proportion exactly.

When you represent the quantity of Bank of England notes to be now only proportionate, as heretofore, to the occasions of the public, do you take into consideration the increased price of all articles and the consequent increase of the amount of payments; and do you assume that the quantity of notes ought to be increased in proportion to that increase of the amount of payments? – The Bank never force a note into circulation, and there will not remain a note in circulation more than the immediate wants of the public require; for no banker, I presume, will keep a larger stock of [the Bank's] notes by him than his immediate payments require, as he can at all times procure them . . .

[Question repeated] – I have taken into consideration not only the increased price of all articles, but the increased demands upon us from other causes.

Minutes of Evidence, Bullion Committee, testimony of Governor
John Whitmore, Bank of England, March 6, 1810

So went the opening exchange between the House of Commons' Select Committee on the High Price of Gold (Bullion Committee), with Francis Horner in the Chair, and the Bank of England, represented by Governor Whitmore. This testimony played an important part in the beginnings of modern monetary theory and the intellectual discovery of central banking. Economists contended that the latter – monetary policy – properly derives from the former, while the central bankers resisted. The events surrounding the inflation that led to Parliament's enquiry are presented in the first section in this chapter, followed by a review of the

Background: People and Events
1793: Beginning of the French Wars; financial panic.
1797: Suspension of convertibility.
1799: Income tax introduced.
1805: Austerlitz and Trafalgar; Napoleon supreme on land, England at sea.
1808: Wellington's Peninsular campaign begins.
1810: Bullion Committee; resolutions voted on, May 1811.
1812: Napoleon invades Russia.
1814: Napoleon abdicates, retires to Elba; Congress of Vienna.
1815: Waterloo.

	Prime Minister	Chancellor of the Exchequer	Political Parties
1783	William Pitt	Pitt	These were Tory
1801	Henry Addington	Addington	governments,
1804	Pitt	Pitt	with the King's support,
1806	Lord Grenville	Lord Henry Petty	between the Whig
1807	Duke of Portland	Spencer Perceval	dominance under the first
1809	Perceval	Perceval	two Georges and its
1812	Earl of Liverpool	Nicholas Vansittart	resurgence in the 1830s.

Note: Short-lived ministries omitted.

Committee's proceedings. Its members stressed in a modern way the effects of an unrestrained central bank on inflation through money creation. In an equally modern way, the Bank's representatives denied responsibility and pointed to other causes.

The third section puts the debate into a longer term perspective by means of the best contemporary analyses of central banks. Henry Thornton explained in Smithian terms that there was much to be gained from a private central bank acting in the enlightened pursuit of its interests. Alexander Hamilton's discussion indicates that similar forces and ideas were at work on the other side of the Atlantic, and prefaces the appearance of American central banking in Chapter 6. The last section reviews the Bank directors' second thoughts about their responsibilities after a change in political circumstances.

War, Inflation, Suspension, and More Inflation, 1793–1810

The Bullion Committee was appointed on a motion by Horner on February 1, 1810, after two years of accelerating inflation, an adverse balance of trade, and a falling exchange rate. Horner, Henry Thornton, and others, although by no means the majority of the House of Commons, attributed these events to an excess of lending by the Bank of England made possible by the suspension in 1797 of its obligation, even its freedom, to redeem its notes for gold. War brought a growing public deficit as the government was slow to find revenue to match its increased spending. The Bank had complained of the government's pressure for funds since 1794. That pressure slackened in 1795 and 1796, but the restoration of gold convertibility in France and uncertainty of British intentions sparked a decline in the Bank's gold reserve from £6 million in February 1795 to £1 million in February 1797. When the drain was turned to panic by rumors of a French invasion and the Bank informed Chancellor of the Exchequer (and Prime Minister) William Pitt that its situation was desperate, he called a Council of State, which declared on February 26

that it is indispensably necessary for the public service that the Directors of the Bank of England should forbear issuing any cash in payment until the sense of Parliament can be taken on that subject and the proper measures adopted thereupon for maintaining the means of circulation and supporting the public and commercial credit of the kingdom at this important juncture.[1]

The order was confirmed by the Bank Restriction Act, passed on May 3, effective until June 24, and kept in force by continuing acts until 1821. Although the Act referred only to the Bank of England, other banks took the opportunity to refuse redemption of their notes, and before the end of the war the number of country banks had tripled.[2] The public acquiesced, and the country's monetary base was transformed from gold to Bank of England notes.

Later estimates (there were no contemporary price indices) indicated average inflation of about 3 percent per annum between 1797 and 1810.[3] The Bank's note and deposit liabilities grew about 6 percent per annum and the value of its notes at Hamburg, the exchange most often quoted, fell at an average rate of 2 percent.[4]

---

[1] Edwin Cannan, *The Paper Pound*, p. ix; see pp. xliii–xlvi for the data referred to here.
[2] John Tritton of Barclay & Co. estimated that the number of country banks had increased from 230 in 1797 to 721 at the time of his evidence to the Bullion Committee (April 9, 1810).
[3] W. S. Jevons, *Investigations in Currency and Finance*, p. 144, reported in Cannan's Table I.
[4] The exchange rate data are from an appendix to the fourth edition of Ricardo's *High Price of Bullion, Works*, iii, p. 121.

One of the leading critics of the inflation, Walter Boyd, pointed to its underlying cause in 1801:

Indeed it is not to be supposed that a corporation whose profits chiefly arise from the circulation of its Notes, and which is exclusively directed by persons partici- pating in the profits, has been, or could possibly be, proof against the temptation which license they have enjoyed since February 1797 has afforded.

> Walter Boyd, *A Letter to the Right Honourable William Pitt on the Influence of the Stoppage of Issues*, p. 4

An obstacle encountered by those – not excluding members of Par- liament – desiring to monitor the Bank was its secrecy. It issued no regular reports until compelled by the government in 1832. In Boyd's time it had partially yielded to pressure with coded versions of its balance sheets, which according to the actuary William Morgan, "would require an Oedipus to decypher them."[5] Pitt told the House of Lords committee of enquiry into the causes of the suspension that he had "received from the Bank confidentially the particulars . . . of their precise situation, and must beg to decline stating those particulars, unless I receive their per- mission."[6] He successfully resisted a motion in the House of Commons for information on "outstanding advances made from the Directors of the Bank to the Government" on the ground that "it would tend to divulge the private transactions of the Bank, and thereby prove injurious to pub- lic credit."[7] (The Bank records for this period used by later students and upon which Fig. 2.1 is based are from the 1832 Bank Charter Committee.) When he thought that he had found a key to the Bank's activities leading up to the suspension, Morgan wrote,

Neither our foreign trade nor our commercial intercourse at home have derived much advantage from the operations of this bank. Its chief energies have been unequivocally directed to another quarter. The advances to Government have generally been four or five times greater than the private discounts. [I]t must appear as if its principal purpose had been to enable a minister to lavish the public revenue much faster than it could ever be collected; and to furnish him with the means of engaging in the most extravagant and ruinous expence before his prodigality could be submitted to the deliberation of Parliament.

> William Morgan, "On the Finances of the Bank"

---

[5] "On the Finances of the Bank," discussed by P. Sraffa, "The 'Ingenious Calculator'," an appendix to Ricardo's *Works*, iv, pp. 415–16; and Judy Klein, *Statistical Visions in Time*, chap. 4.

[6] House of Lords, 1797, p. 7.

[7] Frank Fetter, *Development of British Monetary Orthodoxy, 1797–1875*, p. 61.

Neither the Bank nor the government admitted responsibility for the inflation, but an income tax and then the Peace of Amiens (1802–3) brought a respite.[8] The deficit was still substantial, but the government turned to the capital market. In 1808, the Bank's liabilities were only 20 percent more than in 1801 and were almost unchanged from 1805. Prices and exchange rates had stabilized, the Bank's stock of gold was replenished, and its notes were exchanged for gold at par. Convertibility might have been resumed with little difficulty. "But no Government involved in a great war is willing to give up so potent an engine for surreptitiously fleecing its subjects as an inconvertible currency, whether in its own hands or in that of a bank which it influences," the sound-money Edwin Cannan wrote in 1919 during another suspension.[9]

The year 1809 saw renewed inflation, most strikingly revealed in the price of gold. In his first appearance in print, Ricardo observed,[10]

The mint price of gold is 77 7/8 shillings and the market price has been gradually increasing, and was within these two or three weeks as high as 93s per ounce, not much less than 20 per cent. advance.

David Ricardo, *Morning Chronicle*, August 29, 1809[11]

The price of Bank notes per ounce of gold (par of £3 17s 10½d) paid by the mint before suspension is converted to *shillings*. We will be helped by definitions of the coins and related terms that were used in the bullion debate. Until decimalization in 1971, the pound consisted of 20 shillings of 12 pence each (denoted *d* from the Roman *denarius*.) The English pound, like Charlemagne's *livre*, was originally a troy (after the French city of Troyes) pound of 12 ounces or 240 pennyweights of silver. The principal gold coin at the time of suspension was the *guinea*, which had been minted since 1663 with an elephant, the mark of the African company that supplied it. An increase in the market price of gold had raised its effective exchange value to 21 shillings. The guinea was replaced by the gold *sovereign*, worth 20 shillings, in 1817, although many professional

---

[8] An income tax was introduced in 1799, repealed and reintroduced with the beginning and end of the Peace of Amiens in 1802 and 1803, repealed in 1816, and reintroduced permanently in 1842 (Roy Douglas, *Taxation in Britain since 1660*, pp. 40–52).

[9] Cannan, *op. cit.*, p. xviii.

[10] *David Ricardo* left his father's firm to set up his own business in 1793 after marriage to a Quaker had estranged them from their families; conversion to the Church of England enabled him to serve in Parliament from 1819 to 1823; he retired from business in 1814 to develop his economics, of which he had become the foremost authority; *The Principles of Political Economy and Taxation* was published in 1817.

[11] Ricardo, *Works*, iii, p. 17.

fees continued to be expressed in hypothetical guineas of 21 shillings, now £1.05.[12] "Bullion" refers to bars and ingots whereas "specie" encompasses bullion and gold and silver coin. Money was nominally bimetallic (gold and silver) but had become monometallic (gold) in practice, confirmed by statute on the resumption of convertibility in 1821.

In an application of the quantity theory of money, Ricardo contended that the high price of gold was evidence of a general increase in commodity prices caused by the over issue of Bank notes. The suspension stimulated the premier theoretical controversy in the history of money. The participants were able to use the 18th-century contributions of Richard Cantillon, David Hume, and Adam Smith, although Ricardo and the Bullion Committee may with justice be called the founders of the monetary theory that became part of the Ricardian classical system.[13] They are made even more luminous in monetary histories by their victory over the Bank directors – intellectual victory, that is, because Parliament voted its preference for the Bank's principles over the Bullion Committee's. The directors' statements showed an ignorance of the relations among money, prices, interest rates, exchange rates, and the balance of trade that was shocking in men possessing great influence over them. Walter Bagehot later called their testimony "almost classical by its nonsense."[14]

I argue that this view of the directors, although correct as far as it goes, is incomplete. It is limited to what they did not know, namely the wider, macroeconomic effects of their actions, and neglects what they knew best, and felt most – the financial markets. The Bullion Committee's questions and the Bank's answers, if so they may be called, hardly represented an exchange of views and certainly were not an argument. The two sides occupied different levels: Macroeconomic questions elicited microeconomic responses.

A primary contention of this study is that the language and decisions of the directors closely resembled those of later central bankers, which was almost inevitable in view of their common backgrounds and situations. If one's beliefs and actions are conditioned as much by experience and environment as by abstract arguments, we should not be surprised that central bankers talk and act like bankers. Most of them have been

[12] A. E. Feavearyear, *The Pound Sterling*, pp. 90, 142, 198.
[13] Cantillon, *Essay on the Nature of Trade in General*; Hume, "Of Money" and other *Writings on Economics*, reprinted in Eugene Rotwein. A useful account of early theories of money is by Jacob Viner, *Studies in the Theory of International Trade*, chaps. 1 and 2.
[14] Walter Bagehot, *Lombard Street*, p. 167.

bankers, and they operate in a bankers' milieu. They are slow to see why the practices that have worked in one institution may not apply in another. The Bank of England was to the directors just a large bank, with a special responsibility for financial stability because of its size (and they were not always conscientious in this regard, another reflection of bankers' behavior) but none for such macroeconomic variables as the price level. The directorships were part time, and the governor and deputy governor, who served in each capacity for two years, were short-term central bankers, hardly separated from their own banking and trading houses. We will see in later chapters that their views of economic relationships have been shared by their successors at the Bank and the Federal Reserve.

The Bullion Committee and the Macroeconomic Responsibilities of the Bank of England

The early witnesses before the Bullion Committee – brokers and dealers in gold and merchants in foreign trade – established the state of the currency. There had been a quiet period in the middle of the decade, but the gold market had been active since 1808, and the price exceeded 90s when the Committee met in 1810. The rate of exchange on Hamburg ($34\frac{1}{2}$ before suspension) was 29 Flemish shillings per pound sterling. The Committee believed that the depreciation of the currency was due to the increase in its quantity arising from the excessive credit – in government securities and private discounts – of the Bank of England. The governor came prepared to defend the Bank, which explains his premature response to the second question quoted at the beginning of the chapter. Before going into the Committee's efforts to break down the Bank's argument, we look at the governor's elaboration of its position in a later appearance:

State to the Committee what is the criterion which enables the Bank at all times to ascertain that the issue of Bank notes is kept precisely within the limits which the occasion of the public requires, and thereby to guard the circulation of this country against the possibility of any excess; and in what manner the control necessary for maintaining uniformly an exact proportion between the occasions of the public and the issues of the Bank, is exercised and applied by the Court of Directors. – I have already stated that we never forced a Bank note into circulation, and the criterion by which I judge of the exact proportion to be maintained is by avoiding as much as possible to discount what does not appear to be legitimate mercantile paper. The Bank notes would revert to us if there was any redundancy in circulation, as no one would pay interest for a bank note that he did not want to make use of. (March 13)

This rule – the limitation of loans to "real" transactions of merchants, as opposed to speculation – applied regardless of other terms of lending:

Is it your opinion that the same security would exist against any excess in the issues of the Bank if the rate of discount were reduced from five to four percent?

Mr. Whitmore – The security against an excess of issue would be, I conceive, precisely the same.

Mr. Pearse (deputy governor) – I concur in that answer.

If it were reduced to three percent?

Mr. Whitmore – I conceive there would be no difference, if our practice remained the same as now, of not forcing a note into circulation.

Mr. Pearse – I concur in that answer.

However, the rule was not always applied. The governor had earlier conceded (March 6) that the Bank used discretion:

Antecedently to the suspension of the cash payments of the Bank, was it not the practice of the Directors to restrain in some degree their loans or discounts in the event of their experiencing any great demand upon them for guineas [gold coins]? – The Bank always act with that prudent caution, that their advances to the public upon discount can be called in two months, or at furthest 90 days.

[Question repeated] – A short time antecedently to the restriction upon the Bank, they were seriously alarmed at a diminution of their coin, and did in some degree limit their advances, both to the public and to the Government. I would wish to be understood, that they do now set limits to their advances according to circumstances, and as their discretion may direct them. . . .

This was a last resort, however. The Bank recalled previous applications, particularly just before suspension, with regret:

I perfectly well remember the Bank limiting a certain sum of discount to be made to each commercial house applying for it; that was the mode of diminishing the whole amount of discount. I would also wish to add, that afterwards in the contemplation of many of the Directors, this last was a measure to be regretted under the then circumstances, on account of the very considerable embarrassment and inconvenience by it to the mercantile world. . . .

Thornton's analysis of the effects of credit restrictions will be presented in the next section. For the present, we focus on the Committee's attempt to get the directors to admit the macroconsequences of the Bank's actions, their denials, and their concern for financial stability.

On what principle is it now the practice of the Bank to regulate the general amount of their loans and discounts, and what was the principle antecedent to the restriction; namely, do they endeavour . . . to keep the quantity of Bank of England notes nearly at their usual level, or do they enlarge their advances to merchants when the merchants happen to extend their demands for discount

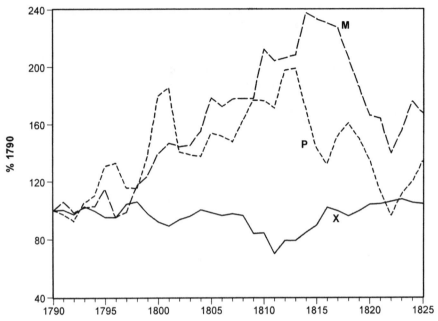

Figure 2.1. Bank of England notes and deposits (*M*), rate of exchange on Hamburg (*X*), and price level (*P*), 1790–1825 (annual averages). *Sources*: B. R. Mitchell, *British Historical Statistics*, pp. 666–67, 702, 721.

[or] by a reference to the state of the exchange, and to the difference between the market price and the mint price of Gold ... ? – We do not comply with the demands for discounts to the extent demanded of us; it has always reference, not only to the solidity of the paper, but to the amount of the accommodation the individual applying for it already has. We never discount without the circumstances being considered; namely the amount already given to the individual, the solidity of the paper, and the appearance of its being used for commercial purposes. ... I do not advert to the circumstances of the exchanges, it appearing upon a reference to the amount of our notes in circulation, and the course of exchange, that they frequently have no connexion ...

The Bank's defenders pointed to the lack of correlation between the quantity and value of the Bank's issue. Figure 2.1 shows that *M* (money) and *X* (the exchange rate) moved oppositely half the time between 1797 and 1809, and between 1809 and 1821.[15] Nicholas Vansittart, government spokesman on the Bullion Report and chancellor of the exchequer from 1812 to 1823, reminded the House of Commons in 1815 that the rise in

[15] Similar data are in R. G. Hawtrey, *Currency and Credit*, p. 283.

the price of gold between 1810 and 1813 had not been accompanied by an increase in the Bank's circulation, the price fell between August 1813 and October 1814 while the circulation rose (the French armies suffered a series of defeats beginning in June 1813, culminating in the rout of the Grand Armée at Leipzig in October), and the "violent fluctuations... in the year of Waterloo," Cannan added, "could certainly not be attributed to changes in the note circulation."[16] Wesley Mitchell later described the sensitivity of greenbacks to military fortunes during the American Civil War: "... fluctuations in the premium on gold were so much more rapid and violent than the changes in the volume of the circulating medium that not even academic economists would regard the quantity theory as an adequate explanation of all the phenomena."[17]

Looking at longer term movements, we observe that the values of sterling and the dollar trended downward during periods of credit expansion and upward during deflations. These short- and long-term deviations are reconciled by letting the demand for money depend on its expected value. For example, Napoleon's defeats in 1813 improved the chances of early resumption. They were explained in the testimony of a "Continental Merchant" who had observed that inconvertibility preceded the depreciation of currencies and that "ultimate results are anticipated by the speculation of individuals" (March 5).[18]

The Bank would not concede that the value of money is affected by its quantity:

Supposing the currency of any country to consist altogether of specie, would that specie be affected in its value by its abundance or by its diminution, the same as copper, brass, cloth, or any other article of merchandise? – I have already said that I decline answering questions as to opinion; I am very ready to answer any questions as to matters of fact.... (March 13)

On his last appearance before the Committee (March 30), the governor alternated between denying that the value of money was related to its quantity and saying that "It is a subject on which such a variety of opinions are entertained, I do not find myself competent to give a decided answer."

The Bank has been accused of a mistaken belief in the real bills doctrine, according to which price stability is assured if the quantity of money

---

[16] Cannan, *op. cit.*, p. xxvii.

[17] Mitchell, *A History of the Greenbacks*, p. 188.

[18] Cannan conjectured that the anonymous "Continental Merchant" was Nathan Rothschild (*op. cit.*, p. xlii), but Piero Sraffa argued that his foreign situation and other evidence pointed to John Parish of Parish & Co. in Hamburg ("Mr. __ of the Bullion Report").

is linked to output by tying bank lending to real transactions.[19] The doctrine is expressed in the equation of exchange, $MV = PT$, where M is the average quantity of money in a period, V (velocity) is its rate of turnover, P is the average price of transactions, and T is the number of transactions or money purchases of goods and services. If M is linked to T, then P is constant – if V is constant. So the doctrine is qualified immediately, although this is not a concern if we want a money rule that does not itself cause price changes.

The limitation of bank discounts to real bills cannot be relied on for price stability, however, because it implies no particular relationship between M and T. A bundle of goods might give rise to several bills of exchange with overlapping lives as it makes its way from manufacturer or importer through merchants to retailers. However, even if there were precisely one real bill, discounted at a bank and outstanding precisely as long as the bundle that it finances is in the marketplace, P would be indeterminate. A unique quantity of money is not tied to a bundle of goods because the amount borrowed and lent on the security of the goods depends on the prices that the parties expect them to fetch in the market. Both M and P depend on expected prices. If inflation is expected, purchases require large loans, and the expectation is realized.

These points had been made by Thornton in 1802 in *An Enquiry into the Nature and Effects of the Paper Credit of Great Britain*. In parliamentary debates on the Bullion Committee's report, he pointed to the similarity between the Bank of England's policy and John Law's land bank that had failed a century before in France.

Mr. Law considered security as everything, and quantity as nothing. He proposed that paper money should be supplied (he did not specify in his book at what rate of interest) to as many borrowers as should think fit to apply, and should offer the security of land. . . . He forgot that there might be no bounds to the demand for paper; that the increasing quantity would contribute to the rise of commodities: and the rise of commodities require, and seem to justify, a still further increase.[20]

Thornton argued that the only way to limit money was to charge interest commensurate with the rate of profit that merchants expected to

---

[19] See, for example, the Bullion Report and Lloyd Mints, *A History of Banking Theory in Great Britain and the United States*, chap. 4.

[20] *Hansard*, xix, May 7, 1811. Rep. in Thornton, *An Inquiry into the Nature and Effects of the Paper Credit of Great Britain*, p. 342. Also see the discussion in Fetter, *op. cit.*, p. 43. John Law urged the issue of money on the security of land in *Money and Trade Considered*. He was given an opportunity to implement his theories in France, but after a period of success they burst with the Mississippi Bubble in 1720.

earn on borrowed money. "Whilst the Bank is willing to lend," Ricardo agreed, "borrowers will always exist, so that there can be no limit to their overissues."[21]

The *Bullion Report* condemned the Bank's behavior in words probably written by Thornton:[22]

[W]hile the convertibility into specie no longer exists as a check to an over issue of paper, the Bank Directors have not perceived that the removal of that check rendered it possible that such an excess might be issued by the discount of perfectly good bills. So far from perceiving this, Your Committee have shown that they maintain the contrary doctrine with the utmost confidence.... That this doctrine is a very fallacious one, Your Committee cannot entertain a doubt. The fallacy upon which it is founded lies in not distinguishing between an advance of capital to Merchants and an additional supply of currency to the general mass of circulating medium.[23]

This last sentence goes some way toward the Bank's intellectual position, which was not that it had an incorrect theory of the price level, but that it had no theory. The Committee had tried to get the directors to consider the macroeconomic effects of their actions, but the latter showed no sign of comprehending even the possibility of such effects. Short-term lending on good security subject to an adequate reserve is sound banking practice. If we look at the Bank of England as a commercial bank, we find consistency and comprehensibility. Its protests of innocence of wider effects are less satisfactory. Nonetheless, they were consistent with a desire not to be derailed from its focus on the banking business and its understanding of its limited public responsibilities that was to continue for many decades. "To those who ... governed and worked in the Bank," Ralph Sayers wrote of the 20 years before 1914, after Bagehot had tried to tell them that they were a central bank, "the daily business appeared almost entirely as the business of a bank – a slightly peculiar bank – with its select groups of customers," the first being the government.

If there had been an articulate Governor (they do not seem to have been born that way) he might have said that fundamentally he had three duties. He had a statutory duty to maintain the convertibility of the note into gold coin; he had a

---

[21] Ricardo, *loc. cit.*

[22] The *Report's* authors were Thornton, partner in the Downe, Free & Thornton bank, whose home was the center of the Clapham Sect that included William Wilberforce; Horner, who founded the *Edinburgh Review*; and William Huskisson, who held several government offices in a long parliamentary career.

[23] Cannan, *op. cit.*, p. 50.

political duty to look after the financial needs of the Government; and he had a commercial duty to maintain an income for the stockholders.

R. S. Sayers, The Bank of England, 1891–1944, pp. 5, 8

The Bank's survival was threatened by government borrowing, and the Bank and Pitt had disagreed about what was excessive. Private lending is also a delicate business. Banks do not like to restrict lending. Borrowers, even issuers of short-term debt, depend on finance for the long haul. Commitments are made months or years in advance, and orders for goods and other financial obligations are undertaken in the expectation of reliable credit. The nonrenewal of loans is liable to bring "stoppages" even by solvent, though illiquid, firms. One stoppage might bring another, and in the complex fabric of finance everyone is at risk. Banks are reluctant to compensate for increased government finance by refusing their private borrowers – especially when business is brisk, borrowers appear sounder than usual, and reserves are not a problem.

The Committee recommended retention of the existing commitment to resumption within six months after the war's end, and asked for convertibility within two years if the war continued. A motion to this effect was rejected by the House of Commons by a 180–45 vote. The majority sided with the Bank in ascribing fluctuations in the exchange rate and the price of gold to factors other than the Bank's credit policies. The House accepted the paper standard, although it resolved to terminate the suspension as soon as "the political and commercial relations of the country" rendered it "compatible with the public interest."[24] These positions are reconciled on practical if not intellectual grounds if Parliament preferred the gold standard "in ordinary times" but would not interfere with war finance.[25]

Banking, Central Banking, Knowledge, and Incentives to the Public Interest

We are all City people and connected with merchants, and nothing but merchants on every side.

Henry Thornton on his brothers' ambitions to society[26]

---

[24] *Ibid.*, p. xxvi.

[25] *Loc. cit.*

[26] Quoted from *Recollections of Marianne Thornton* by F. A. Hayek, "Introduction" to Thornton's *Paper Credit*, p. 12.

Judgment of the Bank's conduct in the crisis of war might reasonably begin with its proper behavior in ordinary times. Thornton's *Paper Credit* still ranks as the best combination of monetary theory and banking practice. It begins: "Commercial credit may be defined to be that confidence which subsists among commercial men in respect to their mercantile affairs." This is not surprising in a banker and former merchant. However, this unusually reflective "commercial man" extends the equation of "credit" and "confidence" beyond individual relationships. This equation forms the foundation of an analytical system capable of explaining aggregate financial flows, interest rates, inflation, exchange rates, and – most important for our purposes – the proper conduct of a central bank. Although Thornton indicated in the preface that his "first intention" was the exposure of "some popular errors which related chiefly to the suspension of the cash payments of the Bank of England, and to the influence of our paper currency on the price of provisions," he had probably begun the project before the suspension.[27] Certainly it transcends the problems of the government and the Bank in 1802.

The elements of Keynes's liquidity-preference theory of interest appear in Thornton's discussions of the motives for holding money and the influences of changes in its quantity on interest rates, and his mechanism of adjustment to international price differences was rediscovered 120 years later as the purchasing-power-parity theory of exchange rates. Later difficulties would have been avoided if the proponents of the Bank Charter Act of 1844 had accepted Thornton's point (and other points, as we will see later) that bank deposits perform the same monetary functions as bank notes. But Thornton's best-known contributions to monetary theory are his proof of the indeterminacy of prices under the real bills doctrine, the doctrine of "forced saving" whereby inflation in combination with rigid wages compels the laborer "to consume fewer articles, though he may exercise the same industry," and his explanation of inflation as a consequence of the divergence between "market" and "natural" rates of interest. Almost a century later, Knut Wicksell placed this divergence at the center of academic discussions of monetary policy, and it influences the Bank of England and the Federal Reserve today.

We will apply these contributions in other places. Our interest in Thornton here stems from his analysis of the role of the central bank in the financial system. Because that role is derived from credit, that is,

---

[27] Thornton, *op. cit.*, p. 67.

confidence, it was necessary to pave the way for monetary policy by first explaining the origins and maintenance of confidence. Most of the analysis applies to any bank and implies strong parallels between the actions proper to bankers and central bankers.

It is "this confidence," Thornton continued from the opening sentence, "which disposes them to lend money to each other, to bring themselves under various pecuniary engagements by the acceptance and indorsement of bills, and also to sell and deliver goods in consideration of an equivalent promised to be given at a subsequent period." Credit is normally manifested in paper – bills of exchange, bank notes, and other securities – that serves "to express that confidence which is in the mind, and to reduce to writing those engagements to pay, which might otherwise be merely verbal." The benefits of credit are great. "The day on which it suits the British merchant to purchase and send away a large quantity of goods may not be that on which he finds it convenient to pay for them." Without credit, "he must always have in his hands a very large stock of money; and for the expence of keeping this fund (an expence consisting chiefly in the loss of interest) he must be repaid in the price of the commodities in which he deals." Credit sets him "at liberty in his speculations: his judgement as to the propriety of buying or not buying, or of selling or not selling, . . . may be more freely exercised."[28]

The credits and payments of the country converged on the Bank of England. Trade was financed by bills of exchange, that is, marketable obligations to pay fixed amounts at fixed times and places. Buyers desiring credit accepted bills drawn on them by sellers. Most bills were drawn on London. That is, payments were made in London, and merchants and bankers outside London maintained connections there to handle their payments and receipts. London was to the whole island, and even to Europe and perhaps the world, "what the centre of a city is to the suburbs." Although Thornton did not apply "central" to the Bank of England, he wrote that banks are

particularly likely to be multiplied in a state like ours, in which the mercantile transactions are extended, the population is great, and the expenditure of individuals considerable; and also where a principal bank exists, which through the necessity imposed on it by its situation undertakes the task of providing a constant reservoir of gold accessible to every smaller banking establishment. The creation of the large bank operates as a premium on the institution of the smaller.

Thornton, *Paper Credit*, pp. 168–69

---

[28] *Ibid.*, p. 77.

The gold reserve had to be available. Because it was concentrated in the Bank, that institution had to be ready to pay it on demand. This sometimes entailed the conversion of its note and deposit obligations into coin or bullion, but more often it meant the willingness to supply its notes, which were regarded "as good as gold," that is, to lend. "The practice had grown up," Ralph Hawtrey wrote, "of the Bank of England acting as the lender of last resort" – the *"dernier resort"* as Francis Baring called it in 1797.[29] Hawtrey writes,

[I]f there was a general shortage of cash, so that the sellers of bills in the market predominated over the buyers, there was no way of providing for the unsold residue of bills unless the Bank of England would take them . . . ; it was expected to discount all eligible bills offered, whether by merchants or by bankers, and any bills on London maturing within ninety-five days and bearing two good English names (one being the acceptor) was eligible.

Hawtrey, *A Century of Bank Rate*, p. 11

The central bank's ability and willingness to satisfy these demands in times of crisis was, with the question of the standard, one of the two main issues of monetary policy in the 19th century. Attention to Thornton's explanation of the importance of maintaining the Bank's circulation would have benefited many future central bankers and legislators:

It has been shewn already that in order to effect the vast and accustomed payments daily made in London, payments which are most of them promised beforehand, a circulating sum in bank notes nearly equal to whatever may have been its customary amount is necessary. But a much more clear idea of this subject will be gained by entering into some detail.

There are in London between sixty and seventy bankers, and it is almost entirely through them that the larger payments of London are effected. . . . The notes in their hands form, probably, a very large proportion of the whole circulating notes in the metropolis. [A] very small proportion of Bank of England notes circulate far from London, and that it is to the metropolis itself that all the larger ones are confined. The amount of the bank notes in the hands of each banker, of course, fluctuates considerably; but the amount in the hands of all probably varies very little; and this amount cannot be much diminished consistently with their ideas of what is necessary to the punctuality of their payments and to the complete security of their houses. Thus there is little room for reduction as to the whole of that larger part of the notes of the Bank of England which is in the hands of the London bankers: the notes which may chance to circulate among other persons, especially among persons carrying on any commerce, if we suppose the usual punctuality of payments to be maintained, and the ordinary system of effecting them to proceed, can admit also of little diminution. . . . A large proportion of the

---

[29] *Observations on the Establishment of the Bank of England*, p. 20.

London payments are, moreover, carried on by a comparatively small quantity of notes; and they, perhaps, cannot easily be effected, with due regularity, by a much smaller number, so complete has been the system of economy in the use of them which time and experience has introduced among the bankers. There is, moreover, no substitute for them.... They serve, at the same time, both to sustain and regulate the whole paper credit of the country. It is plain from the circumstances which have just been stated that any very great and sudden diminution of Bank of England notes would be attended with the most serious effects.... A reduction of them which may seem moderate to men who have not reflected on this subject – a diminution, for instance, of one-third or two-fifths, might, perhaps, be sufficient to produce a general insolvency in London, of which the effect would be the suspension of confidence, the derangement of commerce, and the stagnation of manufactures throughout the country.

Thornton, *Paper Credit*, pp. 113–14

Conditions are likely to be made worse by the hoarding of gold, and although the introduction of substitutes for the Bank's notes might be attempted, their credit would be inferior to the Bank's and have little effect. Rising interest rates and falling prices might attract foreign gold – after the damage had been done. Anticipating the rule in the Bank Act of 1844, Thornton noted,

The idea which some persons have entertained of its being at all times a paramount duty of the Bank of England to diminish its notes in some sort of regular proportion to that diminution which it experiences in its gold is, then, an idea which is merely theoretic.

Thornton, *Paper Credit*, p. 116

Thornton tells us – his criticisms of the Bank are restrained and he takes care not to disturb confidence in the credit system – that the "case which has been put is ... merely hypothetical; for there is too strong and evident interest in every quarter to maintain, in some way or other, the regular course of London payments."[30] Among the most important were the interests of the Bank's owners.

The directors of the bank ... have now, by their exclusive power of furnishing a circulating medium to the metropolis, the means of, in some degree, limiting and regulating its quantity; a power of which they would be totally divested, if, by exercising it too severely, they should once cause other paper to become current in the same manner as their own.

Thornton, *Paper Credit*, pp. 113–14

---

[30] Thornton, *op. cit.*, p. 115.

To the threat of innovation must be added the political danger of increased powers for rival institutions or even the nonrenewal of its charter. Strong natural forces also directed the Bank toward the public interest:

> It may be mentioned as an additional ground of confidence in the Bank of England, and as a circumstance of importance in many respects, that the numerous proprietors who chuse the directors, and have the power of controlling them . . . , are men whose general stake in the country far exceeds that particular one which they have in the stock of the company. They are men, therefore, who feel themselves to be most deeply interested not merely in the increase of the dividends or in the maintenance of the credit of the Bank of England, but in the support of commercial as well as of public credit in general. . . . The proprietors . . . are not likely to approve of any dangerous extension even of their own paper, [but while they] have thus an interest, on the one hand, in limiting the quantity of paper issued, they are also naturally anxious, on the other, in common with the whole commercial world, to give the utmost possible credit to it. . . .
>
> Thornton, *Paper Credit*, pp. 109–110

Conflicts of interest were not eliminated, however, because a great agency threatened the stability of credit. Britain was fortunate in having a principal bank "quite independent of the executive Government," Thornton wrote, more in hope than belief, which, because of its ability to raise funds "without the smallest difficulty" in the capital market, was "under little or no *temptation* either to dictate to the Bank of England, or to lean upon it in any way which is inconvenient or dangerous to the bank itself. . . . In those countries in which the Government is the chief banker or issuer of notes," in contrast, "a temptation arises, on the occasion of every public pressure, either to lessen the quantity of precious metal contained in the chief current coin, as one of the means of detaining it in the country, or to allow paper to pass at a considerable and professed discount. . . . These are evils from which we consider ourselves as happily secured by the established principles of good faith which prevail in Great Britain."[31]

The secretary of the treasury of the new American republic had given a similar lecture a decade earlier in his proposal for a national bank.

> The emitting of paper money by the authority of Government is wisely prohibited to the individual States by the National Constitution. And the spirit of that prohibition ought not to be disregarded by the Government of the United States. Though paper emissions under a general authority might have some advantages not applicable, and free from some disadvantages which are applicable, to the

---

[31] *Ibid.*, pp. 105–6, 190.

like emissions by the States separately; yet they are of a nature so liable to abuse, and it may even be affirmed so certain of being abused, that the wisdom of the Government will be shewn in never trusting itself with the use of so seducing and dangerous an expedient. In times of tranquillity, it might have no ill consequence, it might even perhaps be managed in a way to be productive of good; but in great and trying emergencies, there is almost a moral certainty of its becoming mischievous. The stamping of paper is an operation so much easier than the laying of taxes that a Government in the practice of paper emissions would rarely fail in any such emergency to indulge itself too far in the employment of that resource to avoid as much as possible one less auspicious to present popularity.

Alexander Hamilton, *Report on a National Bank*

The best way to keep government from these temptations was private bank issues redeemable in coin. "While the discretion of the Government is the only measure of the extent of the emissions by its own authority," under the private banking arrangements then current, "there is a limitation in the nature of the thing. . . ." The nation had three banks, but Hamilton wanted a more extensive institution with responsibilities to the national government. The structure of the proposed national bank and Hamilton's understanding of the incentives most conducive to the public interest were influenced by the example of the Bank of England. His rationale of that institution as the best regulator of the currency is consistent with Thornton's:

To attach full confidence to an institution of this nature, it appears to be an essential ingredient in its structure that it should be under a *private* not a *public* Direction, under the guidance of *individual interest*, not of *public policy*; which would be supposed to be, and in certain emergencies, under a feeble or too sanguine administration would really be liable to being too much influenced by *public necessity*. (Hamilton's emphasis)

Hamilton, *Report on a National Bank*

It would be "little less than a miracle" if a *public* bank did not eventually suffer "calamitous abuse." The "only security that can always be relied upon for a careful and prudent administration," Hamilton argued, is the "keen, steady, and, as it were, magnetic sense of their own interest, as proprietors, in the Directors of a Bank, pointing invariably to its true pole, the prosperity of the institution. . . ." To ensure that the Bank would not be used to evade the scrutiny of the people's representatives in Congress, to whom government appropriations had been reserved, he recommended that "No loan shall be made by the bank, for the use or on account of the Government of the United States . . . to an amount exceeding fifty thousand dollars . . . unless previously authorised by a law of the United

States." The act establishing the Bank of England in 1694 contained a similar provision, as we will see in the next chapter. Hamilton got the bank, with a charter for 20 years, but neither it nor its successor were sufficiently circumscribed to survive an opposition, led by President Andrew Jackson, convinced that "such a concentration of power in the hands of a few men irresponsible to the people" threatened the people's freedom.[32]

Returning to the Bank of England, Thornton proposed the following rule:

> To limit the total amount of paper issued, and to resort for this purpose, whenever the temptation to borrow is strong, to some effectual principle of restriction; in no case however, materially to diminish the sum in circulation, but to let it vibrate only within certain limits; to afford a slow and cautious extension of it, as the general trade of the kingdom enlarges itself; to allow of some special, though temporary, encrease in the event of any extraordinary alarm or difficulty, as the best means of preventing a great demand at home for guineas; and to lean on the side of diminution in the case of gold going abroad, and of the general exchanges continuing long unfavourable; this seems to be the true policy of the directors of an institution circumstanced like that of the Bank of England. To suffer either the solicitations of merchants or the wishes of Government to determine the measure of the bank issues, is unquestionably to adopt a very false principle of conduct.
>
> Thornton, *Paper Credit*, p. 259

This is not very different from Federal Reserve Chairman Martin's "leaning against the wind" or the temporary supplies of liquidity following the stock market crash of 1987 and other emergencies.

Rhetoric, Knowledge, and Monetary Policy

What did their first experience with freedom from convertibility tell us about the beliefs and objectives of central bankers? Was the experience special to the time or did it reveal attitudes, adaptations, and rhetoric to be repeated in a durable pattern that defines central banking even today? These questions cannot be answered before considering later experiences, but hints are given by the reflections of the Bank directors.

They did not depart from their 1810 testimony as long as the suspension continued. Their responses to questions from the Commons Committee on the Expediency of the Bank Resuming Cash Payments in 1819 included the usual disclaimer. After "serious consideration," the Court

[32] Veto message, July 10, 1832; see Chapter 6.

of Directors "cannot refrain from adverting to an opinion, strongly insisted on by some, that the bank has only to reduce its issues to obtain a favourable turn on the exchanges and a consequent influx of the precious metals; the Court conceives it to be its duty to declare that it is unable to discover any solid foundation for such a sentiment."[33] However, when asked in 1832 by a Committee on the renewal of the Bank's charter if he believed "that the Bank should conduct itself, in its issues, with reference to the state of the foreign Exchanges and the bullion market," William Ward, a director since 1817, replied, "Certainly; I do not think there is one person in the Bank of England that denies it, or is disposed to act in opposition to it" (Q2073).[34] However, he added that "over and over again I have been responsible myself for violating it when some extraordinary case has arisen." Jeremiah Harman, one of the directors who had denied the principle in 1810, was also asked whether the Bank should contract in the presence of an unfavorable exchange. "Yes; but then comes another question, and that is, the risk that it may occasion to the commercial world . . ." (Q2254). Somerset banker Vincent Stuckey also admitted the relevance of the exchanges for commercial banks. "They serve as a beacon for the general management of our business." Nevertheless, "on extraordinary occasions, and particularly in cases of panic, the principles cannot be acted upon" (Q1015–20). John Richards, governor from 1826 to 1828, said that it might be necessary to expand credit in the face of gold losses caused by poor harvests (Q4973–80). The defense by George Grote, "a banker in the City," of the Bank's assistance to the market in 1825 was a typical subordination of rules to discretion:

In the particular case of 1825, I apprehend that the Bank have in their favour what is the best and most complete justification, the actual result as it ensued. But if I am asked whether, if I had been a Bank Director at that moment, I should have been disposed to approve of such conduct, I cannot answer the question without a variety of considerations which nobody except a Director could have possessed the means of going through, and which could only have been suggested by all of the circumstances taken together at that actual moment.

Q4667

The 1832 Committee was less interested in the Bank's exercise of discretion in special circumstances – although it was criticized for being too slow with critical assistance – than in the evolution of its attitude toward

---

[33] House of Commons, 1819, p. 263.
[34] Also see Fetter, *op. cit.*, pp. 151–52, for the directors' testimony.

the Bullion Committee's proposed rule since its testimony in 1810. The chairman, Lord Althorp, asked Ward,

From what period is it that the Bank Directors have conducted themselves generally upon the principles you mention, of regulating their issues by the state of foreign Exchanges? – It may be recollected that in the year 1819 [the Bank] distinctly denied the principle that the Exchanges were to be regarded in regulating the issue. Subsequently to that period, opinions became changed, and of course, in the working of the machinery, they found the merits of the case such as they really were; and a growing disposition manifested itself to heed in a greater degree than they hitherto had done the principle of exchange and bullion; but in 1827 I moved that that Resolution should be rescinded, and from that moment I have considered it the practice of the Bank, and it was the practice in a great degree even previously to that. I always believed, in Mr. Horner's time, that his principle was completely right.

Q2074

The positions of Bank spokesmen in 1810 and 1832 suggest that economic relationships are minded most when their neglect has costs. This is especially true when, as Boyd had pointed out in 1801, the Bank's interests lay in other directions. When the relationship comes back into force, as in 1821, the Bank has to attend to "the working of the machinery."

We should not take the Bank's protestations of former errors too literally. It was bidding for approval while under attack. What most required explanation, Thomas Tooke observed, was:[35]

How happened it that the Bank, having such powerful motives of interest, with a view to its dividends, . . . being no longer under the check of convertibility, the directors having avowed, moreover, that in the regulation of the amount [of their issue] they disregarded the exchanges, . . . and that their only guide was the demand for discount of good bills at 5 per cent.? How happened it, that with such motives to excess, and under the guidance of opinions so unsound, there was so trifling an increase . . .?

Thomas Tooke, *History of Prices*, i, p. 283

Tooke's answer was the "coincidence between the Bank rate of discount and the market rate of interest for such bills as came within the Bank rules." Either they were lucky or the directors knew more than they let on.

An indication of the influence of the exigencies of public policy and social pressure on the bank's language, possibly more than on its behavior,

---

[35] *Thomas Tooke* was a banker, frequent witness before parliamentary committees, and historian of prices.

is given by the further testimony of Ward. Asked by the chairman whether the Bank had taken the exchanges into account during the suspension, he replied that after "some enquiries" into the Bank's history he was of the opinion

that upon the whole the Bank did not so greatly disregard that principle previously to 1792; but it is necessary to observe that the Bank has not, until latterly, been in a situation exclusively to judge for itself; when it was most in fault, it was most in accordance with the Government and the Parliament and the public at large; I believe the most unpopular tenet that ever was, was the being a bullionist twenty years ago.

Must not the Bank, governed as it is by prudent merchants, always proceed upon the principle of reducing their issues, when they find their treasure greatly diminished? – I think the practice of the Bank would make that inevitable; but the difficulty has been that during the period I have been speaking of, the measures of the Bank have been very much in connection with other things than those it exclusively could influence.

Q2082–83

Althorp's sermon came easily in 1832. He had not as a member of Parliament in 1811 contested Castlereagh's identification (as a former secretary of war) of "winning the war" with rejection of the Bullion Report or his plea to "preserve that system of currency," which has so far enabled "us to confine [Napoleon's] violence to the continent," or Prime Minister Perceval's warning that its adoption would amount to a declaration that the country should not "continue those foreign exertions which they had hitherto considered indispensable to the security of the country [and that] the House, in adopting it would disgrace themselves forever, by becoming the voluntary instruments of their country's ruin."[36]

We may wonder where this leaves the importance that Hamilton attached to an independent bank as a bulwark against spendthrift governments. Our examination of the directors' language and actions suggests that they did about as well as they could in the circumstances. Their policy was to comply with the government while softening the effects on private customers and the financial markets – a policy, allowed by their freedom from convertibility, with which Thornton should not have been too unhappy – and deflecting criticism by denials of inflationary consequences. Seen from this angle, the Bank's behavior is consistent with the explicit maximization of a complicated utility function of public and private arguments subject to economic and political constraints. Or it might have

[36] *Hansard*, May 7–8, 1811; discussed in Fetter, *op. cit.*, pp. 53–54.

been a rough-and-ready bankers' compromise between traditional practices and the accommodation of a demanding principal in the presence of a relaxed but uncertain discipline. Either explanation might apply to the Bank and the Federal Reserve in the second half of the 20th century. We will see in Chap. 4 that Parliament's dissatisfaction with the Bank's structure and rules of behavior followed not from its war finance and its rejection of the Bullion Report but rather from the failure to maintain financial stability after the peacetime resumption of the gold standard.

THREE

Making a Central Bank: I. Surviving

Of all the institutions in the world, the Bank of England is now probably the
most remote from party politics and from "financing." But in its origin it was
not only a finance company, but a Whig finance company. It was founded
by a Whig Government because it was in desperate want of money, and
supported by the "City" because the "City" was Whig.

Walter Bagehot, Lombard Street, p. 90

This chapter continues our backward movement from the Monetary Policy Committee in 1998 to the intellectual origins of central banking in 1810
to the initiation in 1694 of the institution that became the model central
bank. From this point we generally follow the calendar in describing the
growth of central banking.

The Bank of England was not founded as a central bank. The concept
did not exist in the 17th century. The goldsmith bankers of London had
just begun to learn how to manage individual credit relationships and
their new paper money liabilities. It was difficult enough to know how
much coin and bullion to keep for the redemption of one's own notes and
deposits without performing that service for other banks as well. Not until
the end of the 18th century, after the rise of the country banks, did the
Bank become a central bank to whom other banks looked for funds as
their customers looked to them. The public's confidence made the Bank's
liabilities "as good as gold." However, that confidence had to be earned.

The Bank's survival was never assured. Although it possessed valuable
legal privileges, and 180 years later Bagehot thought it "quite natural" that
"With so many advantages over all competitors...the Bank of England
should have outstripped them all," many firms with greater monopoly

---

Background: People and Events

See Table 3.1 for wars.

1640, 1672: Mint and Exchequer "stops."

1660: Stuart Restoration: Charles II to 1685; James II, 1685–89.

1689: Glorious Revolution: Overthrow of James II and accession of William III (1689–1702) and Mary (1689–94).

Queen Anne, 1702–14; George I, 1714–27; George II, 1727–60; George III, 1760–1820.

Long-serving First Lords of the Treasury (also commonly chancellors of the Exchequer): Lord Godolphin, 1700–10; Robert Walpole, 1715–17, 1721–42 (the first "prime minister"); Henry Pelham, 1743–54; William Pitt (the elder, later Lord Chatham), 1757–62; Lord North, 1770–82; William Pitt (the younger), 1783–1801, 1804–6.

1694: Bank of England founded.

1696: Recoinage; threatened Land Bank.

1720: South Sea Bubble.

1745: Invasion of the Young Pretender (Bonnie Prince Charlie, grandson of James II).

1780: Gordon Riots; protest against Parliament's relief of Catholic disabilities led by Lord George Gordon turns to riot, including attack on the Bank of England, which was afterward defended by troops and kept supplies in case of siege.

---

privileges have vanished because of their failures to adapt.[1] The "quiet life," which has been called the "best of all monopoly profits," has not always been conducive to longevity.[2] The Bank got little serenity, however. Its survival owed less to luck than to the efforts of its owners and others who valued its existence. The following discussion is largely a story of how the Bank's directors, though not always wise, were determined to preserve a profitable and prestigious institution, while showing considerable ingenuity under pressure; of how it was supported at critical times by a government dependent on its finance, even though more often than not the government's demands had caused its problems in the first place; and of how a merchant community that depended on the Bank showed forbearance when it was needed.

Although there was little change in the Bank's charter or organization between its founding in 1694 and the revision of 1844, that did not prevent it from adapting and prospering during a financial as well as an industrial revolution. The account of the Bank's first century may help us

---

[1] Walter Bagehot, *Lombard Street*, p. 97.
[2] J. R. Hicks, "The Theory of Monopoly."

to anticipate and appreciate the difficulties that the newly independent central banks with some of the same responsibilities might encounter in the 21st century. The second section, which describes the adjustments of the Bank and the economy as the directors and the government prepared to return to the limitations of the gold standard after the freedom of the paper pound between 1797 and 1819, has analogies with the problems encountered after World Wars I and II and surrounding the independence of the Bank after 1997.

The First Hundred Years

Origins of the Bank
In June 1640, Charles I, "being at his wits' end for money," ordered that nothing should be paid out of the mint until further notice, and the merchants who had deposited silver to be coined would receive 8 percent interest for their "loans."[3] They were repaid, but the incident made a strong impression on the financial community. Samuel Pepys wrote in his diary on August 17, 1666, after a reference to the 1640 incident, "The unsafe condition of a bank under a monarch, and the little safety to a Monarch to have any City or Corporacion alone ... to have so great a wealth or credit ... makes it hard to have a bank here."

The "stop" on the mint encouraged people to keep their cash with the budding goldsmith bankers who were part of the great financial developments of the second half of the 17th century. "In the reign of William," Thomas Macaulay wrote in his *History of England*, "old men were still living who could remember the days when there was not a single banking house in the city of London. So late as the time of the Restoration every trader had his own strong box in his own house, and, when an acceptance was presented to him, told down the crowns and Carolusus on his own counter."[4] By the end of the reign of Charles II in 1685, however, it "was at the shops of the goldsmiths of Lombard Street that all the payments in coin were made. Other traders gave and received nothing but paper," that is, notes and drafts on the goldsmiths. "Oldfashioned merchants complained bitterly that a class of men, who, thirty years before, had confined themselves to their proper functions, and had made a fair profit by embossing silver bowls [and] setting jewels ... had become the treasurers and were fast becoming the masters of the whole city."

[3] A. E. Feavearyear, *The Pound Sterling*, p. 85.
[4] Vol. iv, p. 54.

Pepys was "doubtful of trusting any of these great dealers because of their mortality." However, he wanted 6 percent, and "the convenience of having one's money at an hour's call is very great" (September 12, 1664). When Dudley North returned to England in 1680 after years of trading in the Levant and still preferred to keep his cash at home, he could not go to the Exchange "without being followed round the piazza by goldsmiths, who, with low bows, begged to have the honour of serving him."[5]

The Crown was also active in the market for short-term debt. The Exchequer anticipated receipts with interest-bearing paper issued for goods and services in denominations as small as £1, exchangeable for coin in order of their issue as taxes were collected. William Shaw called these Exchequer orders England's first government paper money, and he said they might have become permanent and thus altered the history of English money and banking, greatly reducing the scope of the Bank of England, if Charles II had been a better manager.[6] His credit was not sufficient for the Dutch War of 1672–74, and a generation after his father's "stop" he was compelled to postpone the redemption of Exchequer orders for a year. It was shortly announced that orders for supplies and those in place of wages and salaries were eligible for redemption, except those that had been assigned to third parties. This meant that banks and other lenders of money on the security of the orders were the losers. There was a run on the banks believed to be heavily involved, and they stopped payment. Most resumed after the king promised to redeem the orders, although they never "really recovered from the shock to their credit, and there was widespread ruin amongst their depositors."[7]

Exchequer orders have been described because they were essentially the same as the Exchequer bills that replaced them at the end of the century and played an important part in the relations between the Bank and the Treasury until Bagehot's time. They accrued interest on a daily basis at rates announced by the Treasury from time to time, and they could be used in payment of taxes or other sums owed to the Exchequer. Interest was raised if the Treasury wished to slow the rate of redemption. Exchequer

---

[5] Macaulay, *History*, iv, pp. 54–55. North was not conservative in his ideas, however, and was Adam Smith's forerunner in opposing legal restrictions on trade and interest rates and especially for arguing in *Discourses upon Trade* that governments would best promote the nation's wealth, which was not measured by its money, by letting trade flourish.

[6] "The 'Treasury Order Book'."

[7] Feavearyear, *op. cit.*, p. 104; J. K. Horsefield, "The 'Stop of the Exchequer' Revisited."

bills were "a subsidiary negotiable paper money standing side by side with and supplementing the note issue of the Bank of England" and in financial crises were employed or threatened by the government when the Bank's efforts were thought to be inadequate – as in 1793 and 1822.[8] They were the main short-term debt of the government until replaced by regular issues of Treasury bills in 1877.

There had been several proposals for a national bank. William Petty expressed a popular view when he argued that a bank would "almost double the Effect of our coined Money" by means of checks and notes secured by fractional reserves of coin and bullion.[9] However, the Bank of England had to wait for a coincidence of circumstances: a government with a low credit rating in need of money, which was a common condition, and confidence on the parts of investors and depositors that the bank would be safe from the depredations of government, which was new. The latter condition was provided by the Glorious Revolution of 1688 that led to a constitutional monarch.

The "financial revolution in public credit" made possible by the political revolution needed a generation or two,[10] but a solid foundation was soon underway, and the Bank of England played a key role. A necessary step was the replacement of the king's purse by the national budget – of the royal debt by the national debt. The old system was unsatisfactory for the safety as well as the liberties of the king's subjects. To keep the king poor risked public services and national security. But to vote him reliable resources had risked the profligacy of Charles II, and the oppression of his financially more prudent younger brother thus made independent of Parliament. Under the new system, the king was voted revenues sufficient for regular expenses, whereas military and other extraordinary expenses were Parliament's responsibility. The other side of the contract was the commitment of property owners to supply revenues on a continuing basis instead of forcing the government to cast about for funds in every crisis. The Glorious Revolution has been seen as a triumph of property in which government was converted from oppressor to protector. The land tax was payment for this protection.[11]

---

[8] The quotation is from Shaw, "The 'Treasury Order Book'."

[9] Petty, *Quantulumcunque Concerning Money*. This was his answer to Question 26: "What remedy is there if we have too little money?" For other contemporary proposals see J. K. Horsefield, *British Monetary Experiments, 1650–1710*.

[10] P. G. M. Dickson, *The Financial Revolution in England*.

[11] This fiscal account is based on Dickson, *op. cit.*; Geoffrey Holmes, *The Making of a Great Power*; and David Ogg, *England in the Reigns of James II and William III*.

Contracts

War with France broke out in 1689, and by 1694 the government had raised taxes "as far as they dared," borrowed from "everyone who would lend," and resorted to tontines and lotteries. "Finally, and almost as a last resource, they founded the Bank of England."[12] There was still considerable fear of a national bank, and several proposals had failed to elicit the necessary support in Parliament. But negotiations between the Bank's projectors and the government led to Parliament's offer, on April 25, 1694, of a corporate charter to "the Governor and Company of the Bank of England" on condition that they raised £1,200,000, one-half by August 1, to be lent to the government at 8 percent. Interest would be secured by "Rates and Duties upon Tunnage of Ships and Vessels, and upon Beer, Ale and other Liquors." The Bank would receive £4,000 for "management," and its charter would expire on payment of the principal, with a year's notice but not before 1706. Eight percent was below the market rate for government loans, and the Bank's stockholders must have been attracted by expectations of profit from banking activities. Earlier proposals had foundered on the right of note issue. This was not mentioned in the Act of 1694, but the new institution followed the goldsmiths' practice and issued notes from the beginning.[13]

To allay fears that the Bank would be a vehicle by which governments circumvented the legislature's control, the Act limited its government loans to those authorized by Parliament and prohibited it from buying Crown lands, which had been an important part of royal finance since Henry VIII. The Bank's management was entrusted to a governor and deputy governor, who were almost always limited to two successive one-year terms until World War I, and 24 directors, most of whom in the early years "were substantial City merchants and members of the leading City companies."[14] Their backgrounds changed with industry and finance, and Bank historian John Clapham wrote of the 1930s that "the London merchant or merchant banker of Victorian type was declining, [and] ships and railways, steel and chocolate, leather and beer, the trades of Canada and South Africa, and the China trade all were, or had been, represented."[15]

---

[12] Feavearyear, *op. cit.*, p. 125. A tontine is a gamble on one's longevity, the pot being divided among survivors on a prearranged date. For the Bank's original charter, see Forrest Capie, *History of Banking*, vol. 6.

[13] J. H. Clapham, *Bank of England*, i, p. 16; and Feavearyear, *op. cit.*, p. 126.

[14] W. M. Acres, *The Bank of England from Within, 1694–1900*, i, p. 21.

[15] Clapham, *op. cit.*, ii, p. 419.

The required capital was subscribed by July 1, and the Bank soon proved its usefulness as a ready source of finance and an efficient manager of payments. The government's needs were substantial, especially for coin to pay the armies on the Continent ranged against Louis XIV. In June 1696, William wrote to his ministers from Holland, "... in the name of God determine quickly to find some credit for the troops here." He wrote in July,

I know not where I am, since I see no resource which can prevent the army from mutiny or total desertion; for it is more impossible to find here than in England money sufficient for their subsistence; so that if you cannot devise expedients to send contributions, or procure credit, all is lost, and I must go to the Indies.[16]

"Here was the crisis of the war," David Ogg wrote, "it was financial."

"There was hard and close bargaining between the Directors and the Committee of the House in the early months of 1697."[17] When the government pressed the directors to take at par £1,000,000 of its outstanding debt then selling at a discount they complained of Parliament's repeal of the tonnage duties that had been the first security of the Bank's loans to the government as well as of some of the securities they were now asked to accept. However, they gave way in exchange for an extension of their charter to 1710 and Parliament's promise to recognize no other "Corporation, Society, Fellowship, Company or Constitution in the nature of a Bank" during the life of the Bank of England.

These negotiations were repeated several times during the next hundred years (see Table 3.1). In 1708, during the War of the Spanish Succession, the charter was extended to 1732, the Bank's allowable capital was doubled, and its privileges were increased by the prohibition of note issues to any association of more than six persons. During another war, in 1781, five years before expiration of the charter, it was extended to 1812; the Bank made a large short-term loan to the government and exchanged £3,000,000 of exchequer bills for a 3-percent annuity. In 1800, the charter was continued to 1833 "on condition of three Millions being advanced for the Public Service, without Interest, for six years ...; the sole right of Banking as a Corporate Body, and the other privileges are fully recited and confirmed."[18]

---

[16] Ogg, *op. cit.*, p. 433.

[17] Clapham, *op. cit.*, i, p. 47.

[18] House of Commons. *Second Report for the Committee on the Public Expenditure...*, 1807, p. 81.

Table 3.1. *Bank of England Charters, 1694–1844*

	Terms	Permanent Public Debt to Bank; National Debt; Military Situation
1694	Charter until 12 months notice after Aug. 1, 1705, and payment of public debt. £1,200,000 loan for annuity of £100,000 and £4,000 for management.	£1,200,000 6,100,000 War with France, 1689–97
1697	Charter continued until 12 months notice after Aug. 1, 1710, on payment, etc. Protection from corporate rivals. Bank takes £1,001,171 of Exchequer bills.	£2,175,028 16,700,000
1708	Charter continued until 12 months notice after Aug. 1, 1732, on payment, etc. Note issue prohibited to associations of more than 6 persons. £400,000 loan without interest; exchanged £1,775,027 of bills for 6% annuity.	£9,375,028 15,200,000 War of the Spanish Succession, 1702–13
1713	Charter continued until 12 months notice after Aug. 1, 1742, on payment, etc. Circulated £1,200,000 Exchequer bills at 3%.	£9,100,000 34,700,000
1742	Charter continued until 12 months notice after Aug. 1, 1764, on payment, etc. "Privileges of exclusive banking" renewed. £1,600,000 loan without interest.	£10,700,000 51,300,000 Wars of Jenkins' Ear & Austrian Succession, 1739–48
1764	Charter continued until 12 months notice after Aug. 1, 1786, on payment, etc. Bank pays £110,000 to Exchequer.	£11,686,000 134,200,000 Seven Years War 1756–63
1781	Charter continued until 12 months notice after Aug. 1, 1812, on payment, etc. £3,000,000 loan at 3%.	£11,686,000 190,400,000 American War, 1775–83

(continued)

Table 3.1 (*continued*)

	Terms	Permanent Public Debt to Bank; National Debt; Military Situation
1800	Charter continued until 12 months notice after Aug. 1, 1833, on payment, etc. £3,000,000 loan without interest for 6 years, later continued to 6 months after peace treaty.	£14,686,000 456,100,000 War with France, 1793–1815
1833	Charter continued until 12 months notice after Aug. 1, 1855, on payment, etc., with proviso that it may be dissolved on 12 months notice after Aug. 1, 1844, on payment, etc. Bank of England notes made legal tender. Bank to deduct £120,000 from charge for management of debt; one-fourth of public debt to Bank to be paid. Joint-stock banks of issue allowed 65 miles from London. Average monthly accounts to be published.	£14,686,100 783,000,000 (National debt peaked at £844 million in 1819; after rising to £812 million in Crimean War, fell to £569 million in 1900)
1844	Charter continued until 12 months notice after Aug. 1, 1855, and annually thereafter on payment, etc. Other banks' note issues prohibited from increasing. Bank notes of £14,000,000 to be issued on securities. Further £180,000 deducted from charge for management of the debt; Issue and Banking Departments separated. Precise weekly accounts to be published.	£11,015,100 794,500,000

Sources: J. R. McCulloch, *Treatise on Metallic and Paper Money and Banks*, p. 42; B. R. Mitchell, *British Historical Statistics*, sec. 14; R. D. Richards, "The First Fifty Years of the Bank of England."

When in the course of the last negotiation, the prime minister suggested that the government share the Bank's profits, Governor Samuel Thornton acknowledged "the advantages which the Bank derive from their Charter, and from their connexion with the Public," but thought it "proper to enumerate the benefits which the Public receive from them in return."[19]

The bank gets large profits from management of the Public Debt; interest on that debt; [and] from their Paper circulation, the issue of which results from the exclusive powers given to them by their Charter. It may be remarked, however, that it is a circulation of which they carefully limit the amount, and on account of which, as well as with a view to the general demands of the State, they are subject to the burden of ordinarily maintaining a large stock of Cash and Bullion, and of providing, except during the suspension of payments in Cash, all the Gold and Silver used for the coinage of Money.

The Bank's charters were contracts in the ordinary sense of explicit agreements between parties, each with something to offer and expecting performance from their counterparties. Governments wanted cheap, re-liable credit, which they came to believe depended on a bank whose size and soundness were unthreatened by competition, and the Bank's stock-holders desired a good return on their investment. These contracts were similar in important respects to the late-20th-century central bank con-tracts mentioned in the first chapter. There were important differences, however, most obviously in the simplicity of the early contracts, which did not encumber the Bank with the various regulatory and macroeco-nomic tasks of modern central banks. Another difference was the Bank's bargaining strength. Modern governments still like the credibility of a conservative central bank, but their greater taxing powers and improved credit ratings have dispensed with the necessity of conciliating central bank investors.

From the 1930s to the 1980s, nearly all central banks were treated as government departments and expected to share the government-of-the-day's aspirations. More recently, their desires for credible low-inflation monetary policies have compelled governments with profligate histories to allow central banks degrees of independence that have given them some of the bargaining power of the Bank of England in the 18th cen-tury. The probable uses of that power will be unclear until we learn the objectives of the newly independent central bankers. The objectives of the Bank directors were clear – or as clear as for any group of investors

---

[19] *Ibid.*, pp. 83, 103.

and managers. The agency problem introduced with central bank independence has been addressed in some countries by the imposition of penalties (dismissal or the embarrassment of public letters) on central bankers for failing to achieve specified inflation targets. The success of these contracts will depend on the commitments of governments to low inflation. It remains to be seen whether electorates will want low inflation as much as the Bank directors wanted profits.

Crises

The goal of financial stability was not written into the Bank's charters, but the previous statement by Governor Thornton, appropriate in Henry's brother, indicates that the directors had come to realize their special position in the financial system. Clapham counted nine occasions of financial distress, sometimes extending to panic, involving the Bank in its first century: 1696, 1701, 1720, 1745, 1753, 1763, 1772–73, 1783, and 1793.[20] The first arose from a shortage of liquidity from a recoinage, combined with fears for the Bank's survival of competition from a new Land Bank approved by Parliament. The Land Bank did not get off the ground, but the scare induced the Bank of England to seek the protection from competition stated in its first contract renewal. The Bank's early attempt to retreat into its shell after the collapse of the South Sea Bubble of 1720 showed that it had not learned its central position in finance. It refused assistance to the goldsmiths and other lenders in difficulty, called loans, and for a time refused all loan requests. It tried to slow the loss of cash (gold) by offering interest-bearing notes payable in three months in exchange for ordinary notes and cash, and survived a run by devious tactics.

Payments were made in light sixpences and shillings, and large sums were paid to particular friends, who went out with their bags of money at one door, to deliver them to people placed at another, who were let in to pay the same money to tellers, who took time to count it over. These persons were, of course, always served first. By this means time was gained, the friends of the Bank rallied round it, and made large subscriptions to support the company. The festival of Michaelmas, at which it was usual at that time to shut up the Bank, came, and, when it was opened again, the public alarm had passed off.

H. D. MacLeod, *The Theory and Practice of Banking*, i, p. 499

Twenty-five years later, in July 1745, Bonnie Prince Charlie landed in Scotland to reclaim his grandfather's crown. Highland clans rallied to his cause and defeated the forces sent against him. When news of the English

---

[20] Clapham, *op. cit.*, i, chap. 7. For another list based on bankruptcies see Julian Hoppit, "Financial Crises in Eighteenth-Century England."

army's defeat reached London on September 26, panic broke out and the Bank of England again resorted to the leisurely payment of small change. "But on that day a meeting of the principal merchants, traders, and bankers took place in which the following resolution was entered into and signed by upwards of 1,100 names."[21]

We, the undersigned, merchants and others, being sensible how necessary the preservation of public credit is at this time, do hereby declare that we will not refuse to receive Bank notes in payment of any sum of money to be paid to us, and we will use our utmost endeavours to make our payments in the same manner.

We are told that "the run ceased, and bank notes circulated with as much ease and credit as before."[22] This was neither the first nor the last time that the Bank's creditors came to *its* assistance.

Other crises came with the beginning or ending of wars. The crisis of 1793 is worth exploring in some detail because it had most of the ingredients of later crises and influenced subsequent discussions. The Bank registered a formal complaint with the prime minister, Lord North, in 1782 about his pressures for advances against Exchequer bills on the dubious legal ground that short-term loans were exempt from Parliament's restriction.[23] William Pitt was no less demanding, for a bad harvest if not for war. After the crop failure of 1792, Pitt asked the Bank to honor £100,000 of Exchequer bills for government purchases of foreign grain. Further pressures on the Bank's resources came from the war between the Continental powers and the wave of business failures that marked the end of the boom.[24] There were 105 bankruptcies in November, more than twice the numbers seen in normal years. The Bank's bullion had fallen from almost £9 million in 1789 to £4 million in February 1793. France declared war the same month, and on the 19th the Bank "refused the paper of Lane, Son & Fraser, who suspended payment the next day, leaving a deficit of a million."[25] Conditions continued to decline, and there were 397 bankruptcies in April and May.

This was the first crisis in which the country banks stood out. In a financial revolution as great as the previous century's, the number of banks outside London (the "country" banks) had grown from a dozen in 1750 to over 300 in the 1790s, and were represented in every part

---

[21] Thomas Fortune, *A Concise and Authentic History of the Bank of England*, p. 12.

[22] *Ibid.*, p. 13.

[23] Clapham, *op. cit.*, i, p. 253.

[24] *Ibid.*, pp. 258–60; Andreades, *History of the Bank of England*, pp. 187–89.

[25] A. Andreades, *op. cit.*, p. 186.

of the island.[26] They were small because of Parliament's limit of note issue, except the Bank of England, to small partnerships. (Not until the next century did the growth of payment by check render this constraint unimportant.) Furthermore, they had not yet become familiar with – or chose not to follow – sound banking principles such as the maintenance of adequate reserves. They relied heavily on the Bank of England to discount their paper. As Vincent Stuckey testified in 1832, "My customers give their money to me, and look to me for it; I do the same to the Bank."[27] Stuckey's was a joint-stock bank under the Act of 1826 and had fourteen branches. The little country banks were more vulnerable.

Scores of banks failed and the Bank of England was blamed – or praised – for "putting them down." Sir Francis Baring criticized the Bank for the severity of its restriction.[28]

The foreign market was either shut, or rendered more difficult of access to the merchant, [and] the country at large had no other resource but London; and, after having exhausted the bankers, that resource finally terminated in the Bank of England.

. . . it might have been right for the Bank to lessen the amount of the accommodation which individuals had been accustomed to receive, but then it ought to have been gradual; their determination, and the extent to which it was carried, came like an electrical shock.

In such cases the Bank are not an intermediate body, or power; there is no resource on their refusal, for they are the *dernier resort*.

Sir Francis Baring, *Observations on the Establishment of the Bank of England and of the Paper Circulation of the Country*, pp. 19–20

This task was too much for the Bank, and on April 23, 1793, Pitt met with eleven "City men," including the Lord Mayor, four Bank directors,

---

[26] See Francis Baring, *Observations on the Establishment of the Bank of England and on the Paper Circulation of the Country*. Baring observed that the increase had been especially rapid since 1772.

[27] House of Commons, *Report . . . on the Bank of England Charter*, 1832. Minutes of Evidence, Q1145.

[28] Francis Baring (1740–1810), son of a German cloth merchant who settled in Exeter, apprenticed to a London merchant in 1755 and began an acceptance business with his brother in 1762, head of Francis Baring and Co., baronet 1793; his son Alexander (1774–1848), 1st Baron Ashburton, 1834, formed Baring Brothers with Thomas and Henry; Francis Thornhill (1796–1866, son of Thomas) was Chancellor of the Exchequer, 1839–41, 1st Lord of the Admiralty, 1849–52, and 1st Baron Northbrook, 1866; Evelyn (1841–1917, son of Henry) was consul general of Egypt and 1st Earl of Cromer 1901; George Rowland Stanley (1918–91, grandson of Evelyn) was 3rd Earl of Cromer, ran Baring Brothers during 1945–61 and 1967–70, and was governor of the Bank of England during 1961–66.

and Baring. They agreed that the government would assist the market by issuing up to £5 million of Exchequer bills to solid merchants on the security of commodities. Although the plan did not pass Parliament and receive the royal assent until May 9, in the meantime the "feeling that credit could be obtained was enough to calm people's fears and to prevent many from actually asking for it."[29] There were 338 requests for a total of £3.8 million; 238 of these were granted for a total of £2.2 million, with 49 refused and the rest withdrawn. Only two of the borrowers went bankrupt, some repaid their debts before they fell due, and the government made a profit of £4,348.

Pitt's statement to the Committee appointed to examine the plan is a clear account of the causes and course not only of the crisis of 1793, but of other payments crises:

The Chancellor of the Exchequer stated . . . – That he had received representatives from many different quarters which induced him to believe that the Failures which had taken place had begun by a run on those houses who had issued Circulating Paper without being possessed of sufficient Capital; but that the consequences had soon extended themselves so far as to affect many houses of great solidity and possessed of funds ultimately much more than sufficient to answer all demands upon them; but which had not the Means of converting those Funds into Money or Negotiable securities in time to meet the pressure of the moment. – That the sudden discredit of a considerable quantity of Paper which had been issued by different Banks in itself produced a deficiency of the Circulating Medium which in the ordinary course of things could not be immediately replaced; and that this deficiency occasioned material inconvenience in mercantile transactions. – That in addition to this immediate effect these circumstances also were represented to have induced Bankers and others to keep in their hands a greater quantity of money than they thought necessary in the usual train of business, and that large sums were thus kept out of circulation, and great difficulty arose in procuring the usual advances on Bills of Exchange, particularly those of a long date. – That many persons were said to be possessed of large stocks of goods which they could not at present dispose of and on the credit of which they could not raise money. – That this occasioned an interruption of the usual orders to Manufacturers; which circumstances, together with the interruptions of the means by which they were enabled to make their weekly payments, tended to prevent the employment of a number of persons engaged in different manufactures. – That these evils were represented as likely rapidly to increase to a very serious extent if some extraordinary means were not adopted to restore Credit and Circulation . . .

Report from the Select Committee Appointed to Take into Consideration the Present State of Commercial Credit . . . , April 29, 1793, p. 4

[29] Andreades, *op. cit.*, p. 189.

This and other crises were remembered by critics of the 1797 suspension. Thomas Fortune observed that "the situation of the Bank of England in February 1797 was by no means new, or without precedent: the rebellion in the year 1745 produced the same effect, but with much more reason for it than at the latter period."[30] The '45 had been a real invasion, whereas the rabble that had been released from French prisons and landed in South Wales in 1797 were soon apprehended, it is said, by farmers with pitchforks. The committee of inquiry appointed in the aftermath of the suspension noted that the Bank's reserve during 1782–84 was less than in 1796, the debt of the government to the Bank was greater in 1780–84 than in February 1797, the drain of coin from the Bank between June 1792 and March 1793 exceeded that of December 1795 to February 1797, and in April 1793 the Bank raised its discounts to more than double their amount in December 1796."[31] A critic of the Bank conceded that the "run was not one that could be checked by ordinary measures. Not having originated in commercial causes, in an excess of paper, or in any doubts with regard to the solidity of the Bank, but in the fear and apprehensions caused by the alarms of invasion, it was clear, that so long as these continued no paper convertible into gold would continue in circulation." The government was "bound to intervene." The "really objectionable part of their conduct consisted in their continuing the suspension after the alarms of invasion which had occasioned the panic had completely subsided; when the confidence of the public in the stability of the Bank stood higher than ever; and there was no longer any thing to fear from a return to cash payments."[32] Baring took the opposite position.

My chief reason is that credit ought never to be subject to convulsions; a change even from good to better ought not to be made until there is almost a certainty of maintaining and preserving it in that position; for a retrograde motion in public credit is productive of consequences which are incalculable. With this principle in view, I am averse to the Bank re-assuming their payments generally during the war whilst there is a possibility of their being obliged to suspend them again.

Baring, *Observations . . .* , p. 69

He believed that Bank notes should be made legal tender for the duration of the war, with limits on their quantity "as a security to the public with regard to the private interest of the Bank," as well as "to preserve

---

[30] *History*, preface.
[31] House of Commons, *Third Report . . . on the Outstanding Demands of the Bank of England*, April 21, 1797, p. 10.
[32] Anonymous, *Note on the Suspension of Cash Payments. . . .*

the independence of the Bank ... to prevent their becoming, either directly or indirectly, the means of introducing Government paper as the circulating medium of the country."[33]

The Resumption of 1821

Background and First Steps
The most painful part of the suspension was the postwar depression. The behavior of the Bank between 1809 and resumption in 1821 was generally consistent with the passive accommodation of credit demands on unchanging terms against a background of fluctuating market rates of interest. The end of the war could not be seen in 1809, and the opening of trade with South America combined with government spending to produce a speculative boom that the Bank joined. Its discounts and advances rose from £28 million in 1808 to £45 million in 1814–15, before falling to £32 million in 1818.[34] Henry Thornton's firm was brought to the brink of ruin in 1815 by the failures of a partner and a borrower who had gambled on commodities.[35] After a period of stability in 1818–19, the Bank's lending plummeted to £17 million in 1822. These movements corresponded closely with its circulation (M) and to a lesser extent the price index (P), seen in Fig. 2.1.

Progress toward resumption was uneven and uncertain. The authorities "were, generally speaking, in favour of a return to cash payments on the old basis – some day."[36] By an Act of 1803, convertibility of the Bank's notes was to be resumed six months after the end of the war. In 1814 this was moved back to July 5, 1815, then to July 5, 1816.[37] Resumption was probably possible on the latter date because the exchanges, having risen as money and prices fell, stood at par. However, neither the government nor the Bank had worked out the mechanics of a return to gold, and it was decided not to attempt resumption on the first favorable turn of the exchanges. It was moved back to July 5, 1818, and Parliament ordered

---

[33] *Observations*, pp. 68–69, 81, and *Further Observations*.

[34] Data sources are with Figure 2.1. See Feavearyear, *op. cit.*, pp. 180–97, for the 1809–14 boom and bust.

[35] The story is told by E. J. T. Acaster, "Henry Thornton – The Banker." Down, Thornton, Free, and Down was salvaged by an infusion of capital, but its successor, Down, Thornton & Co., collapsed in 1825.

[36] Feavearyear, *op. cit.*, p. 204.

[37] See House of Commons, *Second Report . . .* , 1819, p. 3, for the history of acts of restriction and resumption.

"that the Directors of the Bank...make such preparations as to their discretion and experience may appear most expedient for enabling them to resume payments in cash without public inconvenience, and at the earliest period..."[38]

The process began in November 1816 with an offer to redeem small notes issued before 1812 at par. But in September 1817, when the Bank offered to redeem all notes issued through 1816, the public took large amounts of gold. The exchanges had become unfavorable in July (that is, the paper pound had fallen relative to gold), but the Bank took no steps to protect its reserve. It had become accustomed to an inconvertible system under which unlimited credit might be extended without fear of repercussions. "[I]f the Bank directors," Thomas Tooke wrote in *Thoughts and Details of High and Low Prices of the Last Thirty Years*, "had not unfortunately... disregarded in the regulation of their issues the indication by which their predecessors, previous to 1797 professed to be guided, they would have been warned to contract, instead of enlarging, their issues [and so tending] to accelerate the rise of prices..., and so promote the spirit of speculation and overtrading."[39] The Bank applied for a further suspension, and Parliament extended the Restriction Act to July 1819 and appointed committees of inquiry into the method of resumption.

The Question of the Standard

While those wishing to return to the old standard hesitated, others proposed fundamental changes. Before going into those proposals, which are still argued, we need to understand the workings of the gold standard, particularly the determination of the price level. The purchasing power of gold coin (the value of money) is regulated by the relative costs of production of gold and other goods.[40] Their stability over long periods has been called "the golden constant."[41] The quantity of gold money is not rigid but responds to profit opportunities. However, the long-run may be very long. The Australian and California gold rushes of the 1850s followed a quarter-century of falling prices (rising value of gold), as did those in Alaska and South Africa in the late 1890s.

---

[38] *Ibid.*, preamble. Discussed by A. W. Acworth, *Financial Reconstruction*, pp. 72–73.
[39] Pp. 155–56.
[40] A classic statement is Nassau Senior, "On the Quantity and Value of Money."
[41] Roy Jastram, *The Golden Constant: The English and American Experience, 1560–1967*.

The changes proposed to this system fell into three categories: devaluation under the old standard, paper currencies, and a more efficient gold standard with or without devaluation. After the inflation of 1809–10, some urged a return to gold at the prevailing price to avoid the deflation necessitated by a return at the old par. However, the weight of opinion was against them. The Bullion Committee, this time speaking for the majority, called it a "breach of public faith and dereliction of a primary duty of Government."[42] William Huskisson called it "a stale and wretched expedient."[43] Looking back from 1821, however, Ricardo wrote that if inflation had gone far enough and long enough, the balance of justice, considering the parties entering into contracts at high prices, perhaps in the belief that the old par would not be resumed, would be on the side of devaluation. Such a case might have existed in 1813 at the height of the price rise.

I never should advise a Government to restore a currency which was depreciated 30 percent to par; I should recommend . . . that the currency should be fixed at the depreciated value by lowering the standard, and that no further deviations should take place. It was without any legislation that the currency from 1813 to 1819 became of an increased value, and within 5 percent of the value of gold – it was in this state of things and not with the currency depreciated 30 percent, that I advised a recurrence to the old standard.

Ricardo, Letter to John Wheatley, *Works*, ix, p. 72

It is interesting to note that a hundred years later, in December 1919, when the Cunliffe Commission recommended a return to the prewar standard, the pound was 22 percent below its par with the U.S. dollar and gold. At its lowest point two months later, the depreciation was 30 percent.

Gold is not the best way to stable prices, anyway, the advocates of paper money argued. A "steady exchange . . . will cost us too dear if the price to be paid for it is a fluctuating currency," argued Walter Hall.[44] The Birmingham banker and political reformer Thomas Attwood desired an inconvertible paper currency issued by the government.[45] A commission

---

[42] Edwin Cannan, *The Paper Pound*, p. 68.

[43] William Huskisson, *The Question Concerning the Depreciation of Our Currency Stated and Examined*, p. 25.

[44] *A View of Our Late and of Our Future Currency*, p. 56; see Jacob Viner, *Studies in the Theory of International Trade*, p. 215.

[45] Thomas Attwood was a banker and founder of the Birmingham Political Union for extension of the ballot, achieved in the Reform Bill of 1832; he was leader of the Birmingham School favoring an inconvertible currency. William Cobbett was a peasant, soldier, and pamphleteer. His *Political Register*, which reported his tours, later collected as *Rural Rides*, opposed Peel's resumption because it allowed for paper money.

would regulate its quantity under the authority of Parliament by purchases and sales of government securities. The commission would not be limited by "laws of maximum and minimum," but would find it "easy . . . and safe to prevent the depreciation of money, and to preserve prices upon certain fixed relations . . . by judicious legislative operations upon the issue of bank notes, or other national paper."[46] He later admitted that this would not always be an easy task because one cannot simply decree increases in money, most of which would be bank liabilities.[47]

Advocates of paper money – derided as "rags" by William Cobbett[48] – lacked credibility because their aversion to unstable prices was limited to deflation. Attwood believed that the "depreciation of the currency is beneficial to a country in every way that it can be considered. It is only injurious to . . . holders of monied obligations, who ought to be bought up, or compromised with, by the public, rather than suffer the national welfare to be arrested by a crippling of the circulation."[49] A decade after resumption he wrote, "More injustice had been done to, and more misery had been endured by, the productive classes" during each of the contractions of 1819–22 and 1825–28 "than would have been done to or endured by the fundowners if the Government had abolished the whole national debt at once."[50]

Ricardo, who was interested in how to make the gold standard work, accepted that it was not an end in itself but a means to price stability, and not necessarily the best:

A well regulated paper currency is so great an improvement in commerce that I should greatly regret if prejudice should induce us to return to a system of less utility. The introduction of the precious metals for the purposes of money may with truth be considered as one of the most important steps towards the improvement of commerce and the arts of civilised life; but it is no less true that with the advancement of knowledge and science we discover that it would be another improvement to banish them again from the employment to which, during a less-enlightened period, they had been so advantageously applied.

Ricardo, *Proposals for an Economical and Secure Currency*, p. 65

Keynes expressed this sentiment a century later in the midst of another resumption when he called the gold standard "a barbarous relic."

---

[46] Attwood, *Prosperity Restored*, pp. 129–30, 163–64; and Viner, *op. cit.*, p. 213.

[47] *The Scotch Banker*, p. 101.

[48] William Cobbett, *Paper against Gold and Glory against Prosperity*, Letter III; discussed in Frank Fetter, ed., *Selected Writings of Thomas Attwood*, p. xiv.

[49] Attwood, *Prosperity Restored*, p. 163.

[50] Attwood, "Famine," p. 94.

However, Ricardo shared the common fear that unless banks and governments were disciplined by convertibility, inflation and monetary instability might have no bounds. It had to be admitted that "gold and silver are . . . subject to greater variations than it is desirable a standard should be subject to. They are, however, the best with which we are acquainted."[51]

The case can also be made that the gold standard is the most flexible of systems. Britain's ability to finance the war on reasonable terms by the paper pound gave it an advantage over Napoleon, who because of the lack of credibility in France's promises had to pay gold.[52]

The Chamberlain–Bradbury Commission noted in 1925 that "such credit restriction as may become necessary to adjust the general level of sterling prices to a free gold market may well be less drastic than that which would be required in order to maintain a 'managed' pound in the neighbourhood of parity. If the gold standard is firmly re-established, the danger of apprehensions as to the future of exchange leading to sudden withdrawals . . . will be reduced."[53]

Ricardo's compromise standard would have limited the convertibility of paper to ingots. The circulation would be paper and token coins, eliminating the costs of gold and silver coinage and freeing some of the resources tied up in metallic reserves, whereas the effectiveness of the gold standard would remain because notes of £233 could obtain a 60-ounce ingot for export (as provided in the Resumption Act of 1819).

Resumption, 1819–21

The resumption committees submitted recommendations in early May 1819, and the Resumption Act, called Peel's Act after the chairman of the Commons committee, passed before the end of the month.[54] It was the first statutory monetary rule beyond convertibility, if only for a transition. Its provisions are listed in the following. The last was a signal from Parliament that it had reformed and accepted an uninhibited gold standard. It would no longer seek to regulate gold flows by legal restrictions. The first

---

[51] Ricardo, *Proposals for an Economical and Secure Currency*, p. 62.

[52] Michael Bordo and Eugene White, "A Tale of Two Currencies: British and French Finance during the Napoleonic Wars."

[53] T. E. Gregory, ed., *Select Statutes, Documents & Reports Relating to British Banking, 1832–1928*, ii, pp. 377–79.

[54] Robert Peel (succeeded to baronetcy in 1830) was secretary for Ireland during 1812–18 (forming the Irish constabulary, "Peelers"), Home secretary during 1821–29 (organizing the Metropolitan police, "bobbies"), and prime minister in 1834 and from 1841 to 1846. He repealed Catholic disabilities in 1844 and Corn Laws in 1846.

provision was a signal that the government's financial needs no longer posed a threat to the Bank and the gold standard. The others aimed at a gradual reduction of money and prices.

To give the Bank greater control over their issue, provision ought to be made for the gradual repayment of £10 million of its holdings of Government securities.

From February 1, 1820, the Bank shall be liable to deliver, on demand, a quantity of gold of standard fineness of not less than 60 ounces in exchange for the Bank's notes at the rate of £4 1s per ounce;

From October 1, 1820, the rate shall be £3 19s 6d;

From May 1, 1821, the rate shall be £3 17s 10½d [the old par];

The Bank may at any time between February 1, 1820, and May 1, 1821, fix any rate between £4 1s and £3 17s 10½d, but that such intermediate rate having once been fixed by the Bank, that rate shall not be subsequently increased;

From May 1, 1823, the Bank shall pay its notes on demand in the legal coin of the realm; and

The laws prohibiting the melting and exportation of the coin of the realm are repealed.

The Bank resisted. The directors still denied any effects of their issue on gold movements or the exchanges. They registered a protest with Parliament against the burdens of an act that made a private establishment responsible for the national currency under a system that required it to anticipate the future:

If the Directors of the Bank have a true comprehension of the views of the Committees in submitting this scheme to Parliament, they are obliged to infer that the object of the Committees is to secure, at every hazard, and under every possible variation of circumstances, the return of payments in Gold at mint price for Bank Notes at the expiration of two years; and that this measure is so to be managed that the mint price . . . shall ever afterwards be preserved, leaving the market or exchange price of Gold to be controlled by the Bank solely by the amount of their issues of Notes.

It further appears to the Directors, with regard to the final execution of this plan . . . , that discretionary power is to be taken away from the Bank, and that it is merely to regulate its Issues and make purchases of Gold so as to be enabled to answer all possible demands whenever its Treasury shall be again open for the payment of its Notes. . . .

The Directors . . . cannot but feel a repugnance [toward] a System which, in their opinion, in all its great tendencies and operations, concerns the Country in general more than the immediate interests of the Bank alone.

It is not certainly a part of the regular duty of the Bank under its original institution to enter into the general views of Policy by which this great Empire is to be governed, in all its Commercial and Pecuniary transactions, which exclusively belong to the Administration, to Parliament, and to the Country at large; nor is it the province of the Bank to expound the principles by which these views ought to be regulated. Its peculiar and appropriate duty is the management of the concerns of the Banking Establishment as connected with the payment of the Interest of the National Debt, the lodgments consigned to its care and the ordinary Advances it has been accustomed to make to Government.

But when the Directors are now to be called upon, in the new situation in which they are placed by the Restriction Act, to procure a Fund for supporting the whole National Currency, either in Bullion or in Coin, and when it is proposed that they should effect this measure within a given period, by regulating the market price of Gold by a limitation of the Issue of Bank Notes, with whatever distress such limitation may be attended to individuals, or the community at large, they feel it their ... duty to state their sentiments thus explicitly ... to His Majesty's Ministers on this subject that a tacit ... concurrence at this juncture may not, at some future period, be construed into a previous implied sanction on their part of a System which they cannot but consider fraught with very great uncertainty and risk.

It is impossible for them to decide beforehand what shall be the course of events for the next two, much less for the next four years; they have no right to hazard a flattering conjecture, for which they have not real grounds, in which they may be disappointed, and for which they may be considered responsible. They cannot venture to advise an unrelenting continuance of pecuniary pressures upon the Commercial world of which it is impossible for them either to foresee or estimate the consequences.

> *Representation by the Directors of the Bank of England to the Chancellor of the Exchequer*, May 20, 1819[55]

But the political climate had changed. The war was over and sound-money men were ready for a return to "the only true, intelligible, adequate standard of value," as Peel called it in speaking for the committee's resolutions.[56] He had voted against the Bullion Report out of ignorance, he admitted, but had been persuaded that "every consideration of sound policy and of strict justice" – for the laborer, whom depreciation robbed of the value of his wages, as well as for the public creditor – "should induce them to restore the ancient and permanent standard." He was convinced that "the difficulties of our situation would be aggravated" by delay. The only question was one of mechanics – of how to proceed with resumption. General statements and good intentions had not been enough.

The Bank was supported by merchants and bankers frightened of the planned deflation. They shared Governor George Dorrien's concern that "It is very difficult to say when the Bank could with propriety resume its cash payments, it must always be judged of by experience."[57] However, the

---

[55] *British Parliamentary Papers, Monetary Policy, General, 2*, pp. 359–62.

[56] *Hansard*, May 24, 1819.

[57] House of Commons Resumption Committee, *Minutes of Evidence*, p. 32; also see House of Lords Resumption Committee, *Minutes of Evidence*, questions 14–34, and Elmer Wood, *English Theories of Central Banking Control, 1819–58*, pp. 101–6.

government, "piqued by the Bank's intransigence" and tired of waiting, "abandoned" it.[58]

The prime minister, Lord Liverpool,[59] defended the plan by stressing its gradual and therefore "less injurious" operation. In any case, it was time to return to a fixed standard of value. Those who opposed the plan in reality objected "to returning to cash payments at all." Unrestricted paper money had never been adopted "by any civilised country from the beginning of the world." Besides, how would it operate? Everyone "knew the disgraceful measures, reverted to, even in this country, in former times, to depreciate the standard of value; but even that alternative, bad as it was, presented advantages not to be found in the rejection of a standard altogether." He complimented the integrity and patriotism of the Bank of England, but pointed to the "inevitable effect" of releasing it from the obligation of redeeming its notes in the precious metals. "It would, in fact, be to invest them with the unrestrained power of making money."[60]

Would Parliament consent to commit to their hands what it would certainly refuse to the Sovereign on the throne, controlled by Parliament itself, the power of making money without any other check or influence to direct them than their own notions of profit and interest? Nothing could be more unwise than for Government to erect itself into a company of bankers; but it would be more reasonable for Government to take even that course, and issue its own notes, than to give such a power as he had described to any private corporation.

Turning to the argument that the value of gold itself was changeable, and had varied a great deal since the beginning of the war, Liverpool said that departure from a fixed standard

was not only objectionable as between the State and the individual, but must also operate on the engagements between every individual debtor and creditor in the country. It was impossible in either case to enter into calculations of individual loss or gain. Those who entered into the engagement did so at their own risk, and the State, having made or authorised the contract, was bound to see it fulfilled without reference to those who had benefited or who had lost.

---

[58] Boyd Hilton, *Corn, Cash, Commerce*, p. 41n37, referring to Lord Liverpool in the House of Lords, January 21, 1819.

[59] Lord Liverpool (Robert Banks Jenkinson) was master of the Mint in 1799, foreign secretary in 1801, home secretary during 1804–9, secretary of war during 1809–12, and prime minister during 1812–27; he was the son of Charles, 1st Earl, and author of *Coins of the Realm*.

[60] This account of Liverpool's speech is from Charles Yonge, *Life of Lord Liverpool*, ii, pp. 386–87.

The Lords' approval was nearly unanimous. The more spirited opposition in the House of Commons was silenced by Ricardo, recently retired from the Stock Exchange and a member since February. He told the House of Commons that

he was fully persuaded of the truth of the declaration of the hon. Director that the Bank wished to resume cash payments, but he was just as fully persuaded that they did not know how to set about it. When called before the Committee, the Directors individually admitted that the price of bullion and the rate of exchanges were affected by the amount of their issues.[61] But when collected in their own Court they resolved that "they conceive it to be their duty to declare that they are unable to discover any solid foundation for such a sentiment." When they avowed such inconsistent opinions, and after the experience which the House had had of their conduct, it would be the highest indiscretion in Parliament not to take out of their hands the preparations for the resumption of cash payments. [The course chosen should] keep the ministers also under control.[62]

Boyd Hilton described the scene of Ricardo's performance:[63] "The Commons debates on cash payments were curiously unreal. Several members had prophesied disaster when suddenly Ricardo, 'the phenomenon of the night,' transformed the situation. He was wildly cheered throughout, perhaps because he said authoritatively things that his apprehensive audience was only too relieved to hear."

This question was one of immense importance in principle [Ricardo continued], but in the manner of bringing it about was trivial, and not deserving half an hour's consideration of the House. The difficulty was only that of raising the currency 3 per cent in value. [Hear, hear!] And who could doubt that even in those states in which the currency was entirely metallic, it often suffered a variation equal to this without inconvenience to the public. [Hear!] . . .

Till October 1820, the Bank need make no reduction [of its issue], and then a slight one [hear!]; and he had no doubt that if they were cautious they might arrive at cash payments without giving out one guinea in gold. . . .

He was quite astonished that such an alarm prevailed at a reduction of perhaps one million in four years, and could only ascribe it to the indiscreet language of the Bank. [Hear, hear!]

---

[61] Governor George Dorrien and Deputy Governor Charles Pole admitted that "a considerable reduction" (perhaps 7 or 8 millions, that is, 30 percent) of the Bank's issue would affect the exchange. House of Commons, 1819, *Monetary Policy*, pp. 32, 35.

[62] *Hansard*, May 24, 1819; *Works*, v, pp. 9–11.

[63] *Corn, Cash, Commerce*; some additional passages are provided from Ricardo's speech, *Hansard*, May 24, 1819; *Works*, v, pp. 9–17. Hilton's account draws from J. S. Mallet's diary quoted by Piero Sraffa, editor of Ricardo's *Works*, v, p. 17n2.

"The hon. member sat down amidst loud and general cheering from all sides of the House," the debate was adjourned, and the House rose at two o'clock. The next day, "to everyone's amazement, amid turmoil and 'great confusion,' Canning called for unanimity 'to show the public that the House was earnest in its attempts to restore the ancient standard,' and the resolutions were passed 'without a dissentient voice.'"[64]

The resolutions applied Ricardo's ingot plan and he expected a successful experiment to lead to its permanent adoption. They were, he wrote a few days later, a "triumph of science and truth over prejudice and error."[65] His sanguinity regarding their mild and gradual operation was not generally shared by those most directly affected, however. Witnesses before the resumption committees had worried that a severe contraction was planned. John Smith, a London banker with country bank connections, thought that even the gradual reduction of the Bank's issue that was envisioned by the committees "would have the effect of crippling all persons engaged in money transactions, and generally in commerce.... I consider that all persons having very large engagements for future periods would endeavour to diminish them...."[66] Nathan Rothschild and Alexander Baring agreed with Smith that resumption should be phased in over several years – although admitting that this might raise doubts of the government's resolve – and that considerable financial and commercial distress could not be avoided. Peel's father, a textile manufacturer and member for Tamworth in Staffordshire, opposed the bill and urged the House, "before a measure so destructive of the commercial interests of the country was passed," to pause to consider the recent Petition of the Merchants of London in Favour of the Restriction of Cash Payments. He lamented the error of his son.[67]

These fears were increased by the first resolution, which implied a sale over an unknown period of nearly a third of the Bank's securities. Preparations for repayment were announced in July, and in the same month Parliament restored the prohibition against Bank loans to the government for more than three months except on its express authority – which Pitt had persuaded Parliament to suspend in 1793.[68]

---

[64] Hilton, *op. cit.*, p. 47; from R.I. and S. Wilberforce, *The Life of William Wilberforce*, vol. 27, and Canning ms. *Diary*.

[65] Letter to Hutches Trower, May 28, 1819; *Works*, viii, p. 31.

[66] *Second Report...*, 1819, Minutes of Evidence, pp. 219–20.

[67] P. Sraffa, "Notes on the Evidence of the Resumption of Cash Payments," Ricardo's *Works*, v, p. 365.

[68] For a history of Bank loans to the government, often in violation of the law, see MacLeod, *Theory and Practice of Banking*, i, p. 517.

The price of gold dropped to par almost immediately, the Bank's notes and deposits fell, and gold flowed into the Bank. Early in 1821, with the reserve at another record level, the Bank expressed its willingness to resume immediate payments in coin of all its notes at par, and an act was passed permitting it to do so from May 1. Full convertibility had been achieved in less than two years instead of four, and the value of the currency had risen to par in less time than that. Unfortunately, these accomplishments were accompanied by deflation and unemployment. Between 1819 and 1822, prices fell 36 percent, on top of the 7-percent drop between 1818 and 1819, with similar falls in the Bank's currency. The Bank's private discounts fell substantially, and between 1818 and 1822 its government securities fell from £27 million to £13 million.

Ricardo was blamed for what was popularly believed to have been the consequences of his resumption plan, and it was later rumored that he recanted on his death bed.[69] In 1822, in the speech quoted in the frontispiece, he rejected these charges. Resumption had been bungled by the Bank, but "he was as it were put upon his trial – his plan had not been adopted, and yet to it was referred the consequences which were distinct from it; and he was held responsible for the plan that had been adopted, which was not his, but was essentially different from it." All would have gone smoothly if the Bank had reduced its circulation "cautiously," as he and others had recommended, specifically by only as much as would have been necessary to return the currency to par, certainly by no more than 5 percent.

What went wrong? Why did money and prices fall so much? What errors did the Bank commit, and why? Tooke's explanation is persuasive. He began by pointing out that Peel's Act had not forced the 1819–22 contraction of the currency. At the end of August 1819 the Bank's circulation was little different from the preceding several months and the exchange rate was virtually at par. There had been no repayment by the government of its debt to the Bank. In short, restoration had been achieved without action by the Bank or the government. Then what was the cause of the subsequent contraction? "Either the Directors designedly and forcibly contracted the circulation with a view to prepare for paying in gold," which was unnecessary, or they "were simply passive in the regulation of their issues, following the routine by which they were guided previously to 1819." The latter was the case, he declared. "From the fall in the mercantile rate of interest, and the little inducement to speculation," which might be

---

[69] See R. S. Sayers, "Ricardo's Views on Monetary Questions," for the story.

explained by the public's expectations of contraction, "the applications for discount of mercantile bills fell off rapidly," and the government began to pay off its loans while the Bank's rate remained 5 percent.[70]

Ricardo had presented a foolproof rule and been thwarted by the markets and the Bank. The market anticipated resumption, investors believing that this time the authorities meant business. No one would pay 81s for what would soon be available for 78s. However, they were happy to take the opposite position. Ricardo had foreseen this possibility and urged that the Bank in no circumstances accumulate gold. He thought that the operation could be managed with no gold purchases by the Bank. Yet its gold rose (in millions) from £4 in August 1819 to £11 in February 1822, whereas their notes fell from £25 to £18 and their deposits from £6.4 to £5.5.

There might have been nothing the Bank could have done to avert the contraction. There might have been no positive discount rate consistent with the stability of money and prices. Nonetheless, the fact remains that notwithstanding their professed concern for financial distress and their protest against the limits placed on their freedom of action, the directors failed to exercise the discretion left to them. Perhaps the only lessons of this experience are that contracts (including monetary rules) are necessarily incomplete and the ends of inflation are always painful. Ricardo anticipated the government's course in the next resumption a hundred years later when he opposed Charles Western's motion in June 1822 to bring back restriction because of the deflationary consequences of resumption:

[T]he measure of 1819 was chiefly pernicious to the country on account of the unfounded alarms which it created in some men's minds, and the vague fears that other people felt lest something should occur, the nature of which they could not themselves define. That alarm was now got over; those fears were subsiding; and he conceived, that as the depreciation in the value of our currency which a few years ago was experienced could not possibly return upon us in future if we persevered in the measures we had taken, it would be the most unwise thing in the world to interfere with an act, the disturbance of which would unsettle the great principle we had established.[71]

The government had demonstrated its steadiness under pressure. When Nathan Rothschild lobbied for a reversal of policy after the army

---

[70] Tooke, *Letter to Lord Grenville*, pp. 1–11.
[71] Ricardo, *Works*, v, p. 216.

disbursed a public protest in the Peterloo massacre of August 1819, Liverpool responded:[72]

If we are quiet things will come right. I know from a person who has seen Baring within these few days that he is of the opinion that there will be a great reaction as to our funds, and that the French funds cannot rise much beyond their present price.

The point, however, upon which I feel most anxiety is the idea suggested by Rothschild of a continuance of the Bank restriction. I am satisfied that no measure could be more fatal, and that the very notion of its being a matter for consideration would do harm . . .

Let us therefore determine to stand upon our present system, and let no one entertain a doubt that this is our determination. I am persuaded the Bank, for their own interest, when they see we are firm, will not make any improper reduction of their circulation . . .

In 1925, Chancellor Winston Churchill's adviser responded in a similar fashion to his chief's question why resumption should not be delayed:

It would reverberate throughout a world which has not forgotten the uneasy moments of the winter of 1923; and would be the more convinced that we never meant business about the gold standard because our nerve had failed when the stage was set. The immediate consequence would be a considerable withdrawal of balances and investment (both foreign *and British*) from London; a heavy drop in Exchange; and, to counteract that tendency, a substantial increase in Bank rate. We might very easily reap all the disadvantages which some fear from a return to gold without any of the advantages.

With the engine thus reversed, no one could foretell when conditions, political, psychological, economic, would be such that the opportunity would occur again. It would certainly be a long time.

Otto Niemeyer, H. M. Treasury Controller of Finance[73]

---

[72] Yonge, *op. cit.*, pp. 416–17; David Kynaston, *City of London*, p. 40. "Peterloo" (sarcastically after Waterloo) refers to the cavalry charge on a meeting of "radical reformers" at St. Peter's Field, Manchester, on August 16, 1819, in which 11 were killed and hundreds injured.

[73] Donald Moggridge, *British Monetary Policy, 1924–31*, p. 67.

FOUR

Making a Central Bank: II. Looking for a Rule

[N]either the Bank of England nor the country bankers acted upon any rule or principle in their issues. They answered the demand for their issues on such security as satisfied them. I would not trouble the [House] at length upon the effect of such a system. I will merely read to them a summary account of the management of the circulation during the last drain in 1838–9 [when the circulation varied inversely with gold]. Can anybody wonder that under these circumstances this drain was so severe and so prolonged, and I need say no more as to the utter absence of all principle and all rule in the management of our circulation.

Charles Wood, House of Commons, May 20, 1844

Our general rule is to draw a distinction between the privilege of Issue and the conduct of the ordinary banking business. We think they stand on an entirely different footing. We think that the privilege of Issue is one which may be fairly and justly controlled by the State, and that the banking business, as distinguished from Issue, is a matter in respect to which there cannot be too unlimited and unrestricted a competition.

Sir Robert Peel, House of Commons, May 6, 1844

Resumption in 1821 required the Bank of England to relearn the arts of profit making and survival under the constraints of the gold standard. The narrow escapes of its first century would have supported skepticism. Nonetheless, it had survived and prospered in the midst of great economic and political change. The Bank may not always have been intelligent, but it was adaptable. Furthermore, its path would be made easier by the removal of the most troublesome source of financial pressures – the government's war needs. These would be replaced by new pressures, however. The financial system had become more complex with the pyramiding of

		Background: People and Events	

1819: Social unrest; troops disburse protesters at St. Peter's Field, Manchester ("Peterloo").

1819–21: Resumption.

1825, 1837: British and American financial panics and depressions.

1826: Joint-stock banks of issue permitted 65 miles from London. Nonissue joint-stock banks recognized in London in 1833; limited liability extended to banks in 1862.*

1830: Wave of violence, notably rick-burning by agricultural laborers.

1831, 1833, 1842: Factory and Mines Acts directed especially at the safety and hours of women and children.

1832: The Great Reform Bill extended suffrage to the middle classes and shifted parliamentary seats from rotten boroughs to counties and new towns.

1833: Bank Charter Act: Bank of England made more transparent and notes legal tender.

1834: Social agitation and repression; Tolpuddle Martyrs transported for union organizing; New Poor Law increased workhouses.

1838: Chartists agitate for universal male suffrage; mass movement ended by 1848 but goal realized in 1867.

1844: Bank Charter Act: separation of departments, notes tied to gold.

* P. L. Cottrell and B. L. Anderson, *Money and Banking in England*, pp. 241, 304.

	Prime Minister	Chancellor of the Exchequer	Party
1812	Lord Liverpool	Nicholas Vansittart	Tory
1823		F. J. Robinson	
1827	George Canning	Canning	
1828	Duke of Wellington	Henry Goulburn	
1830	Earl Grey	Viscount Althorp	Whig
1834	Viscount Melbourne		
1834	Sir Robert Peel	Peel	Tory
1835	Melbourne	Lord Mounteagle	Whig
1839		Francis Baring	
1841	Peel	Henry Goulburn	Tory/Conservative
1846	Lord John Russell	Charles Wood	Whig/Liberal

Note: Short-lived governments omitted.

monetary claims that was already underway before the restriction. All those claims rested in the end, even more than in Thornton's time, on the Bank. At home, the small, volatile, and more numerous country banks were the greatest concern. International pressures would also grow with the overseas banks and governments that looked to London for their liquidity as well as their long-term finance.

Another change was the extent to which the Bank was regarded as a public institution with responsibilities beyond that of banker to the government. Although the maintenance of the gold standard – convertibility – was still for respectable opinion, its primary objective, the government and the public expected more than this. They also wanted financial stability. The Bank's failure to supply this, sometimes apparently making matters worse, provoked parliamentary inquiries in 1832 and 1840–41, and changes in its charter in 1833 and 1844.

The following discussion begins with the Bank's bumpy reentry to the gold standard in the 1820s that provoked, as we see in the second section, inquiries into its role in the monetary system. The third section examines more crises, the failure of the Bank's attempt to establish a reliable decision rule, new debates over monetary policy, and the political victory of rule over discretion in the Act of 1844. The arguments anticipated latter controversies over the relations between short-run financial stability and long-run price stability, the definition of money, the ability to distinguish between shocks, and the time consistency of optimal plans.

Public Responsibilities

The Bank, the Government, and the Money Supply

The contraction that came with resumption was described in the previous chapter. In February 1822, the government threatened to take monetary policy into its own hands, giving notice that the chancellor would bring a measure to enable the Bank to lend the government funds at 3 percent on Exchequer bills to be secured by poor rates and distributed among the parishes for the relief of agriculture. The prime minister thought the Bank's request for a repayment of £10,000,000 by the government in 1819 "unnecessarily large,"[1] but he had been reconciled to it "by what passed in the [Resumption] Committee with respect to the probability that, in the event of the general circulation being found insufficient, the Bank would lower their rate of discount." It would be better that money be increased through the medium of the Bank's private discounts than by loans to the government. "It does appear very extraordinary to His Majesty's Government, and I imagine must appear very extraordinary to

---

[1] House of Lords, February 26, 1822; A. W. Acworth, *Financial Reconstruction*, pp. 105–6.

your Lordships and to the public, that at this moment when the market rate of interest is not more than 4 percent, the Bank refuse to discount at a lower rate than 5." The situation was rendered "the more inexplicable" by the fact known to everybody that because of the favorable state of the exchanges since 1819 an "immense quantity of treasure . . . must have been flowing into the coffers of the Bank of England."[2]

The government did not need the money for its own use, Liverpool said, but desired simply "to extend and quicken the general circulation." Tooke later observed of the plan that it was "a new and somewhat dangerous doctrine to contend that Government ought to enlarge or diminish [its] debt not according to views strictly financial but according to their notions of the proper amount of the circulating medium."[3]

The government also planned to apply a part of the the sinking fund to the purchase of public securities to reduce interest rates, which would benefit mortgagers and other borrowers, relieving the landed interest. Ricardo objected to this measure first on the basis that it would fail to achieve its objective. The rate of interest depended on other causes, particularly "the profit that could be made upon the employment of capital."[4] The harvests had been overabundant, and the only effective remedy for farmers was "to regulate their supply by the public demand." His main objection was that the measure was another instance of the Government's resort to indirect means to divert the income of the people to unapproved and often wasteful purposes. Ricardo was not against the principle of the sinking fund, but he had

found from experience that while the people were called upon to pay a large proportion of taxes for the maintenance of this fund in the hope that it would be applied to the discharge of their debt, they experienced nothing but disappointment through the manner in which the fund had been appropriated by the ministers. The existence of this fund would serve only to encourage ministers to engage in new wars. [A] fund which ought to be now above £20,000,000 was so reduced that with the addition of £3,000,000 of new taxes it only amounted to £5,000,000. . . . Let us have no sinking fund; let the money remain in the pockets of the people. When the ministers want supplies, whether for carrying on a war, or for any other purpose, let them come down to the House and ask for them, without having any such fund to resort to.[5]

[2] Acworth, *op. cit.*, 105–6; *Hansard*, NS, VI, pp. 714–16.
[3] Thomas Tooke, *History of Prices*, ii, p. 106.
[4] House of Commons, February 18, 1822; *Works*, v, pp. 129–30.
[5] House of Commons, June 1, 1821, February 18, 1822; *Works*, v, pp. 119, 130.

Ricardo's criticism of the sinking fund applied to discretionary public finance in general. Possibly the most dangerous source was the Bank of England.[6] Ricardo was moved to address this issue again, he told the House on April 29, 1822, by the government's intention to use the Bank to manipulate the currency. It was bad enough that the Bank had been created to enable governments to circumvent Parliament, but the bribes that it was paid to perform this service were excessive. He had learned that the government proposed to extend the Bank's charter from 1833 to 1843 in return for its approval of joint-stock banks of issue outside the metropolis. He "had hoped never to have heard of their charter being renewed." He said it "would be a great improvement that the public should be allowed to enter into partnery concerns for supplying their own money transactions. . . ."[7] A month later, he spoke in support of a complaint of the Bank's "immense profits":

Mr. Ricardo did not complain of the Bank directors for making the concern as profitable as possible; but he complained of the ministers for having made such improvident bargains with the Bank as to enable that establishment to make those enormous profits. He should oppose to the utmost the renewal of the Bank charter because he was satisfied that every farthing made by the Bank ought to belong to the public. Even if a paper currency were wanted, ministers could accomplish the object more advantageously for the public without than with the assistance of the Bank of England.

House of Commons, May 31, 1822; *Works*, v, p. 193

Returning to immediate questions of monetary policy, the Bank reduced its rate to 4 percent in June. However, Ricardo did not believe that this would have "any general effect upon the value of money in the market, or upon the price of land, or of any commodity."

If the Bank had doubled its circulation, it still would have no permanent effect upon the value of money. If such a thing had taken place, the general level of interest would be restored in less than six months. The country only required, and could only bear, a certain circulation; and when that amount of circulation was afloat, the rate of interest would find its wholesome and natural level.

House of Commons, July 1, 1822; *Works*, v, p. 222

---

[6] The sinking fund, introduced by Pitt in 1786 and terminated in 1828, is discussed in J. R. McCulloch, *A Select Collection of Scarce and Valuable Tracts and Other Publications on the National Debt and the Sinking Fund*.

[7] House of Commons, April 20, 1822; *Works*, v, p. 156.

Ricardo was less willing than most economists to admit real effects of money.[8] Nevertheless,

he was very glad to hear that the Bank had at length began to discount at 4 percent; and he thought they should have done so long before. Had they persisted in demanding 5 percent, they would have been without a single note to cash.

Boom and Bust, 1822–25

Depression turned to expansion, led by investment in the newly independent countries of South America, and the Bank joined the country banks in its first postrestriction credit expansion.[9] Its gold reserve, which had reached £13.8 million in February 1824, fell to £3.6 million in August 1825. This was practically the country's entire reserve, for "there was but little gold in the provinces.... Add to this the fact that many of the country banks as well as their customers were heavily involved in the purchase of shares in bubble flotations, and it becomes clear," Feavearyear wrote, "that the situation was at least as full of danger as that of 1793 or 1797."[10] In March 1825, Liverpool took the occasion of a debate on joint-stock companies to condemn "that general spirit of speculation which was going beyond all bounds, and was likely to bring the greatest mischief on numerous individuals." He urged them

to reflect what would be the situation of the public if (not to speak of actual war)...any embarrassing event were to occur. Their lordships would recollect that when commercial embarrassment occurred during the late war, bankers and merchants came forward and applied to parliament for aid, which they obtained by issues of Exchequer bills. He wished it, however, to be clearly understood that those persons who now engaged in Joint-Stock Companies, or other enterprises, entered on those speculations at their peril and risk. He thought it was his duty to declare that he never would advise the introduction of any bill for their relief; on the contrary, if such a measure were proposed, he would oppose it, and he hoped that parliament would resist any measure of that kind...

Although it recognized an impending crisis in September, the Bank did not raise its rate until December. Its restriction of credit in November made matters worse. News "that the Bank was returning a considerable portion of the bills sent for discount by even the largest houses" provoked runs on the country banks. "On Sunday, the 27th, partners of the London

---

[8] R. S. Sayers, "Ricardo's Views on Monetary Questions."
[9] William Page, *Historical Review of Economic Conditions*, pp. 69–72.
[10] A. E. Feavearyear, *The Pound Sterling*, p. 219.

houses were fetched from church to supply gold to their desperate provincial customers.... In three weeks sixty-one country banks and six important London houses ceased payment."[11] Although the Bank's help was selective, its own position was desperate. On December 15, it turned to the government for help either in the form of Exchequer bills or for authorization to stop payment. The government refused, telling the Bank to "pay out to the last penny." Bank Director Jeremiah Harman recalled the incident for the Committee of 1832:

Did any communication take place between the Bank and the Government respecting an Order in Council to restrain payment in gold at that period? – Yes, it was suggested by the Bank.

What answer did His Majesty's Government give to that? – They resisted it from first to last.

It was stated by the late Mr. Huskisson... that he as a member of the Administration at that time suggested to the Bank that if their gold was exhausted, they should place a paper against their door stating that they had not gold to pay with, but might expect to have gold to recommence payment in a short period; do you recollect such a suggestion? – There was such a suggestion.

What would, in your opinion, have been the consequences of that paper placed against the door of the Bank, without preparation to support commercial and financial credit? – I hardly know how to contemplate it.[12]

Thrown on its own resources, Harman told the committee, the Bank lent assistance "by every possible means, and in modes that we never had adopted before; we took in stock as security, we purchased exchequer bills, we made advances on exchequer bills, we not only discounted outright, but we made advances on deposit bills of exchange to an immense amount; in short by every possible means consistent with the safety of the Bank; and we were not upon some occasions over nice..." The Bank worked overtime to produce new notes and sent agents into the country to lend them, raising its discounts in a few weeks from £5 to £15 million. The panic was over, the drain of gold from the Bank became a trickle, and by spring it had turned around.

The Joint-Stock Banks

There was no official inquiry into the crisis because its causes were agreed.[13] The Bank had been slow to respond to the situation, but the main fault was the banking system. The hundreds of small issuers had

---

[11] Feavearyear, *op. cit.*, pp. 220–21.

[12] *Committee on the Bank Charter, Minutes of Evidence*, 1832, Questions 2217–30.

[13] Feavearyear, *op. cit.*, p. 223.

been too susceptible to the mood of speculation and too weak to survive the collapse. The government addressed the problem in 1826 by opening the door to joint-stock banks of issue as long as they did not maintain offices within 65 miles of London. The Bank did not get an extension of its charter (that would wait until the current charter had almost lapsed), but it was encouraged to open provincial branches.

The government had begun negotiations for the Bank's agreement to such an act in 1822 in exchange for an extension of its charter and legal tender status for its notes. Although the directors had agreed after some hesitation, the government did not proceed until after the crisis of 1825, "mainly because of the strong opposition in Parliament to the renewal of the Bank's charter."[14] Legal sanctions were given to the joint-stock banks without concessions to the Bank of England.

Another reason for the deterioration of the Bank's position was Thomas Joplin's argument that in contesting the establishment of joint-stock banks the Bank of England claimed a monopoly that it did not possess.[15] The Act of 1708 prohibited companies of more than six partners from issuing "bills or notes payable on demand," but said nothing about banks of deposit.

The Committee of 1832

Trying to Improve the Monetary System without Changing the Bank
As chancellor of the exchequer and leader of the House of Commons, Lord Althorp, better known for his part in securing the Reform Bill of that year, proposed a committee with himself in the chair "to consider the expediency of renewing the Bank's charter."[16] The committee would extend its inquiries into the banking situation as a whole, especially the regulations most appropriate for banks of issue. Information was gathered about the Bank's policies and banking practices in general, but the committee made no recommendations. There was little agreement regarding the need for new legislation or the form that it might take. Although

---

[14] Evelyn Thomas, *Rise and Growth of Joint Stock Banking*, p. 49; Marston Acres, *The Bank of England from Within, 1694–1900*, ii, p. 41.

[15] *An Essay on the General Principles and Present Practice of Banking*, 1822. Joplin's argument and his influence on bank legislation are discussed by Feavearyear, *op. cit.*, p. 223, and Thomas, *op. cit.*, pp. 72–73.

[16] John Charles Spencer, Viscount Althorp by courtesy, was leader of the House of Commons and chancellor of the exchequer, 1830–34. His succession to the earldom (3rd Earl Spencer) in 1834 brought down the government.

the Bank's record was unenviable, the directors described a promising new policy rule, and no politically acceptable alternative was put forward. Opponents of the gold standard were vocal but had no influence in Parliament, and neither did Ricardo's plan for the displacement of private currencies (including the Bank's) by a national bank.[17]

The government focused on impediments to the Bank's monetary control: competing note issues and the legal ceiling on the Bank's interest rate. The remaining portions of the Bank Charter Act of 1833, which were addressed to the transparency of monetary policy, will be discussed along with the governance of the Bank after we look at those directed at financial stability.

Althorp introduced the bill with the statement that the first objective of the legislation, as well as of the Bank of England and other banks, was convertibility. "It is only on that principle that they can pretend to say that the paper issued by them is valuable as a medium of exchange" (May 31, 1833). Subject to this condition, the government sought to end the evils of an "irregular and fluctuating medium." Althorp proposed that the Bank's interest rate be made a more flexible instrument by eliminating the 5-percent ceiling. Bank Director George Warde Norman repeated Thornton's observation of 30 years before when he told the committee, "If the rate of interest should rise much above 5 percent, the Bank must either over-issue or be obliged to resort to measures to contract its discounts, which might lead to very serious effects, such as rejecting private paper capriciously for no other reason than because enough had been discounted already" (Question 2430). Governor Horsley Palmer made the same argument, linking overissue to the price level and exchange rates. "Over-issue means excess of prices having relation to the prices of other countries." Asked "By what test would you generally measure an over-issue?," he replied, "By the foreign exchanges" (Q371–72). Ralph Hawtrey's *Century of Bank Rate* began "with the recommendation of the representatives of the Bank of England in 1832 for the repeal of the laws against usury, and ... ended with the reduction of Bank rate to 2 percent on the 30th June 1932," where except for two months in 1939 it remained until 1951.

To mitigate runs on gold, the Bank Charter Act of 1833 made the Bank's notes legal tender for all payments of £5 and above except at the Bank. Althorp had wanted to go further by eliminating the country bank issues, but he could not muster the necessary support. "The outcry of the

---

[17] David Ricardo, *Plan for the Establishment of a National Bank.*

country bankers caused the Cabinet to yield to them, and Lord Althorp was so mortified at being deserted by his colleagues that he wished to resign."[18] The joint-stock companies showed their political muscle by obtaining recognition of the right to operate within the 65-mile radius of London if they did not issue currency. By the 1850s, at least three joint-stock banks in London had deposits greater than the Bank of England's.[19] The Bank's charter was renewed until such time as the government gave a year's notice and paid its debt to the Bank, but not before 1844, and if the government's option was unexercised then, not until 1855.

The Palmer Rule

The removal of the limit on Bank rate was necessary to the new policy that Palmer and Norman revealed to the 1832 committee. It had been discussed in the Bank and efforts were made to apply it after the crisis of 1825–26, but it has been given the name of the governor who first described it. The Palmer Rule was more sophisticated and more automatic than the Bullion Committee's recommendation that the Bank respond to the exchange rate. It bore similarities to Ricardo's plan for a monetary commission and later colonial currency boards as well as to the Act of 1844. The public was permitted to operate on the exchanges while the Bank stood ready to engage in gold transactions initiated by the public. An overissued, depreciated currency would lead to the cashing in of notes for gold to export. Deflation and undervaluation would have the opposite effect. Either way, notes would change one-for-one with gold. Effects would not be immediate, however, and imbalances might continue for some time. An ample reserve was necessary.

Palmer's testimony is as interesting for the Bank's admission of responsibility for the circulation as for its consideration of a rule. It anticipated Bagehot's lender-of-last-resort recommendation without committing itself.

What is the principle by which in ordinary times the Bank is guided in the regulation of their issues? – The principle, with reference to a period of a full currency, and consequently a par of exchange, by which the Bank is guided in the regulation of their issues (excepting under special circumstances) is to invest and retain in securities . . . a given proportion of . . . deposits and . . . notes . . . , the remainder being held in coin and bullion; the proportions which seem to be desirable

---

[18] A. Aspinall, *Three Early Nineteenth Century Diaries*, p. 343.
[19] Jacob Viner, *Studies in the Theory of International Trade*, p. 219.

under existing circumstances may be stated at about two-thirds in securities and one-third in bullion, the circulation of the country, so far as the same may depend on the Bank, being subsequently regulated by the action of the Foreign Exchanges.

By the circulation of the country, do you mean the whole circulation of the country, and not the country circulation? – The whole circulation of the country.

When you say that as a general principle you think it desirable to have one-third of bullion in your coffers against your circulation you mean to include in that circulation not only your paper out but all deposits . . .? – Yes.

In short, all liabilities to pay on demand? – Yes. . . .

[D]o not the Directors of the Bank of England possess the power of regulating the whole circulation of the country? – The Bank are very desirous not to exercise any power, but to leave the Public to use the power which they possess, of returning Bank paper for bullion.

Would the Exchanges be corrected if the amount of currency was left wholly in the hands of the Public? – They have been principally corrected under that management.

Is the Bank exposed to no inconvenience by waiting to have the correction take place in this method, in preference to itself interfering by that power to diminish the circulation in case of a fall of Exchange? – No; provided they are adequately supplied with bullion when the Exchanges are at par, and which proportion I have stated to be about one-third.

Q72–80

The Bank could "forcibly" expand or contract its liabilities by pur-chases and sales of securities, but Palmer would rather, "except under special circumstances, . . . leave it to the Public to act upon the Bank" (Q82–83).

What has come down as the Palmer Rule of monetary control was only half the policy described by Palmer. The other half was concerned with financial stability and was the part that most depended on a flexible Bank rate. Palmer wanted a combination of discipline and power that would inhibit the Bank from contributing to overexpansions, whereas enabling it to support the credit market in times of need. The Bank should in ordinary times stand aside from the discount market, relying for most of its earnings on government securities. Althorp asked whether Palmer believed "that the Bank of England ought to confine itself to public transactions and the management of the currency of the country, and not to interfere in the general commercial discounts in the Metropolis . . ." Palmer replied,

I entertain . . . an opinion that in ordinary times the leading functions of the Bank of England have been to furnish, upon a stated principle, an adequate supply of paper money convertible into coin and bullion upon demand, and to act as a bank for safe deposit of public and private money, and in so acting, that it is not deemed to be desirable to attempt to regulate the amount of issues of the Bank in London through commercial discounts, but that there are occasions and circumstances when the functions of the Bank as a bank for commercial discounts in the Capital have been and ever must be of the first importance to the country.... If the Bank were required to hold no other securities than commercial bills, they would be under the necessity of acting in common with all other parties, viz. by competition in the purchase of bills of exchange at the existing market rate of interest. It is that competition with private bankers and individuals in London which seems to me to be so objectionable.

Q477

If the Bank is ready to lend to private individuals on good security at all times at a rate above the market rate (whereas maintaining the circulation by means of the automatic mechanism described previously), it stays aloof from speculation. "[S]till that public rate is always open to individuals if circumstances should arise to render such applications necessary... The Bank *then* becomes the main support of the commerce of the country" (Q559, 477). Palmer reminded the committee that "as a commercial body, [the Bank] is at all times enabled to judge the character of the application so made, though they should be only occasional, yet they are at times of very considerable importance to the parties making such applications, and so far beneficial" (Q559).

The Transparency of Monetary Policy and the Bank's Governance
The Bank Charter Act of 1833 ordered the payment of a quarter of the public debt to the Bank and required it to publish a monthly report of its average bullion, securities, notes, and deposits over the preceding three months. The Bank's secrecy and lack of accountability were discussed in Chapter 2. However, because most violations of its charters had been concessions to governments under protest, the publication of its accounts is best interpreted as a signal from the government of its own new commitment to financial rectitude. Publication of the accounts of the previous 40 years, which Althorp managed to pry from the Bank, and the Bank Charter Act of 1833 combined an admission of past sins with a promise of good behavior – like the Bank of England Act 165 years later.

It was provided, "in consideration of the Privilege of exclusive Banking given by this Act," to deduct £120,000 from the Bank's charges to the government "for the Management of the Public Debt." This was intended to capture the profits from the probable increase in the Bank's circulation arising from its new legal tender status, and accorded with Ricardo's view that the profits of the currency belonged to the public. The late renewal of 1833 was a departure from the practice of negotiating extensions well in advance of the expirations of existing charters in exchange for financial concessions. The Bank's first 120 years were almost entirely years of war or preparations for war. By 1832 there had been 17 years without a major war, and none loomed on the horizon. The government could afford the luxury of an independent central bank, and these provisions of the act should probably be understood more as a public announcement of the new relationship than as a monitoring or enforcement mechanism. The cut in the government's debt signaled the new arms-length relationship. Nevertheless, Althorp admitted that its legal privileges continued the possibilities of "a harmful connexion between the Bank and the Government."

Now, he thought that the blame which was often attributed to the Bank was often attributable to the action of the Government upon the Bank. He likewise was of the opinion that the Bank ought not to change its operations to accommodate the Government. . . . Now, he put it to the House whether that publicity [which he had proposed] would not have a direct tendency to check the connexion between the Bank and the Government. . . . He could not conceive that with a publicity of accounts there was any danger of the connexion between the Government and the Bank again producing the evils which had been so justly lamented (August 9, 1833).

Part of the House of Commons wanted the Bank's position to be published more frequently and in more detail. Althorp replied that the method proposed "would enable the public to ascertain whether the Bank acted upon sound principles as completely as it could be ascertained in any way whatever" without being injurious by sometimes creating "a mistaken impression . . . when the demand for bullion, arising from particular circumstances, became great. . . ." Henry Warburton retorted that "the arguments of the noble Lord . . . might have been used on behalf of any Government which conducted its transactions in secret." The government stood its ground, and only the information required for the purposes of the Bank Charter Act of 1833 was demanded of the Bank. The popular rationale for the publication of the Bank's position – "the diffusion of confidence" – applied only if the reserve was "enough to tranquillise people," which in Bagehot's opinion seldom happened.[20] When the Act of 1844 imposed a precise and continuous currency rule on one department of the Bank (the Issue Department), both departments were required, over the Bank's protests, to submit exact weekly accounts.

The Committee of 1832 was also interested in the Bank's governance, and although no changes were required, this is a convenient place to

[20] Walter Bagehot, *Lombard Street*, p. 303.

consider the Bank's organization and its relationship to monetary policy.[21] Management was in the hands of the governor and deputy governor. Twenty-four directors, collectively called the Court of Directors, met weekly to review policy. The typical new director, Bagehot wrote four decades later, was "a well-conducted young man who has begun to attend to business, and who seems likely to be fairly sensible and fairly efficient twenty years later."[22] The deputy governor was selected from the directors primarily on the basis of seniority and succeeded the governor. Both were elected for one-year terms and almost always served a second year in each capacity.

There was a one-third turnover of directors each year, but the eight who stepped down were taken from among those who had not "passed the chair" (been governor), and they usually returned the next year. The two-year limit for senior management and the two-thirds ceiling on the annual succession of directors were rejected by the directors in 1694 but imposed by Parliament in 1697 to discourage the perpetuation of cliques. The attempt was eventually abandoned, and the Bank took advantage of an 1872 Act that permitted the reelection of seven-eighths of their number and the power conferred in 1896 to end rotation altogether. The senior advisory body was the Committee of Treasury, consisting of the directors who had passed the chair, so-called because it was originally formed to "attend the lords of the Treasury," the Bank's main customer.

These arrangements were thought by the directors to be best for the country and the Bank. We have seen that Governor Palmer was aware of the Bank's responsibility for "the whole circulation of the country." However, he also believed with Thornton that the circulation should be in the hands of "a commercial company, independent of the Government." This arrangement made it "less liable to abuse" from political interests – using the leading phrase of Althorp to which Palmer assented (Q551–54). Palmer added in opposition to Attwood and Ricardo, although he did not mention names, that he did not believe "that a bank formed of political individuals, or of commissioners, would have the same general knowledge of the commercial transactions of the country as a body formed of commercial persons" (Q555).

---

[21] For example, see Horsley Palmer's testimony in T. E. Gregory, *Select Statutes*, i, pp. 8–18. Much of the following discussion is from R. S. Sayers, *Bank of England, 1891–1944* (pp. 594–96 and app. 2, 39); J. H. Clapham, *Bank of England* (i, p. 108; ii, pp. 358–79); and Marston Acres, *op. cit.*, i, pp. 13, 36; ii, pp. 524–42, 613.

[22] Bagehot, *op. cit.*, p. 200.

The requirements of knowledge and interests dictated management of the currency by "a company of merchants" after all. Harman, who had been a director between 1794 and 1827 and a supporter of the governor and deputy governor before the Bullion Committee, indicated to Althorp that there was no conflict between their private and public responsibilities:

Will you state the principles which guided the Bank in their issues of paper, during the different periods of the time you were in the Bank direction? – The first principle, was attention to the security of the Bank itself, in which we considered the safety of the public, of course, very much involved; to render as much service as we could to the commercial community with propriety, always having reference to the means which we possessed of fulfilling our engagements.

Q2151

The same attitude is implicit in the second paragraph of the chancellor's 1844 letter to the Bank quoted in the following. However, both were aware of conflicts of interest. The exchange between Althorp and Palmer (Q249–50) went as follows:

Is it not the fact that the Directors of the Bank of England for many years past have thought it right not themselves to be very large holders of Bank stock? – I do not believe that any Director of the Bank of England holds more than his qualification [the £2,000 minimum required of Directors since 1694].

Is it not true that in the month of May 1816, when the Bank made a most magnificent donation to the proprietors, the Bank Directors remained just as they did before, small proprietors of stock? – I believe so.

Perhaps the ownership commitment required of management by the outside owners was offset, or had to be seen to be offset, by considerations of the public interest. But the directors might sometimes have bent too far backward. When Althorp asked when they had begun "to act upon what you regard to be the sound principle" (that is, the regulation of their issue by the state of the exchanges), William Ward, a director since 1817, answered,

I think I must correct it in this way: The Bank had been accused of rapacity, and of not meeting the resumption of cash payments from grounds of cupidity, which certainly was not a tenable accusation; but being so challenged, and so much said upon the subject, I think their feeling was that they would at least go far enough in avoiding abundance of gold that they would rather procure too much gold than too little, so that they might be able at least to assert that it was not from interested motives that we have not complied with what Parliament requires; then, till they had accomplished that object, they did not look so minutely at the principle as might have been advisable, but little by little, after the year 1819, they adverted more frequently to that consideration, and they eventually found that the practice pretty nearly corresponded with the theory.

Q2076

Time persuaded Bagehot of the Bank's inability to grasp its functions. He saw the problem less as a conflict of interest than as a lack of knowledge – failures of training and experience. What was needed was banking expertise. He believed that the Bank needed a permanent chief executive, or at least a permanent deputy who was a banker.[23] On the other hand, it could be said in response to Bagehot that existing practice provided the permanency of culture, if not of individuals, into which successive managers were expected to grow.

Long terms in Bank management did not come until Walter Cunliffe, governor since 1913, continued to the end of the war. That was the death knell of the two-year rotation, although no one else has come close to the 1920–44 tenure of Montagu Norman. Deputy governors were selected in the traditional way and served for two years until the practice was broken by Sir Ernest Harvey and Basil Catterns, career servants of the Bank who held the office from 1929 to 1936 and 1936 to 1945, respectively.[24] Bagehot's proposal for requiring top management to have banking experience before assuming control of the Bank was never adopted. The practice of excluding commercial bankers from the directorship because they had originally been the Bank's competitors, although they had since become its largest customers, was also preserved throughout its history as a private institution.

The Bank Charter Act of 1844

Instability Unchecked

Monetary stability did not improve in the 1830s, and there was little evidence of either part of Palmer's Rule. The "exceptional circumstances" requiring departures from the rule were disturbingly frequent.[25] Although the Bank's gold and liabilities varied in the same direction every year from 1833 to 1840, the changes never approximated one-for-one, and in

---

[23] For other late-19th-century discussions of this issue, including the problems arising in the 1890s from the lack of control of a long-serving insubordinate chief cashier, see Clapham, *op. cit.*, pp. 358–79.

[24] See Richard Roberts and David Kynaston, *The Bank of England: Money, Power and Influence, 1694–1994*, appendix 2.

[25] Viner, *op. cit.*, p. 227.

the middle of the decade the Bank joined the railway boom. In May 1839, after the collapse of the inflationary boom on the Continent and large imports of grain were underway, the Bank rate was raised to 5 percent, then to 5½ percent in June and to 6 percent in August. But the reserve continued to fall, reaching £2.5 million in October. There was a wave of country bank failures and the Bank turned to the Bank of France for a credit of £2 million, "with which it was able gradually to stem the outflow of gold and restore confidence...."[26]

The price index rose from 84 to 113 between 1835 and 1839, and fell back to 84 in 1843. The Bank's liabilities fluctuated less than this, although the 13-percent rise of 1832–36 and 23-percent fall of 1836–41 were not small. In any case, as after the boom and bust of the preceding decade, there was much finger-pointing by the Bank of England and other banks, although this time the other banks were the rising joint-stock companies. The Bank had refused to take bills bearing the names of these banks during the crisis, and Palmer complained that their excess issue had neutralized the Bank's contraction. Unless firm measures were taken by the government, "a repetition of the pressure will no doubt recur with increased violence.... So dangerous does the system appear, *as it now stands*, that it becomes questionable whether the Bank of England and the [unregulated joint-stock banks] can permanently exist together."[27]

The London and Westminster Bank's J. W. Gilbart responded that the Bank of England ignored its own guidelines. It had not kept outside the discount market during the boom and waited too long to raise its rate. The country was indebted for such stability as existed to the joint-stock banks and "the public confidence they enjoy."

Previous to their establishment, whenever the Bank of England reduced their circulation, crack went the banks – away went the merchants – down went prices – and the exchanges were righted speedily. But now, when the Bank of England contracts the circulation, the banks won't go, and prices won't go, but the gold will go. How provoking this! If half the Joint-Stock Banks in the country would just have the kindness to stop payment whenever the Bank of England wanted to turn the exchanges, it would be of great assistance towards attaining the object. Mr. Palmer has eulogized the private banks, of whom, he states, about 150 failed about the year 1810, and about 80 more in 1825. But the Joint-Stock Banks cannot be so easily crushed. They are able to support public credit even under an adverse

---

[26] *Loc. cit.*

[27] Horsley Palmer, *Causes and Consequences of the Pressure upon the Money Market,* pp. 49–50.

state of the exchanges, and hence it is their strength, not their weakness, that makes the Bank of England their enemy.

> J. W. Gilbart, *An Inquiry into the Causes of the Pressure on the Money Market during the Year 1836*, p. 45

Samson Ricardo continued his brother's campaign to take money powers from both groups to remove private interests. He asked, "May not a slight consideration for the Bank-Stock proprietors sometimes interfere with a strict adherence to the principle laid down?"[28] When the rule and the public interest imply in a particular circumstance that the "proprietors must submit to a reduction of dividend," he observed that "means are ... taken to increase the paper circulation: money is made still more abundant; this engenders and excites speculation, prices rise ... " He did not "accuse the Bank Directors of intentionally sacrificing the interests of the public to those of the Bank-Stock proprietors. Their position is a difficult one, and the fault is in the system which places those interests in collision." These problems could only be solved by transferring the power of money creation from profit-seeking bodies with conflicting goals to a public board of commissioners with a single task and no other interests.[29]

The Currency and Banking Principles and the Committees of 1840 and 1841[30]

Notice was not required for a change in the Bank's charter until 1843, but dissatisfaction with the structure and performance of monetary institutions in general and the Bank in particular foretold the near certainty of fundamental changes, and "the division of opinion among the experts and ... the absence of any agreed first principles" meant that time was needed for an examination of the alternatives. So said the chancellor when he moved the appointment of a Committee on Banks of Issue:

> [T]he question to which their attention ought to be specially called was as to the existence of a bank having any particular privileges – whether the existence of that bank was right and proper – whether it would not be more advisable to introduce

---

[28] Samson Ricardo, *Observations on the Recent Pamphlet of J. Horsley Palmer*, p. 27.

[29] Samson Ricardo, *A National Bank*, pp. 12, 14, 19.

[30] For the development of the Currency and Banking Principles, see Keith Horsefield, "Duties of a Banker." His main argument begins with the origins of the "Banking Principle" in Adam Smith's (*Wealth of Nations*) exposition of the real bills doctrine and the "law of reflux" and ends with Thornton (*Paper Credit*) and Wheatley (*Remarks on Currency and Commerce*) and the conflict between the alternative views contained in the Report of the Parliamentary committee appointed to inquire into the Irish circulation, which anticipated the Bullion Report of 1810 (Frank Fetter, *The Irish Pound, 1797–1826*).

the system called free banking; whether, if they conceded that a bank ought to exist, sufficient powers had been given to it to perform those functions which they expected a bank to perform. And then again there was the question, whether it were advisable at the present moment to reconstruct the whole system and have but one bank of issue.

Francis Thornhill Baring, Chancellor of the Exchequer,
House of Commons, March 10, 1840[31]

The principal contending answers to these questions were classified as the Currency and Banking Principles, with the latter skirting the edges of free (unregulated) banking.[32] There was diversity within these schools of thought, but our discussion focuses on the witnesses before the Committees of 1840 and 1841, which though formally separate, had substantially the same charge and membership.

First consider Samuel Jones Loyd, leader of the Currency School, whose testimony provided the outline and much of the detail of the Bank Charter Act of 1844.[33] Loyd stated the objective of monetary policy in response to the question, "What, in your opinion, is the sound principle according to which the circulation should be regulated?"

A metallic currency, I conceive, by virtue of its own intrinsic value, will regulate itself; but a paper currency, having no intrinsic value, requires to be subjected to some artificial regulation respecting its amount. The use of paper money is resorted to on account of its greater economy and convenience, but it is important that a paper currency should be made to conform to what a metallic currency would be, and especially that it should be kept of the same value with the metallic currency, by being kept at all times of the same amount.[34]

Committee of 1840, Q2654

The "artificial regulation" proposed by the Currency School was the legal imposition of a rule on the Bank of England. Paper money should enter the system only as a substitute, shilling for shilling, for gold. The principal issuer of paper money was the Bank of England, but that duty was confounded by its other activities. "The principles of currency are in themselves simple enough," Loyd said, "but by mingling the management

---

[31] *Hansard, Parliamentary Debates*, p. 1118; Gregory, *op. cit.*, i, pp. xvi–xvii.

[32] For summaries of this controversy, see Marion Daugherty, "Banking-Currency Controversy;" Feavearyear, *op. cit.*, chap. 10; Gregory, *op. cit.*, i, Introduction, and Viner, *op. cit.*, chap. 5.

[33] Samuel Jones Loyd served with his father in the London bank, Jones, Loyd, and Co., which was merged into the London and Westminster Bank in 1834. He retired in 1844, served as chairman of the Irish Famine Committee in 1845, was a promoter of the Great Exhibition of 1851, and became 1st Baron Overstone in 1850.

[34] Gregory, *op. cit.*, i, pp. 27–28.

of circulation with banking operations great confusion has arisen; for instance, the charges against the conduct of the Bank in 1835 seem to me to be entirely founded upon the confusion between what was their duty in managing their circulation and what was their duty in their banking capacity." It was claimed at various times and by various people that it was the duty of the Bank to regulate prices; or to regulate the rate of interest; or to regulate the country issues by the supposed wants of their respective districts; and so on; "all of which seem to me to spring out of the want of a due separation, in the minds of those who write upon the subject, of the functions of issue and of banking" (Q2736).

What was needed was to concentrate the power of issue in a single body with no other function. That power might be given to a body of public commissioners or it might – and this was the course taken – be administered as a separate account in the Bank of England. The Act of 1844 modified Loyd's plan by allowing other banks of issue to continue their issues subject to the restriction that their monthly average would not exceed the average of the 12 weeks preceding April 27, 1844. Nonissuing banks could not initiate issues, and those of banks that closed or voluntarily relinquished their rights of issue passed to the Bank of England.

Loyd's system would rid the country of the troublesome expansions and contractions of the currency arising from the Bank's urge to "support the public credit" (Q2784), although it neglected the short-run stabilizing functions of Barings's *dernier resort* and Thornton's maintenance of the circulation. Matthias Attwood, the committee member most hostile to Loyd, suggested that stability in the short term should take precedence over the supposed long-term benefits of the gold standard. Loyd was not moved.

But the whole question at issue is this: I believe that a great deal of the severity of the commercial crises in this country, and of the evils that attend them, are attributable to the want of contraction of the paper circulation of the country in correspondence with the bullion; and I believe, firmly, that no parties would be more benefited by a contraction of the circulation in correspondence with the bullion than the bankers themselves. I believe that it would be eminently calculated to give steadiness, regularity, security, and a satisfactory character to their business; I say so from considerable experience.

Q2729

This dispute has carried over to the present, for example, in Anna Schwartz's support of Loyd's position in "Why Financial Stability Depends on Price Stability." Loyd pointed to his experience as a banker in four crises. But the Attwoods were bankers, too, and Matthias might have quoted his brother's letter to Lord Liverpool protesting the Act of 1819:

> It is extraordinary ... to observe the coolness with which the Committees [of inquiry of the Houses of Parliament regarding the "expediency of resumption"] speak about the Bank of England, and country bankers, having sufficient time "to call in their accommodations." One of the greatest evils of the division of labour is that it so concentrates men's minds and habits upon particular objects of pursuit that few people know any thing at all beyond the range of those immediate objects; and this is the case of the two Committees. They know nothing at all of the business of banking. "To call in accommodations" may be sport to them, and to the bankers, but it is death to the public. I wish that the Committees were to spend twelve months in a banking house during the period of a general "calling in of accommodations." They would get more knowledge of human life and of its ways and means in that short period than is to be learnt in all the books that ever were written from the beginning of the world.
>
> Thomas Attwood, *A Letter to the Earl of Liverpool... on the Questions of the Bank Restriction Act*

History's main criticism of the Currency School concerns its specification of money, which was limited to coin and bank notes.[35] This was accepted by Peel and by Charles Wood, Chairman of the Committee of 1841, who were the main speakers for the Act of 1844 in the House of Commons. Bank notes were money whereas bank deposits and bills of exchange were not money, Loyd argued, because only the former was "the common medium of exchange for the adjustment of all transactions, equally at all times, between all persons, and in all places. It has further the quality of discharging those functions in endless succession" (Q2663). This position involved Loyd in protracted arguments, and Tooke complained that the committee's time was consumed by "mere verbal definitions and distinctions" that "elicited hardly any facts, or any information of value on the practice of banking."[36]

Tooke's rejection of monetary rules relieved him of the necessity of specifying money. The advocates of those rules, on the other hand, are obliged to specify money and the mechanism by which it is to be controlled. Loyd's money was the generally accepted, routinely circulated means of final payment.[37] If we accept this definition, claims that Loyd's

---

[35] For example see Daugherty, *op. cit.*; Viner, *op. cit.*, chap. 5; and J. A. Schumpeter, *History of Economic Analysis*, pp. 698–700.

[36] Tooke, *History of Prices*, iii, pp. 351–52.

[37] This discussion of the definitions and identifications of money is indebted to the concise but comprehensive treatments of Dale Osborne: "Ten Approaches to the Definition of Money" and "What Is Money Today?"

specification of money should have included bank deposits are incorrect. Deposits are not means of final payment any more than bills of exchange. Both are debts. My check is a promise that my bank will pay cash to your bank. This was also true of bank notes. If, however, the Bank of England was given a monopoly of notes that could only be issued for gold, the nation's money specified as notes and gold outside banks would be linked one-for-one to changes in its monetary gold stock. This was what he wanted. In a purely metallic system, the monetary base (or "high-powered money" or simply "money"), the "foundation" of the system, was "distributed to the different countries of the world by the operation of particular laws, which have been investigated and are now well recognized" (Q2666, 2663). He wished to eliminate the powers of individuals to interfere with those laws.

In the event, other bank notes were allowed to remain. Gilbart had warned "that the abolition of the country circulation would cause very considerable distress." In another departure from Loyd's system, the existing balance sheet of the Bank of England and the need for the Banking Department to open with a reserve of notes were recognized in the Issue Department's "fiduciary issue," backed by securities, of £14,000,000 – to expand as the country issues were relinquished. Early "returns" of the Bank under the 1844 Act are shown in the next chapter.

To adherents of the Banking School, the Currency Principle revealed ignorance of the role of money in the credit system and the importance of flexible banking to the maintenance of credit. Nonetheless, the Banking Principle was defeated almost without a fight. With few exceptions, primarily Gilbart, whose purpose was to advance the interests of the joint-stock banks, its proponents joined the fray after the political issue was settled.[38] Even Tooke, the leader of the Banking School in the eyes of later generations, did not find fault with the Currency Principle until the 1840s, and he did not oppose it in print until 1844, when he wrote,[39]

It was held by most writers of any authority on the subject of the Currency, till within the last few years, that the purposes of a mixed circulation of coin and paper were sufficiently answered, as long as the coin was perfect and the paper constantly convertible into coin; and that the only evils to be guarded against by regulation were those attending suspension of payment and insolvency of the banks, a large proportion of which blend an issue of promissory notes with their other business.

[38] Daugherty, *op. cit.*

[39] See Gregory ("Introduction" to Tooke and Newmarch's *History of Prices*) for the development of Tooke's thought.

This . . . is what is understood in general terms as the banking principle, and is that upon which our system of currency is constructed and conducted.

Thomas Tooke, *An Inquiry into the Currency Principle*, p. 1

All that was needed for a stable currency was for banks to operate on sound banking principles, particularly by attending to their "proportion of reserve in treasure and in immediately convertible securities." Tooke believed that the restrictions of the Currency School were unnecessary and potentially destabilizing.

Gilbart supported Tooke before the 1841 Committee in arguing that banks were obliged to maintain money and credit. This meant the neutralization of gold flows – not their reinforcement as prescribed by the Currency Principle. The strict application of the Currency Principle even prevented the amelioration of seasonal fluctuations arising from government receipts and payments and the crop cycle (Q917–31). The surest way to avoid these pressures was for banks, especially the Bank of England, to keep reserves sufficient to be able to withstand gold losses without restricting credit.

A large reserve would buy the time necessary to recognize the causes of those losses and to take appropriate action "without producing alarm and disturbance of the money market on the one hand, or endangering an extreme and unsafe reduction of the Bank treasure on the other."[40] It was important to distinguish between an internal drain due to mistrust (a liquidity crisis), which called for an expansion of credit, and an external drain. Palmer had made a further distinction between temporary, self-correcting external drains, such as harvest failures, which did not call for the contraction of credit, and "a deranged state of prices between this and other countries," which required "an adjustment of prices."[41] To those who said that such distinctions were too fine to be recognized in practice, J. S. Mill later contended that they were "matters of public notoriety. Everyone knows whether there has been a bad harvest [and] all persons who pay attention to commercial transactions know well when there has been an inflation of credit and great speculation going on in goods."[42]

---

[40] Tooke, *op. cit.*, iii, p. 187, discussed by D. E. W. Laidler, "Thomas Tooke on Monetary Reform."

[41] He stated this to the *Committee of 1840*, Q1625. See Viner, *op. cit.*, pp. 261–64, for a discussion of these issues.

[42] This was in response to a question from Sir Charles Wood: "Do you think that the Bank can, with sufficient certainty, distinguish between the separate causes of drain, so as to be able to pursue a different course according to the cause which, in their opinion, produces the drain? (*Committee on Bank Acts, 1857*, Q2106; rep. *Works*, vol. 5). Also see Mill's *Principles*, book 3, chap. 24.

Mill's point is relevant to recent discussions that assume because central bankers do not recognize these distinctions they must commit either to an interest or a money rule.[43]

Yet more could be done than simply keeping a large reserve. The pressure of gold drains on money and credit might be relieved by investments in foreign securities. To an exasperated Peel, who had asked if "the Bank of England should take any step whatever to guard against the ultimate consequences of that state of things [which in two years had caused a fall in bullion from ten million to four million pounds] by restricting the paper circulation," Gilbart answered, "I think in ordinary times the Bank of England might hold foreign securities, by which they would bring gold back to this country, and thus prevent any necessity for a contraction of the circulation" (Q953). He might have referred to the Bank's 1839 credit from the Bank of France (to be repeated in 1890). These instruments of stability in the face of international gold flows were overlooked by Bagehot (whose purpose was to impress upon the Bank of England the importance of a large reserve), but they were eventually recognized.

Palmer and Norman opposed foreign credits before the 1840 Committee except in unspecified "extreme" cases (Q1599, 1936). Norman admitted that they would "be the same as giving us a portion of gold which paid interest" but doubted that it would be possible to "find good securities that would be marketable on all occasions" (Q1942–47). Gilbart did not see why, asking, "When a large amount [of foreign securities] is held by private individuals, ... may not a certain amount be held by the Bank of England?" (Q1062). Loyd disapproved of foreign securities and presumably other secondary reserves on principle: "I had much rather that the safety of our paper circulation was sought from its legitimate source, proper contraction, at the proper time, and to the proper extent, than that we should rely upon an expedient of this nature, which is only a last resource in extreme difficulty" (Q2849). The Bank should not offset gold flows, whatever the source. That would be too much like "supporting the market," which he thought had been the Bank's principal mistake. The Bank should wait to "be acted upon, and not act itself" (Q2848). Only in this way could overissue be avoided – and this required the discipline of a legal currency rule. Loyd had written that the neglect of the Palmer Rule was due to the overpowering of the directors by outside

---

[43] William Poole, "Optimal Choice of Monetary Policy Instruments in a Simple Stochastic Model."

pressures from the market and the government "which they cannot resist."[44]

The man who, because he had accumulated an unusual quantity of water, thought he could therefore fill with it a tub which had lost its bottom was not more absurd than the Bank, in thinking that the accumulation of specie put it in a position to make some effectual progress towards a return to cash payments without any previous or accompanying measures for putting a bottom to its tub by regulating the exchanges.

Loyd, *Remarks on the Management of the Circulation*, pp. 51–52

It was further argued by Norman that the supposed short-term benefits of Bank interventions were self-defeating in the long term. The pursuit of stabilization by relying on the Bank to be the lender of last resort was time-inconsistent, to use a modern term.[45] Although it was true that "the refusal of the Bank to afford accommodation at periods of pressure" might cause "great inconvenience," that was because the "public have always looked to the Bank for assistance in such cases with too much confidence, and entertained what I consider such exaggerated views as to the means and duties of the Bank." Palmer's response to Charles Wood's pursuit of the point follows:

Do you conceive that parties have been induced to neglect precautions which they otherwise would have taken in consequence of their reliance upon that assistance . . .? – I have no positive means of knowing; but I should think so.

Q1770

This implied that there should be no contingency plan for the currency rule's suspension under pressure. Unless it is "strictly adhered to," Loyd insisted in another place, it "becomes a nullity."

A general conviction that [the rule] will not be suspended on such occasions [of pressure on the money market] is essential for producing throughout the community that cautious forethought and that healthy tone of self-reliance upon which the safety and utility of the measure must materially depend. Any special provision . . . for suspending its application at critical periods must prove mischievous by weakening the conviction that the measure will be adhered to, and

---

[44] Samuel Jones Loyd, *Remarks on the Management of the Circulation*, p. 85.

[45] The term was used by Finn Kydland and Edward Prescott ("Rules Rather Than Discretion: The Inconsistency of Optimal Plans") in reference to situations in which the optimal plan chosen each period (e.g., inflation to achieve low unemployment by means of a surprise reduction in the real wage) is suboptimal in the long term (because wage-setters anticipate the plan).

thus checking the growth of the feelings and habits which are intimately connected with its success.

Loyd, *Thoughts on the Separation of the Departments . . .* , p. 439

The Banking School was tarred with the same inflationist brush as the antibullionists – certainly, credit contractions worried them more than expansions – and Gilbart found himself on the defensive during much of his testimony. He denied that banks had the power to expand their liabilities beyond the public's desire to hold them, a discipline that was most effective in a system of many competitive banks. A too-liberal bank would soon find its notes returned to it by other banks. He was directly opposed to the Currency School, for whom monetary control required a single issuer tied to a rule. "A single issuer might be easy to deal with," Norman wrote, "but how are we to deal with five hundred?"[46] Gilbart considered the Bank of England a greater threat than other banks because the status of its notes allowed their expansion "till the foreign exchanges become unfavourable, and gold is wanted for exportation" (Q1362, 1368).

The Committees of 1840 and 1841 made no recommendations, simply referring Parliament to the evidence with two brief observations (in 1840): that the rule described by Palmer in 1832 "has not been adhered to; and doubts have been expressed as to the soundness of its principle, as applicable to the Bank of England, for the mixing up deposits and circulation" and that the directors had been fettered on occasion by the impression that the "rule has received some sort of legislative sanction." They offered the following piece of advice:

Without entering into the question either of the soundness of the rule, or of the degree of sanction which it may be supposed to have received from the Legislature, Your Committee are clearly of the opinion that such an impression on the part of the Directors of the Bank of England ought not to prevent them from adopting any other principle of management which, after their further experience, and upon mature consideration, they may consider to be adapted for the primary object of preserving, under all circumstances, the convertibility of their notes.[47]

Parliament left these issues in abeyance until the Bank's charter approached its end. However, Peel, who became prime minister in 1841, had made up his mind even if the committees had not.[48] After he had

---

[46] *A Letter to Charles Wood* (1841), quoted by Feavearyear, *op. cit.*, p. 245.

[47] House of Commons, 1840, pp. iii–v.

[48] For the progress of Peel's ideas see Horsefield, "Origins of the Bank Charter Act."

persuaded the cabinet to the substance of the Currency Principle, they asked the Bank's opinion.

From the Chancellor of the Exchequer to the Governor and Deputy Governor of the Bank, April 26, 1844.

Gentlemen,

As ... the 1st of August is the day after which it will be competent to the House of Commons to give a notice to the Bank as to the termination ... of their present exclusive privileges, Her Majesty's Government judge it advisable to endeavour to come to an understanding with the Bank as to their future relations to the Government, rather than to terminate the existing arrangements ...

I would premise that the main object of the Government in any new arrangement is one in the success of which the Bank can be scarcely less interested than the Government; namely, to place the general circulation of the country on a sounder footing, and to prevent as much as possible fluctuations in the currency of the nature of those which have at different times occasioned hazard to the Bank and embarrassment to the country.[49]

The chancellor asked if the Bank would be willing to divide its business "into two distinct and separate departments," issue "a certain amount of notes ... on Securities and that all other notes required beyond that amount should be issued only in exchange for bullion," fill the void created by the ceiling on competing note issues, publish weekly "the state of both the Issue and Banking Departments," and accept a charter for 10 years from August 1845, which would subsequently be "terminable at any time upon a notice of twelve months." The profit of the additional issue would go to the government. These proposals, which reflected the Currency Principle, became the Bank Charter Act of 1844.

The Bank wondered whether publication of "the banking accounts can be regarded as essential," especially as other banks only had to report their circulations, and thought that 10-year charter extensions after 1855 were preferable to the one-year extensions suggested by the chancellor: "It seems to us that sufficient power of control would thus be retained by the Government, and that the inconvenience arising from repeated, if not annual discussions on the subject, would be avoided." But the main quarrel concerned the chancellor's estimate of the net profit from the circulation to be paid to the government. After another exchange of letters, the chancellor split the difference between the £240,000 that he had originally proposed and the £120,000 that the Bank already thought excessive.

---

[49] "Correspondence between the Government and the Bank of England Concerning the Renewal of the Bank Charter," Gregory, *op. cit.*, pp. 117–18.

The other terms were retained as set forth in the chancellor's original letter. In particular, he thought that annual charter renewals would be less troublesome than 10-year renewals because "the necessity of reviewing what was otherwise to be for so long a time irrevocable could scarcely be denied."

The smooth passage of the plan was hardly disturbed when George Muntz, successor to Thomas Attwood's Birmingham seat, asked the prime minister, "What would happen in consequence of there being such an export of gold as would render it impossible for the Bank to pay its liabilities in gold and thereby affect the circulation of the country?" The implication of the question was that under the bill the Bank might be prevented from issuing its own notes in a crisis even if they would be acceptable to the public. Peel replied that he "would rather decline answering such questions which were merely speculative, and the answers to which could not tend to any practical result....He, however, by no means anticipated such a contingency as that which had entered into the speculative mind of the honourable Gentleman."[50]

Tooke argued that such a contingency was inevitable. The artificial separation of accounts made it possible for the Issue Department to be solvent (with plenty of gold) whereas the Banking Department was insolvent (without gold or means of supplying notes to the public).

> A most absurd, however disastrous a state of things. But it would be too disastrous, and too absurd to be allowed to take its course. If such a crisis were to happen, as most probably it would at the time when the dividends on the public funds became due, the Government would be imperatively called upon to interfere and prevent so ridiculous, however lamentable, a catastrophe. And the only interference that could meet the emergency would be to authorise a temporary transfer of coin from the issuing to the banking department.
>
> Tooke, *An Inquiry* . . . , p. 109

He believed that the failure to develop contingency plans heightened the uncertainties already inherent in the bill because its suspension was thus subjected to the discretion of the government of the day.

> If an emergency should occur, such as in 1797 or 1825, it would depend entirely upon the character of the ministry of the day whether they would not authorise the issuing department to assist the banking department. . . . I should much sooner rely for security against such a calamity on the prudence of a set of directors, having

---

[50] *Hansard*, May 6 and June 6, 1844.

no sinister interest, and enlightened by the experience of the effects of former mismanagement." (pp. 160–61)

Tooke's fears were realized in 1847 when the Banking Department's reserve fell almost to £1,000,000 and it was forced to restrict credit even though the Issue Department's gold exceeded £8,000,000, considered an ample reserve under the old system.

FIVE

Making a Central Bank: III. Means and Ends

[T]he Act of 1844 has worked satisfactorily because it did not work in the way designed.

> P. Barrett Whale, "A Retrospective View of the Bank Charter Act of 1844"

If we ask how the Bank of England has discharged this great responsibility, we shall be struck by three things: *first*, ... the Bank has never by any corporate act or authorised utterance acknowledged the duty, and some of its directors deny it; *second* (what is even more remarkable), no resolution of Parliament, no report of any Committee of Parliament (as far as I know), no remembered speech of a responsible statesman, has assigned or enforced that duty on the Bank; *third* (what is more remarkable still), the distinct teaching of our highest authorities has often been that no public duty of any kind is imposed on the Banking Department of the Bank; that, for banking purposes, it is only a joint stock bank like any other bank; that its managers should look only to the interest of the proprietors and their dividend; that they are to manage as the London and Westminster Bank or the Union Bank manages.

> Walter Bagehot, *Lombard Street*, pp. 153–54

Lombard Street

The "great responsibility" that Bagehot referred to in his classic study of the position and duties of the central bank that the Bank of England had become was the possession and management of the country's – even the "civilized world's" – reserve. The "key to our whole system," he wrote, is "that no bank, in London or out of it, holds any considerable sum in hard cash or legal tender (above what is wanted for its daily business), except

Background: Ideas and Events

1845: First of a series of failures of the Irish potato crop.

1846: Repeal of the Corn Laws (which had protected domestic grain).

1847: Poor harvest, end of railway boom, government permission for Bank suspension.

1848: European revolutions; J. S. Mill, *Principles of Political Economy*.

1849–51: Beginning of California and Australia gold rushes.

1850–73: The Great Victorian Boom.[*]

1851: The Great Exhibition (of British industry, organized by Prince Albert).

1853–56: Crimean War.

1857: American financial crisis spreads to Britain; Bank suspends payment.

1866: Failure of Overend, Gurney; permission for Bank to suspend.

1871: Trade Union Bill recognized unions as not "in restraint of trade."[†]

1871: Germany adopts gold standard, followed by other major countries by the end of the century.

1873: *Lombard Street*.

1873–96: The Great Depression (prices fell 40 percent), ended by gold production in South Africa and the Yukon.[‡]

1890: Baring Crisis; Alfred Marshall, *Principles of Economics*.

1899–1902: Boer War.

Sources: [*] Roy Church, *The Great Victorian Boom, 1850–73*.
[†] A. V. Dicey, *Law and Public Opinion in England*, pp. 267–68.
[‡] S. B. Saul, *The Myth of the Great Depression*.

	Prime Minister	Chancellor of the Exchequer	Party[†]
1846	Lord John Russell	Sir Charles Wood	Liberal
1852	Earl of Derby	Benjamin Disraeli	Conservative
1852	Earl of Aberdeen	William Gladstone	Liberal
1855	Viscount Palmerston		
1858	Derby	Disraeli	Conservative
1859	Palmerston	Gladstone	Liberal
1865	Earl (John) Russell[*]		
1866	Derby	Disraeli	Conservative
1868	Disraeli	G. Ward Hunt	
1868	Gladstone	Robert Lowe	Liberal
1874	Disraeli	Sir Stafford Northcote	Conservative
1880	Gladstone	Gladstone	Liberal
1882		H. C. E. Childers	
1885	Marquess of Salisbury	Sir Michael Hicks–Beach	Conservative
1886	Gladstone	Sir Wm. Harcourt	Liberal
1886	Salisbury	Randolph Churchill	Conservative
1887		G. J. Goschen	
1892	Gladstone	Harcourt	Liberal

	Prime Minister	Chancellor of the Exchequer	Party[†]
1894	Earl of Roseberry		
1895	Salisbury	Hicks–Beach	Conservative
1902	A. J. Balfour	C. T. Ritchie	
1903		Austen Chamberlain	
1905	Sir Henry Campbell–Bannerman	Henry Asquith	Liberal
1908	Asquith	David Lloyd George	
1915		Reginald McKenna	

[*] Elevated to peerage in 1861.

[†] Political parties became more distinct between the 1830s and 1850s. Tories and Whigs tended to become Conservatives and Liberals, respectively (Llewellan Woodward, *The Age of Reform, 1815–70*, pp. 92–110).

the Banking Department of the Bank of England.... All London banks keep their principal reserve on deposit at the Banking Department... The London bill brokers do much the same." And so do the "Scotch and Irish bankers....: all their spare money is in London.... And therefore the reserve in the Banking Department of the Bank of England is the banking reserve not only of the Bank of England, but of all London; and not only of all London, but of all England, Ireland, and Scotland too." Furthermore, since the suspension of specie payments by the Bank of France after the Franco–German War, "London had become the sole great settling-house of exchange transactions in Europe...."[1]

In consequence, all our credit system depends on the Bank of England for its security; on the wisdom of the directors of that one joint-stock company it depends whether *England shall be solvent or insolvent*. This may seem too strong, but it is not: all banks depend on the Bank of England, and all merchants depend on some banker. If a merchant has £10,000 at his bankers, and wants to pay it to some one in Germany, he will not be able to pay it unless his banker can pay him; and the banker will not be able to pay if the Bank of England should be in difficulties and cannot produce his "reserve."

Walter Bagehot, Lombard Street, p. 36

Lombard Street was primarily a criticism of a position in a banking text taken by Thomson Hankey, long-time director and former governor of the Bank of England. Hankey had rejected "the most mischievous doctrine ever broached in the monetary or banking world in this country;

---

[1] Walter Bagehot, *Lombard Street*, pp. 27–34.

viz., that it is the proper function of the Bank of England to keep money available at all times to supply the demands of bankers who have rendered their own assets unavailable."[2] This passage was directed at Bagehot's interpretation of the Bank's statements and behavior in the *Economist*, of which he was editor, after the crisis of 1866. Bagehot had observed that although the Bank always in the end supplied the market's credit needs in times of crisis, its refusal to admit that such assistance was one of its functions and its threats to withhold assistance caused needless uncertainty and more severe panics than if it communicated clearly that it could be counted on. Hankey responded that sound principles should be observed by all banks. They should keep their own legal tender reserves instead of relying on the Bank of England for the performance of that elementary duty.

Bagehot conceded that Hankey might be correct about what "ought to be," but he had missed the point at issue – of what "is." The *Economist* had not said that "a single bank reserve was a good system, but that it was the system which existed, and which must be worked, as you could not change it."[3] Whatever Hankey and the other directors might say, they were not "like any other bank." They held more reserves than any other bank. Bagehot had stated the problem and its resolution in 1866: ". . . the anomaly of one bank keeping the sole banking reserve is so fixed in our system that we cannot change it if we would; the great evil to be feared was an indistinct conception of the fact . . . [A]nd that is now avoided," he wrote after the governor had described how the Bank had risen to its duty during the crisis of 1866. However, now that duty was denied by Hankey, "a very experienced and attentive director [who, Bagehot thought] expresses more or less the opinions of other directors." (George Warde Norman, for example, had written to the *Economist* in support of Hankey in 1866.[4])

Bagehot did not advocate a change in the law. His denial of revolutionary intentions probably owed something to a desire not to be seen by practical politicians and businessmen as a visionary. It also had impressive logical and empirical foundations. His limited policy proposal – that the Bank of England should recognize, and be seen to recognize, its special position – followed from his belief that systems worked best

---

[2] Thomson Hankey, *The Principles of Banking, Its Utility and Economy; with Remarks on the Working and Management of the Bank of England*, p. 25.

[3] Hankey, *op. cit.*, chap. 7.

[4] J. H. Clapham, *The Bank of England*, ii, p. 285.

when they were permitted to evolve under the pressure of events and in the hands of those who worked them and depended on them. This was particularly true of a system that generally had performed well. A multiple-reserve system might in some sense be more "natural," and it was easy to conceive of a system of many reserve banks of more-or-less equal size that was more stable than the English system, which was the result of an unnatural government interference with banking. The English system of money and credit was nevertheless a marvelous achievement – "by far the greatest combination of economical power and economical delicacy that the world has ever seen," more impressive than could have been imagined even at the time of the Act of 1844. "We have entirely lost the idea that any undertaking likely to pay, and seen to be likely, can perish for want of money; yet no idea was more familiar to our ancestors, or is more common now in most countries."[5] All this had been achieved in spite of the Act of 1844, the importance of which was greatly exaggerated. The Act was "only a subordinate matter in the money market." It had not retarded the financial system or economic growth, Bagehot wrote at the height of British financial and industrial preeminence. People would be better advised to learn how to work the system as it was, including the Act of 1844, than to risk confusion, or worse, by more official fiddling.

We run great risks if we try to force financial arrangements into a preconceived theoretical mold. Well-functioning credit systems, like effective governments, are not invented. They evolve. Bagehot compared "credit in business" with "loyalty in government – you must take what you can find of it, and work with it if possible." Because "we know that the House of Commons is the real sovereign, and any other sovereign is superfluous," a theorist might easily devise a scheme of government that dispensed with the monarch. But he would be running a great risk because "Queen Victoria is loyally obeyed, without doubt and without reasoning, by millions of human beings: if those millions began to argue, it would not be easy to persuade them to obey Queen Victoria or anything else." In a similar manner, "an immense system of credit, founded on the Bank of England as its pivot and its basis, now exists; the English people, and foreigners too, trust it implicitly."

Every banker knows that if he has to *prove* that he is worthy of credit, however good may be his arguments, in fact his credit is gone; but what we have requires

---

[5] Bagehot, *op. cit.*, pp. 6–7.

no proof – the whole rests on an instinctive confidence generated by use and years. . . . A many-reserve system, if some miracle should put it down in Lombard Street, would seem monstrous there; nobody would understand it or confide in it. Credit is a power which may grow, but cannot be constructed; those who live under a great and firm system of credit must consider that if they break up that one they will never see another, for it will take years upon years to make a successor to it.

Bagehot, Lombard Street, p. 68

It is interesting that in 1913 Congress sought to force the opposite of Bagehot's theoretical ideal onto the American banking system, namely, the conversion of a "many-reserve" system into a federal reserve.

The development of the English financial system and of monetary policy between 1844 and 1914 provide case studies of the dominance of fundamental forces over artificial legal devices set in their path. The following sections describe suspensions of the Act of 1844, Parliament's refusal to provide for suspensions for fear of inducing them, the continuation of monetary policy along pre-1844 lines despite the Act and Bagehot's advice, and underlying forces that stabilized the financial system. The concluding section describes monetary policy in the heyday of the gold standard. Tables 5.1 and 5.2 highlight some of the important data.

Table 5.1. *Bank of England Return, September, 7, 1844*

Issue Department			
Government securities	£11,015,100	£28,351,295	Notes
Other securities	2,984,900		
Gold coin and bullion	12,657,208		
Silver bullion	1,694,087		
Assets	£28,351,295	£28,351,295	Liabilities
Banking Department			
Government securities	£14,554,834	£ 3,630,809	Government deposits
Other securities	7,835,616	8,644,348	Other deposits
Notes	8,175,025	19,148,083	Other liabilities and
Gold and silver coin	857,765		capital
Assets	£31,423,240	£31,423,240	Liabilities and capital

Note: The Bank's return was ordered to be published weekly in the *London Gazette* and was also published in the *Economist*. Items have been rearranged and some have been renamed in conformity with modern usage.

Table 5.2. *Selected Bank of England Returns, September 1846 to December 1847, £ million*

Date	Issue Department			Banking Department				Public's Notes
9/5/46	Securities	14.0	Notes 29.8	Gov. secs	13.0	Public dep.	7.3	20.6
	Coin & bullion	15.8		Other secs	12.5	Other dep.	8.6	
				Notes	9.2	Other liabs. & capital	19.3	
				Coin	5.0	capital		
4/17/47	Securities	14.0	Notes 22.8	Gov. secs	11.7	Public dep.	3.0	20.2
	Coin & bullion	8.8		Other secs	17.1	Other dep.	10.0	
				Notes	2.6	Other liabs. & capital	18.9	
				Coin	5.0	capital		
6/19/47	Securities	14.0	Notes 23.6	Gov. secs	11.7	Public dep.	9.3	17.9
	Coin & bullion	9.6		Other secs	17.9	Other dep.	8.2	
				Notes	5.7	Other liabs. & capital	18.8	
				Coin	9.0	capital		
10/23/47	Securities	14.0	Notes 21.9	Gov. secs	10.9	Public dep.	4.8	20.4
	Coin & bullion	7.9		Other secs	19.5	Other dep.	8.6	
				Notes	1.5	Other liabs. & capital	19.0	
				Coin	4.0	capital		
12/25/47	Securities	14.0	Notes 25.6	Gov. secs	11.1	Public dep.	9.2	17.8
	Coin & bullion	11.6		Other secs	17.0	Other dep.	8.2	
				Notes	7.8	Other liabs. & capital	19.0	
				Coin	5.0	capital		

The Crisis of 1847

The cut in its lending rate from 4 to $2\frac{1}{2}$ percent when the Act of 1844 came into effect has been cited as evidence that the Act succeeded in shifting the Bank toward Peel's view that it should behave "like any other bank." Certainly, this was the lowest rate in the Bank's history to that time. On the other hand, there is little doubt that it would have expanded credit under any system because of its recent accumulations of gold. In September 1844, the Bank's coin and bullion reserve was almost half its note and deposit liabilities, the highest ratio since 1790. Furthermore, under the new system the relevant reserve ratio for the Banking Department (notes and coin as a proportion of deposits) was nearly three-quarters. This compares with a typical ratio of one-third in later years. It seldom again reached one-half.

The Bank's positions in September 1844 under the old and new systems are shown in Table 5.1. Under the old system, taking the Bank as a whole, its specie (coin and bullion) reserve was £15.2 million, compared with net liabilities (notes and deposits owed outside the Bank) of £32.5 million. Under the new system, the Issue Department's notes outstanding (to the Banking Department and outside the Bank) were backed one-for-one by securities of £14 million (the fiduciary issue) and specie. The Banking Department's reserve (notes and coin) was £9.0 million, compared with deposit liabilities of £12.3 million.

By summer 1846, private loans had risen 60 percent (from £7.8 million to £12.5 million), much of it for railway construction, which became, according to Feavearyear, a "mania." "Within a short while there was scarcely a possessor of capital in any part of the country who was not holding more railway stock than common prudence would have permitted him to hold," Feavearyear wrote.[6] The Banking Department's note reserve was maintained, however, as there was little change in the public's demand for notes, and the Issue Department actually gained gold.

Gold began to flow out of the country when the poor harvests of 1845 and 1846 increased grain imports whereas "the rise of price produced a wave of speculation and an inordinate number of corn bills, which the banks were called upon to discount. . . . The Bank of England, having supplied the market with from 7–10 millions of floating funds by discounts and by market loans, was in a bad position both for curbing speculation and for checking the drain. As soon as it attempted to do so there was

---

[6] A. E. Feavearyear, *The Pound Sterling*, p. 261.

bound to be a shrinkage of credit and a risk of panic."[7] Several witnesses before the parliamentary committees on the distress of 1847, including the governor and deputy governor of the Bank, stated "that earlier steps in Autumn 1846 and Spring 1847 by the Bank of England might have obviated the necessity for more stringent measures later."[8] The Bank raised its rate from 3 to 4 percent in January and to 5 percent in April. But its note reserve fell from £9.5 million in December to £2.6 million on April 17. The public thwarted the currency principle by maintaining a steady demand for Bank notes at just over £20 million, and the loss of gold impinged only on the Banking Department's reserve and deposits.

The Bank's (that is, the Banking Department's) reserve was low, but it could not force the return of notes by calling in or not renewing loans without risking a crisis. It stopped the drain at the end of April by informing customers that its discounts would be cut in half. However, signs of weakness among debtors caused it to relax the pressure, and easy conditions returned.

The problem shifted to agricultural prices. The large imports of grain and prospects of a good harvest in 1847 brought the price of wheat down from 14 to 8 shillings a bushel. The Bank's lending continued to grow, but in August grain merchants began to fail. By mid-September, the crisis had spread to the bill brokers and panic was beginning to affect all trades and industries. "Early in October, with the payment of dividends, [the note reserve] fell to £3,409,000, and Bank rate was raised again to $5^1/_2$ percent. At the same time, the Bank announced that no further advances would be made on public stocks, which set many people who had used the latter as collateral security selling frantically, and caused a panic on the Stock Exchange."[9]

The country banks felt the pressure of the Bank's tight monetary policy and asked for assistance. The Bank's gold exceeded £8 million, a respectable amount by historical standards, but it was not available. The relevant reserve was now Bank notes in the Banking Department, and on October 23 these had fallen to £1.5 million, a mere 11 percent of deposits. Debtors wanted credit, and the assurance of credit, and promised the Bank that its debt would not be converted to notes, but the Bank would not take the chance.

---

[7] *Ibid.*, p. 261.
[8] House of Commons, 1848, p. iv.
[9] Feavearyear, *op. cit.*, p. 263.

The public turned to the government, and for "a fortnight the Chancellor of the Exchequer, Sir Charles Wood, who had played so important a part in the passing of the Act, was occupied continuously in meeting the arguments and pleadings of those who wanted the Act suspended. Again and again he refused."[10] He told the House (November 30), "Parties of every description made applications to us for assistance [saying] 'We do not want notes, but give us confidence.'... They said, 'We have notes enough, but we have not confidence to use them; say you will stand by us, and we shall have all that we want; do anything, in short, that will give us confidence. If we think that we can get bank notes, we shall not want them. Charge any rate of interest you please, ask what you like.'"

When the Bank Charter Bill was before the House of Commons in 1844, Horsley Palmer and Henry Bosanquet, the latter a director of the London and Westminster Bank, warned Peel that the limitation of the note issue would interfere with the Bank's ability to assist the market. Bosanquet sympathized with the long-term objectives of the Bill. "But I feel confident that in the practical working of the system of currency acting (as it is proposed) as if it were exclusively composed of metal, there will be moments when sudden voids will be created in the circulation,... which if not in some way provided for, may be the cause at times of a total suspension of business throughout the country...." He proposed that "during the first five years of the new system, whenever the rate of interest at the Bank of England shall have risen to eight percent, it shall be lawful for the Issue Department to make advances at that rate of interest on the deposit of Exchequer Bills; the loans to be repaid and the bills sold whenever the rate of interest shall have fallen below eight percent." Thirty London bankers made a similar request. Peel dismissed it in a letter to the Governor:[11]

My confidence is unshaken that we are taking all the precautions which legislation can prudently take against the recurrence of a monetary crisis. It *may* occur in spite of our precautions, and if it does, and *if it be necessary* to assume a grave responsibility for the purpose of meeting it, I dare say men will be found willing to assume such a responsibility. I would rather trust to this than impair the efficiency and probable success of those measures by which one hopes to control evil tendencies in their beginning, and to diminish the risk that extraordinary measures may be necessary.

[10] Feavearyear, *op. cit.*, p. 263.
[11] These letters are reported in C. S. Parker, *Peel*, iii, 1899, pp. 140–41.

The government's hand was forced by the failure of several large banks during the week beginning Monday, October 18. On Saturday the chancellor told the Bank to lend as freely as it wished, and if this involved an increase in the fiduciary issue beyond the legal maximum, an act of indemnity would be asked of Parliament. He suggested that a rate of interest of at least 8 percent be charged. The letter confirming this direction tried to reconcile the government's refusal to admit the inadequacies of the 1844 Act with the necessity of its suspension.

Downing Street, 25 October 1847

To the Governor and Deputy Governor of the Bank of England.
Gentlemen,

Her Majesty's Government have seen with the deepest Regret the Pressure which has existed for some Weeks upon the commercial Interests of the Country, and that this Pressure has been aggravated by a Want of that confidence which is necessary for carrying on the ordinary Dealings of Trade.

They have been in hopes that the Check given to Transactions of a speculative Character, the Transfer of Capital from other Countries, the Influx of Bullion, and the Feeling which a Knowledge of these Circumstances might have been expected to produce, would have removed the prevailing Distrust.

They were encouraged in this Expectation by the speedy Cessation of a similar State of Feeling in the Month of April last.

These Hopes have, however, been disappointed, and Her Majesty's Government have come to the Conclusion that the Time has arrived when they ought to attempt, by some extraordinary and temporary Measure, to restore Confidence to the mercantile and manufacturing community.

For this Purpose, they recommend to the Directors of the Bank of England, in the present Emergency, to enlarge the Amount of their Discounts and Advances upon approved Security; but that, in order to retain this Operation within reasonable Limits, a high Rate of Interest should be charged.

In present Circumstances, they would suggest that the Rate of Interest should not be less than Eight per Cent.

If this Course should lead to any Infringement of the existing Law, Her Majesty's Government will be prepared to propose to Parliament, on its Meeting, a Bill of Indemnity. They will rely upon the Discretion of the Directors to reduce as soon as possible the Amount of their Notes, if any extraordinary Issue should take place . . .

Her Majesty's Government are of opinion that any extra Profit derived from this Measure should be carried to the Account of the Public, but the precise Mode of doing so must be left to future Arrangement.

Her Majesty's Government are not insensible of the Evil of any Departure from the Law which has placed the Currency of the Country upon a sound Basis; but they feel confident, that, in the present Circumstances the Measure which they have proposed may be safely adopted, and at the same Time the main Provisions of that Law, and the vital Principle of preserving the Convertibility of the Bank Note, may be firmly maintained.

> We have the Honour to be, Gentlemen, Your obedient humble servants,
> J. Russell (Prime Minister), Charles Wood[12]

News of the Act's suspension restored confidence immediately, and gold and notes, now that they could be had, were no longer wanted. The new notes quickly printed by the Bank were not taken, and the fiduciary issue was not exceeded. The Bank's position at the end of the year is presented in Table 5.2, which shows a reduction of one-eighth in the public's note holdings since October 23, similar to that following the Bank's ease in April.[13]

Tooke's prophecies had been fulfilled, but Peel and Wood denied that the Act of 1844 was to blame. Although it had not been as effective on all fronts as Peel had hoped, most of the Act's goals were secured. "Its first object was that in which I admit it has failed, namely, to prevent by early and gradual [steps] severe and sudden contraction and the panic and confusion inseparable from it."[14] However, in "two other objects of at least equal importance ... my belief is that the Bill has completely succeeded," namely the preservation of convertibility and the prevention of the aggravation of speculation by the abuse of paper money (House of Commons, December 3, 1847).

The Act's defenders pleaded that the crisis would have occurred under any system:

All legislation – every system – proceeds upon the supposition that men will be actuated by the ordinary motives of human action; and against the consequences of their conduct, when it is influenced by other motives, no system and no legislation can provide. It is no fault of the principle of the Act of 1844 that it was unable to provide against that state of things against which no other principle and no other system that has ever yet been advocated for the regulation of our currency could have protected us.

> Sir Charles Wood, House of Commons, November 30, 1847

The Act was as good as the wit of man allowed. But no one could tell the future. In simultaneously defending the Act and the government's

---

[12] House of Lords, *Report from the Secret Committee . . .* , 1848; reprinted in T. E. Gregory, *Select Statutes*, ii, pp. 7–8.

[13] See House of Commons, 1848, appendices 5 and 24.

[14] [. . .] substitutes a word possibly omitted from Hansard.

decision to break it, the chancellor said that the government had followed the course recommended by the best authorities. Quoting Loyd, he said,

> For all contingencies which can be reasonably anticipated, and which are susceptible of being previously defined by law, the firm application of the provisions of the Bill is essential, and against the occurrence of these contingencies which are not capable of being foreseen and defined by law, but which are not altogether impossible, the Bill itself affords the best protection than can be obtained. Should a crisis ever arrive 'baffling all ordinary calculations' and not amenable to the application of any ordinary principle, the remedy must be sought not in the previous provisions of the law, but, quoting Mr. Huskisson's words, "in the discretion of those who may then be at the head of affairs, subject to their own responsibility, and to the judgment of Parliament."[15]
>
> Samuel Jones Loyd, *Thoughts on the Separation of the Departments of the Bank of England*, pp. 439–40

Anyway, he said, again quoting Loyd,

> To guard against commercial convulsions is not the direct or real purpose of the Bill. To subject the paper issues to such regulation as shall secure their conformity in amount and value with and consequently their immediate convertibility at all times into metallic money, is the purpose to which the provisions of the measure are avowedly directed.
>
> *Thoughts . . .* , p. 388

"I should have little faith in any system of currency," he added, "which professed to accomplish more than to regulate the circulation."

Contingencies and Commitments

Wood and Peel thus denied the "main object" of the Act as stated in the chancellor's letter to the Bank in April 1844 (quoted in Chapter 4). The earlier statement accorded with John Stuart Mill's later interpretation of the Act. He wrote for the 1857 edition of *The Principles of Political Economy* that "I think myself justified in affirming that the mitigation of commercial revulsions [rather than the convertibility of the issue] is the real, and only serious, purpose of the Act of 1844. No Government would hesitate a moment" to stop convertibility to assure the continuity of the Bank of England's support of the financial system "if suspension of the Act of 1844 proved insufficient. . . ."[16] The House of Lords recommended

[15] Huskisson, *The Question Concerning the Depreciation of Our Currency*, p. 88.
[16] Book 3, chap. 24.3, p. 657n.

that this be recognized by amending the Act to deal with crises. Its 1848 Committee on the Commercial Distress questioned

whether the Restrictions of the Act of 1844 are not attended with grievous and unnecessary Evils. [An] attempt to enforce by Law, under all Circumstances, one fixed and inflexible Rule for the Management of a national Bank of Issue seems inconsistent with the best written Authorities, with the general Principles of Economic Science, as well as with the Testimony of many Witnesses of Practical Knowledge and Experience....[17] It has been shown that an Enlargement of the Issues of the Bank under a favourable Foreign Exchange, would frequently be expedient at Times, when, under the Provisions of the Act, no such Enlargement would be possible, and even in Cases where by the Act a compulsory Contraction would be enforced.[18]

There was no better evidence of this, in the judgment of the committee, than the government's letter of October 25, 1847. Although the necessity of abrogating the Act was unquestioned, it raised problems:

But even if those Restrictions were originally defensible when enacted, their Hold on Opinion, as well as their Authority in Practice, have been materially impaired by the Letter by which they were superseded – by its acknowledged Necessity and by its undeniable Success. The Precedent is established, and its Application will inevitably be called for on other Occasions; and it may so happen that the Principle of Relaxation will be applied under Circumstances less urgent and less justifiable than those which occurred in 1847. The Committee are therefore of the opinion that it is expedient for the Legislature to provide specifically for the Manner and the Responsibility of relaxing these Restrictions in Times when it can be done consistently with the perfect Convertibility of the Note – an Obligation which should never be forgotten.[19]

We understand the time-inconsistency of optimal plans, the committee was saying. We understand that offers of assistance raise the probabilities of, even guarantee, their necessity. Nonetheless, once assistance is forthcoming in conditions that are likely to be repeated, why not provide for it?

They saw support in the admissions of the Act's defenders. Loyd had testified, "You cannot build up in this Country an enormous and complicated System of Credit without being occasionally, under some very peculiar and extraordinary Combination of Circumstances, exposed to the

---

[17] The *Report*'s "authorities" were Francis Horner's "Review" of Thornton's *Paper Credit* and Huskisson's elaboration of *The Bullion Report* (*The Question Concerning the Depreciation of Our Currency Stated and Examined*).

[18] Gregory, *op. cit.*, p. 37.

[19] *Ibid.*, pp. 27–28.

Possibility of Panics seizing the Public Mind, which cannot be regulated by any systematic legislative Provisions, but which must be met, according to the Exigency of the Moment, by some extraordinary and exceptional Measure." William Cotton, who had been governor when the Act was passed, believed that "such Contingencies will not be unfrequent," but "you could not make Provision in the Act for an Exception like that of a Panic, which may arise once in Five or Six Years, or not even that." Their lordships wondered what had happened to the rule of law:

To leave these Cases, when they do arise, to be dealt with by the irregular Exercise of the mere Authority of the Crown and its Advisers, setting aside 'once in Five or Six Years,' or even at Periods more remote, the express Provisions of a distinct Statute, appears wholly inconsistent with that Fixity and Order which it is, or ought to be, the Object of all Law to secure.[20]

It seemed that there were two alternatives: Repeal the Act or continue it subject to a "discretionary relaxing Power." The second had more support, but to whom should the power be given? Not the government because of "the Danger that all Governments are liable, more or less, to be influenced in such Cases by political rather than by economical Considerations. It may also be apprehended that the Exercise of an undefined and extraordinary Power would depend too much on the personal Character or the political Position of the Minister for the Time being." Nor jointly to the government and the Bank because they would be inclined to cast the responsibility on each other, "and in this Conflict the Interests of the Public would be forgotten or defeated." That left the Bank alone, although this course also had some potential failings. It was "apparent from the Evidence that the immediate pecuniary Interests of the Proprietors as a trading Company may at Times supersede or control larger and higher Considerations." Was it suggested, contrary to Thornton, that the informed self-interest of the directors might not be consistent with the public welfare? Not necessarily, but the committee was impelled to remind the Bank of the public responsibilities that went with the "great Privileges and exclusive Powers" that Parliament had conferred on it. The Bank "differs from an ordinary trading Corporation; and, consequently, is bound always to keep in view the real and permanent Interests of the Commercial Classes, and of that great Community of which it forms a Part. The true Interests of the Proprietors of Bank Stock can never be prejudiced by being considered in connexion with these larger principles."

[20] *Ibid.*, p. 39.

However, to increase the probability that the Bank would be governed by these principles the committee recommended changes in its governance that will be summarized following their statement that in the final analysis discretionary monetary policy could not be avoided.

In conclusion, the Committee think it right to add, that, whilst they feel deeply the Necessity of a sound System of Legislation for the Bank of England, and for all other Establishments entrusted with the Privilege of issuing Notes as Substitutes and Representatives of the current Coin of the Realm, they are far from suggesting that it is upon Laws, however wisely framed they may be, that Reliance can or ought exclusively to be placed. The best Banking System may be defeated by imperfect Management; and, on the other hand, the Evils of an imperfect Banking System may be greatly mitigated, if not overcome, by Prudence, Caution and Resolution. In the Confidence universally and justly placed in the Bank of England the fullest Testimony is borne to the Integrity and good Faith with which its great Transactions have been conducted; and the Opinion of the Committee in this respect is best shown in their Desire to see vested in the Bank a wider Discretion than they possess under the Act of 1844 – a Discretion which the increased Knowledge produced by Experience and Discussion, and in which the Bank of England can hardly fail to participate, will enable them to exercise to the Advantage of their own Corporation, to their own Honour, and to the permanent Benefit of the Public, and more especially of the Commercial Classes of England.[21]

Even so, the committee thought that some reorganization, "to obviate" criticisms of the Bank, would not be amiss. It was glad to hear from Cotton that the Court of Directors had decided to abandon the principle of election by seniority and to select "as Governor and Deputy Governor the Directors they consider best qualified for the Situation." They also learned "that in order to secure the services in the Committee of Treasury of a Director [George Warde Norman], the ordinary preliminary conditions of having filled the Chair was dispensed with when the health of the party rendered his appointment as Governor inexpedient." Furthermore, Governors Palmer and Cotton had been reelected for another year because "continuity of action was required in consequence of the pending renewals of the charter." The committee was also attracted by a proposal of the banker witness, G. C. Glyn:

I consider that it would be well that the Bank Court should have in it certain Persons not elected by the Proprietors, who should be appointed under Act of Parliament for a limited Time, or in any other Way which may be deemed advisable, not immediately by the Government or the Proprietors, and not removable

---

[21] *Ibid.*, p. 46.

by the Government, and that they should have, not an absolute Veto upon the proceedings of the Bank Court, but if they dissented from the Majority their Reasons for that Dissent should always be submitted in Writing, and that they should be laid before Parliament, if Parliament saw fit, from Time to Time. I think that the Introduction of these Commissioners and their Protests and Influence would exercise a very wholesome Control upon the Body of Governors, and at the same Time would not deprive them of that Power of which as representing the Proprietors it would not be right that they should be deprived.[22]

Public directors waited eighty years, and public disclosures of policy discussions a century and a half. There were no significant changes in the Bank's governance until the next century. Nor, despite inquiries after the crises of 1857 and 1866, were formal provisions made for exceptions "baffling all ordinary calculations" until 1928. In June 1873, the month *Lombard Street* appeared, Chancellor Robert Lowe introduced a bill "to provide for authorizing in certain contingencies a temporary increase of the amount of Bank of England Notes issued in exchange for securities" subject to the condition that the chancellor and prime minister were satisfied, first, that the Bank rate was not less than 12 percent, second, that the foreign exchanges were favorable, and third, that "a large portion" of outstanding notes was "rendered ineffective for its ordinary purpose by reason of internal panic."[23] The bill got nowhere, the banker–economist R. H. I. Palgrave believed, because its terms were too "cumbrous and exacting."[24] *Bankers Magazine* thought that Lowe had picked a high trigger rate to discourage its use.[25]

Clapham wrote that "indifference to banking reform [in the 1870s] was no doubt a testimonial to the combined skill and good fortune of the Bank" in a variety of situations since the crisis of 1866 – "from the quiet times of the late sixties through continental war, Parisian revolution, post-war trade boom and subsequent collapse. . . . "[26] This was not so after 1925. The Loyd–Peel–Wood aversion to the legal provision for contingencies carried over to the next resumption in the Gold Standard Act of 1925. However, Parliament's declining confidence in the Bank's skill or good fortune led it in the Currency and Bank Notes Act of 1928 to adopt the recommendation of the Lords' Committee 80 years earlier. The 1844

---

[22] *Ibid.*, p. 43.
[23] Quoted from Clapham, *op. cit.*, ii, p. 289.
[24] R. H. I. Palgrave, *The English Banking System*, p. 178. Lowe's bill is also reproduced in Palgrave, *Bank Rate and the Money Market*, pp. 91–93.
[25] July 1873.
[26] Clapham, *op. cit.*, ii, p. 290.

principle of a fiduciary limit was retained, provided that "the Treasury may authorise the Bank to issue bank notes" beyond that limit if the Bank represents "to the Treasury that it is expedient" to do so, subject to the requirement that "Any minute of the Treasury authorising an increase of the fiduciary issue under this section shall be laid forthwith before both Houses of Parliament."

Gregory observed that the "exact significance" of this contingency clause "depends not only upon the terms of the legislation itself but also upon certain 'undertakings' given by the Governor of the Bank of England as to the manner in which the Bank intends to interpret the spirit of the Act."[27] These undertakings were revealed to Parliament through the medium of Sir Laming Worthington-Evans, who moved and spoke for the Act of 1928 on behalf of the government.

Responding on May 14, 1928, to questions about the conditions under which the fiduciary issue might be increased, Worthington-Evans said, "I do not pretend to be able to forecast every contingency which may cause the Governor of the Bank to make the application and which may make the Chancellor of the Exchequer of the day agree to an increase in the fiduciary issue . . . ." But he pointed to "a new kind of emergency" arising from the sterling area. "Now that foreign banks have adopted the practice of accumulating a large reserve of sterling bills it is possible that owing to a change of policy on their part a large sum of gold might be withdrawn in a short time." On May 22 he reported to the House that "the Governor of the Bank has read what I said . . . and he has authorised me to say that that does represent the general intention of the Bank." The *Economist* observed (May 12, 1928) that there are "many unknowns" in the new world of scarce gold and high and fluctuating prices, but "We think the country may rely upon those to whom discretion is given to see to it that industrial recovery is not penalised for the sake of forcing our currency into a rigid mould."

The fiduciary issue was raised from £260 million to £275 million on August 5, 1931, to avoid a contraction of credit from a gold loss and a holiday increase in the note circulation – a few weeks before Parliament's suspension of convertibility on September 21.[28] The Bank's reserve was still substantial (notes of £56 million, 41 percent of deposits, in the Banking Department) and it had gold of £135 million. However, the £200 million withdrawn from London since mid-July had been met by drawing on

[27] Gregory, *op. cit.*, i, lix–lx.
[28] *Economist*, August 8, 1931, p. 254.

£130 million of foreign credits from France and the United States. Further attempts to maintain convertibility would involve a needless waste of the remaining gold, and the government was unwilling to allow credit restrictions in the face of 22-percent unemployment. "If, in the language of 1848, the price of convertibility of the note was to be a further disemployment of labour," Ralph Hawtrey wrote, "the position had become untenable."[29]

Central Banking after Bagehot

An opinion appears to have been entertained by some persons, though not by the Governor and Deputy-Governor of the Bank of England, that the Bank is released by the Act of 1844 from any obligation, except that of consulting the pecuniary interests of its Proprietors.

It is true that there are no restrictions imposed by law upon the discretion of the Bank, in respect to the conduct of the Banking, as distinguished from the Issue Department. But the Bank is a public institution, possessed of special and exclusive privileges, standing in a peculiar relation to the Government, and exercising, from the magnitude of its resources, great influence over the general mercantile and monetary transactions of the country.

House of Commons, *First Report from the Secret Committee on Commercial Distress*, June 8, 1848

Monetary Policy and the Act of 1844
James Morris and Henry Prescott, respectively governor and deputy governor of the Bank, testified before the House of Commons Committee on the Commercial Distress in March 1848, of which Francis Thornhill Baring, grandson of the founder of Barings and the chancellor of the exchequer who had called the Committee of 1841, was chairman:

Q2651. (*The Chairman*) Will you state to the Committee what you consider the effects of the Act of 1844 upon the responsibility of the Bank? – (*Mr. Morris*) The effect of the Act of 1844 was to create a separation between the two departments, the issue department and the banking department; over the issue department we have no control whatever, and the effect of the Act of 1844 is to oblige us in the banking department to look to the amount of our deposits, and the amount of reserve that we have for meeting our deposits.

Q2652. Do you consider that the Act of 1844 relieved you entirely from any responsibility as regarded the circulation? – Entirely.

---

[29] R. G. Hawtrey, *A Century of Bank Rate*, p. 143. For the 1931 crisis and departure from the gold standard, see the *Economist*, especially September 26, 1931.

Q2653. With regard to the banking department, in what condition did the Act place you? – It placed the Bank of England in the condition of any other bank, except that we were carrying on business on a much larger scale, and we had also Government deposits to deal with.

How can these answers, and the chapter's introductory statement by Bagehot, be reconciled with the Committee report quoted at the beginning of this section and the following testimony?

Q2654. It has been stated that the effect of the Act of 1844 was to relieve you from any other responsibility than that which you had to your own shareholders, with the view of making the dividend for them as large as it could be made; do you consider that the Bank was relieved from all responsibility as regards the banking department with reference to the public interest? – ... we have a duty to the public to perform, and a duty to perform to the proprietors; our duty to the proprietors would lead us to make the best dividend we could for them; but in doing that we are bound to take care, considering the power that the Bank have, as a large body, not to interfere generally with the monetary affairs of the country. I have always considered that the two interests were united, the proprietors' interest and the public interest; I have always found that whenever a step has been taken to promote the interests of the proprietors at the cost of the public, it has invariably fallen back upon us, and instead of bettering ourselves we have put ourselves in a worse position. – (*Mr. Prescott*) I should say that in all the important measures of the Bank, such as in reducing or raising the rate of interest, the first thing that the directors look to is the public interest rather than the interest of the proprietors of the Bank.

Q2655. That is, you consider that the managers of the Bank are bound to look to the public interest more than to the particular interest of the proprietors? – They are bound to consider both.

Q2656. (*To Mr. Morris*) You consider that the two interests coincide? – Yes; I do not see how the two interests can very well clash.

The attitude of what was good for the Bank – or General Motors – was good for the country would in the next century be a source of amusement and alarm. However, in 1848 the spirit of Thornton and Smith was abroad, and at least for the Bank of England it had considerable logic. The Bank's disclaimer of responsibility for the quantity of money was not new. It was present in the director's testimony in 1810 and 1819. Nevertheless, they could not escape the credit markets. Lenders are pressed by special responsibilities in payments crises; they must show forbearance or bring the structure down around their heads. Their survival is tied to the public interest. Attempts to impose both responsibilities – for the money supply and financial stability – on the Bank thus generated distinct reactions by the directors: disavowals of the first and acceptance of the second. These were not changed by the Act of 1844.

Monetary Policy after Bagehot

The editor of the *Economist* proposed three changes to the policies of the central bank to avert crises and alleviate them when they came. Most important, "There should be a clear understanding between the Bank and the public that since the Bank hold our ultimate banking reserve, they will recognize and act on the obligations which this implies; that they will replenish it in times of foreign demand as fully, and lend it in times of internal panic as freely and readily as plain principles of banking require." The second proposal was necessary to the effectiveness of the first: Because "the mind of the monetary world would become feverish and fearful if the reserve in the Banking Department ... went below £10,000,000," it "ought never to keep less than £11,000,000," and "must begin to take precautions when the reserve is between £14,000,000 and £15,000,000." Third, "We should diminish the 'amateur' element [in Bank management]; we should augment the trained banking element; and we should insure more constancy in the administration."[30]

None of these recommendations was accepted. Addressing them in reverse order, we have seen that notwithstanding the good intentions expressed to the Lords Committee in 1848, there was no change in the appointment procedure or tenure of the Bank's managers until World War I, when the gold-standard system that the recommendations assumed had ceased to exist.

A larger Bank reserve had been recommended by Gilbart and Tooke. Nevertheless, the Banking Department did not raise its reserve until the increase in the world's gold production and its liabilities in the 1890s. Palgrave argued in 1903 that the country's note and gold reserves were as inadequate as in 1844. The average note/deposit reserve ratio of the Banking Department was virtually the same (46 percent) during the three decades after *Lombard Street* as between 1844 and 1873.[31]

In correspondence with Professor Bonamy Price, H. H. Gibbs, governor from 1875 to 1877, rejected Bagehot's notion of a minimum reserve. He believed that the Bank's reserve should be governed by the nature of the liabilities.[32] Pressnell saw in this position the meaning of the Bank's claim that it was like other banks, which "strictly meant no more than the maintenance, like any other properly run bank, of adequate liquidity to meet its liabilities at any time. It is, indeed, only by regarding it as a

---

[30] Hawtrey, *op. cit.*, pp. 70–72, 307–9.

[31] Palgrave, *Bank Rate and the Money Market*, pp. 82–83.

[32] Bonamy Price, *Chapters on Practical Political Economy*, appendix, pp. 519, 530.

bank, certainly with unique liabilities and assets but still a bank, that it is possible to glimpse more rationality in the Bank's activity than some of its heavier critics allowed."[33]

Criticisms of "the inadequacy of the nation's banking and gold reserves" increased after the Baring crisis of 1890. Governor William Lidderdale begged Chancellor of the Exchequer G. J. Goschen to say nothing in a forthcoming speech "that might imperil our 'very inadequate Banking Reserves.'" Goschen had been pressing for a larger reserve, but Lidderdale noted that "the larger the Bank's own reserves, the less the bankers like to keep *their* money unused." He had spoken plainly to the bankers after the crisis in a speech at the Guildhall, and now "almost regretted having prevented the panic threatened" by his "assault" – "they are a stiffnecked and rebellious race, each caring only for his own corporation." He observed that the banks sensed danger when the Bank's reserve fell below £10,000,000. Several times when the reserve had approached £9,000,000, "the demand on the Bank of England was *very* heavy." The governor asked the chancellor to press the banks to keep greater reserves. If the banks would not keep more, he would "look round for compensation in other ways, and these ways must produce the same result (less profit to the bankers, more to the Bank) as their leaving more money here."[34]

"Anxiety about the national gold reserve was in no way abated" in the new century:

For the four peace years, 1903–6, the Issue Department treasure averaged only £33,000,000, at a time when countries with fewer liabilities and a less delicately balanced financial system carried far greater quantities, as indeed they long had; at a time too when almost the whole civilized world was on the gold basis, so that, through the international banks, claims might be made on London from any, or all, of half a dozen or more financial centres. A centre so new, remote and incalculable as Tokio now kept very large balances in London.

J. H. Clapham, The Bank of England, ii, p. 379

The Bank's exposure was not so different in the 1920s as Worthington-Evans and the governor suggested. However, some things had changed. Inflation, the loss of export markets, unemployment, and the decline of *laissez faire* had weakened the commitment to the gold standard. The Act

---

[33] L. S. Pressnell, "Gold Reserves, Banking Reserves, and the Baring Crisis of 1890."

[34] Letter from Lidderdale to Goschen, January and February 1891, quoted from Clapham, *op. cit.*, ii, pp. 344–45. Goschen's speech is in Duncan Ross, ed., *History of Banking*, iv. For other discussions of the Bank's inadequate reserve, see R. S. Sayers, *Bank of England Operations*, p. 10, and *The Bank of England, 1891–1944*, i, p. 33.

of 1928 may be seen less as a change in attitude toward contingency plans than as preparation for throwing in the towel.

This brings us to the Bank's performance of its alleged responsibility as lender of last resort. Although it never followed Bagehot's recommendation to acknowledge that responsibility, it is conceivable that the market expected the Bank to come to its aid.[35] Such expectations, however, were not put to the test. The Bank had come to the support of large firms before Barings, and under more difficult circumstances. The Bank believed that Barings, in spite of its bet on Argentine securities, was solvent.[36] That had not been true of Overend Gurney in 1866, when, Hawtrey wrote, "there was so much unsound business . . . that something like a crisis was probably in any case inevitable; the trouble could hardly have been got over with such smoothness as that of 1890."[37]

Furthermore, there remained considerable uncertainty regarding the Bank's proper behavior under stress. Bagehot agreed, indeed emphasized, that it is not easy to know when to build the reserve and when to use it. "The practical difficulties of life often cannot be met by very simple rules: those dangers being complex and many, the rules for encountering them cannot well be single or simple."[38] Hankey never abandoned the circumspect attitude that had been criticized by Bagehot. The offending passage in the first edition was unchanged in the fourth edition of 1887. In 1903, Palgrave complained of the absence of a system for the Bank rate: "A distinct statement of policy on the part of the Bank as to the course of action they would follow in any time of business pressure, as well as on many other points, is now greatly needed."[39] We have seen that Lidderdale almost regretted the Bank's assistance, and in 1875 *Bankers' Magazine* thought the Bank might reasonably refuse assistance to "a deputation from Lombard Street, which, after having turned their backs on the Bank for perhaps several years, might come on any day like the Black Friday of 1866, with a message like this, 'our reserve is nearly exhausted, what can you do to help us?'"[40]

---

[35] For example, see Feavearyear, *op. cit.*, p. 285. However, this view was not shared by Clapham (*op. cit.*, ii, pp. 286–90) or Sayers (*Bank*, 1891–1944, i, p. 3, and "Central Banking after Bagehot"), who thought the development of central banking in the 19th century "hardly conscious."

[36] Clapham, *op. cit.*, ii, p. 329.

[37] Hawtrey, *A Century of Bank Rate*, p. 110.

[38] *Lombard Street*, pp. 300–1.

[39] *Bank Rate and the Money Market*, p. 61.

[40] "Prestige, and the Position of the Bank of England," January 1875; discussed by Clapham, *op. cit.*, ii, p. 343.

The pre-1914 Bank refused – before and after 1844 – to make a commitment to the market. Its statements and actions, the "faltering way" that Bagehot condemned, were consistent with an unwillingness to leap before looking, a determination to judge the actions appropriate to each situation, and a belief that crisis claims on its assistance might be avoided by raising doubts of its availability.[41] Loyd, Peel, Hankey, G. W. Norman, Gibbs, and Lidderdale understood "the Bagehot problem," as the moral hazard inherent in an unconditional lender has been called.[42]

Financial Stability after Bagehot

The Bank was again authorized to break the law in 1857 and 1866, and in the former case, following exports of gold to meet a financial crisis in the United States, the fiduciary issue was actually exceeded. There was, however, no financial crisis between 1866 and 1914, the "Baring crisis" being "noteworthy," Hawtrey wrote, as the crisis that did not occur.[43] Because every decade from the 1820s to the 1860s experienced a serious crisis, it is natural to wonder why none occurred the next half-century. We have seen that the improvement cannot be credited to legislation or the policies of the central bank, but there are plausible explanations connected with developments in financial institutions, the structure of production, and government finance.

The three main instigators of crises between the founding of the Bank and the middle of the 19th century were crop failures that necessitated food imports, war finance, and fragile financial institutions. The first problem was solved by the repeal of the Corn Laws (tariffs and other restrictions on grain imports) in 1846, the decline in shipping costs, abundant North American wheat, and improvements in domestic agriculture. Crop failures became less common, and less important when they occurred. The proportion of wheat consumption supplied by imports rose from one-twelfth before the repeal of the Corn Laws to one-half in 1870 and four-fifths in 1914.[44] The development of international finance and the credibility of the gold standard also made it possible to finance trade deficits without resort to gold shipments and credit restrictions.

---

[41] *Lombard Street*, p. 64.

[42] Fred Hirsch, "The Bagehot Problem"; see also Hugh Rockoff, "Walter Bagehot and the Theory of Central Banking," and John Wood, "Bagehot's Lender of Last Resort: A Hollow Hallowed Tradition." Angela Redish noted that "Lender of Last Resort Policies: From Bagehot to Bailout" were addressed to legal restraints.

[43] Hawtrey, *op. cit.*, p. 105.

[44] C. Ó Gráda, "Agricultural Decline, 1860–1914."

The pressures on London caused by the demands of the country banks in the 1790s, 1820s, and 1830s led to the elimination of legal obstacles to large banks beginning in the 1820s and culminating in limited liability in 1862. By 1873, Bagehot could write that "The joint-stock banks of this country are a most remarkable success." They were just getting started. The years after the crisis of 1866 "witnessed a rapid change in the structure of the banking system." From the distribution of a relatively small volume of credit among a large number of banks, "by the growth of the joint-stock banks and by the process of amalgamation, a much larger volume of credit [was by 1914] concentrated in the hands of a very few banks."[45] The number of banks fell from nearly 400 to 66, and the number of joint-stock banks from 121 to 43.[46] The stability of the new banks contrasted sharply not only with the domestic situation earlier in the century but also with the contemporary United States, which maintained severe branching restrictions. The development of fiscal conservatism and professional management in government finances also contributed to financial stability and the security of the Bank. Regular budgetary surpluses meant that the Bank was not pressed to overextend itself as before 1815. Peace, a high credit rating, and alternative sources of funds through the Post Office Savings Banks opened in 1861 and the regular issue of Treasury bills beginning in 1877 all contributed to Gladstone's objective of making the chancellor "independent of the Bank and the City power when he has occasion for sums in seven figures."[47] He "now never had to beg." The "still times" following 1866, when, according to Bagehot, "The Money Market took care of itself," followed "Gladstone's longest and greatest spell at the Exchequer (1859–66)."[48]

Conclusion: Central Banking under the Gold Standard

There can be no doubt that under the Act of 1844 a sudden exportation of gold must cause a sudden contraction of the notes in circulation. This 'self-acting' machine acts by jerks, like a steam-engine without a fly-wheel; and its advocates look to the banking department to supply the fly-wheel, and to cause the machine to move smoothly and equably. It may be doubted whether the banking department

---

[45] Feavearyear, *op. cit.*, p. 292.

[46] See Clapham, *An Economic History of Modern Britain*; Francois Crouzet, *The Victorian Economy*; and William Ashworth, *An Economic History of England, 1870–1939*.

[47] John Morley, *Life of Gladstone*, i, p. 651.

[48] Clapham, *Bank of England*, ii, pp. 272–74. See David Kynaston for more on the "The Bank and the Government."

has the power of doing this. But when this is not done, the advocates of the act throw the blame upon that department. They resemble the court preceptor, who, when the royal pupil did anything wrong, inflicted the beating on his fellow student.

J. W. Gilbart, *A Practical Treatise on Banking*, i, 1856, p. 141

The machine *was* made to run fairly smoothly, and the Bank deserves some of the credit. However, its contributions arose more from doing what came naturally than to the conscious construction of an optimizing policy to fit the new legal environment. "Peel's Bank Act . . . seemed [to Barrett Whale] exceptional in English legislation because it did not represent an attempt to deal piecemeal with the immediate practical problems, giving support in this direction, imposing restrictions in that, but gave effect to a clear-cut theory – that banking ought to be separated from the control of the currency." Nevertheless, the financial system continued on the course that had been set. It could hardly have done otherwise. It is almost impossible that a whole new system can be imposed successfully on a complex and changing economic and social structure. The effects of such an attempt might in various respects be good or bad, but they will be unpredictable.

In the case of the Act of 1844, it can reasonably be argued that the attempt had almost no effect. If inevitabilities in human behavior exist, they include bankers' concerns for their reserves and the maintenance of their credit. The Bank Charter Act did little if anything to interrupt the Bank's development of a policy that, to the best of its ability in an uncertain world, balanced the competing goals of profits and safety – with attention, however imperfect, to the ramifications of the actions of a large reserve bank. Although Gilbart (who knew better but had his own axes to grind) and others blamed subsequent crises on the Act, they were neither more frequent nor substantially different than before. Bagehot opened *Lombard Street* with a pledge not to weary the reader by another book on the Act of 1844, the effects of which had been greatly exaggerated. It was "only a subordinate matter in the money market," which could be studied independently of the Act's irrelevant principles and unrealized purposes. Modern readers will soon be able to determine whether the central bank contracts adopted in the 1990s, with their focus on macrorules, will also be bypassed because of their lack of attention to more fundamental commitments to the financial markets.

Not only did the financial structure develop, to the admiration of Bagehot, independently of the Act of 1844, but monetary policy also showed, as he deplored, substantial continuity with the past. The Bank's lending behavior at the end of the century would have been familiar to

Horsley Palmer. As in his time, the Bank had found that a Bank rate equal to the market rate – or even below the market when its reserve was large – might in optimistic times invite unsustainable expansion. However, a rate high enough for safety meant the loss of customers. So in 1878 the Bank "announced, in effect, that henceforth, however large the reserve might be, money would never be available *ab libitum* to all and sundry at market rate. To its own regular customers ... discounts would be granted at the competitive rate. But to the market generally, the other banks and bill-brokers, accommodation would be available only at Bank rate, which, it was understood, would in future bear no definite relation to the competitive rate and would as a general rule be higher."[49] Evaluated from the standpoint of a private banker, this enabled the Bank to maintain customer relationships, while maintaining control of its reserve. It was also conducive to the possibility of lender of last resort.

The Bank held a smaller reserve than Palmer would have liked – although he might have adjusted, as the Bank did, to the increasing effectiveness of the Bank rate. The main reason that Bagehot gave for a large reserve was that the Bank rate worked weakly and slowly; "for experience shows that between £2,000,000 and £3,000,000 may ... be withdrawn from the Bank store before the right rate of interest is found which will attract money from abroad, and before that rate has had time to attract it."[50] The progress of the century saw skepticism about the effectiveness of the Bank rate turn to wonder. The increasing sophistication of the financial markets might have been the source of its increased power. A related explanation was that "Probably this growing sensitiveness was partly due to traders having learnt what to expect. If, when Bank rate rose to 6 percent, they all expected one another to become reluctant buyers, they would become reluctant buyers, and business would decline without the rate being raised any higher."[51] The Bank was accused of overconfidence. It got away with a small reserve by means of an active Bank rate. It had learned how to manage its reserve *and* earn profits. The "ultimate answer to Bagehot's problem," R. S. Sayers wrote, "was ... a powerful Bank Rate weapon with a 'thin film of gold.'"[52]

But there were costs. Palgrave, the banker, complained that the Bank rate was changed too often, Hawtrey, the economist, that it was not changed often enough. An increase in Bank rate tended to operate by

[49] Feavearyear, *op. cit.*, p. 283; from the *Economist*, June 15, 1878, p. 693.
[50] Bagehot, *op. cit.*, p. 309.
[51] Hawtrey, *op. cit.*, p. 61.
[52] Sayers, "The Development of Central Banking after Bagehot."

reducing aggregate demand, incomes, and finally the public's transactions demand for money, including gold. The effects required time, and the Bank was slow in taking action. Hawtrey believed that "an incipient expansion can always be checked by a rise in Bank Rate. If the adjustments of Bank Rate are wisely and promptly applied, quite small changes will suffice."[53]

The Bank was not unaware of the costs of Bank rate. A private lender who withdraws credit does not have to be told of its effects. When in 1848 Horsley Palmer was asked by Thomas Baring (who knew the answer) how an increase in Bank rate exerted its influence, he replied:

> It presses upon all branches of commerce in a way that is most prejudicial to them; the raising of the rate of interest I am given to understand stopped very largely the mercantile transactions of the country – exports as well as imports.
>
> It is by the interference with trade that it acts, and not merely by the inconvenience that it occasions to holders of bills? – It causes the stoppage of trade.[54]

The Cunliffe Report of 1918, in which the government declared its intention to return to the prewar standard as soon as possible, acknowledged that an increase in Bank rate restricted credit, demand, and employment. However, Hawtrey, Keynes, and other economists believed that the postwar Bank and Treasury had forgotten the magnitudes of these effects. Hawtrey harped on the point that 19th-century monetary policy exerted its influence by acting on domestic demand, reporting the exchange between Baring and Palmer. Keynes reminded the government in "The Economic Consequences of Mr. Churchill" that "Deflation does not reduce wages 'automatically.' It reduces them by causing unemployment. The proper object of dear money is to check an incipient boom. Woe to those whose faith leads them to use it to aggravate a depression."

When Keynes wrote in 1930 that "it may be too much to expect that . . . countries will voluntarily sacrifice what they believe to be their own interests in order to pursue . . . the rules of the gold standard game," he was referring to a Bank and government that – in direct opposition to the direction of social change – had reversed the priorities of convertibility and commercial well-being that Mill had discussed and, in their eagerness for convertibility, produced a reaction against long-term objectives that still influences monetary policy.[55]

---

[53] Ibid., p. 275.

[54] Q2007, 2113; see Hawtrey, *op. cit.*, pp. 27–28.

[55] J. M. Keynes, *Treatise on Money*, ii, pp. 273–74.

SIX

Central Banking in the United States, 1790–1914

A central bank is a banker's bank. It affords to the other banks of the community, the competitive banks, the same facilities as they afford to their customers. The competitive banks make payments to one another by drawing on balances at the central bank,... and they replenish their balances, when low, by borrowing from the central bank.

These facilities being secured to them, the competitive banks are relieved from responsibility for the provision of currency. They still have to keep their position liquid, but this they can do by maintaining sufficient assets of the kind that can be pledged or rediscounted with the central bank. The exclusive responsibility for seeing that the supply of currency in the community is adequate, and no more than adequate, devolves upon the central bank.

R. G. Hawtrey, *The Art of Central Banking*, p. 116

Whether it likes it or not, whether it admits it or not, a central bank is responsible for the currency, Hawtrey tells us, because it is the lender of last resort. Henry Thornton and Francis Baring recognized this as a crucial role of the Bank of England at the end of the 18th century. "Monetary authority" might be a better description than "central bank" because later organizations that were designed or grew to perform this role have been called central banks even when they have not been banks, let alone bankers' banks. The Independent Treasury as it operated between the Second Bank of the United States and the Federal Reserve System has been called a central bank because it affected bank reserves – sometimes intentionally – by shifting coin between its vaults and commercial banks. The New York City money market banks, taken together, were more like the Bank of England because they were bankers for banks outside the

Background: People and Events
1790–91: Hamilton's Reports on Public Credit, A National Bank, and Manufactures.
1791–1811: First National Bank of the United States.
1812–15: War of 1812; beginning of currency suspension.
1816–36: Second National Bank of the United States.
1832: Jackson vetoes renewal of the National Bank; begins removal of government deposits from the Bank in 1833.
1846: Independent Treasury Act.
1857: The New York Clearing House and the Independent Treasury respond to panic – one of several times.
1861: Federal issue of currency (greenbacks) for war finance.
1862–78: Suspension of convertibility.
1863: National Bank Act, amended 1864 and 1865.
1890–93: Passage and repeal of the Silver Purchase Act.
1896: Bryan's Cross of Gold speech.
1900: Gold Standard Act.
1907: Panic, Aldrich–Vreeland Act, National Monetary Commission.

	President of the United States	Secretary of the Treasury[*]	Party[†]
1789	George Washington	Alexander Hamilton	Federalist
1795		Oliver Wolcott, Jr.	
1797	John Adams		
1801	Thomas Jefferson	Albert Gallatin	Democrat–Republican
1809	James Madison		
1814		Alexander Dallas	
1816		William Crawford	
1817	James Monroe		Republican
1825	John Q. Adams	Richard Rush	No designations
1829	Andrew Jackson	Samuel Ingram	Democratic
1831		Louis McLane	
1833		Roger Taney	
1834		Levi Woodbury	
1837	Martin Van Buren		
1841	William H. Harrison	Thomas Ewing	Whig
1841	John Tyler	Walter Forward	
1843		John Spencer	
1844		George Bibb	
1845	James K. Polk	Robert Walker	Democratic
1849	Zachary Taylor	W. M. Meredith	Whig
1850	Millard Fillmore	Thomas Corwin	

	President of the United States	Secretary of the Treasury[*]	Party[†]
1853	Franklin Pierce	James Guthrie	Democratic
1857	James Buchanan	Howell Cobb	
1860		Philip Thomas	
1861	Abraham Lincoln	Salmon Chase	Republican
1864		William Fessenden	
1865	Andrew Johnson	Hugh McCulloch	
1869	Ulysses S. Grant	George Boutwell	
1873		William Richardson	
1874		B. H. Bristow	
1876		Lot Morrill	
1877	Rutherford B. Hayes	John Sherman	
1881	James A. Garfield	William Windom	
1881	Chester A. Arthur	Charles Folger	
1884		Walter Gresham	
1884		Hugh McCulloch	
1885	Grover Cleveland	Daniel Manning	Democratic
1887		Charles Fairchild	
1889	Benjamin Harrison	William Windom	Republican
1891		Charles Foster	
1893	Grover Cleveland	John Carlisle	Democratic
1897	William McKinley	Lyman Gage	Republican
1901	Theodore Roosevelt		
1902		Leslie Shaw	
1907		George Cortelyou	
1909	William H. Taft	Franklin MacVeagh	

[*] Some briefly serving secretaries are omitted.

[†] Washington and Adams did not call themselves Federalists, although many of their supporters (or, more appropriately, supporters of Hamilton and opponents of Jefferson) were Federalists and shared a desire for a strong central government. The early Republican/Democrats and Republicans marked steps in the development of the modern Democratic party.

metropolis, and with the aid of their clearinghouse supported the system – that is, behaved as lenders of last resort – in times of stress. The federally chartered Banks of the United States (1791–1811 and 1816–36) might have grown into something like the Bank of England. However, although they affected money and credit by their sometimes conservative, restraining policies, they were not regular repositories of the reserves of those banks or dependable lenders of last resort.

This chapter is concerned with the influences of these central institutions on aggregate money and credit. Their existence and powers were controversial from Alexander Hamilton's *Report on a National Bank* in

1790 to the founding of the Federal Reserve in 1913. The main contest was between those who believed that a national institution was necessary to a uniform and stable currency and opponents who believed either that it would be ineffective or too powerful – destabilizing or a tool of bankers or irresponsible governments.

The controversies over central banking and monetary policy in Britain were also alive in the United States. Congress, the Treasury, and financial institutions disputed rules and discretion, and restrictive laws provoked extra-legal clearinghouse currencies and Treasury open market purchases. The American resumptions after the War of 1812 and the Civil War were comparable with Britain's after the Napoleonic Wars and, looking ahead, the two world wars.

The National Banking System described in the last section was a Civil War finance measure, but it also sought a uniform currency backed by U.S. bonds. In the end, spurred by a variety of political and economic forces, the president and Congress decided that none of these devices was competent to regulate money, and in 1913 they erected a version of the European public banks that will be introduced in the next chapter.

New England Central Banks, 1824–1866

The Suffolk Bank System showed how banks in a trading area may develop a credit system and a uniform currency that is centered on a major institution. It was replicated, often with multiple central banks, in other areas, and some of its features are with us today in correspondent banking.

The system was a response to the notes of "country" banks that had worried Boston banks since the 1790s. Boston merchants depended on sales outside the city, and because the redemption of country notes at their source was inconvenient and Boston banks would not accept these "foreign" notes except at substantial discounts, and sometimes refused them altogether, Bostonians found it convenient to hold and do business with country notes while paying off their bank loans, making deposits, and obtaining coin with "city" notes. In 1824 the Suffolk Bank of Boston estimated that country notes made up 96 percent of the city's circulation (see its letter).[1] The problem as seen by the Boston banks was worsened by the country-bank practice of lending their notes through Boston agents in

---

[1] Donald Mullineaux suggests that the Suffolk Bank exaggerated and that the notes of Boston banks exceeded country notes ("Competitive Monies and the Suffolk Bank System").

violation of the Massachusetts law against branch banking. Boston banks sporadically tried to restrain the country banks by sudden demands for redemption of wagonloads of notes. However, this was expensive, unpopular, and not always supported by the courts. (Like other creditors, disappointed noteholders had to sue banks for compensation.)

The Suffolk Bank's offer to be agent for other Boston banks in handling country notes was taken up, and it began to accept the notes of country banks willing and eligible to join the system at a uniform small discount and to bear the costs of redeeming them when they became excessive. The notes of these "members" circulated at par throughout New England.

The cost of membership was an interest-free deposit sufficient to redeem the member's notes and compensate the Suffolk Bank for operating expenses (tantamount to a reserve requirement). In addition to making a market for a nearly uniform currency, the Suffolk Bank was the principal holder of the region's reserve and provided overdraft privileges for members with deficient balances. The relative mildness of New England's depression following the Panic of 1837 probably owed something to the Suffolk Bank's "central bank-like" lending.[2]

New York banks followed suit and provided competition in the process. They cooperated in an agency that "redeemed the notes of New York country banks at . . . $\frac{1}{4}$ of 1%, New England notes at 1/8 of 1%, and Pennsylvania and New Jersey notes at $\frac{1}{4}$ of 1%. Country banks which kept deposits with the organization paid 10¢ per $100 of redeemed notes."[3]

A *letter from the Suffolk Bank to the other Boston banks,* on April 10, 1824,[4]

The subscribers, having been chosen by the directors of the Suffolk Bank a committee for the purpose of conferring with the other banking institutions in the city concerning the measures which it might be expedient for them in common to adopt, with the view of checking the enormous issues of country, and especially Eastern, paper, and of securing to the bills of the Boston banks a just proportion of the circulation, beg leave to call the attention of your board to the following statement of facts.

That of the whole incorporated banking capital of New England, amounting to no less than $20,000,000 dollars, the eleven banks in this city possess $10,150,000. That estimating the circulation of the country banks at only seventy-five per cent of their capital, which they believe to be a moderate computation, these banks furnish $7,500,000 of the circulating medium, while the banks in the city, with a capital equal to all the rest, keep in what may be fairly termed permanent

[2] Arthur Rolnick et al., "The Suffolk Bank and the Panic of 1837."
[3] Fritz Redlich, *The Molding of American Banking*, p. 79.
[4] Herman Krooss, *Documentary History of Banking and Currency*, pp. 630–32.

circulation only $300,000. That this prodigious credit thus enjoyed by the country banks is not owing to any superior confidence in the stability of these institutions, or in their ability to redeem their promises in gold and silver, but may be attributed to a discount founded on the very difficulty and uncertainty of means of enforcing this payment. Such would not be the natural operation of these causes were these institutions what they profess to be, – establishments for the discount of country notes and the convenience of country traders. Their bills would then circulate only in their own immediate vicinity. The farmers, who come to this city to dispose of their produce, would take back Boston bills, which the traders would in their turn bring down to pay for foreign or domestic merchandise. The superior stability and security of our banks would insure this result. But under the existing circumstances we presume that a very great proportion of the discounts of the country banks are made in Boston. Loans to an immense amount are made by their agents here at reduced rates of interest, payable in three or five days after demand, so that they can be in funds at very short notice, and in this manner necessarily deprive us of much valuable business. . . .

With these views we make the following proposals. That a fund . . . , to be assessed in proportion to their respective capitals, be raised by the several banking institutions who may agree to the arrangement, to be placed at the disposal of one or more banks for the purpose of sending home the bills of the banks in the State of Maine, in such way as may be deemed expedient. That this capital shall be paid in the bills of the several banks, which shall be indiscriminately paid out for the purchase of Eastern money. That the profit or loss shall be in common, after charging a reasonable compensation for any extra service rendered by the officers of the bank receiving them.

Signed: John A. Lowell and William Lawrence

The Bank of Mutual Redemption

New England country banks eventually formed a cooperative to divert the Suffolk Bank's profits to themselves. Historian Fritz Redlich called the Bank of Mutual Redemption "America's first bankers' bank" in the sense that its stock was "subscribed and held exclusively by New England banks. . . ."[5] It was chartered in 1855 "to redeem our currency at par in Boston," and by requiring smaller deposits and paying higher interest it drove the Suffolk Bank from the field. Whereas the venerable Suffolk Bank "handled the foreign money business in a dignified, routine fashion, the Bank of Mutual Redemption pushed it with a very undignified aggressiveness," going so far as to employ an agent to "solicit subscriptions."[6] It took "at par from any party the notes of banks which kept their accounts with it and the notes of all other New England banks at a rate of

[5] *Ibid.*, p. 76.
[6] *Ibid.*, p. 77.

twenty cents per thousand dollars" and grew rapidly, extending to New York and beyond.[7]

These services ended when state bank notes were terminated by the federal tax imposed on them in 1866 to force state banks into the new national system. National bank notes needed no more support than the government bonds that backed them.

The First and Second Banks of the United States, 1791–1836

It is the desire of the President that the control of the banks and the currency shall, as far as possible, be entirely separated from the political power of the country as well as wrested from an institution which has already attempted to subject the Government to its will. In his opinion the action of the General Government on this subject ought not to extend beyond the grant in the Constitution, which only authorizes Congress "to coin money and regulate the value thereof;" all else belongs to the States and the people, and must be regulated by public opinion and the interests of trade.

> President Andrew Jackson on removing public deposits from the Bank of the United States, September 18, 1833[8]

The First Bank

Until the Civil War, the chartering and regulation of banks was left to the states – with two exceptions. The first Bank of the United States began in 1791 with a charter for 20 years, and after its failure to secure renewal, the second Bank of the United States opened in 1816 with a charter that also expired after 20 years without renewal. The first Bank was established by Congress along lines proposed by Treasury Secretary Alexander Hamilton, who believed that the advantages of a national bank included assistance "to the Government in obtaining pecuniary aids, especially in sudden emergencies . . . , facilitating of the payment of taxes," and the promotion of industry by enabling gold and silver to "become the basis of a paper circulation."[9] It was privately owned to prevent the abuse of its credit that would follow from government control, but had a special relationship with the government, including the latter's pledge to accept its notes in all payments to the United States, a privilege accorded no other bank. Congress also promised to establish no other bank during the life of the Bank of the United States.

---

[7] *Loc. cit.*
[8] Krooss, *op. cit.*, p. 940.
[9] Hamilton, *Report on a National Bank*, 1790, Krooss, *op. cit.*, pp. 231–33.

The national banks were surrounded by legal and political conflicts from their beginnings. John Marshall wrote in his *Life of George Washington* that Hamilton's economic measures, especially his plan for a national bank, "made a deep impression on many members of the legislature; and contributed, not inconsiderably, to the complete organization of those distinct and visible parties, which, in their long and dubious conflict for power, have since shaken the United States to their centre."[10] The most vocal opposition to the establishment of the first national bank came from two overlapping groups: rural elements, especially in the South, who disliked banks in general because they were associated with trade and manufactures and threatened a way of life, and constitutionalists, also primarily southern, who perceived national banks as part of the central government's infringements of states' rights and personal liberties. There was also a strong if inconsistent hostility from the finance-starved western regions that liked credit but disliked creditors.

In 1791, Congressman James Madison objected to the proposed national bank because it would expose the public "to all the evils of a run on the bank," and its charter "did not make so good a bargain for the public as was due to its interests. The charter to the Bank of England had been granted only for eleven years, and was paid for by a loan to the Government on terms better than could be elsewhere got. Every renewal of the charter had, in like manner, been purchased; in some instances at a very high price."[11]

However, Madison's main concern was the bank's legality. The United States Constitution was a "limiting" document, he told the House of Representatives, in which "particular powers" had been granted to the federal government, "leaving the general mass in other hands." The Tenth Amendment provided that "The powers not delegated to the United States by the Constitution or prohibited by it to the States, are reserved to the States, respectively, or to the people." The Constitution did not mention banks. He "well recollected that a power to grant charters of incorporation had been proposed in the general convention, and rejected." Congress undoubtedly had the "power to make all laws which shall be necessary and proper for carrying into execution" its expressed powers, including the powers to "collect taxes," "borrow money," and "coin money [and] regulate the value thereof" (Art. 2, Sec. 8). However, Madison

---

[10] Vol. iv, p. 244. For support of Marshall's account of the origin of American political parties, see Charles Beard, *Economic Origins of Jeffersonian Democracy*, pp. 109–13.

[11] House of Representatives, February 2, 1791, Krooss, *op. cit.*, pp. 262–63.

did not see that these implied, or made "necessary," a national bank. Necessary instruments were specified for the other powers. The power "to declare war" is supported by the power "to raise and support armies," and the power "to regulate the value of money" is supported by the power to punish counterfeiters. Nothing is said about the power to establish a national bank.

The bill passed the House by a vote of 39 to 19, with 34 of 35 representatives from above the Mason–Dixon Line in favor compared with 5 of 23 Southerners. (Senate proceedings were not published at the time.) President Washington consulted Attorney General Edmund Randolph and Secretary of State Thomas Jefferson, both Virginians and both of the opinion that the bank was unconstitutional, but the secretary of the Treasury (from New York) prevailed.[12] He believed that it was sufficient that the bank had a "natural relation" to the powers of collecting taxes, regulating trade, and providing for the common defense. "Now it appears to the Secretary of the Treasury that this general principle is inherent in the very definition of Government and essential to every step of the progress to be made by that of the United States; namely, that every power vested in a Government is in its nature *sovereign*, and includes, by force of the term, a right to employ all the means requisite and fairly applicable to the attainment of the ends of such power and which are not precluded by restrictions and exceptions specified in the constitution or not immoral, or not contrary to the essential ends of political society." Washington set aside the veto message that he had asked Madison to prepare and signed the bill.

The Bank's services were in demand from the beginning, and it seems to have been successful in all aspects of its business. It performed efficiently as a fiscal agent for the government, managed a conservative but profitable portfolio, and maintained the convertibility of its liabilities into coin.[13] Nonetheless, its charter was not renewed.

The lineups for and against the Bank changed during its life. As President, Madison came around to its support because of its "expediency and almost necessity," and he defended its constitutionality on the basis of "deliberate and reiterated precedents." It had "throughout a period of twenty years with annual legislative recognitions" received "the entire

---

[12] See Krooss, *op. cit.*, pp. 273–306, and M. St. Clair Clarke and D. A. Hall, *Documentary History of the Bank of the U.S.*, chap. 2, for Washington's concerns and advice.

[13] See Curtin Nettels, *The Emergence of a National Economy*, pp. 118–20, 300–1, and the references cited there for the content of this paragraph.

acquiescence of all the local authorities as well as the nation at large."[14] In contrast, some of the business interests that had thought the Bank useful at the beginning increasingly resented its competition. The Bank was a creditor of the state banks, and when it presented their notes for payment in coin it acted "as a brake on credit expansion [and] antagonized sanguine entrepreneurs who sought loans for their speculative ventures."[15]

Some agrarians had been reconciled to banking but were on guard against federal intrusions. Congressman Richard Johnson of Kentucky complained that the Bank "would contract very much the circulation of the State bank notes, and would, in many other respects, come in collision with state rights. Every State has a right to regulate its own moneyed concerns."[16] Others joined the administration and conservative bank and business interests in praise of the Bank's restraint. Georgia Senator William Crawford warned that the check exerted by one state bank against another's "excessive discounts and emissions" was not sufficient – they could both double their discounts without anyone being the wiser until the damage had been done....[17] Renewal of the Bank's charter was defeated by one vote in the House of Representatives and in the Senate by the tie-breaking vote of Vice President George Clinton of New York.

War, Suspension, and Resumption

The condition of the circulating medium of the country presents another copious source of mischief and embarrassment. The recent exportations of specie have considerably diminished the fund of gold and silver coin; and another considerable portion of that fund has been drawn, by the timid and wary, from the use of the community, into the private coffers of individuals. On the other hand, the multiplication of banks in the several States has so increased the quantity of paper currency that it would be difficult to calculate its amount, and still more difficult to ascertain its value with reference to the capital on which it has been issued. But the benefit of even this paper currency is in a great measure lost, as the suspension of payments in specie at most of the banks has suddenly broken the chain of accommodation that previously extended the credit and the circulation of the notes which were emitted in one State into every State of the Union. It

---

[14] From a letter to C. J. Ingersoll of Pennsylvania, June 25, 1831, explaining his apparent inconsistency toward the constitutionality of the Bank, Clarke and Hall, *op. cit.*, pp. 778–80.

[15] Nettels, *op. cit.*, p. 301.

[16] Clarke and Hall, *op. cit.*, p. 232.

[17] Krooss, *op. cit.*, p. 393. More of the speech is in Clarke and Hall, *op. cit.*, pp. 302–15.

may, in general, be affirmed, therefore, that there exists, at this time, no adequate circulating medium common to the citizens of the United States. The moneyed transactions of private life are at a stand, and the fiscal operations of the Government labor with extreme inconvenience.

> A. J. Dallas, Secretary of the Treasury, "Recommendations for a National Bank," October 14, 1814[18]

Former Secretary of the Treasury Albert Gallatin,[19] who had supported the United States Banks in the Jefferson and Madison cabinets, estimated that between 1811 and 1816 the number of banks increased from 88 to 246, and their circulations rose from $23 million to $68 million, whereas their metallic-reserve ratio fell from 42 percent to 28 percent.[20] These developments were not entirely due to the loss of the restraining influence of the national bank, however, because the War of 1812 (declared in June 1812, although there had been hostilities at sea for some time, and was officially ended in December 1814 by the Treaty of Ghent) was financed entirely by debt, mostly bonds purchased with state bank notes. Federal revenues actually fell between 1811 and 1814, which was not surprising because they were mainly customs duties and the administration avoided internal taxes. The national debt, which had been reduced from $83 million to $45 million between 1800 and 1811, reached its pre–Civil War peak of $127 million in 1815.

The British invasion of the late summer of 1814 – remembered for the burning of Washington and the shelling of Baltimore – occasioned suspensions of specie payments by the Treasury and banks outside New England. (Alienated by Jefferson's embargo, New England bought little government debt and was less vulnerable to fears of government default.) As in England, banks continued to operate and their notes circulated at discounts.[21]

---

[18] Response to the Ways and Means Committee's request for ways to revive the public credit, Krooss, *op. cit.*, pp. 396–400.

[19] Albert Gallatin immigrated from Switzerland and settled in western Pennsylvania. He was clerk of a meeting of the "Whiskey rebels" in 1792, served in the U.S. Congress during 1790–92 and 1795–1801, was secretary of the treasury from 1801 to 1814, negotiated the Treaty of Ghent in 1814, was minister to France and Great Britain during 1815–23 and 1826–27, and was president of the National Bank of New York City (later Gallatin's Bank, 1831–39).

[20] Albert Gallatin, *Considerations on the Currency and Banking System of the United States, Writings*, iii, pp. 286, 291, 296. See also *U.S. Department of Commerce, Historical Statistics of the United States*, p. 1018, and Comptroller of the Currency, *Annual Reports, 1876*, p. xl, and *1920*, ii, p. 846.

[21] Gallatin, *op. cit.*, pp. 283–84, Nettels, *op. cit.*, pp. 332–34.

President Madison called it "essential . . . that the benefits of an uniform national currency should be restored to the community. The absence of the precious metals will, it is believed, be a temporary evil; but until they can again be rendered the general medium of exchange, it devolves on the wisdom of Congress to provide a substitute."[22] If the state banks could not do the job, a national bank deserved consideration. An alternative, more a threat than a proposal, was government currency.

Congress also wanted a national bank, but the two branches had not agreed on its powers. Toward the end of 1814, Secretary Dallas proposed a national bank (in the previously quoted message) that "shall loan $30,000,000 at an interest of six percent at such periods and in such sums as shall be convenient." This was rejected by Congress as not sufficiently limiting, and its own version was vetoed by the president. "The objection of Congress to the original plan," Bray Hammond wrote, "had been that the Bank had too much of the Government in it. President Madison's objection was that in the Bank proposed by Congress the Government was left out."[23]

In his veto message of January 15, 1815, Madison complained that the capital of Congress's Bank – a substantial proportion of which, as in all the new proposals as well as for the first Bank, could be subscribed in the form of government bonds – was insufficient "to produce, in favor of the public credit, any considerable or lasting elevation of the market price. . . ."[24] Furthermore,

the bank proposed will be free from all legal obligation to co-operate with the public measures; and whatever might be the patriotic disposition of its directors to contribute to the removal of those embarrassments, and to invigorate the prosecution of the war, fidelity to the pecuniary and general interest of the institution, according to their estimate of it, might oblige them to decline a connexion of their operations with those of the national treasury. [News of the December peace treaty did not reach Washington until February 1815.] Temporary sacrifices of interest, though over balanced by the future and permanent profits of the charter, not being requirable of right in behalf of the public, might not be gratuitously made; and the bank would reap the full benefit of the grant whilst the public would lose the equivalent expected from it. For it must be kept in view that the sole inducement to such a grant on the part of the public would be the prospect of substantial aids to its pecuniary means at the present crisis.

---

[22] *Annual Message* to Congress, December 5, 1815, Clarke and Hall, *op. cit.*, p. 609.
[23] Bray Hammond, *Banks and Politics in America from the Revolution to the Civil War*, p. 232.
[24] Krooss, *op. cit.*, pp. 401–3.

Daniel Webster said of the administration's proposal that it

looks less like a bank than a department of Government. It will be properly the paper-money department. Its capital is Government debts; the amount of its issues will depend on Government necessities. . . . The Government is to grow rich because it is to borrow without the obligation of repaying and is to borrow of a bank which issues paper without liability to redeem it. . . . Other institutions, setting out perhaps on honest principles, have fallen into discredit through mismanagement or misfortune. But this bank is to begin with insolvency. It is to issue bills to the amount of thirty millions, when everybody knows it can not pay them. It is to commence its existence in dishonor. It is to draw its first breath in disgrace.[25]

American debates about the monetary standard and the roles of government and public and private banks paralleled those across the Atlantic and had generally the same results: a private national bank acting for financial stability with a longer term goal of a uniform currency. Although some legislators shared Madison's view of a national bank as primarily a source of government finance, William Findley of Pennsylvania probably spoke for the majority when he said that "the erection of a Bank was not so desirable on account of the Government as for the general convenience of the country," by which he meant the resumption of convertibility.[26] By the end of 1815, with the war over and government finances improving, the president agreed. Although hardly necessary to the purpose (except as a political buffer, as we will see), the second Bank of the United States was adopted primarily as a means of forcing resumption on the state banks. Their profits were reputed to be large and their specie reserves adequate, but they were not inclined to resume payment and state legislatures were not inclined to compel them.

The Second Bank
In shepherding the Bank bill through the House of Representatives, John Calhoun turned the earlier constitutional objection around. He said that the Constitution required Congress to establish an agency for the regulation of the currency. "No one . . . could doubt that" the power (and responsibility) "to coin money [and] regulate the value thereof" meant "that the money of the United States was intended to be placed entirely under the control of Congress." Although not foreseen by the founders, money now consisted principally of paper currency that had been allowed to develop in a way that defied the Constitution. "By a sort of under-current" in the

---

[25] January 2, 1815; Clarke and Hall, *op. cit.*, pp. 563–67.
[26] April 2, 1814; Clarke and Hall, *op. cit.*, p. 475.

form of a "revolution in the currency . . . , the power of Congress to regulate the money of the country had caved in, and upon its ruins had sprung up those institutions which now exercised the right of making money for and in the United States." The States were prohibited from issuing money, but "In point of fact," added Speaker Henry Clay, "the regulation of the general currency is in the hands of the state Governments, or, which is the same thing, of the banks created by them." It was "incumbent upon Congress to recover . . . control," Clay said, and although direct regulation of the state banks was impracticable, a sound currency might be regained by the restraining influence of a national bank.[27] The vote for the Bank was 80–71 in the House and 22–12 in the Senate. The geographical distribution of votes was the reverse of 1791, with most of the opposition coming from the Northeast, where state banking was strongest.

Webster argued that a national bank was unnecessary and that the situation only needed compulsory redemption. He obtained a resolution that the government would accept payment only in coin or redeemable bank notes, and it would keep no deposits in "any bank which shall not pay its notes, when demanded, in the lawful money of the United States."[28] The resolution was adopted in April 1816, the month the Bank's charter was approved, effective the next February.

The Bank's charter was a compromise between the government's desire for a line of credit and those wanting a bank large enough to regulate the currency but not so large that it threatened individual liberties or the state banks. Its capital was $35,000,000 (compared with $10,000,000 for the first Bank and the $50,000,000 desired by Madison), loans to the government were limited to $500,000, and the Bank could not "at any time suspend or refuse payment in gold or silver of any of its . . . obligations." If it did "at any time refuse or neglect to pay on demand any bill, note or obligation . . . according to the contract . . . , the holder of any such bill, note or obligation . . . shall . . . be entitled to receive and recover interest . . . until the same shall be fully paid and satisfied, at the rate of twelve per centum per annum. . . ."

---

[27] March 9, 1816, *ibid.*, p. 672. The speeches of Calhoun and Clay and votes on the Bank charter are on pp. 630–34, 669–72, 681–82, and 706. For the parts played by four financiers (John Jacob Astor, David Parish, Stephen Girard, and Jacob Barker) and two public men (Dallas and Calhoun) in the agitation for and organization of the second Bank, see Raymond Walters, "The Origin of the Second Bank of the United States."

[28] *Annals of Congress*, 14th Congr., 1st sess., April 30, 1816, pp. 1440, 1919. R. C. H. Catterall, *Second Bank of the United States*, p. 23.

The Bank was a center of controversy throughout its history. The resumption of 1817 was "neither universal nor genuine,"[29] and the Bank participated in a credit boom as fully as the state banks that it was supposed to restrain. It expanded rapidly, establishing 18 branches by the end of 1817, which the head office failed to control. The notes of any branch were redeemable at all, and some of them, especially Baltimore, vied to see who would be largest. The Bank was also for a while, under prodding from Secretary of the Treasury William Crawford, tolerant of the state banks' tardiness in redeeming the notes presented to them. However, prices had increased and gold had left the country during the boom, and the Treasury's resumption had begun to bite. Unlike Britain, where resumption was in the hands of the Bank of England, in the United States it was governed by the Treasury, but with no less pain. The government's postwar surplus was paid with redeemable bank notes and Treasury notes issued during the war. These were high-powered money, material of the recent credit expansion, and were disappearing.[30]

Bank reserve losses were aggravated by the leisurely pace with which the Treasury deposited its specie receipts. There was a scramble for liquidity, and failures almost included the United States Bank, whose "grim efforts" to collect its debts aroused a popular hatred that "was never extinguished."[31] Parts of the Bank's balance sheet are depicted in Fig. 6.1. Its notes and private deposits fell more than one-half between mid-1818 and early 1820. By July 1821 it was a net debtor to the state banks. Although he might better have blamed the Treasury, Andrew Jackson's bank-hating adviser, William Gouge, wrote of this episode that "The Bank was saved and the people were ruined."[32]

Jackson's opponents made the Bank a campaign issue in 1832 by passing a bill for the renewal of its charter four years before its expiration. Old Hickory obliged them with a veto, and after reelection he withdrew the government's deposits from the Bank, which was compelled to look after its own position to the neglect of the banking system.[33]

An appraisal of the Bank's conduct under normal conditions must be limited to the period from 1823, when it had recovered from the

---

[29] W. B. Smith, *Economic Aspects of the Second Bank of the U.S.*, p. 104.

[30] William Crawford served as senator from Georgia (1807–13), minister to France (1813–15), secretary of war (1815–16), and secretary of the treasury (1816–25).

[31] Hammond, *op. cit.*, p. 259; also Murray Rothbard, *The Panic of 1819*, chap. 1.

[32] William Gouge, *A Short History of Paper Money and Banking in the United States*, part ii, p. 110.

[33] The bill to renew the charter passed the House 107–85 and the Senate 28–20.

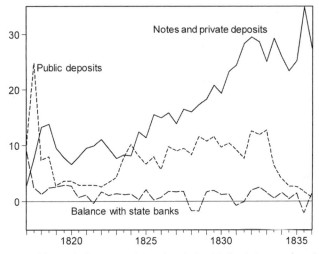

Figure 6.1. Position of the second Bank of the United States (semiannually, January 1817 to January 1836, in millions of dollars). *Source:* Catterall, *The Second Bank of the United States*, pp. 502–503.

vicissitudes of resumption, to 1832. Hammond preferred 1823–30, before it became embroiled in politics, as the period of the Bank as a central bank in the sense of a regulator of aggregate bank credit.[34] The former year saw Nicholas Biddle's assumption of the Bank's direction. Biddle was more committed to (at least more outspoken about) a stabilizing role for the Bank than his predecessors, and he was in a stronger position to act on it.[35] "I think," he had written in 1819, "that experience has demonstrated the vital importance of such an institution to the fiscal concerns of this country and that the Government, which is so jealous of the exclusive privilege of stamping its eagles on a few dollars, should be much more tenacious of its rights over the more universal currency, and never again abandon its finances to the mercy of four or five hundred banks, independent, irresponsible, and precarious."[36]

[34] Hammond, *op. cit.*, p. 300.

[35] Nicholas Biddle was a director of the Bank of the United States from 1819 to 1823 and its president, from 1823 to 1839, including its three years with a Pennsylvania charter. It failed in depression shortly after his retirement.

[36] This was written in response to an inquiry from the House committee investigating the Bank, just before he was appointed director by President Monroe; Hammond, *op. cit.*, p. 301.

His larger view seemed to be borne out by the Bank's maintenance of its credit in the face of the gold drain of 1831. "Not only did it expand loans, notes, and deposits while reserves fell," Richard Timberlake wrote, "but it practiced forbearance in presenting notes of other banks for redemption.... The bank clearly acted like a central bank in 1831."[37] Biddle told a congressional committee that his bank had never "oppressed" the state banks. However, he continued with what Hammond called "perhaps the most profound descent into indiscretion he ever made." "There are very few banks," Biddle told the congressmen, "which might not have been destroyed by an exertion of the power of the Bank. None have ever been injured. Many have been saved. And more have been, and are, constantly relieved when it is found that they are solvent but are suffering under temporary difficulty."[38]

"This is enough! Proof enough!" exclaimed Senator Thomas "Old Bullion" Benton of Missouri, "for all who are unwilling to see a moneyed oligarchy established in this land and the entire Union subjected to its sovereign will. The power to destroy all other banks is admitted and declared; the inclination to do so is known to all rational beings to reside with the power! Policy may restrain the destroying faculties for the present; but they exist; and will come forth when interest prompts and policy permits."[39]

The Bank's supporters defended its contributions to stability and sound money, and historians have suggested that it was the first conscious central bank.[40] The record is less favorable to the central banking hypothesis if we look for a consistent *policy*.[41] As a counterexample to the 1831 episode, in 1825 the Bank (like the Bank of England) sought self-protection by contracting credit while the country was losing specie.[42] Nor is the

---

[37] Richard Timberlake, *Monetary Policy in the United States*, pp. 38–39.

[38] U.S. Congress, 22nd Congr., 1st sess. *Reports of Committees, House Report* no. 460, April 30, 1832.

[39] Benton made these statements in support of a resolution "That the charter of the Bank of the United States ought not to be renewed," February 2, 1831. Benton justified his submission of the resolution five years before the charter expired to allow "the people" a "hand in the decision" before its supporters saw "a chance ... to gallop the renewal through Congress," citing a precedent in the 1824 House of Commons debate over the Bank of England's charter expiring in 1833. The resolution was defeated 23–20. Krooss, *op. cit.*, pp. 698–737.

[40] Catterall, *op. cit.*, pp. 453–77; Hammond, *op. cit.*, pp. 286–325.

[41] This view was shared by Jacob Meerman, "The Climax of the Bank War," and Peter Temin, *The Jacksonian Economy*.

[42] Timberlake, *op. cit.*, p. 38; Smith, *op. cit.*, p. 140; and chap. 4 above.

Benton–Jackson monopolistic-predator hypothesis supported by the data. The Bank tended to move with the state banks, expanding in good times (reducing its reserve ratio) and contracting in hard times, but more conservatively. It did not expand at the expense of the state banks by returning their notes with increasing frequency. The Bank's behavior is more consistent with a third hypothesis that falls between the supportive central bank and the predatory monopolist proclaimed by its supporters and detractors, namely, that it was a large corporation seeking survival as much as profit.[43]

In any case, whatever the Bank might or might not have done, its capacity for damage was too much for its enemies. It also lacked friends apart from those who saw it as a political weapon against Jackson. It was intended to provide special facilities to the government as its depository and collector and disburser of public moneys as well as to regulate the currency. However, with the public debt nearly paid off, there would soon be "no moneys to transfer," and the currency did not now need the Bank. It was also a source of war finance. Henry Clay opposed the renewal of the first Bank in 1811, but by 1816 he had learned "that war could not be carried on without the aid of banks."[44] However, "Times have changed," Benton declared in 1831. "The war made the bank; peace will unmake it."[45]

Money Centers and Clearinghouses, 1853–1913

Shortly after the panic or currency famine of 1893...there was issued fully $100,000,000 of clearing-house certificates used in settlement between banks, of certified checks, certificates of deposit, cashier's checks in round amounts (as $1, $5, $10, $20, and $50), due bills from manufacturers and other employers of labor, and clearing-house certificates, . . . , all designed to take the place of currency in the hands of the public. Clearing-house certificates, issued and used in settling debit balances between banks, were in no wise prohibited, but all of the other above-described evidences of debt which were issued to circulate among the public as money, were clearly subject to the ten per cent tax enacted for the purpose of getting rid of state bank circulation. This temporary currency, however, performed so valuable a service in such a crucial period, in moving the crops and keeping business machinery in motion, that the Government, after due deliberation, wisely

---

[43] Richard Highfield et al., "Public Ends, Private Means: Central Banking and the Profit Motive."

[44] Recalled by Clay in another debate on a proposed national bank, July 15, 1841, *Congressional Globe*, 27th Congr., 1st sess., p. 177.

[45] Krooss, *op. cit.*, p. 736.

forbore to prosecute. In other words, the want of elasticity in our currency system was thus partially supplied. It is worthy of note that no loss resulted from the use of this makeshift currency.

A. Barton Hepburn, *History of the Coinage* . . . . , p. 374[46]

The New York Money Market: Call Loans and the Nation's Reserve
The improvement in England's financial stability after 1866 was not matched by the United States, and much of the blame rests with the antibranching laws that produced a system of thousands of small undiversified local banks. The developing British system of large banks with branches throughout the country enabled transfers of funds from surplus to deficit areas, and rapid deliveries to those temporarily short of cash. Nevertheless, New York City almost shared London's importance as the nation's central money market. The importance of New York to the nation's trade and communications, preserved and, in fact, increased by the canals, railroads, and telegraph as the population moved west, meant that as soon as the developing regions had banks they had accounts in New York.

Just as the English country banks and later the joint-stock banks kept their reserves in London, banks in the American interior kept their reserves in New York, mainly on deposit with New York banks. In the 1830s, nearly $2 million from Ohio was kept in New York. Banks in Boston, Philadelphia, Baltimore, Charleston, and New Orleans passed funds from banks in their regions to New York. Much was sent to banks outside New York. Like London, New York served as an intermediary between surplus and deficit areas, between the savings of the low-interest East and the investment opportunities of the West. Large amounts were also lent on call to stock purchasers, much of it through the "money desk" of the New York Stock Exchange. The call loan market "gradually became the final reservoir for the banking reserves of the nation," Margaret Myers observed in her history of the *New York Money Market*, "and upon it, in emergency, fell the final responsibility for providing banks with funds."[47] When country banks withdrew their balances from central banks to finance crop movements in the autumn, the latter called in loans from the stock market. Autumn was frequently a period of financial stringency and

---

[46] A. B. Hepburn was a bank examiner, assemblyman, and superintendent of banking for New York (1880–92), comptroller of the currency (1892–93), and executive successively of the Third National Bank of New York, National City Bank of New York, and Chase National Bank (1893–1911).

[47] Margaret Myers, *The New York Money Market*, p. 135.

high interest rates, and if an additional strain occurred, the money market was hard-pressed to deal with it.

The New York Clearing House

London had a cooperative central mechanism for settling interbank claims in 1775. New York followed in 1853 and soon "had a stabilizing effect in forcing banks to make daily, rather than weekly, settlements, and in preventing the accumulation of large adverse balances, with the consequent dangerous lowering of reserves and scramble for funds in the call market."[48] The New York banks acquired the position of the Bank of England in the monetary system. As the ultimate bankers' banks, they were custodians of the nation's gold reserve, and they financed the money markets, being pulled into the role of lender of last resort without benefit of the privileges of that Bank. They had no monopoly of the government's financial business or of the note issue. The New York banks presented a picture of how London might have developed if the Bank of England had not been protected.

Clearinghouse Money

The Clearing House exercised a stabilizing influence in the natural course of affairs by limiting interbank debt, but it was soon asked to do more. "The panic of 1857 was so severe and so prolonged that the Clearing House was practically forced into action, and it began timidly to feel its way towards an emergency technique."[49] Reserves were leaving New York in August, as usual, when news of the stoppage of payment by the New York branch of the Ohio Life Insurance and Trust Company induced the country banks to increase their withdrawals.[50] The collapse of Ohio Life, in which western banks had deposited half-a-million dollars, followed the default of a substantial portion of its call loans after a fall in stock prices.

On September 2, the Mechanics' Bank was suspended from the Clearing House because of its failure to meet the daily settlements, and the worries of other banks about their own positions deepened. Myers noted,

---

[48] *Ibid.*, p. 95.

[49] *Ibid.*, p. 97.

[50] The freedom of trust and insurance companies from many of the restrictions on commercial banks, including interstate branching, was a source of complaint by the latter but was not seriously addressed by public policy until the failures of the former in 1907.

The instinct of each one was to curtail its loans in order to protect its reserves, yet nothing was more certain to intensify the panic. The banks, therefore, on September 20, agreed that all would increase their loans so that the Clearing House balances of all of them would be increased proportionately and would cancel each other without reducing their slender stock of specie.

Margaret Myers, *The New York Money Market*, p. 97

Despite such action the drain continued, and the banks held back from expanding or even maintaining their loans. The uncertainty in the policy of "I will if you will" is obvious even with daily settlements. Something more was needed. Clearing House certificates, used in settlements as evidences of claims on specie, had declined with specie. Finally,

the Clearing House committee decided to issue certificates also against notes of New York state banks [which were building up in New York]. This group of banks agreed to pay 6 per cent interest on the notes ..., and the city banks were willing to hold them on those terms.

Margaret Myers, *The New York Money Market*, p. 98

The Clearing House banks earned interest on the country notes, which they could not have redeemed, anyway, and transformed them into certificate claims on specie. These steps did not prevent the suspension of specie payments between October 13 and December 13, but they enabled the country and city banks to continue lending.

These loan certificates were used again in future crises. When the Treasury stopped issuing gold certificates in 1893 because of a decline in its gold reserve, "again the Clearing House filled the gap with an issue of its own gold certificates."[51] "In every instance, though, some new wrinkles were added."[52] In 1860, collateral was extended to New York State and U.S. Treasury bonds. In 1873, irredeemable certified checks were issued, based on neither deposits nor collateral. Any member of the Clearing House might put them into circulation, stamped or written "Payable through the Clearing House." Other "banks accepted them as settlement media by common consent through their clearinghouse association, but did not have to redeem them with legal tender."[53]

The acceptance of clearinghouse certificates depended on agreements to share their risk – so that Bank B, for example, was spared the loss of all of its claims on an insolvent Bank A. The system spread beyond

---

[51] Myers, *op. cit.*, p. 257.
[52] Timberlake, *op. cit.*, p. 200.
[53] O. M. W. Sprague, *History of Crises under the National Banking System*, p. 54; Timberlake, *op. cit.*, p. 201.

New York, and the risk-sharing agreement of the Boston clearinghouse became the model:

> The Associated Banks of the Clearinghouse severally agree with the others that the Bills received instead of specie at the Clearinghouse from the Debtor Banks...shall...be and remain at the joint risk of all the Associated Banks in proportion to the amount of their Capitals respectively.[54]

Clearinghouse loan certificates allowed banks to maintain their loans and deposits despite gold losses, thus violating legal reserve requirements. They were effectively additions to bank reserves. "The banking industry simply reinstituted itself as an *ad hoc* central bank."[55] The certificates were often in sufficiently small denominations that they could be used as currency. This did not go unnoticed by the authorities, such as Comptroller Hepburn, who as we saw in the previous quotation, only winked, and became a bank executive. His successor, James Eckels, also praised the clearinghouse issues, issuing an official denial that they were currency. If they had been used as currency, he reasoned, the offending banks would have been fined. Eckels became president of the Commerce Bank of Chicago on leaving the Comptroller's office.[56]

Make Them Honest?

O. M. W Sprague[57] suggested that by the means of their loan certificates, the clearinghouse banks "were converted, to all intents and purposes, into a central bank, which, although without power to issue notes, was in other respects more powerful than a European central bank because it included virtually all the banking power of the city."[58] It will be recalled that the effectiveness of Bank rate depended on the cooperation of the joint-stock banks and that the support of Barings in 1890 was a joint effort. The general acceptance of their emergency issues would seem to have made a logical next step in the endorsement of their central banking functions.

---

[54] See Redlich, *op. cit.*, p. 159, and Gary Gorton, "Private Clearinghouses and the Origins of Central Banking."

[55] Timberlake, "The Central Banking Role of Clearinghouse Associations."

[56] U.S. Controller of the Currency *Annual Report*, 1907, p. 64; Timberlake, *Monetary Policy*, p. 207.

[57] O. M. W. Sprague, Harvard 1908–41, advisor to the Bank of England 1930–33, wrote *History of Crises under the National Banking System* for the National Monetary Commission.

[58] Sprague, *History of Crises*, p. 90.

Businessman Theodore Gilman supplied an argument when he wrote that the system needed a "grade of banks higher than our ordinary commercial banks" that could support the latter. He suggested the formalization of existing practices by the federal incorporation of a clearinghouse in each state. The notes of these clearinghouses would be guaranteed first by security collateral, second by the individual banks issuing them, and third by the clearinghouse associations. This would be better than a separate reserve held outside the banking system because it might never be needed. "[I]t should not be provided by capital withdrawn from productive use. It will cost nothing and will be just as serviceable if it is provided by law as a power which may be used in case of need." Clearinghouse committees would be "conservative" in their issues because of their "pecuniary interest as stockholders in banks." Furthermore, the 6-percent interest charge to banks issuing clearinghouse currency "would act as a check upon their issue, and they would not be taken so much for profit as for protection and necessity."[59]

The New York Clearing House's record in alleviating panics was mixed. It responded quickly and effectively in 1884 and 1890, but fell short in 1873, 1893, and 1907 because, Wicker suggested, it was unable to develop an incentive-compatible approach that was equal to major needs.[60] Plans for its support or extension were bypassed in favor of a new institution, the Federal Reserve, patterned on the public banks of continental Europe.

The Independent Treasury, 1846–1914

Be it enacted . . . , Sec. 6. That the treasurer of the United States . . . and all public officers of whatsoever character . . . are hereby required to keep safely, without loaning, using, depositing in banks, or exchanging for other funds than as allowed by this act, all the public money collected by them . . . till the same is ordered by the proper department or officer of the Government to be transferred or paid out. . . .

Sec. 18. That on January 1, 1847, and thereafter, all duties, taxes, sales of public lands, debts, and sums of money accruing or becoming due to the United States . . . shall be paid in gold and silver coin only, or in treasury notes. . . .

Sec. 19. That on April 1, 1847, and thereafter, every officer or agent engaged in making disbursements on account of the United States . . . shall make all payments

---

[59] Theodore Gilman, *A Graded Banking System*, pp. 44–45, 71, 157; Timberlake, *Monetary Policy*, pp. 205–6.

[60] Elmus, Wicker, *Banking Panics of the Gilded Age*, pp. 114–38.

in gold and silver coin, or in treasury notes if the creditor agree to receive said notes...

The Independent Treasury Act, August 6, 1846[61]

Origins and Effects

The Act of June 1836 to Regulate the Deposits of Public Money provided that the deposits of the federal government be distributed among the states "in proportion to their respective representation in the Senate and House of Representatives of the United States."[62] Because most federal revenues were customs duties deposited in banks in the port cities, the Act required a transfer of "specie from the place where it was most wanted, in order to sustain the general circulation of the country, to places where it was not wanted at all," Gallatin wrote, and "the monetary affairs of the country were convulsed."[63] Others have argued that the Panic of 1837 and the subsequent depression owed more to the previous credit expansion and international gold flows than to the government's choice of depositories.[64] But the potential for harm in the hands of the secretary of the treasury and accusations that "pet bank" depositories were the benefactors of political favoritism led to movements in Congress to require the Treasury to keep its money in its own, "sub-treasury," vaults.

Webster attacked the "independent Treasury" in the Senate:

The use of money is in the exchange. It is designed to circulate, not to be hoarded. All the Government should have to do with it is to receive it today, that it may pay it away tomorrow. It should not receive it before it needs it, and it should part with it as soon as it owes it. To keep it – that is, to detain it, to hold it back from general use, to hoard it, is a conception belonging to barbarous times and barbarous Governments.[65]

He recalled that in 1833 the Treasury had "admonished and directed" its bank depositories "to extend their accommodation to individuals, since the public moneys in their vaults would enable them to give such additional accommodation. Now, Sir, under this bill, any officer who shall do

---

[61] Krooss, *op. cit.*, pp. 1163–73.

[62] Section 13; Krooss, *op. cit.*, p. 972.

[63] Gallatin, *Suggestions on the Banks and Currency*, in *Writings*, iii, pp. 391; Edward Bourne, *History of the Surplus Revenue of 1837*, pp. 36–37.

[64] See Hammond, *op. cit.*, p. 457; Peter Temin, *The Jacksonian Economy*, pp. 172–73; and Timberlake, *Monetary Policy*, chap. 5.

[65] *Congressional Globe*, 25th Congr., 2nd sess., March 12, 1838, appendix, p. 2.

any one of the same things, instead of being praised, is to be . . . adjudged guilty of embezzlement and of a high misdemeanor, and is to be confined, for aught I know, in cells as dark and dismal as the vaults and safes which are to contain our metallic currency." The bill was passed in 1840 but repealed the next year by the Whig Congress in preparation for a third national bank, which, however, was vetoed by President Tyler. The Independent Treasury was reestablished in 1846 and managed the government's cash until the Federal Reserve became its fiscal agent.

The new system exposed the monetary base to shocks from federal budgets. Seasonal movements in net Treasury receipts often took reserves from circulation in active times such as the autumnal crop movements. The fiscal surpluses common to peace had longer term deflationary effects. During the two decades of falling prices preceding 1896, Treasury balances rose from $51 million to $258 million, which were significant compared with the average monetary base of $1 billion.

However, the Treasury sometimes supplied funds in times of stress by early payments of interest and debt redemptions, that is, open market purchases. Secretary James Guthrie reported in the summer of 1853 that[66]

the amount still continuing to accumulate in the Treasury, apprehensions were entertained that a contraction of discounts by the city banks of New York would result, . . . and . . . might have an injurious influence on financial and commercial operations. With a view, therefore, to give public assurance that money would not be permitted to accumulate in the Treasury, a public offer was made on the 30th of July to redeem . . . the sum of $5 million of the loans of 1847 and 1848 . . .

Secretary Howell Cobb carried Guthrie's activism into the Panic of 1857 until the Treasury's balance, further depleted by the sudden turn in the budget to a deficit, neared the $6,000,000 regarded as a minimum. Cobb defended his halt to debt purchases in the 1857 *Treasury Report*:

There are many persons who seem to think that it is the duty of the Government to provide relief in all cases of trouble and distress . . . and their necessities, not their judgments, force them to the conclusion that the Government not only can, but ought to relieve them.[67]

War, Suspension, and Resumption
The lack of a fiscal plan that matched the needs of the war led to runs on gold and suspension by banks and the Treasury at the end of 1861. The

---

[66] *Congressional Globe*, 33rd Congr., 1st sess., appendix, p. 250.
[67] Pp. 11–12.

fears of those demanding gold were justified. Four-fifths of government war spending was financed by debt, one-fifth of which was nonconvertible currency – "greenbacks" – and the dollar price of gold doubled between 1861 and 1864. The prices of goods in general rose 75 percent. Resumption of dollar convertibility at its prewar value would require substantial deflation.

Three approaches to resumption were considered. Some groups, including the Greenback Party, opposed deflation. Their position overlapped with the silver interests that later took the lead in the fight against the gold standard. Congress at first took the opposite view, and in December 1865, a House resolution stating "the necessity for a contraction of the currency with a view to as early a resumption of specie payment as the business interests of the country would permit" passed by a vote of 144–6.[68] This suited Secretary of the Treasury Hugh McCulloch, whose "chief aim," he told his staff on taking office, would "be to provide the means to discharge the claims upon the Treasury at the earliest date practicable, and to institute measures to bring the country gradually back to the specie basis, a departure from which . . . is no less damaging and demoralizing to the people than expensive to the Government."[69] However, the House "resolution soon proved not to reflect the real sentiment of the people," historian Davis Dewey observed.[70] The secretary set about his task too energetically to suit most people.[71] He was denounced as an impractical and dangerous theorist who expected to achieve specie payments by a "few legislative *whereases* and *be it enacteds*," whereas industry was paralyzed by his "species of experiment," to take a sampling of letters to Congress.[72] In April 1866, Congress restricted purchases to $10,000,000 a month for the next six months and $4,000,000 a month thereafter. McCulloch protested: "How rapidly [the currency] may be retired must depend upon the effect which contraction may have upon business and industry, and can be better determined as the work progresses." He thought Congress's

---

[68] *Ibid.*, 39th Congr., 1st sess., p. 75; Irwin Unger, *The Greenback Era*, p. 41.

[69] *Banker's Magazine*, April 1865, p. 783; as quoted in Unger, *op. cit.*, p. 41.

[70] Davis Dewey, *Financial History of the United States*, p. 335.

[71] Hugh McCulloch, from the State Bank of Indiana during 1835–63, went to Washington to protest the National Bank bill and accepted Secretary Chase's offer to be the first comptroller (1863–65). He was secretary of the Treasury during 1865–69 and 1884–85, in 1869 he became partner in the London house of Jay Cooke, McCulloch & Co., reorganized after the Panic of 1873 as McCulloch & Co.

[72] Quoted from letters to Pennsylvania Congressman Thaddeus Stevens and Maine Senator William Fessenden, January 1866; see Unger, "Businessmen and Specie Resumption."

limit could be doubled "without injuriously affecting legitimate business.... There is a great adaptability in the business of the United States, and it will easily accommodate itself to any policy which the Government may adopt."[73]

McCulloch proceeded as rapidly as he was allowed; he had cut the greenbacks almost in half when Congress stopped him in February 1868 by freezing them at the amount then in circulation – $347 million. Republican leader James G. Blaine of Maine summarized the pressures on Congress:

> Mr. McCulloch, in trying to enforce the policy of contraction, represented an apparently consistent theory in finance; but the great host of debtors who did not wish their obligations to be made more onerous and the great host of creditors who did not desire that their debtors should be embarrassed and possibly rendered unable to liquidate united on the practical side of the question and aroused public opinion against the course of the Treasury Department. In the end, outside of banking and financial centers, there was a strong and persistent demand for repeal of the Contraction Act. [A]lthough it might be admitted that the entire nation would be benefited by the ultimate result, the people knew that the process would bring embarrassment to vast numbers and would reduce not a few to bankruptcy and ruin.
> James G. Blaine, *Twenty Years of Congress*, ii, p. 328

The middle way advocated by John Sherman of Ohio, chairman of the Senate Finance Committee, was that resumption should occur naturally by letting the country grow into the currency. This became, with fits and starts, the official policy. To sound-money historians, "Unofficially, procrastination became the norm; and after a few years many congressmen were paying only lip service to the resumption ideal."[74]

The resumption period can be separated into two parts according to the direction of changes in the stock of money: 1865–68 and 1875–78, on the one hand, which saw declines in money, the latter very slight (Fig. 6.2), and price falls of 4.5 percent and 3.8 percent per annum; and the "procrastination" years 1868–75, when money grew at a rate of 4.3 percent and deflation slowed to 2.4 percent per annum. Output was strong, falling only one year, by less than 1 percent in 1874.

President Grant's first secretary of the treasury, George Boutwell (1869–73), was unwilling to let the market fend for itself. He helped it with early security redemptions, especially in the autumn, and in October 1872 he stretched the law to reissue $5,000,000 of the retired greenbacks. Sherman protested, but his committee sympathized with Boutwell's

---

[73] Secretary of the Treasury *Annual Report*, 1865; Krooss, *op. cit.*, pp. 1467–68.
[74] Timberlake, *Monetary Policy*, p. 91.

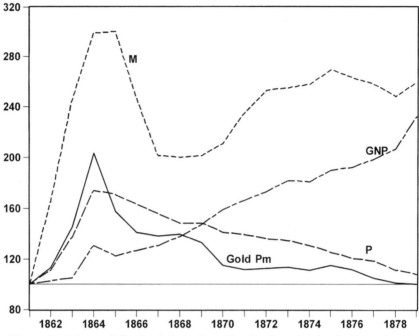

Figure 6.2. Money (M), the dollar value of gold, the price level (P), and real GNP (1681 = 100), 1861–79. *Sources:* Gold value (Wesley Mitchell, *Greenbacks*, table 1), money (Friedman and Schwartz, *Monetary History*, table A1), P and GNP (Gordon and Balke, appendix B).

response that relief from panics had never been attained even in England "without the personal intervention of men possessing power." Furthermore, deflation ought to be avoided because "we have no right morally to alter debtor-creditor relations." His use of the greenback reserve was

in its effect . . . substantially what is done by the Government of Great Britain through the Bank of England. The Secretary furnished temporary relief . . . by adding to the circulation of the country, diminishing its value . . . and changing the relations of debtor creditor. . . . Clothed with authority by law, . . . the Secretary of the Treasury could not sit silent and inactive while ruin was blasting the prospects of many and creating the most serious apprehensions in all parts of the country. It was a great responsibility; but it is a responsibility which must be taken by men who are clothed with the authority . . .[75]

[75] These words were spoken in the Senate, to which he had been elected in 1872. *Congressional Record*, 43rd Congr., 1st sess., appendix, p. 19, January 22, 1874.

Congress was unwilling to interfere, and Sherman chided his colleagues for their gestures to resumption whereas allowing money to increase and the premium on gold to continue.[76] The premium had fallen from 100 percent at the end of the war to 11 percent in October 1870, and it remained near that point for six years. Sherman did not push for a more rigorous policy, however, until after the 1874 elections in which the Democrats won control of the House and gained several seats in the Senate. The Republican majority of the lame-duck Congress decided that their loss had been caused by the conflicts between its hard- and soft-money wings, and in the interest of party unity, looking toward the 1876 elections, they adopted a compromise resumption plan: The limit on national bank notes (described in the next section) was removed; the Treasury was directed to redeem greenbacks at the rate of 80 percent of increases in national bank notes, with the proviso that greenbacks, which had risen to $382,000,000, would not be reduced below $300,000,000; and "on and after January 1, 1879, the Secretary of the Treasury shall redeem, in coin, the United States legal-tender notes then outstanding, on their presentation for redemption, at the office of the assistant treasurer of the United States in the city of New York, in sums of not less than fifty dollars."[77]

The Resumption Act of January 1875 was received with a mixture of skepticism and indifference. Financial writers were unclear whether it was inflationary or deflationary and thought its purposes purely political. A date had been set for resumption, but they saw nothing in the act to bring it about.[78] Resumptionist Senator Carl Schurz asked whether some of the notes redeemed by the Treasury would be reissued, as in the past. Sherman answered that he would leave the interpretation of "redeem" to future Congresses, when greenbacks were down to the target of $300,000,000. "The case that is put . . . may never arise. . . . But if there is any doubt upon that question, I leave every Senator to construe the law for himself; and if there is a doubt about it, I say it is not wise as practical men dealing with practical affairs, seeking to accomplish a result, to introduce into this bill a controversy which will prevent that unity that is necessary to carry out the good that is contained in this bill."[79] The hard-money Democratic Senator Allen Thurman complained that "it is very difficult to find what is in [the bill]. We know that there is a great deal of omission but the least

---

[76] *Congressional Record*, 43rd Congr., 1st sess., p. 700, January 16, 1874.
[77] *Resumption Act*, January 14, 1875, Krooss, *op. cit.*, pp. 1683–84.
[78] See Unger, *Greenback Era*, pp. 260–62, and Timberlake, *Monetary Policy*, pp. 110–12.
[79] *Congressional Record*, 43rd Congr., 2nd sess., December 22, 1874, p. 196.

possible amount of commission that ever I have seen in a great public measure."[80]

Antiresumptionists were unable to get the two-thirds majority to override the inevitable presidential veto, and the measure remained on the books until, to nearly everyone's surprise, it was implemented as written. The plan was more restrictive than expected, especially in the hands of Sherman, who became Rutherford Hayes's secretary of the treasury (1877–81) to apply the law that he had written. Although the $80 reduction in greenbacks for every $100 increase in national bank notes sounded mildly inflationary, it forced a significant contraction because the greenbacks were high-powered money – fractional reserves upon which an inverted pyramid of deposits rested. Furthermore, Sherman did not reissue greenbacks; when he redeemed them they stayed redeemed.

A Comparison of Resumptions

Of the resumptions that ended the four wartime suspensions of the gold standard in Britain (1813–21 and 1918–25) and the United States (1816–23 and 1865–78), the last mentioned was least painful. The obvious explanation – that it was the longest – has a good deal of merit.[81] Nature was generally allowed to take its course. Congress and the Treasury by and large waited for the economy to grow into the money stock. History (including Wesley Mitchell's *Business Cycles* and Willard Thorp's *Annals*) has labeled 1873–79 a depression, but that accorded with the traditional association of deflation and depression.[82] As noted, annual aggregate output fell only in 1874, and average growth exceeded 4 percent.

But the question remains: Why did resumption take so long? The answer seems to be that a large cross section of the electorate – acting through Congress – was involved in the decision, and that although feelings ran high, important groups were disposed to moderation. They wanted resumption *sometime*, like the British businessmen and economists of the 1920s, but not at the price of present pain. Sherman and the country were fortunate in the favorable trade balance and gold inflow

---

[80] Timberlake, *Monetary Policy*, p. 197.

[81] One can argue about these dates, especially in the United States, where regional differences were considerable and convertibility was often difficult in practice, but this does not affect the relative lengths of the resumptions.

[82] For this point in relation to Britain, see S. B. Saul, *The Myth of the Great Depression, 1873–1896*.

that coincided with the targeted resumption date.[83] His record suggests, however, that he would not (and could not) have forced resumption against an unfavorable tide. His political survival did not permit it. Ohio was a swing state, the geographical center of the nation's population most of the last half of the 19th century, and its politicians did not have the luxury of an eastern hard-money or western easy-money position. Furthermore – and this may be the most important reason – there was no third party, no central bank, whom the politicians could assign to administer the medicine.

This was the era of what the young Woodrow Wilson called *Congressional Government*.[84] "The checks and balances which once obtained," he wrote, "are no longer effective." The federal courts were under the appointive power of Congress, and the Supreme Court had declared its reluctance "to interfere with the *political discretion* of either Congress or the President." The president's cabinet had been made "humble servants" of Congress. In line with its British heritage, Congress in the course of exercising its power of the purse expected the secretary of the treasury to be its agent. While speaking for the Morrison resolution that prescribed the Treasury's cash management in detail, Senator James Beck of Kentucky reminded his colleagues that whereas the laws creating the other executive departments enjoined their secretaries to advise and act under the direction of the president, the secretary of the treasury was required "to make report and give information to either branch of the Legislature . . . and generally to perform all such services relative to the finances as he shall be directed to perform. . . . We with the Secretary of the Treasury manage the purse; the president and the other secretaries control the sword."[85] The Congress of the 1870s exercised its constitutional authority over the currency directly. In the previous American resumption a strong secretary was able to use the national bank. "The Bank supplied the machinery, the secretary supplied the brains," Hammond wrote, and the Bank got the blame.[86] We will see that a strong Bank of England imposed an early and idealistic resumption over the protests of those affected in the 1920s, but in the United States during 1865–79, the legislators were directly

---

[83] See *Historical Statistics . . .* , ser. U15 and U24, for the positive trade balance of 1876–81 and gold inflows of 1876–88, which resumed in 1896.

[84] Written in 1883–84 while a graduate student at Johns Hopkins University. The following quotations are from the "Introductory" chapter.

[85] *Congressional Record*, 49th Congr., 1st sess., p. 7675, July 29, 1886.

[86] Hammond, *op. cit.*, p. 249.

accountable for the currency. These are the reasons – the political costs of imposing pain – that are usually given for divorcing the politicians from money. Devotion to the monetary theory of the day carries costs of its own, however.

Discretionary Monetary Management: Treasury Bank Deposits and Open Market Operations

The Independent Treasury was intended to keep the government's money from banks. In the 1880s, as in the 1850s, however, the Treasury had a greater reserve than seemed necessary and its secretaries were sensitive to the money market. There was no legal reserve or special resumption fund, although "by tradition public sentiment adopted $100,000,000 as the line of demarcation between safety and danger."[87] Some used a loophole supplied by an 1861 amendment "to allow the Secretary of the Treasury to deposit any of the moneys obtained on any of the loans now authorized by law . . . in such solvent specie-paying banks as he may select."[88] The amendment was quickly made irrelevant by the war suspension, but Secretary Charles Fairchild (1887–89), who "always considered the needs of banks," used it to justify an expansion of Treasury bank deposits from $13 million to $54 million.[89] The increases, as well as Treasury debt purchases, were timed for the autumn and other periods of financial stringency. The *Commercial and Financial Chronicle* noted the following:

The time was when our banks provided beforehand for the fall trade and so trimmed their sails through the summer months to avert a storm by preparing themselves for the crop demand. Of late years they have looked to the Treasury wholly and have gone through the summer trenching on their reserves regardless of any increased drain sure to come later on.[90]

Sometimes they were disappointed. Secretary William Windom (1889–91), "a strict observer of the letter of the Law of 1846," according to Esther Taus, "believed that the policy of depositing public money in banks was wholly unjustifiable" and cut the Treasury's bank deposits to $21 million.[91]

---

[87] Dewey, *op. cit.*, p. 441.

[88] Krooss, *op. cit.*, p. 1174.

[89] Esther Taus, *Central Banking Functions of the U.S. Treasury*, pp. 80–82, 269. The amounts are for June 30 nearest the beginning and end of the secretaries' terms.

[90] December 6, 1890, Taus, *op. cit.*, p. 88.

[91] Taus, *op. cit.*, p. 82. Fairchild had already begun the reversal on learning that Congress was about to reaffirm the Appropriation Act of 1881, which called for surplus funds to be used for debt retirement.

Congressmen complained of the large sums in Treasury vaults that might be used to save interest expenses, and the Appropriation Act of 1881 gave the Treasury discretion to redeem government debt. But balances remained high, and they further rose during the Cleveland administration (1885–89), which desired a "prudent" reserve.[92] In 1886, those wanting easier money secured House and Senate agreement to the Morrison resolution calling on the Treasury to apply its "surplus or balance . . . over $100,000,000 . . . to the payment of the interest-bearing indebtedness of the United States" at a maximum rate of $10,000,000 a month.[93] A. J. Warner of Ohio quoted Lord Overstone (Samuel Jones Loyd): "In adopting a paper circulation we must unavoidably depend for a maintenance of its due value upon the adoption of a strict and judicious rule for the regulation of its amount." He asked why it was necessary to "hoard $228,000,000 in the Treasury of the United States? Is it to purchase the favor of Wall Street and the banks? If so it is altogether too dear a price."[94] Senator Beck argued that it was Congress' responsibility to direct the secretary to relieve him of temptation and political embarrassment. Nelson Dingley of Maine, however, objected to Congress' interference "with a question which exclusively pertains to administration. This is the first attempt, I think, in the history of this Government to determine by a legislative resolution what should be the working balance of the Treasury. . . . No cast-iron rule can be laid down on a matter of this kind." Conservatives got a contingency balance of $20,000,000 in the resolution and authority for the secretary to suspend debt purchases in emergencies. Benjamin Butterworth of Ohio believed that the secretary's discretion was "indispensable to the maintenance of the national credit," and called the Treasury reserve "the ballast which keeps our monetary ship steady as she moves through the sea of financial troubles which constantly threaten."[95]

The Silver Question

Instead of being a steadying influence, the Treasury used its discretion "erratically and unpredictably," according to Milton Friedman and Anna

---

[92] Cleveland's first secretary of the treasury, Daniel Manning (1885–87), wrote to Congressman Frank Hiscock that it would not be "prudent" to reduce the Treasury balance; Timberlake, *Monetary Policy*, p. 154.

[93] Introduced July 13, 1886, by William Morrison, Chairman of the House Ways and Means Committee.

[94] *Congressional Record*, 49th Congr., 1st sess., July 13, 1886, pp. 6884, 6887.

[95] *Op. cit.*, July 29, 1886, p. 7675; July 14, 1886, p. 6937; August 4, 1886, p. 7998.

Schwartz. It assisted the money market in the panics of 1873, 1884, and 1890, but itself needed assistance in 1893.[96] The Sherman Silver Purchase Act of 1890 required purchases of 4.5 million ounces of silver a month with Treasury notes issued for the purpose and redeemable in gold or silver coin.[97] The policy coincided with falls in exports and government receipts. Both contributed to gold exports – the first through the balance of trade and the second by depressing investor confidence in the country's ability or desire to remain on the gold standard.

The crisis led President Cleveland to call a special session of Congress in the summer of 1893. He told it that the Sherman Act "may be regarded as a truce, after a long struggle, between the advocates of free silver coinage and those intending to be more conservative."[98] The struggle had been tipped, he might have added, by the shift in power caused by the admission of six western states to the Union between 1886 and 1890. The price of silver had continued to fall despite the government's purchases. "This disappointing result has led to renewed and persistent effort in the direction of free silver coinage," but the "evil effects" of the government's promotion of silver had already gone too far. The insistence of the United States, alone among the great trading nations, to commit to a constantly depreciating standard "has resulted in such a lack of confidence at home in the stability of currency values that capital refuses its aid to new enterprises.... Foreign investors, equally alert, not only decline to purchase American securities, but make haste to sacrifice those which they already have." The market price of gold relative to silver had risen from 18 in the 1870s to 20 in the late 1880s, accelerating to 26 in 1893 and eventually to 40 in 1902.[99] The result of the requirement to redeem silver notes in gold at a fixed price must be an end to the Treasury's ability to pay these notes in gold,

and their discredit and depreciation as obligations payable only in silver.... I earnestly recommend the prompt repeal of the provisions of the act passed July 14, 1890, authorizing the purchase of silver bullion, and that other legislative action may put beyond all doubt or mistake the intention and the ability of the Government to fulfill its pecuniary obligations in money universally recognized by all civilized countries.

---

[96] *Monetary History of the United States, 1867–1960*, p. 128; also see Taus, *op. cit.*, p. 89.
[97] See Krooss, *op. cit.*, pp. 1917–18 and 1952–60, for these acts and the repeal of the latter.
[98] Krooss, *op. cit.*, pp. 1915.
[99] *Historical Statistics . . .*, ser. M270.

It is noteworthy that Cleveland's call for monetary restraint came during the most severe American depression between the 1830s and the 1930s. He believed, like Herbert Hoover four decades later, that a condition of recovery was confidence in the currency.

Sherman defended the reversal of his position:

Sir, "give the devil his due." The law of 1890 may have many faults, but I stand by it yet, and I will defend it, not as a permanent public policy, not a measure that I take any pride in, because I yielded to the necessity of granting relief, but I do say that the beneficial effects that flowed from the passage of the law were infinitely greater even in the percentage of money than the loss we have suffered in the fall in the price of silver. Without it, in 1891 and 1892 we would have met difficulties that would have staggered us much more than the passing breeze of the hour.... The immediate result of the measure was to increase our currency, and thus relieve our people from the panic then imminent, similar to that which we now suffer. The very men who now denounce from Wall Street this compromise were shouting "Hallelujah!" for their escape by it from free coinage.[100]

Congress repealed the Sherman Act, but the gold standard was not assured. The gold reserve still fluctuated, and when it approached $100,000,000, the Treasury went to the market for gold, borrowing from banks and selling securities. It "finally recognized the futility of selling bonds for gold, most of which was shortly drawn out of the Treasury by the presentation of legal-tender notes for redemption," Dewey wrote, and in February 1895, it turned to J. P. Morgan.[101] He undertook to place 30-year, 4-percent bonds for 3,500,000 ounces of gold, at least half to be procured abroad. However, "the reserve remained near the traditional danger line. In July 1896, it fell to $90,000,000 because of hoarding due to popular apprehension as to the success of the silver movement [led by the Democratic nominee William Jennings Bryan] in the November presidential election."[102]

Bryan's defeat and the rise in world gold production ended concerns about the gold convertibility of the dollar, and the country formally turned from bimetallism in the Gold Standard Act of 1900. The Treasury would issue and redeem notes for gold, and it would hold a reserve fund of $150,000,000 in gold coin and bullion. If the "fund shall at any time fall below $100,000,000, then it shall be [the secretary's] duty to restore the

---

[100] Marion Miller, *Great Debates in American History*, xiv, p. 398.

[101] Dewey, *op. cit.*, p. 441.

[102] *Ibid.*, p. 454.

same to the maximum sum of $150,000,000 by borrowing money on the credit of the United States," specifically by issuing bonds "to be payable, principal and interest, in gold coin of the present standard value. . . ."

A Central Bank?

The decade 1899 to 1909 – under Secretaries Lyman Gage, Leslie Shaw, and George Cortelyou – is regarded as the heyday of the Treasury's monetary policy, in which, according to Friedman and Schwartz, its "central-banking activities . . . were being converted from emergency measures to a fairly regular and predictable operating function."[103] The time was auspicious. Gold accumulated, the federal budget was close to balanced (usually in surplus), and the gold reserve varied from $276 million to $422 million, giving ample scope for open market operations and variations in bank deposits.

The secretaries were eager to engage the monetary system. The gold standard was a political issue to which the party in power was committed, and they knew that it functioned neither perfectly nor automatically. In his *Report* for 1899 Secretary Gage said that "Stability [of the] currency should be safely guarded, [but] *flexibility* – the power of needful expansion – must also be provided," and referred to the flow of funds from New York to the country banks the previous autumn that wreaked "havoc . . . in the regular ongoing of our commercial life." They were innovative. Faced with the constraint that customs receipts had to be kept in the Treasury, Secretary Shaw declared depository banks to be offices of the Treasury. When his actions were condemned as autocratic and primarily for the relief of "a ring of powerful Wall Street speculators," he answered, "It has been the fixed policy of the Treasury Department for more than half a century to anticipate monetary stringencies, and so far as possible prevent panics," which he likened to pestilences.[104]

The effectiveness of the Treasury as a central bank is difficult to judge. It may have moderated financial movements. Certainly it tried. Shifts of funds to banks in years of pressure, especially 1907, were large. However, although the first decade of the new century was more prosperous than the depressed 1890s, there is little evidence of improved financial stability. There were as many "major panics" and more "minor panics" in the later

---

[103] Milton Friedman and Anna Schwartz, *op. cit.*, p. 149; also Taus, *op. cit.*, pp. 100–33, and David Kinley, *The Independent Treasury of the United States*, p. 110.

[104] Address to the American Bankers' Association, 1905; Timberlake, *Monetary Policy*, p. 192.

decade as in the earlier, and notwithstanding the secretaries' pride in assisting crop movements, seasonal fluctuations in interest rates were not reduced.[105]

The secretaries felt the inadequacy of the tools at their disposal. Cortelyou thought that a monetary framework that would "adapt the movement of currency more nearly automatically to the requirements of business" would improve upon his discretion, and Gage anticipated the Federal Reserve System when he asked, "Can not the principle of federation be applied, under which the banks as individual units, preserving their independence of action in local relationships, may yet be united in a great central institution?" Shaw claimed in his 1906 *Report* that if the secretary of the treasury had the powers over bank reserves and reserve ratios that were later given to the Federal Reserve, "no panic as distinguished from industrial stagnation could threaten either the United States or Europe that he could not avert."[106]

The National Banking System

The National Bank Act of 1863 was first of all a war finance measure. It established the Comptroller of the Currency to charter and regulate "national" banks whose most signal features were investments in government currency as "reserves" and government bonds as security for note issues. Most of these (the "country") banks had to hold reserves of at least 15 percent of their deposits, with at least two-fifths of this percentage in "lawful money" (gold, silver, or greenbacks) and up to three-fifths in the national banks of 17 "reserve" cities.[107] Reserve city banks had a reserve requirement of 25 percent, of which, for those outside New York City, up to half could be kept with national banks in the metropolis. All the latter's reserves had to be "lawful money."

---

[105] E. W. Kemmerer, *Seasonal Variations in the Relative Demand for Money*, pp. 222–23, Jeffrey Miron, "Financial Panics, the Seasonality of the Nominal Interest Rate, and the Founding of the Fed," and Sprague, *op. cit.* For interest rates, the average annual difference between the high and low monthly average stock exchange call loan rate was 7.40 percent during 1900–1910 compared with 4.90 during 1890–99 (Federal Reserve Board, *Banking and Monetary Statistics, 1914–41*, p. 448). Wicker (*op. cit*, p. xii.) thought that Kemmerer and Sprague exaggerated the number of panics.

[106] *Treasury Report 1901*, p. 77 (Gage); 60th Congr., 1st sess., Senate Doc. 208, *Response of the Secretary of the Treasury . . . In Regard to Treasury Operations*, p. 32 (Cortelyou); *Treasury Report 1906*, p. 49 (Shaw); Timberlake, *Monetary Policy*, pp. 186, 195–96.

[107] Originally called "redemption" cities.

The Act sought a "uniform currency" of national bank notes secured by U.S. bonds deposited with the treasurer of the United States. The notes had a standard design with the name of the issuing bank.[108] National bank notes peaked at 32 percent of the currency in 1915, the remainder being gold and silver certificates and greenbacks. They were succeeded by Federal Reserve notes as the principal currency during World War I, and these were phased out after Congress ceased to issue bonds eligible as security for them and provided for their retirement by Federal Reserve purchases.[109]

The National Banking System got underway too late for the war effort, but it was also a reform measure. Secretary Chase said that "the time has arrived when Congress should exercise" its authority to regulate money:

The value of the existing bank note circulation depends on the laws of thirty-four states and the character of some sixteen hundred private corporations. It is usually furnished in the greatest proportions by institutions of least actual capital.

Secretary of the Treasury, *Annual Report*, 1861

Chase proposed a system that would provide safe banks, adequate circulation, and convenience for the government. It acceptance was disappointing, however, as banks preferred their state charters. Congress responded in 1865 with a 10-percent tax on state bank notes.[110] In the 12 months following June 1865, the ratio of national to state banks turned from 467/1,089 to 1,294/349. With the growth of deposit banking (stimulated by the tax), most small banks reverted to state charters and their less costly regulations, specifically, lower reserve and capital requirements. City banks, on the other hand, were attracted by their role as depositories. By 1914, 70 percent of commercial banks had state charters, although national banks had half the deposits.[111]

---

[108] Ross Robertson, *The Comptroller and Bank Supervision*, p. 51. The Acts of 1863 and 1864 are reproduced in Krooss, *op. cit.*, ii. The second Act contained several small revisions but did not differ greatly from the first.

[109] *Historical Statistics* ..., ser. X425–37. The rest were mainly U.S. silver certificates. For a history of national bank notes see Glenn Munn and F. L. Garcia, *Encyclopedia of Banking and Finance*, p. 636.

[110] Robertson, *op. cit.*, pp. 53–54.

[111] There were 17,992 state banks of a total of 25,510, with deposits of $8,830 million of a total of $17,390 million. Federal Reserve Board, *Banking and Monetary Statistics, 1914–41*, pp. 16–17.

An Inelastic Currency

The national banking system came to be seen as a too-rigid form of monetary control that contributed to financial panics. Its critics wanted an "elastic" money supply unrestrained by the high and rigid cash reserve requirements of national banks or the U.S. bond collateralization of the currency.[112] When Carter Glass introduced the Federal Reserve bill in September 1913, he referred to the "intense dissatisfaction with the prevailing national banking and currency system."

Financial textbook writers of Europe have characterized our American system as "barbarous," and eminent bankers of this country who, from time to time, have appeared before the Banking and Currency Committee of the House have not hesitated to confess that this bitter criticism is merited. . . . Five times within the last 30 years financial catastrophe has overtaken the country under this system; . . . The System literally has no reserve force. The currency based upon the Nation's debt is absolutely unresponsive to the Nation's business needs. The lack of cooperation and coordination among the more than 7,300 national banks produces a curtailment of facilities at all periods of exceptional demand for credit.[113]

Glass proposed that the country's reserve be concentrated in a new institution, away from the "stock gambling operations" of New York, that would supply it when needed. It is ironic that the foremost service of Glass's creation (after war finance) in its first 20 years was support of the New York banks when their stock-exchange loans collapsed.

---

[112] The availability of eligible U.S. bonds did not limit national bank notes, which were never more than 30 percent of the amount permitted. John James attributes this to the greater profitability of bank loans, which were usually extended in the process of deposit creation, than of collateral bonds ("The Conundrum of the Low Issue of National Bank Notes").

[113] *Congressional Record*, 63rd Congr., 1st sess., pp. 4642–51; Krooss, *op. cit.*, pp. 2343–46.

SEVEN

Before the Crash: The Origins and Early Years of the Federal Reserve

When I began a study of the history of Federal Reserve monetary policy several years ago, I assumed that its interpretation could be shaped primarily by familiar criteria such as the behavior of the money supply, interest rates, and price levels, and that the well-known descriptions of monetary behavior represented by such labels as real-bills, gold standard, and managed money were adequate. But I finally realized that the traditional framework could not possibly do justice to the myriad strands of thought – professional and amateur, political and personal – entering into the complex process of monetary decision making. How could it? For a considerable period of Federal Reserve history the responsibility for decision making had been in the hands of men with little understanding of central banking theory and with little or no experience of central bank administration except that gained on the spot.

Elmus Wicker, *Federal Reserve Monetary Policy, 1917–1933*, p. vii [1]

The new central bank was unlike any previous American institution. It was not adapted from the Independent Treasury or private clearinghouses, although it took over some of their functions. Nor was it a bank. Unlike the Bank of England or the first and second Banks of the United States, it did not lend to or maintain accounts for private citizens. Existing banks did not want competition from a large national bank that enjoyed a special relationship with the government. The banking interests that had supported Andrew Jackson's veto of the second Bank were still formidable, although they saw the benefits of a public institution that would lend to them and bear the costs of the nation's reserve.

---

[1] Seymour Harris also found the Federal Reserve to be generally ignorant and ineffective its first 20 years (*Twenty Years of Federal Reserve Policy*, p. vii).

Background: People and Events

1913: Federal Reserve Act.

1914–18: World War I; U.S. at war, April 1917 to November 1918.

1918–21: Treasury pressure for bond support; price level rises one-third in 1917–18 and another one-third in the 21 months after the war, and falls 20% between the third quarter of 1920 and the first quarter of 1921. (Gross national product and deflator from Robert Gordon and Nathan Balke, appendix.)

1922: Governors Committee on open market operations formed by the Reserve Banks.

1922: Board members increased from 5 to 6 (not counting the Secretary of the Treasury and the Controller of the Currency, who were *ex officio* members until 1936) to give "due regard" to financial and agricultural as well as commercial and industrial interests.

1922, 1926: Unsuccessful bills to require price stability as a Federal Reserve goal.

1923: Credit model in Board *Annual Report*.

1921–29: Dow-Jones Industrial stock price index rises from 64 to 381. Real gross national product grows 4.6% per annum; price level unchanged. Recessions in 1923–24 and 1926–27. Farm depression after agricultural price rise and fall during and after the war; failures reduce the number of banks from 30,000 to 25,000. Monetary gold stock rises from $3.4 billion to $4 billion, after rising from $1.5 billion in 1914.

	President of the United States	Secretary of the Treasury	Chairman of the Federal Reserve Board
1913	Woodrow Wilson	William McAdoo	Charles Hamlin
1916			W. P. G. Harding
1919		Carter Glass	
1920		David Houston	
1921	Warren Harding	Andrew Mellon	
1923	Calvin Coolidge		Daniel Crissinger
1927			Roy Young
1929	Herbert Hoover		

The Federal Reserve Act of 1913 was made possible by the intersection of the traditional Federalist–Whig–Republican broad interpretation of the national government's constitutional powers (which had seen limited successes in the Banks of the United States and the National Bank Act) and the capture of the Democratic Party by Woodrow Wilson's New Freedom. The populist fear of a monster central bank that had moved Jackson and Benton was relegated to the fringes, and the large banks and progressives got most of what they wanted. Wilson's price for the new bankers' organization was the location of its "capstone" – the Board – in the political capital, away from the financial markets. He also wanted it free of politics even though interests, experience, and knowledge are inextricably bound to the public's detriment (but not always, if we believe Thornton and Hamilton). Old Hickory had believed that the conflicts were irreconcilable. Contradicting both views, Wilson's creation was founded on the conviction that goodwill and the spirit of public service carried with them the correct goals and the knowledge of how to achieve them.

The first section in this chapter brings together the forces that erected the new institution: the money-center bankers who wanted cooperation in managing the country's reserve and stability in money and interest rates; the innovators who looked to Europe for a model; political reformers who carried the message to the heartland; crises that called for change; and the president who saw the program through.

Another plan that balanced political accountability with bankers' knowledge and incentives is discussed in the second section. Keynes's proposal for an Indian central bank might have been a model for the Federal Reserve (the Fed). The third section examines the handicaps that plagued the Fed at its outset, including the lack of expertise, information, and clear goals, as well as an overbearing Treasury. The fourth section is concerned with the internal conflict over the usefulness of interest rates to regulate credit. The reliance of the regional bankers on market forces exceeded the "capstone's" in Washington with a Treasury wanting cheap finance at its elbow.

The next two sections review an early and perhaps the most advanced internal articulation of a policy model based on the credit markets that took notice of the price level while resisting a legislated rule. The last two sections review the Fed's organizational and conceptual problems on the eve of the Crash.

Origins: Who Wants a Central Bank?

Problems

The major monetary problem at the end of the 19th century, after the settlement of the standard, was the inelasticity of the currency.[2] A principal

---

[2] For political, economic, and social forces leading to the Federal Reserve Act, see Gabriel Kolko, *The Triumph of Conservatism: A Reinterpretation of American History,*

culprit was thought to be the National Banking System's requirement that bank notes be backed by U.S. bonds. Banks were unable or unwilling to extend credit in times of stress because of the insufficient supply or attractiveness of these securities. Laurence Laughlin of the University of Chicago wrote, "An elastic banknote circulation, slowly rising, but expanding and contracting sharply with seasonal demand is imperative. Our present national bank circulation does not provide for this elasticity."[3]

The problem was exacerbated by the dispersion of gold reserves. "In a modern system constructed on credit," investment banker Paul Warburg argued,[4] "cash must be centralized as far as possible into one big reservoir from which everyone legitimately entitled to it may withdraw it at will and into which it must automatically return whenever it is not actually used."[5] This view differed from that of Walter Bagehot, who regarded the centralization of the reserve as a source of instability. The purpose of *Lombard Street* was to instruct the Bank of England, the accidental repository of the reserve, on how to soften the effects of that encumbrance. However, Warburg was not alone in ascribing European financial stability to their central banks, overlooking the more serious defect of American finance: that thousands of small banks had failed at rates similar to that of the English country banks at the beginning of the century. The latter had been absorbed into nationwide systems, but antibranching laws prevented a similar evolution in the United States.

Warburg, who had been an investment banker in his family firm in Germany before coming to the United States in 1902, proposed a remedy for American monetary instability that presumed money markets on European lines. Some reformers had wanted bank notes secured by assets arising in the ordinary course of commercial banking. These would provide sufficient security for noteholders if banks made sound loans and would allow a more elastic issue. However, Warburg was skeptical of the

1900–1916; James Livingston, *Origins of the Federal Reserve System: Money, Class, and Corporate Capitalism, 1890–1913*; and Robert West, *Banking Reform and the Federal Reserve*, 1863–1923.

[3] Laurence Laughlin, *Banking Reform*, p. 61.

[4] Paul Warburg started with Warburg & Co., Hamburg, in 1888, serving there until 1914. He worked at Kuhn and Loeb, New York (1902–14), served on the Federal Reserve Board (1914–18), was chairman, International Acceptance Bank (1921–32), was on the Federal Advisory Council (1921–26), and wrote a history of the Federal Reserve.

[5] From an article in *Financial and Commercial Chronicle* about Paul Warburg's speech, "The Financial Situation," November 19, 1910; reprinted in Warburg, *The Federal Reserve System: Its Origin and Growth*, i, pp. 43–48.

quality of American bank loans. Many were long term and illiquid and subject to interest-rate risk, and bank short-term paper consisted mainly of unsecured "single-name" promissory notes that were effectively long term because they were routinely rolled over.[6] Warburg wanted the two-name, self-liquidating real bills discountable at central banks that he had known in Europe. They would allow "fluidity of credit. . . . A sound financial system must mobilize its commercial paper and make it a quick asset instead of a lock-up." The central reservoir by which this would be accomplished, the United Reserve Bank, would be filled by the "power to request banks to keep with it cash balances proportionate to the amount of their deposits. . . ."

Although the framers of the Federal Reserve Act found it politically useful to fictionalize an opposition from the "money trust," the strongest advocates of a central bank were the large New York banks, who wanted to break loose from the restrictions of the National Bank Act. The United States was the world's largest economy and greatest trading nation, but most of its trade was financed in Europe or through private bankers instead of deposit-taking commercial banking corporations. The 1863 Act was interpreted by the comptroller to prohibit national banks from "accepting" bills of exchange, that is, from commissions for "guaranteeing" them. The big banks wanted entry into this line of international finance with a central bank to support the market. A central bank would also "free them, as holders of the nation's ultimate bank reserves, from responsibility for the stability of the U.S. banking system."[7] The New York banks envied the profits that accrued to the London banks that let the Bank of England keep the gold reserve.

Banks outside the money centers were cool to the idea of a central bank. The suspicions of small-town bankers of proposals from New York were shared by their fellow citizens. The Baltimore and Indianapolis plans of 1894 and 1900 for increasing the elasticity of the currency by letting bank assets be the basis for notes had significant input from New York, but they were marketed as proposals from middle America. The National Citizens League for the Promotion of a Sound Banking System was formed in 1911 to promote the Aldrich plan, which was named after Senate Finance Committee chairman Nelson Aldrich but was essentially

---

[6] Davis Dewey and Martin Shugrue, *Banking and Credit*; Waldo Mitchell, *The Uses of Bank Funds*.

[7] Vincent Carosso and Richard Sylla, "U.S. Banks in International Finance."

Warburg's proposal for a United Reserve Bank.[8] Laughlin was the principal spokesman for the League, "which is made up of business men," and explained its existence by the fact "that the reform affects the borrowing business man more than the lending bank. . . . The reform should not take the shape of a dominant central bank, nor should it be a creature of politics. For this reason the Government of the United States should not enter the discount and deposit business of banking; but . . . should supervise and regulate a cooperative means of assistance, like an enlarged clearinghouse association, in the common interest. . . ."[9] The League backed away from Aldrich and New York in 1912 when the Republican Party's problems (the Taft–Roosevelt split) made it apparent that any plan associated with it would fail.[10]

Few would have predicted that a central bank would owe its creation to a Democratic president, the leader of the party traditionally most jealous of federal encroachments on the rights of individuals and states. A central bank was far from inevitable in the early years of the century. It is true that there was considerable support for such an institution and for monetary reform generally, but that had always been the case, and the reformers had seemed no stronger than on other occasions since Jackson's veto of the second Bank. A national bank had less support from Republicans in the early 1900s than from Whigs in the 1830s and 1840s. Main Street Republicans were almost as wary of Wall Street as their Democratic neighbors. "Banking reform at the beginning of 1912 seemed a dead issue, of interest only to a few bankers and a seriously divided National Citizens' League for Sound Banking."[11]

After the rise of government intervention and the part played by Woodrow Wilson, subsequent generations have seen the Federal Reserve as a natural consequence of the post–Civil War crises that finally spurred Congress to action. There is more to the story, as we have seen, but something can be said for this view because the Panic of 1907 heightened awareness of currency problems and made the monetary system a logical object of the reform administration coming to power in 1913.

---

[8] Nelson Aldrich, businessman and banker, served on the Providence, RI, city council (1869–74), was a member of the State House of Representatives (1875–76), was a Republican congressman (1879–81) and U.S. senator (1881–1911), served on the Committee on Finance (1897–1911), and was chairman of the National Monetary Commission (1908–12).

[9] Laughlin, *op. cit.*, pp. iii–iv.

[10] Livingston, *op. cit.*, pp. 208–12.

[11] Kolko, *op. cit.*, p. 217.

*The Panic of 1907, the Aldrich–Vreeland Act, the Aldrich Plan for
a National Reserve Association, and the Federal Reserve Act*

The panic of 1907 and a widespread suspension of payments brought the usual palliatives, including clearinghouse loan certificates, increased Treasury bank deposits, and an emergency pool arranged by J. P. Morgan.[12] However, 1907 differed from previous crises in the response of Congress. Senator Aldrich proposed a plan for emergency currency expansions, as well as, looking toward fundamental solutions, a National Monetary Commission "to inquire into and report to Congress at the earliest date practicable what changes are necessary or desirable in the monetary system of the United States or in the laws relating to banking and currency. . . ."[13] The Aldrich–Vreeland Act of 1908 authorized banks to form National Currency Associations to issue temporary currency secured by U.S. bonds and commercial paper "if, in the judgment of the Secretary of the Treasury, business conditions in the locality demand additional circulation."[14] Eligible commercial paper was limited to "notes representing actual commercial transactions [bearing] the names of at least two responsible parties."

The Act came into play once before its expiration in 1915, in an effort to counteract the currency withdrawals by Europeans in 1914. In addition to clearinghouse loan certificates of $212 million, $400 million of Aldrich–Vreeland currency were issued. "The maximum amount outstanding on any one date was $364 million," Friedman and Schwartz report, "which was nearly one-quarter of the total amount of currency in the hands of the public before the outbreak of war, and nearly one-eighth of total high-powered money. The availability of the emergency issue probably prevented a monetary panic and the restriction of payments by the banking system."[15]

The Aldrich–Vreeland Act may be best remembered for the studies of the American monetary system and foreign central banking sponsored by the National Monetary Commission, including those used in this history by O. M. W. Sprague, *History of Crises under the National Banking*

---

[12] See Milton Friedman and Anna Schwartz, *Monetary History of the United States*, pp. 156–68; O. M. W. Sprague, *History of Crises under the National Banking System*, chap. 5; and Piatt Andrew, "Substitutes for Cash in the Panic of 1907."

[13] Sections 17 and 18 of the Aldrich–Vreeland Act, May 30, 1908; Herman Krooss, *Documentary History of Banking and Currency in the United States*, pp. 2098–99.

[14] Edward Vreeland, banker and businessman, was a Republican congressman from New York (1899–1913), chairman, Banking and Currency Committee (1909–11), and vice chairman, National Monetary Commission (1908–12).

[15] Friedman and Schwartz, *op. cit.*, p. 172.

System; R. H. I. Palgrave, *The English Banking System*; E. W. Kemmerer, *Seasonal Variations in the Demand for Money and Capital in the United States*; and David Kinley, *The Independent Treasury of the United States*.[16] Their ostensible purpose was to provide the background for legislation, although the bill that Aldrich submitted in 1912 had been outlined by Warburg before the Commission was formed.[17]

Except for the composition of the central board and its authority over the branches, the Aldrich bill resembled the Federal Reserve Act of December 1913.[18] The Aldrich bill provided for a National Reserve Association (NRA) of 15 branches owned by subscribing commercial banks. Day-to-day credit operations would be performed by the branches, primarily by discounting real bills. The NRA had no nonbank private customers, doing business only with banks and the government. It could invest in U.S. bonds and short-term obligations of U.S. states and foreign governments and issue currency in the course of its loans and security purchases. Member bank reserves could be held as either Reserve Association currency or deposits in the Association; reserve ratios were the same as under the National Banking System. The new currency would replace national bank notes and, like them, be redeemable in gold.

The NRA was envisioned as a corporate body, with the central board of directors having authority over the branches, including the determination of the uniform discount rate. The central board would have 46 members. There were two directors elected by the board of directors of each branch, one of the two a nonbanker to "fairly represent the agricultural, commercial, industrial, and other interests of the district"; nine directors elected from the branches at large (with votes weighted toward the big banks but no more than one director from any district); and seven *ex officio* members: the chairman of the board and governor of the NRA, appointed by the president of the United States for a 10-year term from a list of three provided by the NRA board; two deputy governors elected by the board for seven years; the secretaries of the treasury, agriculture, and commerce and Labor; and the comptroller of the currency.

The Aldrich plan was unfortunate in its timing. Republicans lost control of the House in the election of 1910 and would also lose the Senate and the

---

[16] William Dewald, "The National Monetary Commission: A Look Back."
[17] For example, see "A Plan for a Modified Central Bank" (November 1907), reprinted in Warburg, *op. cit.*, ii, pp. 29–36.
[18] A juxtaposition of the two bills is in Warburg, *op. cit.*, i, pp. 178–369.

presidency in 1912. Democrats associated Aldrich with the "money trust" and took a stand against his plan in the 1912 campaign. However, the banking community continued to push for reform and found an ally in Carter Glass of the House Banking and Currency Committee.[19] Festus Wade, a St. Louis banker and member of the American Bankers Association (ABA), promised Glass the ABA's cooperation "in devising a financial system for this country." He favored the Aldrich bill, but "any bill you submit will be a vast improvement on our present system." George Reynolds, a Chicago banker and president of the ABA, said that he was opposed to a true central bank (that is, a bankers' bank with branches throughout the country competing with existing banks) but that Glass could "count on at least good treatment and a reasonable measure of cooperation by the ABA [for an] organization with branches located in various sections of the country dealing only with banks and the Government."[20]

Glass's cooperation was conditional, however. He objected to the centralization in the Aldrich bill, and with the assistance of Laughlin's former student, Parker Willis, imposed on the Aldrich plan an organization of privately controlled independent regional banks. He hoped to break Wall Street's dominance by rival concentrations of power.[21] The president-elect was favorably disposed to Glass's plan when it was explained to him in December 1912, but he thought it needed a capstone – a central board – to control and coordinate the system. Glass was privately aghast at this backward step toward the centralization of the Aldrich plan,[22] but he accommodated Wilson with a Federal Reserve Board of six public members appointed by the president and three bankers chosen by the regional banks, although the bankers had to be dropped to placate William Jennings Bryan and his populist following. Bryan also prevailed over the protestations of Wilson and Glass to make Federal Reserve currency a liability of the United States instead of the regional Fed banks. Wilson's biographer Arthur Link noted the weakness of

---

[19] Carter Glass, a newspaperman from Lynchburg, was a Virginia state senator (1899–1903) and U.S. congressman (1902–18). He was chairman, Banking and Currency Committee (1913–18), secretary of the treasury (1918–20), and a U.S. senator (1920–46).

[20] From House Banking and Currency Committee *Hearings on Banking and Currency Plans*, January 1913, 62nd Congr., 3rd sess.; also Kolko, *op. cit.*, p. 226; and Carter Glass, *An Adventure in Constructive Finance*, 1927, p. 86.

[21] H. P. Willis, *The Federal Reserve System*, pp. 142–43. The idea for a decentralized system is usually traced to Victor Morawetz (*The Banking and Currency Problem in the United States*), who is given credit by Warburg, *op. cit.*, i, p. 36.

[22] Arthur Link, *Wilson: The New Freedom*, p. 212.

Wilson's resistance, who was evidently swayed by the argument of his advisor Louis Brandeis that

The power to issue currency should be vested exclusively in Government officials, even when the currency is issued against commercial paper. The American people will not be content to have the discretion necessarily involved vested in a Board composed wholly or in part of bankers; for their judgment may be biased by private interest or affiliation.... The conflict between the policies of the Administration and the desires of the financiers and of big business is an irreconcilable one.[23]

"Let bankers explain the technical features of the new system," the president wrote to the chairman of the House Ways and Means Committee.

Suffice it here to say [that]... it provides a currency which expands as it is needed and contracts when it is not needed: a currency which comes into existence in response to the call of every man who can show a going business and a concrete basis for extending credit to him.

More than that, the power to direct this system of credits is put into the hands of a public board of disinterested officers of the Government itself who can make no money out of anything they do in connection with it. No group of bankers anywhere can get control; no one part of the country can concentrate the advantages and conveniences of the system upon itself for its own selfish advantage. The board can oblige the banks of one region to go to the assistance of the banks of another. The whole resources of the country are mobilized, to be employed where they are most needed. I think we are justified in speaking of this as a democracy of credit.[24]

The Federal Reserve Act had something for everyone. The burden of the nation's reserve was shifted to a public institution that did not compete with privately owned banks. Legal impediments to bank participation in international finance were lessened, as Aldrich had seen his promise of a plan "to make the United States the financial center of the world" made good in the Fed's commitment to make a market in bankers acceptances.[25] Although national banks were compelled to join the Federal Reserve System, the pain was softened by lower reserve requirements. In fact, membership was not compulsory because national banks could switch to state charters, and opposition from state banks had been circumvented by letting their membership be voluntary. These benefits and concessions

---

[23] Brandeis to Wilson, June 14, 1913, *Papers of Woodrow Wilson*, vol. 27.

[24] Letter to Congressman Oscar Underwood, October 17, 1914, *Wilson Papers*, vol. 31.

[25] Speech on *The Work of the National Monetary Commission* to the Economic Club of New York, November 29, 1909; Senate Doc. 406, 61st Congr., 2nd sess.

may explain why bankers were not more forceful in pushing for the development and legal recognition of clearinghouse currencies, for which they had to bear the risks. Finally, the populists and progressives were persuaded to accept the bankers' organization by involving the government in the Washington "capstone" and substituting government currency for bank notes.

The opposition in Congress focused on the dangers of political and big-bank control of the monetary system exercised through the central board. Glass defended it in the House:

> The Federal reserve board, technically speaking, has no banking function. It is strictly a board of control, properly constituted of high Government officials, doing justice to the banks, but fairly and courageously representing the interests of the people.
>
> *Congressional Record*, 63nd Congr., 1st sess., September 10, 1913, p. 4645

It would be "an altruistic institution." Our understanding of the Federal Reserve Act and its founders is improved by J. M. Keynes's analysis of the issues that they ignored or denied.

Another Way: Keynes's Plan for a State Bank for India

The Royal Commission on Indian Finance and Currency met in 1913 to inquire into, among other things, whether the quantity of gold coin circulating in India was sufficient for an effective gold standard. One of its members was the young Keynes, who had just described in *Indian Currency and Finance* how the subcontinent had "drifted" into a monetary system with neither "contemplation" nor "explanation."[26] The 1898 prophecy by A. M. Lindsay, deputy secretary of the Bank of Bengal, had been fulfilled: By an "almost imperceptible process the Indian currency will be placed on a footing which Ricardo and other great authorities have advocated as the best of all currency systems, viz., one in which the currency media used in the internal circulation are confined to notes and cheap token coins, which are made to act precisely as if they were bits of gold by being made convertible into gold for foreign payment purposes."[27] Because "one of the objects of a good currency is to combine cheapness with stability," Keynes wrote to the *Times* in 1912, India's

---

[26] P. 3.

[27] Testimony before the Indian Currency (Fowler) Committee of 1898, quoted by Keynes, *Indian Currency and Finance*, pp. 3–4. The quotation from Lindsay that follows is from p. 24.

establishment "of a gold standard without encouraging the circulation of gold," and the investment of "a part of their reserves in London earning interest," should be objects of admiration rather than the criticism it had received.[28] An official had called it "far too clever for the ordinary English mind with its ineradicable prejudice for an immediately tangible gold backing to all currencies."[29] Nonetheless, Lindsay saw that "they *must* adopt my scheme despite themselves." Keynes called attention to the fact that because "the Indian system has been perfected and its provisions generally known, it has been widely imitated both in Asia and elsewhere. In 1903 the government of the United States introduced a system avowedly based on it into the Philippines."[30]

However, there was room for improvement, and Keynes advocated a central bank. The disadvantages of the "existing 'Independent Treasury System,'" by which, whenever the Government balances are swollen, deliberately or not, large sums are taken off the money market," would be remedied by "a large public or semi-public institution with which large balances could be safely and properly deposited," managed by civil servants pursuing "a policy of discretionary loans out of the balances.... India and the United States of America are now practically alone among the great trading countries of the world in possessing no central bank ... and also alone in having no rediscount market, no elasticity in the note issue, no bank rate policy, and an 'Independent Treasury System' in place of a Government banker."

Keynes's *Memorandum on Proposals for the Establishment of a State Bank in India*, submitted to the Commission in October 1913, is an interesting contrast to the Federal Reserve Act then under consideration, especially in its analysis of the effects of organization on the knowledge and incentives of central bankers.[31] He was not optimistic about the possibility of an effective central bank in the United States.

In America the 1907 crisis served to demonstrate that such a system is indefensible. And the country is now engaged in remedying these defects so far as is possible

---

[28] November 14, 1912; *Writings*, xv, pp. 91–94.

[29] Thomas (Lord) Farrer, permanent secretary of the Board of Trade, 1867–86, cited by Keynes, *Indian Currency*, p. 24.

[30] *Indian Currency*, pp. 24–25. For a survey of the operation of the gold exchange standard in India and elsewhere and a recommendation for its adoption by China and Mexico, see U.S. Congress, HR Doc. 144, 1903.

[31] *Writings*, xv, pp. 151–211.

in the very difficult circumstances which arise out of the presence of innumerable small banks, on the one hand, all with vested interests and a terror of anything which might conceivably diminish their profits, and of a public, deeply suspicious of all moneyed interests and of anything which might strengthen their power, on the other. In India the obstacles are far less to the introduction of the recognised preventives for the diseases of the financial body.[32]

Keynes's Indian proposal dealt with the same conflicts that surrounded the structure of the Federal Reserve, including its location(s), the degree of central control, and whether it should be publicly or privately owned and managed. His primary objective was the moderation of interest rate fluctuations through a more elastic currency. He rejected the Bank of England as a model, arguing that the "Constitutions of the principal state banks of Europe and Japan [point] overwhelmingly to the conclusion that the higher executive officers responsible for the policy and administration of the Bank must be appointed by Government and rest under its ultimate authority." However, this should be combined "with a high degree of day-to-day independence for the authorities of the bank, [whose] duty it would be to take a broad and not always a purely commercial view of policy, and at the same time to make use of the commercial instincts and commercial knowledge of representatives of the shareholders." The Bank would be directed by a central board consisting of a governor appointed by the king, a deputy governor and the managers of the three Presidency [regional] banks appointed for specific terms by the viceroy, and a representative of the government. Decisions would be made by majority rule subject to the emergency power of the government representative to delay implementation of any decision until it had been reported to the viceroy, "with whom shall lie an ultimate right of veto."

An operationally independent state bank would allow the government to resist popular and commercial pressures for increased lending. It "would never admit, for example, the faintest degree of responsibility for the precise level of the bank rate at a particular moment." Such a bank might "get the best of both [private and public management] worlds. . . . Representatives of the public interest must have the ultimate control [while] the alliance of the State with private shareholders serves to keep the executive of the Bank in close touch with commercial opinion, and introduces that element of commercial self-interest from which, in the

[32] Keynes, "Memorandum on Proposals for the Establishment of a State Bank in India," pp. 198–99.

present economic arrangement of affairs, a State bank as well as private institutions may derive a real advantage." The governor and deputy governor "should invariably be persons of commercial or banking, not administrative or official, experience, and should be appointed, so far as may be possible, or convenient, from the staffs of the Presidency offices." An objection to locating the board in Delhi was that "this location would place the Bank too much under the direct influence of government, and . . . the officers of the Bank would be too little in touch with commercial opinion."

The Commission endorsed Keynes's view of India's gold exchange standard, but not his central bank. India did not get a central bank until the Reserve Bank of India in 1935. An attempt in 1927 failed for lack of a compromise between the proponents of government and private ownership and control. The plan accepted eight years later was essentially Keynes's.[33]

Getting Started

Handicaps: Inexperience Reinforced by Unclear Objectives, Instruments, Incentives, and Sources of Information

The Federal Reserve began with disadvantages that were fatal for the monetary system that it was supposed to cure. Its founders differed over the purposes of the institution they were creating. It had been advanced initially as a support mechanism for clearinghouses during financial panics – "a clearinghouse for the clearinghouses," Warburg declared in 1907. Republican Congressman Everis Hayes of California noted that if the objective was in fact an elastic currency, simple adjustments to existing clearinghouse arrangements would be sufficient. He declared, "I believe that it would be safer to make efforts at the reform of our system more strictly along the lines of our own financial evolution than by borrowing from some foreign system."[34] However, by the fall of 1913 Congress was being asked to consider a radical departure, setting up "the most powerful banking institution in all the world," with "the control and management of the banking and the credits of this country," lamented Republican Frank Mondell of Wyoming.[35]

---

[33] J. S. G. Wilson, "The Rise of Central Banking in India."

[34] *Congressional Record*, 63d Congr., 1st sess., p. 4652, September 10, 1913.

[35] *Ibid.*, p. 4691.

Mondell wondered how the proposed powers would be exercised. The framers of the bill "will, no doubt, wax heatedly vociferous and flamboyantly eloquent in their declarations . . . that the people, through their Government, alone have the right to control the issue of currency and supervise the business of banking. The gentlemen may as well save themselves that kind of effort, for they will fool nobody whose opinion is worthwhile. . . ." Supervision "so far as is necessary for the benefit and protection of all the people" is generally accepted. However, "the people pretty clearly understand nowadays that control through a Government bureau, by political appointees, is not synonymous with control by the people and for the people. Neither do people of ordinary intelligence confuse regulation and management. We regulate the railroads, we do not manage them. We regulate the packing of meats, we do not appoint the men who run the business." Speaker Champ Clark had promised that presidents would "appoint men only of ability, character, and patriotism on the Federal reserve board, and then keep close watch on them to the end that all the people may be treated impartially and that our prosperity may increase." Mondell spoke for the minority and the 19th century when he pleaded for a self-regulating system under the law. The "Speaker unwittingly suggests the strongest argument against the proposed plan when he [takes] the view that it is wise or necessary to add to the present tremendous power of the presidential office a further 'stupendous trust' which he can only hope to properly fulfill by keeping a 'close watch' on his appointees."[36]

Some of its proponents expected the Federal Reserve's powers to be scientifically limited by the discipline of commercial paper. Section 13 of the Federal Reserve Act guided lending as follows: "Upon the indorsement of any of its member banks, any Federal reserve bank may discount notes, drafts, and bills of exchange arising out of commercial transactions. . . ."

Robert Owen of Oklahoma, manager of the bill in the Senate, looked to the Fed "to fix the rate of interest" so that "the business men of the country can hope to ascertain and know reasonably in advance what money will cost them in their enterprises. . . ." In place of the high and fluctuating interest rates experienced by the United States, "we are going to have, in the future, the same stability of interest rates that prevails in Europe. I

---

[36] *Ibid.*, p. 4692.

call your attention, for example, to the fact that for 75 per cent of the time the rate of the Bank of France has not exceeded 3 per cent, . . . that the bank of Belgium has not exceeded 6 percent in 50 years, [and] the interest rates in Germany and in England have been of wonderful stability."[37] A generous interpretation of Owen's position is that he hoped to prevent the high interest rates associated with liquidity crises, and he referred particularly to 1907. However, his letters to the Federal Reserve Board in 1920 protesting an increase in the discount rate to 6 percent at a time when Fed credit and commodity prices were rising more than 20 percent per annum and call money rates had reached 11 percent suggest that what he really wanted was permanent easy money. In 1921, he informed the Board that "the Reserve Banks can well afford to make [loans] to whatever extent required by the country." He did not see why they should not set interest rates by the same criteria as commercial banks, which were "justified in charging six and seven per cent because they pay two and three per cent for deposits. . . . If the Reserve Banks would be content with the same margin of profit, . . . they would be charging a rate of between three and four percent."[38]

Warburg had not advocated central bank rediscounting of real bills in the belief that it was an automatic means to price stability. Rather, they were part of a plan for recasting American credit markets in the European mold. These sound and liquid credit instruments would be encouraged if the central monetary institution assured a market for them. Hopes for bankers' acceptances as a means of international finance were realized, but bills did not get off the ground domestically. Warburg was behind financial developments even in Europe. American borrowers had long preferred direct relationships with their banks, a preference upon which the Fed's willingness to discount "real (eligible) paper" made no dent. Observers wondered at the Federal Reserve Act's attempt to "change the commercial credit practices of this country in directions thought to be an improvement."[39] The shortage of eligible paper was cited by Fed officials as an obstacle to credit expansion in the Great

[37] *Ibid.*, pp. 5992–6002, November 24, 1913; reprinted in Krooss, *op. cit.*, pp. 2419–35. Also see the Senate Majority Report on the Federal Reserve Bill, Senate Report No. 133, 63rd Congr., 1st sess., pp. 6002–9, November 22, 1913; reprinted Krooss, *op. cit.*, pp. 2377–402.

[38] W. P. G. Harding, *The Formative Period of the Federal Reserve System*, pp. 195–200.

[39] Luther Harr and Carlton Harris, *Banking Theory and Practice*, p. 433.

Depression, although this was disputed by Milton Friedman and Anna Schwartz.[40]

Whatever the policy instrument, there was no clear understanding of what it should be aimed at. House Majority Leader Oscar Underwood declared that the issue "resolved itself into faith in the President's Board, the whole question being whether the board was angel or devil." So the president controlled the Board, Texas Democrat Oscar Callaway ridiculed, and the Board in combination with the banks controlled the currency, but "Where," he asked, "will the people come in? We are told to ask no questions; have faith, simple faith.... Faith, faith, faith; faith in man, fallible man, swept by all the passions, prejudices, and ambitions, mental misgivings, shortsightedness, and misconceptions of man." The country had experienced discretionary government, and "Who usually gets a hearing, the man on the ground or the trusting man?"

The line of command was also unsettled. The Board's control of the Reserve Banks was not as complete as Callaway supposed. Changes in discount rates required Board approval, and it might temporarily suspend reserve requirements and require member banks to discount each others' paper at rates fixed by the Board. It was otherwise limited to the "general supervision" of the Reserve Banks. The Reserve Banks could control the quantity of loans at existing discount rates and engage in open market operations and, it would appear, determine aggregate money and credit. Confusion between the Banks and the Board over lines of authority would engender animosity and even paralysis.

Appointments to the Board were for 10 years, a term expiring every 2 years. It also included the secretary of the treasury and the comptroller of the currency. A substantial portion of the conflicts between the Board and the Reserve Banks may be attributed to diverse motives and knowledge arising from the different backgrounds and environments of their members. The greater political sensitivity of the Board is explained by its physical proximity to the president and Congress as well as to the considerable Washington seasoning of most of its members. In contrast, many Reserve Bank heads were bankers, and they all functioned in a bankers' milieu, in daily contact with bankers and the financial markets. Their greater reliance on market forces, particularly interest rates, compared with the frequent preference of the Board either for inaction or

---

[40] E. A. Goldenweiser, *American Monetary Policy*, pp. 159–60. Friedman and Schwartz's denial is in *op. cit.*, pp. 399–406.

quantitative controls, can be traced to the experiences of the presidents with market forces and their greater distance from political influences.

Whatever their experience, its relevance was diminished by the break in institutions. New lessons had to be learned and old ones unlearned or at least revised. The Federal Reserve System raised these problems in an extreme form because it was a completely new organization with unprecedented powers and unclear objectives and lines of authority. Even if the financial and political backgrounds of the decision makers of this new force had been "correct," much learning would have to have occurred before a high level of performance could reasonably have been expected. The Federal Reserve had not evolved in the course of adapting to circumstances, and a culture of behavior could only develop with time. The Bank of England, which had weathered storms for more than a century, failed to recognize important implications of the changes in its surroundings and structure after 1797 and 1844. It is not surprising that the Federal Reserve failed its first big test, which came in less than two decades.

Government Money Machine

Problems of goals, knowledge, and incentives were soon placed in abeyance by war. Three-quarters of the large increase in government spending during World War I was financed by borrowing, which continued at a high rate for several months after the November 1918 armistice. Sixty percent of Federal Reserve credit during 1917–19 consisted of purchases of U.S. securities or discounts of bills secured by those securities. These bills were made eligible for Fed discounting by an amendment to the Federal Reserve Act in September 1916.[41] A later research director for the Board described wartime monetary policy as follows:

[T]he Federal reserve banks were guided in their rate policy chiefly by the necessity for supporting the Treasury. The level of discount rates was kept low and preferential rates were granted on loans secured by Government obligations . . . and the discount rate was thus not used as a means of credit control – but as a method of helping the Government to raise the funds necessary for the prosecution of the war. It was not until the summer of 1919 that the use of the discount rate as a means of credit control received serious consideration.

E. A. Goldenweiser, *Federal Reserve System in Operation*, p. 40

The Board had considered rate increases as early as January 1919. However, the Treasury was in the midst of a conversion of short-term to

---

[41] Krooss, *op. cit.*, pp. 2479–85.

long-term debt, and there was "considerable sympathy within the Board for the problems facing the Treasury."[42] In response to Reserve Bank requests for rate increases in April, Board Chairman W. P. G. Harding replied that the secretary of the treasury had communicated to him that the "failure" of the government's loans "would be disastrous for the country. The Board, therefore, did not approve any advance in rates."[43] Nor did it do so in July.[44] Carter Glass, initially, as we have seen, an opponent of central control of the System, had become secretary of the treasury in December 1918, and he shared the desire of his predecessor for low interest rates. Both preferred to resist inflation by credit controls that distinguished between essential (productive) and nonessential (speculative) credit. Assistant Secretary of the Treasury Russell Leffingwell wrote that the Treasury was "honor bound" to avoid the infliction of capital losses on the patriotic citizens that had financed the war effort.[45]

Fed officials, including Governor Benjamin Strong[46] of the New York Reserve Bank, had to consider the "strong outcry in Congress for the protection of the interests of holders of the previous loans, Liberty loans, which had suffered a decline in the market," although Strong had "a feeling – possibly because I do not live in the atmosphere of Washington – that it could have been resisted."[47]

The Board's attitude toward direct controls wavered between sympathy and weak resistance, but stronger opposition emerged from the Reserve Banks. The Board was caught in the middle of an acrimonious debate between Strong and the Treasury in October 1919, but it sided with the latter despite Strong's threat of a public protest unless an increase in the discount rate was approved. Strong believed that attempts to ration credit were futile whereas Leffingwell was convinced that speculative credit expansion should be attacked by "a firm discrimination in

---

[42] Elmus Wicker, *Federal Reserve Monetary Policy, 1917–33*, p. 30.

[43] Harding, *op. cit.*, p. 148.

[44] W. P. G. Harding was president, 1st National Bank, Birmingham, AL (1902–14), served on the Federal Reserve Board from 1914 to 1922 (chairman, 1916–22), and was governor, Federal Reserve Bank of Boston (1923–30).

[45] See "Discussion" of Sprague, "The Discount Policy of the Federal Reserve Banks."

[46] Benjamin Strong worked for Cuyler, Morgan (1891–1900), Metropolitan Trust (1900–3), and Bankers Trust (1903–14). He worked with J. P. Morgan in relief of the Panic of 1907 and served as governor, Federal Reserve Bank of New York during 1914 to 1928.

The chief operating officers of the Reserve Banks were called governors until 1936 and presidents thereafter.

[47] U.S. Congress, *Agricultural Inquiry*, 1922, pp. 503–4; Wicker, *op. cit*, p. 34; Benjamin Strong, *Interpretations*, p. 87.

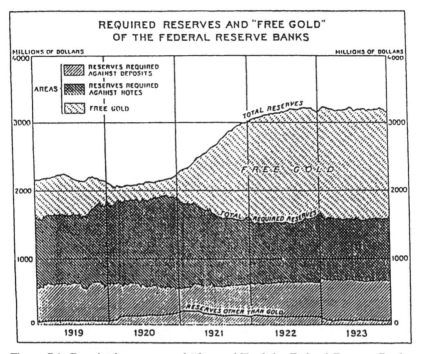

Figure 7.1. Required reserves and "free gold" of the Federal Reserve Banks, 1919–23. *Source:* Emanuel Goldenweiser, *Federal Reserve System in Operation,* fig. 11.

making loans." He was "weary of the copybook texts," which claimed that credit was reduced by making it more expensive. Glass, angered by Strong's attempt "to dominate" the Treasury and the Federal Reserve, threatened to seek his removal.[48]

Increases in the discount rate – from 4 to 4¾ percent in November 1919 and to 6 percent two months later – came when the Treasury informed the Fed that its support of the government bond market was no longer required.[49] The increases were apparently dictated by the Fed's concern for its gold reserve: "the margin [free gold; see Fig. 7.1] was quite narrow," Goldenweiser noted.[50]

[48] Wicker, *op. cit.,* pp. 37–38. For policy conflicts during 1919–20, also see Lester Chandler, *Benjamin Strong: Central Banker,* pp. 135–69, and Friedman and Schwartz, *op. cit.,* pp. 222–39.

[49] Chandler, *op. cit.,* p. 162.

[50] Wicker, *op. cit.,* p. 90. If the gold reserve fell below 40% of Federal Reserve notes, taxes were levied on the Reserve Banks in violation (Sec. 11c, Federal Reserve Act).

Unfortunately, the economy peaked in January 1920, but the rate was raised again in June, to 7 percent, where it remained until it was reduced to 6 percent in April 1921, and then in steps to 4½ percent at the end of the year although the economy had turned up in the autumn.

Harding later defended the Fed against "the contention that . . . rates should have been substantially lowered in April or May, 1920." The drastic falls abroad required a "corresponding fall of prices in this country." Furthermore, he stated,

> The United States was a free gold market, and had it remained at the same time the cheapest money market in the world, our financial structure would have been subject to the severest strain. The Board in that event would have been forced to suspend the reserve requirements, which would probably have resulted in the presentation of large amounts of Federal Reserve notes for redemption in gold for hoarding, which would have reduced reserves still further. In such circumstances prices would have been sustained only in terms of irredeemable paper money.
> W. P. G. Harding, *Formative Period of the Federal Reserve*, pp. 165–66

And that, Harding feared, would have led to progressive inflations of credit and the currency. Certainly the reserve problem was soon resolved, as we see in Fig. 7.1. It has been argued that the Fed's restriction might not be fully explained by its concern for gold, and that it was also influenced by its theory of the appropriate relationship between credit and output. The most extensive official expression of that theory – in its 10th *Annual Report* – is examined later in the chapter. Side-by-side with indecision regarding policy objectives was the conflict over the tools by which credit policy should be implemented – interest rates or persuasion. We have already observed the Board's tendencies to resist and the Reserve Banks to rely on the price mechanism. The minutes of a conference in the spring of 1920 show that the same contrast existed in a more marked degree between the Board and commercial bankers.

Regulating Credit: Interest Rates or Discrimination?

Reserve Banks have nine directors composed of three classes, each with three members: Class A directors elected by the member banks (who own stock in the Reserve Banks); Class B directors, also elected by the member banks but representative of agriculture, commerce, or industry; and Class C "public" directors chosen by the Federal Reserve Board.[51]

---

[51] *Federal Reserve Act*, Sec. 4, Krooss, *op. cit.* p. 2440.

Directors recommend discount rates and choose chief executive officers (governors, later presidents), both subject to Federal Reserve Board approval. They also elect one representative (usually a banker) from each of the 12 Reserve Bank districts to the Federal Advisory Council, which is empowered to meet with and make recommendations to the Federal Reserve Board. Thomas Havrilesky reported evidence that the Council's advisory "directives" (which tended to oppose changes in interest rates, especially on the downside) helped to predict Fed policy.[52]

The "very considerably extended credit position" in the spring of 1920 spurred the Board to go further than usual in getting bankers' views by inviting the Class A directors to the quarterly meeting of the Board and the Advisory Council.[53] It opened with remarks by Board Chairman Harding. There was "no occasion . . . to be unduly disturbed over the situation," he soothed, but from "the 1st of April, 1919, to the 1st of April, 1920, the expansion of bank credit was about 25 per cent, [accompanied] by an advance in commodity prices of about 25 per cent [and] a decline in essential production during the year 1919 of about 10 per cent."

It is evident that the country can not continue to advance prices and wages, to curtail production, to expand credits and to attempt to enrich itself by nonproductive and uneconomic operations without fostering discontent and radicalism, and that such a course, if persisted in, will eventually bring on a real crisis.

The Red Scare, with Attorney General Palmer's raids on suspected Bolsheviks, was at its height. The economic problem as Harding saw it was "the disruption of the proper proportion or relationship between the volume of credit and the volume of goods," for which there were two remedies: contracting credit, which was unpleasant but sometimes necessary, or letting production catch up with credit. Harding then referred to the "lack of liquidation" of debts that normally came at the end of the fall season. The "extravagant spirit has not yet been checked."

There ought to be a recrudescence of our old war-time spirit, of doing something that is worthwhile, and we should get down to work and solid business. There should be a general spirit of cooperation on the part of the Federal reserve banks, the member banks, the non-member banks, and the public to work out a policy which will result in greater production, less unnecessary consumption, and greater economy; all unnecessary borrowings for the purpose of pleasure and

[52] *The Pressures on American Monetary Policy*, chap. 8.

[53] Reported as *Federal Reserve Board Conference*, Senate Doc. 310, 67th Congr., 4th sess.; minutes presented by Senator Glass, February 1923. For accounts of the conference see Harding, *op. cit.*, pp. 171–80, and Federal Reserve *Bulletin*, June 1920.

luxury should be restricted as far as possible and the liquidation of long-standing, nonessential loans should proceed.

We should be careful, however, not to overdo this matter of liquidation, because too drastic a policy of deflation, which might result in crowding to the wall and throwing into bankruptcy legitimate enterprises, however unessential their operations may be, would have a tremendously bad effect and would defeat the purpose of the very policy which we are trying to have established. There must always be a wise and discriminating judgment used.

Whose judgment? The Board's rulings on eligible paper were limited by the Federal Reserve Act, and it was not empowered to distinguish "essential" from "nonessential" loans. Attempts to do so by various government boards had "experienced difficulties" even during the war, "when the problem was simpler than it would be now because there was a general underlying principle that anything essential must be something that was necessary or contributory to the conduct of the war. . . . A Federal reserve bank is in a much better position to undertake this than is the Federal Reserve Board," Harding admitted, "but even here there are difficulties in the way." The needs of communities differed, and "it seems to the board that that whole question of discrimination might very properly be left for solution at the source, as a matter between the individual banker and his own customer." Because of his knowledge of the customer, who relies on his advice, the banker "can often restrict the amount of a loan before it is made and can persuade a customer in very many cases that he really does not need the money after all." This may be difficult "in the case of the hoarder, who for selfish and profiteering purposes wishes to hold back from the mouths of hungry people essential articles of food and clothing. [But] every good banker should exert every influence within his power to force people of that kind to turn loose their hoards. Here is an opportunity for wise discrimination, and this discrimination can be exercised more intelligently and effectively by the individual banker himself than by any Government board."

After calling for a program of education to "inculcate in the minds of the people a sense of the importance of steady, everyday production and distribution, and to encourage the avoidance of waste and the elimination of extravagance," and appealing to "the sound, sensible, and reasonable member banks [to] pull together for sound economic and financial principles," Harding turned to the bankers for their views. The tone of the meeting changed. The spirit of cooperation gave way to the price system. Maine banker Edward Kennard urged "that the rates for money should continue on a high level with the hope of causing liquidation in commodities." James Alexander of New York City's National Bank of Commerce distinguished the present situation from the rationing of coal and other essentials during the war, when "we could go to the users of these commodities and say to them 'You must restrict yourself.'" He said that education was all very well, but "I think now is the logical time . . . to bring this credit situation home to the users of credit. . . . Speaking for myself – and I think I voice the sentiment of the entire board of the Federal reserve district of New York – we think that at the present time the commercial rate, the discount rate, should be raised; that it should not be raised to $6\frac{1}{4}$ or $6\frac{1}{2}$ per cent as a measure of our treatment of the situation, but that the rate should be 7 per cent on commercial paper."

Harding wondered whether the burden of the increase might not be unfairly distributed, for example, whether it might not "penalize anybody who could not liquidate on account of lack of transportation facilities . . .?" Labor disputes had disrupted rail traffic.

"Well, I am afraid somebody is bound to be penalized," Alexander replied. "I do not think we need to consider that question unduly, Governor Harding, any more than we need to unduly consider the position of those who bought Government bonds and who have seen them fall to 85." (Captain Truman's fell to 82, he told Bill Martin during a discussion of the same issues three decades later, recorded at the end of the next chapter.)

Harding yielded to the group's preoccupation with interest rates: "I think it would be well for each director, as he arises, to give his views on the discount rate in his respective district. That is one of the things that we want to take into consideration."

Alexander's New York colleagues expressed their "hearty accord" with his recommended rate increase. However, John Skelton Williams, comptroller of the currency and ex officio member of the Federal Reserve Board, asked if "one of the effects of a 7 per cent rate . . . would be to discourage essential industries?" He suggested that "if you put the rate at 7 per cent, that would not deter the profiteers who are making 70 per cent profit, 20 per cent or 50 per cent. My apprehension and wonder is whether a higher rate of interest would not in the long run discourage the essential producers and at the same time have no effect at all upon the profiteers, upon the men who are making exorbitant and extortionate profits."

To Alexander's defense that high interest would make "a profiteer understand that credit is a luxury," Williams retorted, "But you can do that better by saying, 'We won't let you have the money' than by letting them have the money, even at 10 per cent."

Toward the end of the meeting, Board member Henry Mohlenpah remonstrated with the bankers about the virtues of education, which would make them "something better than bankers; you will become community leaders and not just community advisers, but you will become community directors. The very nature of your business in discriminating upon your loans will make you that, and that is a good thing. It is just exactly, to my mind, what this situation needs; not a contraction that is going to hurt."

Harding, Williams, and Mohlenpah had been bankers. The sharp differences between Harding and Williams and the current bankers in the room might to some extent be explained by their lengthy immersion in the political capital: Harding was a member of the Board since 1914 and Williams was assistant secretary of the treasury at the beginning of Wilson's administration and comptroller since 1914. Mohlenpah, in contrast, had arrived only in November 1919 to serve the remainder of a term expiring in August 1920. It is an interesting question whether the environment had repressed their reliance on interest rates as a primary means of rationing credit (very quickly in Mohlenpah's case) or their language had adapted to the political environment.

Returning to the active bankers, George Reynolds of the Continental and Commercial National Bank of Chicago, after making the obligatory nod to "education," observed the following:

Now, in the Chicago district, where we found business rather overextended, we began to ask these people to reduce their loans, and they rather thought we were joking with them. There was a question as to whether or not we were really serious and whether or not there was a real necessity for our asking them to cooperate with us. . . .

I am ready and willing to do anything and everything necessary to help correct the situation. But I would not be honest with myself if I did not express my own frank opinion on some of the questions that have been raised here. I have not lost my belief in the theory that the yardstick is the interest rate, which is after all the best means for controlling the demand for money.

Reynolds's comments on the kinds of loans that banks made under stringent conditions are also instructive. In times of crisis, correspondent banks in communities affected by deposit losses "have come to us for help, and we have had to give them help because they have had reserve balances. We regard it as our duty to help those banks and to prevent failure. They come to us and say frankly, 'We have got to have help . . . and we can not give you paper that is eligible.'" Money-center banks provided at least some of their traditional assistance after the advent of the Federal Reserve, and sometimes, like the Bank of England a century before, "were not over-nice" respecting collateral. "In every institution in this country there is a large amount of paper which is not eligible for rediscount at the Federal reserve bank, but at the same time it represents the very cream of paper in so far as the question of safety is concerned – I do not say liquidity...." Other claims on bank credit came from U.S. securities, which the Treasury "wanted us to carry," and corporate taxes due in June.

I said to a banker the other morning, "How do you like being a banker nowadays?" He said, "Sherman said, 'War is hell';" but, he said, "I would rather be in the trenches on the other side than loaning to the banks these days." That illustrates the state of mind toward the people and in our institutions in Chicago, and I think in all institutions we do not go down so deep to analyze to any great extent as to whether this is a nonessential or an essential, but we take it right by the scruff of the neck and try to determine whether that fellow must have that money, and if he does not have to have it, even though it is essential, we put him on the waiting list....

Adolph Miller, a member from 1914 to 1936 and the only economist or academic on the Board before the 1950s, said that the advocacy of interest rates to regulate credit revealed "a more optimistic view of the problem with which we are confronted than I think conditions actually warrant." The bankers' statements amounted to little more than "trust in God," when what was needed was a "delicacy of discrimination in undertaking to apply a test to the legitimacy of credit demands.... I think the country will accept that as on the whole indicating a temperate and responsible attitude on the part of the Federal Reserve system and member banks of the country in dealing with this problem...." Discrimination in credit was necessary to "the production of things that immediately are more important and the postponement of things that for the moment are less important."

Comptroller Williams agreed, "...speaking of extravagance and the production of nonessentials and luxuries, ... I was very much disgusted the other day to hear of my chauffeur buying about three silk shirts at $10 apiece."

A Model of Monetary (Credit) Policy? The Federal Reserve Board's 1923 Annual Report

Those who see central banks as regulators of the money stock call their policies "monetary," but that is not how central bankers have seen their job. Bankers first and foremost extend credit. This does not deny their concern for the quantities of their liabilities (money) as the public's willingness to hold a bank's deposits is essential to its credit. The "credit view" of monetary effects that calls attention to the interruption of credit arrangements, such as the banking collapse of 1930–33, has recently been presented as a contributor to the Great Depression.[54] However, bankers and central bankers have always emphasized credit, as was illustrated by the Bank Directors in 1810 and the Federal Reserve conference in 1920. A self-conscious example was the essay on "Credit Policy" in the Federal Reserve Board's *Annual Report* for 1923, in which it revealed a new responsibility for macroeconomic stability following its independence from the Treasury and the prosperity of 1922 and 1923 – good years in which price stability and moderate interest rates accompanied rising output.

The *Report's* argument resembled Keynes's *Tract on Monetary Reform* published a few months earlier and opened with the premise that the traditional guidelines for monetary policy had become inoperative.[55] This was particularly true of "the reserve ratio," which "can not be expected to regain its former position of authority until the extraordinary international gold movements which, in part, have occasioned and in part have resulted from the breakdown of the gold standard, have ceased and the flow of gold from country to country is again governed by those forces which in more normal and stable conditions determine the balance of international payments." The *Report* followed the tendency current in official circles – both British and American – to exaggerate the automaticity and effectiveness of the prewar system, in which "the movements of gold among the money markets of the world exercised a corrective influence on exchange rates, tended to equalize money rates in various countries, and to keep domestic price levels in line with the world price level. In these circumstances, changes in the reserve ratios of the various central banks served as valuable indicators of the changes in the credit and trade relations of the countries and were consequently important guides in the shaping of discount policies."

---

[54] Ben Bernanke, "Nonmonetary Effects of the Financial Crisis in the Propagation of the Great Depression."

[55] The 1923 *Annual Report* with sections on "Credit Policy" and "Open Market Operations" (Krooss, *op. cit.*, pp. 2526–41) was published in early 1924. Keynes's *Tract* appeared in December 1923. Parts of the *Tract*, though not chap. 4 ("Alternative Aims in Monetary Policy," the most relevant to the Board's discussion), were revisions of articles for supplements to the *Manchester Guardian Commercial* in 1922.

If the gold reserve is an inadequate guide – and the Federal Reserve Act only specified minimum reserve ratios – what are the criteria for action? The *Report* first considered the goal of price stability, which had figured prominently in public discussions. However, "price fluctuations proceed from a great variety of causes, most of which lie outside the range of influence of [Federal Reserve] credit.... No credit system could undertake to perform the function of regulating credit by reference to prices without failing in the endeavor." Furthermore, because the "price index records an accomplished fact," a policy based on it would lack timeliness, and attempts to predict it would be unreliable.

No statistical mechanism alone, however carefully contrived, can furnish an adequate guide to credit administration. Credit is an intensely human institution and as such reflects the moods and impulses of the community – its hopes, its fears, its expectations. The business and credit situation at any particular time is weighted and charged with these invisible factors. They are elusive and can not be fitted into any mechanical formula, but the fact that they are refractory to methods of the statistical laboratory makes them neither nonexistent nor unimportant. They are factors which must always patiently and skillfully be evaluated as best they may and dealt with in any banking administration that is animated by a desire to secure to the community the results of an efficient credit system. In its ultimate analysis credit administration is not a matter of mechanical rules, but is and must be a matter of judgment – of judgment concerning each specific credit situation at the particular moment of time when it has arisen or is developing.

Fortunately, there were "among these factors a sufficient number which are determinable in their character, and also measurable, to relieve the problem of credit administration of much of its indefiniteness, and therefore give to it a substantial foundation of ascertainable fact." Those factors were "in large part recognized in the Federal reserve act, [which] therefore, itself goes far toward indicating standards by which the adequacy or inadequacy of the amount of credit provided by the Federal reserve banks may be tested." The act had "laid down as the broad principle for the guidance of the Federal reserve banks and of the Federal Reserve Board in the discharge of their functions with respect to the administration of the credit facilities of the Federal reserve banks the principle of 'accommodating commerce and business.'" How do we know when commerce and business, as opposed to "speculation," are accommodated? The act suggested a further guide to Fed credit by limiting its discounts to real bills, but, as Harding had indicated in 1920, that was insufficient. The Board recognized with Henry Thornton that there were "no automatic devices or detectors for determining, when credit is granted by a Federal reserve bank in response to a rediscount demand, whether the occasion of the rediscount was an extension of credit by the member bank for nonproductive use. Paper offered by a member bank when it rediscounts with a Federal reserve bank may disclose the purpose for which the loan evidenced by that paper was made, but it does not disclose what use is to be made of the proceeds of the rediscount." Therefore "the technical administrative problem presented to each reserve bank is that of finding the ways and means best suited to ... informing itself of ... the extension of credit for speculative purposes."

"The administrative problems presented to the Federal Reserve Board are of a different character and require a different technique." The Board did not make loans but was a supervisory body. "In the discharge of the responsibility placed upon it by the act for the 'review and determination' of the discount policy and discount rates of the Federal reserve banks 'with a view of accommodating commerce and business,' the Federal Reserve Board must look for guidance primarily to information concerning the state of industry and trade and the state of credit."

Policy is still undetermined. There remains the problem of determining when credit is excessive or deficient relative to production and trade. We are given an insight into the Board's understanding of this relationship by its concern for prices and speculation earlier in the *Report*. Although "the interrelationship of prices and credit is too complex to admit of any simple statement, still less of a formula of invariable application, [they may] be regarded as the outcome of common causes that work in the economic and business situation. The same conditions which predispose to a rise of prices also predispose to an increased demand for credit." The *Report*'s concern for "nonproductive credit" and the "undue accumulation or exhaustion of stocks" brings us to the price speculation that worried the Board in 1920. We come back to prices in the end.

The Federal Reserve's interest in price stability is described in the next section. Even before the Great Depression there were suggestions of a lack of symmetry. Speculative accumulations were unreservedly bad but liquidations might be beneficial.

Price Stabilization

I believe that it should be the policy of the Federal Reserve System, by the employment of the various means at its command, to maintain the volume of credit and currency in this country at such a level so that, to the extent that the volume has any influence upon prices, it cannot possibly become the means for either promoting speculative advances in prices, or of a depression of prices.

> Benjamin Strong, speech to the Farm Bureau Convention, December 13, 1922[56]

Although it rejected responsibility, the Fed was interested in price stability between 1921 and 1929. The low volatility of the price level was comparable with other steady-price periods of similar length. The gross national product deflator was about the same in 1929 as in 1921, and the average annual percentage change was about 2.4 percent, which was close to the experiences of 1885–93, 1902–10, 1951–59, and 1956–64. The method of monetary policy was a monetary base rule. In June 1923, Strong wrote the following to Professor Charles Bullock:

If I were Czar of the Federal Reserve System I'd see that the total of our earning assets did not go much above or below their past year's average, after deducting an amount equaling from time to time our total new gold imports.[57]

The czars of all the Russias might have envied Strong's power. Figure 7.2 shows that in every year from 1921 to 1929, except 1924, Fed credit tended toward the sterilization of gold flows.[58] British hopes that the United States would allow its large gold holdings to raise American prices and the exchange value of sterling were disappointed. The exception, which came during the 1923–24 recession, was interpreted by Lester Chandler, Strong's biographer, as deliberate countercyclical monetary policy, although Wicker could find no indication in their statements that Fed officials were concerned about the decline in output or believed they should do anything about it. "The program of security purchases begun at the December 3, 1923, meeting of the Open Market Investment Committee was designed originally to rebuild [by sales to offset gold inflows] a depleted investment portfolio."[59] Strong thought that "a suitable volume of Government securities of short maturities" was needed to put the Fed "in a position to exert an influence from time to time by the purchase and sale of such securities in the open market."[60]

---

[56] Chandler, *op. cit.*, p. 200.

[57] *Op. cit.*, p. 191.

[58] For a similar chart for 1922–26 by a New York Reserve Bank official, see Randolph Burgess, *The Reserve Banks and the Money Market*, p. 247.

[59] Wicker, *op. cit.*, p. 80.

[60] *Board Records*, Open Market Investment Committee, December 3, 1923, minutes. From Wicker, *op. cit.*, p. 80.

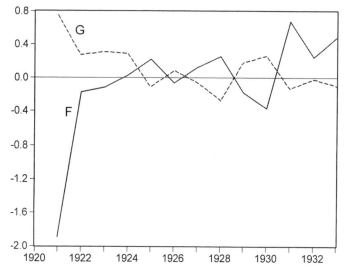

Figure 7.2. Changes in Federal Reserve credit (F) and U.S. official gold (G) (between end years; in billions of dollars), 1921–33. *Source:* Federal Reserve Board, *Banking and Monetary Statistics*, 1914–41, pp. 369–71.

On the other hand, Strong's advisor, Randolph Burgess, had written on November 30,[61]

> There would be very general agreement to the principle that the Reserve Banks should purchase securities at periods when liquidation in business seems to be going faster than fundamental conditions warrant, and that obversely we should sell securities when business is moving forward so rapidly that the tendency has become unduly speculative in nature.

However, Burgess was not sure that the situation was serious enough for the Fed's intervention. Figure 7.2 shows that the opposite movements of gold and Fed credit continued into the 1930s. The principal change from the 1920s was that the latter more than offset the former during 1931–33, and the monetary base rose by one-sixth, the largest increase since the war.

Some economists and legislators believed that price stability was the proper goal of monetary policy. That was Keynes's position in *A Tract on Monetary Reform*, and more rigidly Irving Fisher's in *Stabilizing the Dollar*. In 1922, Maryland Congressman Alan Goldsborough introduced a bill based on Fisher's advocacy of a "compensated dollar" that linked

---

[61] Memorandum to J. H. Case, Deputy Governor of the New York Reserve Bank, *Board Records*, Open Market Investment Committee, Wicker, *op. cit.*, p. 81.

the price of gold to an index of the price level. The bill did not attract much support at the time, but another effort by Goldsborough passed in the House in 1932 before failing in the Senate.

In an attempt aimed directly at the Federal Reserve, a 1926 bill would have required the discount rate to be set "with a view to accommodating commerce and promoting a stable price level for commodities in general." It stipulated that "all of the powers of the Federal reserve system shall be used for promoting stability in the price level."[62] Although Governor Strong and other Fed officials admitted the desirability of stable prices and the Fed's considerable impact on the price level, they resisted responsibility, believing that an unqualified, price-level goal conflicted with other goals, financial stability in particular. Strong wrote the following to Carl Snyder of his research staff in 1923:

Now I don't like to talk about stabilizing gold, the purchasing power of money, or prices being stabilized by the Federal Reserve System, at all. It is bound to lead to confusion, heartburn and headache. . . .

Our job is credit. It makes no difference if it's a deposit or a bank note. If we regulate and keep fairly constant the volume of this credit, – always with due regard to gold imports and exports, which is a part of the credit problem – we are doing our whole duty. Other price influences may then be dealt with by [secretary of commerce] Hoover, et al. They are not our job. Of course we should watch prices – and production and consumption and speculation, and lots of things – to insure that our "play" is correct in regulating volume. To come boldly forward, and volunteer to take the price problem onto our backs, and then *fail*, as we would surely do – is just criminal suicide.[63]

Strong elaborated on this point in congressional hearings. He stressed that "the amount of gold produced in the world has an effect upon prices," and he reminded congressmen of the informational and incentive problems of central banking. The "assumption that the Federal reserve system has powers of great magnitude in the control of prices ought to be considered not alone from the standpoint of economics, but from the standpoint of human nature to some extent." Even if it is assumed, he said, possibly thinking of the "quantity theory extremists" of which he sometimes complained, that the Fed "has the power to raise or lower the price level by some automatic method, by some magic mathematical formula, what safeguards are we going to introduce in regard to ignorance,

---

[62] H.R. 7895, 69th Congr., 1st sess, pp. 2338, 4301, January 18, 1926, February 20, 1926 (Krooss, *op. cit.*, p. 2667). The bill, which was similar to a provision in an early draft of the original Act (Willis, *op. cit.*, pp. 1585, 1605), was introduced on the former date and Congressman Strong's supporting speech came on the latter date.

[63] Chandler, *op. cit.*, pp. 202–3.

stupidity, and bad judgment in the exercise of this power? How are we to deal with the problem of divided counsels in the system, where no action is possible because of differences of opinion?" He also feared that such power would be the object of irresistible political pressures. What is the appropriate price index? The obligation to fix prices will be interpreted by each group as an obligation to "fix their prices."[64] Under "such a mandate," he had written to Professor Bullock in 1923, "within the past six months or so we would first have gone to jail for high sugar prices, and as soon as out on bail, been rearrested for low wheat prices (not to mention gasoline, building costs, wages, freight rates, professors' salaries and such like)."[65]

His fears seem justified when we examine the attitude of the proposer of the 1926 stable-price bill, Kansas Congressman James Strong, who seemed more interested in validating the war-time commodity inflation for his indebted constituents than in price stability. "Our yardstick has a stable number of inches and our money should be stabilized in its purchasing power," Chairman Strong told the House. "The price level now stands at 160, a drop from 251," referring to the wholesale price index at its peak in 1920 rather than the 160 of mid-1916 or the 100 of 1913.[66]

Sixty years later, in another agricultural depression, another Kansan urged that monetary policy be directed at the stabilization of a basket of commodity prices. At his "confirmation hearing before the Senate Banking Committee," Wayne Angell's "voice rose in indignation – nearly cracking at one point – when he described how sagging farm prices were affecting agricultural lenders. (He shared in the ownership of two small banks before joining the Fed.)" Angell had been a state legislator, and after failing in a bid for the Republican nomination to the United States Senate, Senate Majority Leader Robert Dole, also of Kansas, "vigorously lobbied the White House" for him as "a perfect candidate to represent agriculture on the Board."[67]

[64] U.S. Congress, *Stabilization*, 1926.

[65] Chandler, *op. cit.*, p. 203.

[66] *Congressional Record*, 69th Congr., 1st sess., January 18, 1926, pp. 4301–3. The supporting speeches of Loren Wheeler and William Arnold of Illinois also dwelt on farm problems.

[67] *Wall Street Journal*, April 24, 1986, p. 64. For more statements by and articles about Angell, see *Wall Street Journal*, April 24 and November 27, 1986; *American Banker*, May 27, 1992, and January 20, 1994; and *Forbes*, February 24, 1986. An editorial in the last agreed with Angell's contention that commodity prices were good predictors of inflation, but researchers were unable to find statistical corroboration; e.g., Thomas Fullerton, Richard Hirth, and Mark Smith, "Inflationary Dynamics and the Angell–Johnson Proposals," and Fred Furlong and Robert Ingenito, "Commodity Prices and Inflation."

Chairman Alan Greenspan followed in the footsteps of Benjamin Strong when he told a congressional committee, "We must . . . be wary of special factors that may affect the prices of individual commodity price averages significantly in the short run. Especially when the causes are of a transitory character – for example, a temporary supply disruption – the proper macroeconomic policy responses may well be different from those appropriate to major cyclical booms in commodity markets. For this reason the coverage of any index used in the international context should be broad."[68] Annual averages of the prices of farm products and fuel fell about 12 and 30 percent, respectively, between 1981 and 1986, the year of Angell's testimony, whereas the overall producer price index rose 2 percent, and the consumer price index and the gross national product deflator rose 23 percent.[69]

Conflicts in the Federal Reserve System

The major disputes between the Board and the Reserve Banks, especially the New York Bank, concerned the Fed's primary instruments: open market operations and discount rates. These are considered in turn.

Open Market Operations

The Reserve Banks were empowered to buy and sell U.S. securities and eligible bankers' acceptances and bills of exchange. However, that power was not exercised in connection with monetary policy (credit control) until the 1920s. Before 1922, their investments were made to support Treasury securities or bankers' acceptances, or for revenue. In May 1922, they agreed to coordinate their purchases and sales through a Committee of Governors on Centralized Execution of Purchases and Sales of Government Securities. Decisions were not binding, but cooperation was substantial, and not only in open market operations. The Committee's deliberations extended to credit policy in general, including discount rates.

Federal Reserve policy was coordinated, and the center was New York. The Board was determined to gain control. In April 1923, claiming the supervisory powers in Section 14 of the Federal Reserve Act, the Board declared the Governors Committee to be superseded by a new Open-Market Investment Committee of the Federal Reserve System, with the same membership and responsibilities but whose actions were to be regulated

---

[68] *Federal Reserve Bulletin*, February 1988, p. 104.
[69] U.S. Department of Commerce, *Business Statistics, 1963–91*.

by the Board. The Board declared that its supervision was necessary to assure compliance with the Federal Reserve Act, specifically,

that the time, manner, character and volume of open-market investments purchased by Federal Reserve Banks be governed with primary regard to the accommodation of commerce and business, and to the effect of such purchases or sales on the general credit situation.[70]

The Reserve Banks submitted, but they retained the option to undertake limited purchases and sales independently. Disagreements between the Reserve Banks and the Board regarding the scale of open market operations did not become serious until the 1929 crash. Before then, they fought over discount rates.

Discount Rates
Worries about stock market speculation increased, and in February 1929, despite weakness in general retail and wholesale prices, the New York Reserve Bank requested approval of an increase in its discount rate above the 5 percent that had been in effect since July. Preferring direct pressure, the Board wrote to the Reserve Banks that "a member bank is not within its reasonable claims for rediscount facilities at its Federal reserve bank when it borrows either for the purpose of making speculative loans or for the purpose of maintaining speculative loans." The Reserve Banks were asked to report "(a) as to how they keep themselves fully informed of the use made of borrowings by their member banks, (b) what methods they employ to protect their institution against the improper use of its credit facilities by member banks, and (c) how effective these methods have been."[71] The Bank governors repeated the old answers. They could not tell the uses of credit, whose price was the effective control.[72]

"At ten subsequent meetings" following their February 14 request, Friedman and Schwartz wrote, "the last on May 23, 1929, the New York Bank directors again voted to raise discount rates, each time requesting the Board to approve or disapprove the same day. Each time, the Board disapproved, though by a steadily narrowing margin – on February 14, the

---

[70] The quotations in this discussion are from the minutes of the Governors Conference in March 1923 as reported in Chandler, *op. cit.*, pp. 215–35, and Richard Youngdahl, "Open-Market Operations." Also see "Review of the Month," Federal Reserve *Bulletin*, May 1923.

[71] Federal Reserve Board *Annual Report*, 1929, p. 3; Friedman and Schwartz, *op. cit.*, p. 257.

[72] See the statements at the Governors' Conference of November 1919 quoted by Chandler, *op. cit.*, p. 156–57.

final vote by the Board was unanimously adverse; on May 23, the adverse vote was 5 to 3."[73]

Strong had died in 1928, and the New York Reserve Bank was led by his protégé, George Harrison, who campaigned directly by phone, telegraph, and meetings, and indirectly through the Treasury and other potential influences to get the Board to approve a rise in rates. He was supported by virtually the entire Federal Reserve System outside Washington. The Governors Conference and the Federal Advisory Council unanimously recommended higher rates.

Before the Board could be moved, however, signs of an economic slowdown caused the Reserve Banks to back away from their requests for higher rates. The stock market was still advancing rapidly, but on May 31, the New York Bank wrote the following to the Board: "In view of recent changes in the business and credit situation,... it may soon be necessary: To establish a less restrictive discount policy [and] be prepared to increase the Federal Reserve bank portfolios if and when any real need of doing so becomes apparent." The Board shared the desire to ease, and on August 9 it approved New York's compromise plan to raise its discount rate to 6 percent "as a warning against the excessive use of credit" and to encourage member banks to reduce their indebtedness to the Fed, but also to increase Fed credit by open market purchases. It was understood that no other Reserve Bank would raise its rate. The reasoning behind the plan seemed to be that a higher New York discount rate would check stock market speculation whereas open market purchases would reduce market rates and encourage business. This suggested to Wicker that "many officials did not understand that the method of injecting reserves did not determine the use to which reserves were put."[74] In the event, the rise in Fed credit was slight and interest rates were generally unchanged until after the October stock market crash.

Federal Reserve Knowledge and Incentives on the Eve of the Crash

The Fed has been criticized for not being ready with a policy model to combat the Great Depression. However, quite apart from the wide disagreements about the "right model" even after the event, Fed apologists might point to the System's rough consistency with respectable

---

[73] Friedman and Schwartz, *op. cit.*, p. 259.
[74] *Federal Reserve*, p. 143.

opinion at the time.[75] Fed officials were not alone in their sympathy with the liquidationist approach to contractions. Economic expansions tend to be associated with speculative accumulations of inventories and fixed and financial assets, and the 1928–29 boom was no exception. Lionel Robbins wrote in 1934 that "Both in the sphere of finance and in the sphere of production, when the boom breaks, these bad commitments are revealed. Now in order that revival may commence again, it is essential that these positions should be liquidated . . ."[76] His colleague at the London School of Economics, F. A. Hayek, wrote the following in 1932:[77]

It is a fact that the present crisis is marked by the first attempt on a large scale to revive the economy . . . by a systematic policy of lowering the interest rate accompanied by all other possible measures for preventing the normal process of liquidation, and that as a result the depression has assumed more devastating forms and lasted longer than ever before.

Adolph Miller of the Board testified to a Senate committee in 1931 that the Fed's easy-money response to the 1927 recession was

one of the most costly errors committed by it or any banking system in the last 75 years. I am inclined to think that a different policy at that time would have left us with a different condition at this time. . . . That was a time of business recession. Business could not use and was not asking for increased money at that time.[78]

Attempts to delay the needed liquidation would only result in more speculation, inflation, and, Governor George Norris of the Philadelphia Reserve Bank told the Open Market Committee in June 1930, "further increases in productive capacity and further overproduction."

The liquidationist position was countered by the price-stabilization goal. Strong's support of this goal in the 1920s forms a basis of the belief that the Federal Reserve would have pursued a vigorously expansive monetary policy after 1929 if he had lived.[79] But we have seen that his approach to monetary policy was not unequivocal. He thought the

---

[75] For the Keynesian-monetarist debate, see Peter Temin, *Did Monetary Forces Cause the Great Depression?*

[76] *The Great Depression*, p. 118.

[77] "The Fate of the Gold Standard." The quotations in this section are from David Wheelock (*The Strategy and Consistency of Federal Reserve Monetary Policy, 1924–33*), who summarizes the monetary theories of Fed officials before and during the Great Depression along with economists' critiques of their policies.

[78] Senate Committee on Banking and Currency, *Operation of the National and Federal Reserve Banking Systems*, p. 134.

[79] Irving Fisher, Hearings, House Committee on Banking and Currency, *Banking Act of 1935*, p. 534; Friedman and Schwartz, *op. cit.*, pp. 411–19.

1920–21 liquidation was beneficial and was not behind anyone in the Federal Reserve System in his commitment to the gold standard. The Fed's caution in 1930–32 has been linked to its concern for gold.[80] It is unlikely that Strong's survival would have broken that link. The Fed lost a courageous and enterprising leader when Strong died, but Wicker was more to the point when he wrote, "Lack of knowledge, not lack of courage, was the real explanation for the deficiencies in [the Fed's] policy."[81]

The narrow circumscription of the Board's knowledge and its interests and incentives must be laid at the door of the Fed's founders. Whatever the disadvantages of the Treasury, clearinghouses, and congressional monetary policy (and there is no guarantee that those pre-1913 arrangements would have made better decisions than the Federal Reserve in the 1930s) their histories admit little doubt that their policies at least would have been more responsive to business, consumers, and the electorate. Chicago Congressman A. J. Sabath would not have had to ask his colleagues, as he asked Chairman Eugene Meyer in 1931, "Does the board maintain that there is no emergency existing at this time?"[82]

---

[80] Barry Eichengreen, *Golden Fetters*.
[81] *Federal Reserve*, p. 94.
[82] From a letter entered into the *Congressional Record*, 71st Congr., 3rd sess., January 19, 1931, p. 2619.

EIGHT

The Fall and Rise of the Federal Reserve, 1929–1951

> The Federal Reserve Board was the primary agency of the Government in matters of banking and currency.... I concluded it was indeed a weak reed for a nation to lean on in time of trouble.
>
> Herbert Hoover, *Memoirs*, ii, pp. 210, 212

The Great Depression was the greatest economic disaster in American history, perhaps in the history of the industrial world. American production fell 30 percent between 1929 and 1933 and did not recover its previous high until 1939 (in annual averages). Unemployment rose from 1.5 million to 12.8 million, 25 percent of the labor force, and was still 8.1 million in 1940. Money and prices fell between a quarter and a third. Domestic investment and international trade fell more than one-half and did not recover until after the war.

Some have blamed the depth and length of the Great Depression on the Federal Reserve's failure to stop or moderate the decline in money. Others believe that the Fed's damage was small. They contend that the depression was initiated by a collapse in aggregate demand and that the fall in money was a consequence. However, nearly all agree that the Fed did not contest the downturn. Even for those who believe that money and credit cannot be forced, the Fed's sins of omission are great.

This chapter makes no attempt to settle this issue. The effects of the Fed's actions and inactions are not its primary concern. Rather, our interest lies in the reasons for the Fed's behavior. The case will be made that the organization established in 1913, consisting of a political body in Washington and bankers and former bankers in the urban centers, acted as might have been expected. Without censuring their humanity or sense

Background: People and Events

(International policies and events in Chap. 9.)

1929: Hoover becomes president with Republican majorities of 267–167 and 56–39 in the House and Senate, respectively. October stock crash.

1930: Election gives 220–214 Democratic majority in the House and 48–47 Republican majority in the Senate.

1932: *Glass–Steagall Act* and *Reconstruction Finance Corporation. Goldsborough Bill* to direct the Federal Reserve to use "all available means," including revaluing the gold content of the dollar, to maintain the price level passes in the House 289–60 but emasculated in the Senate.

1933: March: Bottom of contraction; from end of 1929, output, consumer prices, and money fell between 25% and 35%, stock prices fell 75%, short-term interest rates fell from 6% to 2%, unemployment rose from 1.5 to 13 million (of 49 million labor force) and 10,000 banks failed.

   March 4: Franklin Roosevelt becomes president with majorities of 310–117 and 60-35; Democrats hold majorities until the Republicans win both Houses in 1946.

   March 5: President declares private "hoarding" of monetary gold illegal, closes banks, and calls Congress to special session on March 9. The 99-day session enacts much of the New Deal: *Emergency Banking Act* ratifies actions taken under an emergency war-powers act, organizes Federal Open Market Committee (FOMC), allows Federal Reserve to lend to nonmembers, and establishes the Federal Deposit Insurance Corporation (FDIC); *Thomas Amendment* to *Agricultural Adjustment Act* authorizes the president to reduce the gold content of the dollar up to 50% and the Treasury to issue $3 billion in greenbacks (unbacked currency; the latter power is not used). *Joint Resolution* abrogates gold clauses in contracts.

1934: Gold devaluation of the dollar.

1935: *Banking Act* reorganizes Federal Reserve Board and FOMC, gives Board power over reserve requirements, and expands FDIC.

1936–37: Board doubles reserve requirements.

1937–38: Recession; after rising to its 1929 level, real GNP falls 12% between 1937:II and 1938:I.

1942: April: Federal Reserve announces Treasury bill peg at 3/8 of 1% (continued to June 1947). National debt rises from $48 to $240 billion, between 1941 and 1945, money stock rises from $46 to $98 billion. Because of wartime rationing and price controls, reported prices rise 25% between 1941 and 1945, and 32% the next two years.

1945: Gold backing of Federal Reserve notes reduced from 40% to 25% (eliminated in 1968).

1946: *Employment Act.*

1950: North Korea invades South Korea.

1951: March: Treasury–Federal Reserve Accord. April: General Douglas MacArthur fired.

	President of the United States	Secretary of the Treasury	Chairman of the Federal Reserve Board
1929	Herbert Hoover	Andrew Mellon	Roy Young
1930			Eugene Meyer
1932		Ogden Mills	
1933	Franklin Roosevelt	William Woodin	Eugene Black
1934		Henry Morgenthau, Jr.	Marriner Eccles
1945	Harry Truman	Fred Vinson	
1946		John Snyder	
1948			Thomas McCabe
1951			William McChesney Martin, Jr.

of public service, the agricultural wastelands and lines of hungry people that represented the Great Depression for most of the population did not weigh heavily on the Fed's decisions. The first section describes the Fed's immediate response to the crash of October 1929 and its responses – or lack thereof – to the events of the next three and one-half years. Consistent with the forecasts of critics in 1913 and its behavior in the 1920s, it focused on the financial markets.

The second section relates the responses of Franklin Roosevelt's administration to the failures of the Federal Reserve and of the monetary system in general. The dollar was devalued in 1934 and the New Deal severed gold's restraints. The government took control of monetary policy, a step that was also taken in Britain.

Power in the Federal Reserve System was moved toward the political center by the Banking Act of 1935, which was soon used to "mop-up" excess reserves to restrain speculation, although monetary policy was generally dominated by the Treasury from 1933 to 1951. The chapter concludes with the Fed's postwar battle for monetary control with an administration that regarded it as a source of cheap finance in peace as well as war.

After the Crash

What the Fed Did. . . .
The New York Reserve Bank responded vigorously to the crash. The Dow Jones Industrial Average had risen from 64 to 191 between August 1921 and February 1928, and it doubled the next 17 months to its peak in

early September 1929. The fall was orderly for a while, and on Saturday, October 26, the index closed at 299. Panic broke out on Monday, and in the greatest two-day crash in its history, the Dow plummeted to 212 at its low on Tuesday. The crash might have been worse according to the foremost monetary history of the Great Depression:

> The situation was greatly eased... by the willingness of the New York banks to take over the loans. In the first week after the crash, those banks increased their loans to brokers and dealers by $1 billion and the rest of their loans by $300 million.... Accordingly [they] had to and did acquire additional reserves,... partly by borrowing from the Federal Reserve Bank of New York, which in [Governor] Harrison's words, kept its "discount window wide open and let it be known that member banks might borrow freely to establish the reserves required against the large increase in deposits resulting from the taking over of loans called by others."
>
> Milton Friedman and Anna Schwartz, *A Monetary History of the United States, 1869–1960*, pp. 335, 339

After a 3 A.M. meeting with his directors, Governor Harrison informed the Stock Exchange Clearing Committee before it met to announce the call loan rate Tuesday morning that the New York Fed was prepared to buy $100 million of government securities. In the event, it bought $132 million, exceeding the amount authorized by the Open Market Investment Committee. Because of these "timely and effective" actions, according to Friedman and Schwartz, "there were no panic increases in money market rates such as those in past market crises, and no indirect effects on confidence in banks which might have arisen if there had been any sizable defaults on security loans." The market rallied to 230 by Tuesday's close and 274 on Thursday. Harrison defended New York's actions:[1]

> [I]t is not at all unlikely that had we not bought Governments so freely, thus supplementing the reserves built up by large additional discounts, the stock exchange might have had to yield to the tremendous pressure brought to bear upon it to close on some one of those very bad days, the last part of October.

The Board's Adolph Miller "was indignant" and said the banks should have been forced to discount. Fellow Board member Charles Hamlin was "inclined to agree with Miller but excused the New York bank on grounds that it was a critical emergency."[2] The majority of the Board acquiesced to New York's actions but did not wish to go further. It denied Harrison's

---

[1] Harrison papers, November 27, 1929, Milton Friedman and Anna Schwartz, *A Monetary History of the United States, 1867–1960*, p. 339.

[2] Hamlin *Diary*, Elmus Wicker, *Federal Reserve Monetary Policy*, p. 145.

request for purchases of $200 million to reduce member bank indebtedness to the Fed, and granted New York's request to cut its discount rate from 6 to 5 percent on the condition that it make no more open market purchases except with the Board's approval or in an emergency. Harrison protested to Board Chairman Roy Young "that more and more the Board has taken to itself not supervisory powers but the equivalent of operating functions and the responsibility for the detailed transactions of the various Federal reserve banks."[3]

I told him that the logical consequence of his point of view . . . was that the Federal Reserve Board would become a central bank operating in Washington . . . [H]is only comment was that the Federal Reserve Board had been given most extraordinarily wide powers, that as long as the Board had those powers, they would feel free to exercise them and Congress could determine whether they objected to having a central bank operating in Washington.

Open market purchases were limited to $25 million a week during November under authority from the Board given in September. Harrison finally got the Board's approval, by a 4-to-3 vote, for additional purchases in December, and bought $155 million that month. The effect on bank reserves was more than offset by a reduction in member bank borrowing from the Fed. By the end of the year, Federal Reserve credit had fallen 10 percent from the end of October and was one-eighth less than at the end of 1928. The increase in the last quarter of the year was the smallest since 1926, which had also marked the beginning of an economic downturn. However, no more open market purchases were permitted until March.

The Index of Industrial Production had peaked in July 1929, and after falling 4 percent the next three months, it dropped 10 percent in November and December. Nevertheless, at the January 28 meeting of the Open Market Policy Conference, eight Reserve Bank governors voted against Harrison's policy of "affirmative ease" through open market purchases. They thought loan liquidation should be allowed to proceed and that the Fed should not hasten the fall in money rates.[4]

This was consistent with the 1923 *Annual Report* and Miller's 1928 testimony (in Chap. 7) that although easy money might stimulate business in the early stages of an expansion, when credit was wanted, it would be wasted in a decline. Worse, it might lead to renewed speculation.

---

[3] Harrison papers, November 15, 1929, Friedman and Schwartz, *op. cit.*, p. 365.
[4] Wicker, *op. cit.*, pp. 147–48.

Nevertheless, the Board narrowly gave its approval in March for security purchases up to $50 million and another reduction in New York's discount rate. Miller was moved by Research Director Goldenweiser's "very pessimistic" summary of business conditions, which persuaded him that "the depression was much graver than he anticipated and [that] we ought to consider whether the System could not be helpful...."[5] However, this sentiment was neither general in the Federal Reserve System nor long-lived at the Board. When the Open Market Policy Conference met on March 24, most Reserve Bank governors declared the open market purchases "unwise," and they suggested that money rates had been eased too rapidly. New York's application for a reduction of its discount rate to 3 percent in April was unanimously refused by the Board for three reasons:[6]

1. There is no evidence of money not being available to business on reasonable terms, and no reason to believe that further reductions in rates will help to revive business.
2. Further ease in money would probably result in further increasing speculative activity. (New York bank loans to brokers are at the highest level on record.)
3. Gold is coming from the Orient and Brazil – not Europe. (Harrison was concerned that high interest rates in the United States might drain gold from Europe.)

A few days later, the Board voted 4 to 3 to approve New York's request after the Banks of England and France had cut their rates to 3 percent. Harrison vainly pressed for open market purchases through the summer of 1930, but by September he had come around to the position of the Board and the majority of the Reserve Banks. After a brief recovery in January, industrial production had fallen 13 percent between February and August, over half of that the last two months. Nevertheless, at the Open Market Policy Conference on September 25, Harrison voted with the 9-to-3 majority for the status quo. Permission was sought only for the purchases needed to offset gold exports.

The course of the depression may be seen in Fig. 8.1. The low interest rates throughout the decade reflect the lack of interest in credit and investment, which in 1939 was still almost 40 percent less than in 1929. The

[5] Hamlin *Diary*, Wicker, *op. cit.*, p. 150.
[6] Goldenweiser papers, April 24, 1930, Wicker, *op. cit.*, p. 151.

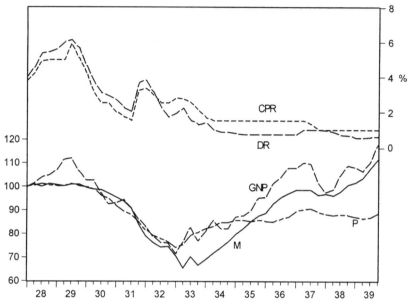

Figure 8.1. Real gross national product (GNP), price level (P), and money supply (M) (percentage of 1928); prime commercial paper rate (CPR) and Federal Reserve Bank of New York discount rate (DR) (quarterly average). *Sources:* Federal Reserve Board, *Banking and Monetary Statistics, 1914–41*; Gordon and Balke, appendix B.

temporary jump in rates at the end of 1931 was a response to the British departure from gold and fears of a liquidity crisis. The Federal Reserve's fears of speculation and inflation throughout the period must be seen in light of falling and then, after a brief rise, relatively stable prices, high unemployment, low interest and investment, and generous gold reserves. The monetary gold stock was near $4 billion throughout 1929–33, never falling below $3.5 billion, compared with $1.3 billion and $2.5 billion at the ends of 1913 and 1920, respectively.

Friedman and Schwartz attributed the Fed's failures during the Great Depression to an absence of leadership; they contrast the conviction and leadership qualities of Benjamin Strong with the modest bureaucratic qualities of his successor. After two years of strenuous efforts against the alternately active opposition and inertia of the majority, Harrison "reverted to his natural character, that of an extremely competent lawyer and excellent administrator, who wanted to see all sides of an issue and placed great value in conciliating opposing points of view and achieving harmony."[7]

This may underrate the man's determination and misjudge his purposes. Harrison fought the majority for a longer continuous period than Strong (with his delicate health) and did not rest in 1930 until his objective had been secured.

Based on accounts of the meetings of the New York Reserve Bank directors in 1930–31, they worried most about the bond and mortgage loan markets.[8] Their immediate objective was "to keep the member banks in the principal money markets of the country practically out of debt at the Federal Reserve Banks, and to preserve a condition of credit ease in those markets."[9] "It was Harrison's opinion," according to Wicker, "that so long as the New York member banks remained practically out of debt, there was no justification for forcing further funds upon the market. To this position he adhered unswervingly throughout 1930 and 1931."

From an average of (in millions) $329 in July 1929, the discount window borrowing of New York City banks fell to $9 in July 1930.[10] The change for Chicago banks was from $48 to zero, and for the 62 Reserve cities it was from $399 to $36. Country bank borrowing remained high whereas that of the money centers was small during the rest of the depression.

The Federal Reserve was quiet after its immediate reaction to the October 1929 crash until after the inauguration of the new president in 1933, except for two short bursts. The first followed Britain's suspension of convertibility on September 21, 1931, and the hike in Bank rate to 6 percent. A number of financial crises in 1931 – including the failure of Austria's Kredit Anstalt in May, the closing of Germany's banks for two days in July, and the acceleration of American bank failures between February and August – increased the restlessness of gold, and several countries were compelled to accompany Britain off the gold standard. The big gainers of gold were France, Belgium, the Netherlands, and Switzerland, all who stayed on gold. The biggest loser was the United States, having its gold reserve reduced from $4.7 to $4.2 billion between August and the end of

---

[7] Friedman and Schwartz, *op. cit.*, p. 414.

[8] Wicker, *op. cit.*, p. 153.

[9] *Harrison Papers*, Discussion Notes, i, memorandum of meetings of Board of Directors, July 17, 1930; Wicker, *op. cit.*, p. 153.

[10] Unless otherwise indicated, the bank and monetary data used here are from Federal Reserve Board, *Banking and Monetary Statistics, 1914–41*; Friedman and Schwartz, *op. cit.*; and U.S. Bureau of the Census, *Historical Statistics of the United States*.

the year, although it was still above $3.9 billion at the end of 1929. The gold movements might be seen as the capture of their share of the recent increases in the world's gold stock by the European countries committed to gold. Eighty percent of the $1 billion increase in the world's monetary gold between December 1929 and August 1931 came to the United States. By early 1932 America's gold reserve had fallen back to the $4 billion average of the late 1920s, where it remained until the 1934 devaluation.

The New York Fed raised its discount rate from $1\frac{1}{2}$ to $2\frac{1}{2}$ percent on October 9, 1931, and to $3\frac{1}{2}$ percent on the 16th, quickly followed by the other Reserve Banks. Discounting had begun to rise in August, and by the end of the year had risen from about $200 million to $1 billion. The $800 million increase in Federal Reserve credit more than offset the $500 million gold loss, but not enough to offset the $700 million increase in the public's currency holdings. The public did not seem worried about the gold standard, that is, the solvency of the Treasury or the Federal Reserve. There was no run on gold. However, they were mightily concerned about the solvency of banks, especially small banks. Member banks lost 35 percent of their reserves between August and December 1931. The smallest losses were for New York City at 13 percent; the largest were 47 percent for the country banks. Two-thirds of these losses were replaced by discounts at the Fed, which continued to grow for the shrinking country banks. New York City banks, in contrast, had recovered their reserves by May 1932 while repaying their debts to the Fed. This is not to say that all was well in New York. A quarter of its 48 banks failed between mid-1931 and mid-1932, and assets and liabilities fell in the same proportion. The city's excess reserves rose from 1 percent to 30 percent of its total reserves.

Its actions the last part of 1931 were explained by the New York Reserve Bank in a paper prepared for the Open Market Policy Conference on November 30:[11]

In the past three months the United States has gone through an extraordinary financial crisis in which were combined the largest gold export movement in the history of the country and a heavy domestic withdrawal of currency continuing a movement of almost a year's duration. These foreign and domestic drains upon bank reserves were met in the classic way by increases in discount rates combined with a policy of free lending. This is the method of meeting such an emergency described by Walter Bagehot in his *Lombard Street* in the following terms: "Whatever persons – one bank or many banks – in any country holding the

---

[11] Wicker, *op. cit.*, p. 165.

banking reserve of that country, ought at the very beginning of an unfavorable foreign exchange at once to raise the rate of interest ... "

High-sounding words, but the Fed's response to the internal drain was half-hearted. The following spring, Congressman James Strong suggested to Board Chairman Eugene Meyer (who had replaced Young in September 1930) that "if we had commenced along in October or November and bought Government securities, would we not have been apt to have checked those failures that happened in January and prevented the recession in bank credits?" It was not as easy as that, Meyer replied,

There were so many other complications, Mr. Strong; ... Within a few weeks after September 21, $750,000,000 was withdrawn by foreign countries from their balances here and taken in the form of gold. No country in the history of the world has ever been able to stand that kind of drain of gold ... [The] purchase of securities by the reserve banks at that time were impracticable. We could not undertake anything of that character in October without increasing the loss of gold.... You will remember at that time we had to raise the discount rate from $1\frac{1}{2}$ to $2\frac{1}{2}$ and $3\frac{1}{2}$ percent. Purchases at that time would not have had a stabilizing effect. They would have tended to neutralize the effect of the advances in the discount rate, which was an important intrinsic and also an important psychological factor at that time.

The occasion of this exchange was a renewal of the efforts of some members of the House Banking and Currency Committee to commit the Federal Reserve to price stabilization.[12] Congressman Goldsborough submitted a bill to that effect and chaired hearings in March and April 1932. Committee member Strong pressed the case to Meyer:

You know I have a great deal of confidence in your judgment ... ; but I do think, in the operation and use of these powers of the Federal reserve system, ... we should give them a measure to follow. For instance, I think ... we should direct them to use their powers toward stabilization of the purchasing power of money ...

Now I want to ask you this question: The Reconstruction Finance Corporation and the Glass–Steagall bill have for their purposes the enlargement of the credit structure so as to bring more credit into use, and in a manner an inflation, or what probably you might term a reflation of the deflation; is that not as practical a thing as if we directed you to use the powers to stabilize the purchasing power of money?

Meyer would not be pinned down, and alluded to the uncertain effects of any particular course. Strong then connected reports of an end of the fall in bank credit to the Fed's new policy of open market purchases.

---

[12] U.S. House of Representatives, *Stabilization of Commodity Prices*, Hearings.

"If . . . you keep on buying $25,000,000 a week, a turn will probably come, will it not?" Meyer resisted the implied cause and effect and raised various difficulties, finally saying, "I do not think we can do anything more than we are doing. . . . "

The other burst of Federal Reserve activity was prodded by the president and Congress. Hoover had not called a special session (although he met congressional leaders in October) but when Congress convened in December 1931, he declared that "the time is ripe for forward action to expedite our recovery" and submitted an 18-point legislative program.[13] The necessity of a balanced federal budget was first in the president's plans – as it would be in Roosevelt's 1932 presidential campaign – but the bulk of his program sought to promote credit while taking care of the gold standard. The Reconstruction Finance Corporation and loan programs for farms, home mortgages, relief, and public works were slaps at the failure of the Federal Reserve, which was encouraged to act by relaxing eligibility requirements for discounting. Hoover also wished to authorize the Fed "to expand credit further by open market operations and lowered discount rates so as to counteract the credit stringencies caused by foreign withdrawals. While we knew that Reserve action had been futile in stopping booms, we hoped it might have some effect by expanding credit in depression."

Little love was lost between the president and Congress, but Hoover got most of his program, including the parts dealing with monetary policy.[14] Both wanted an expansion of credit, although Hoover thought Congress had insufficient regard for the gold standard. "Added to the sabotage and delays of our constructive financial measures were the bills passed or introduced from the opposition side tinkering with the currency" including the Goldsborough plan, which he derided as the "rubber dollar."[15]

A meeting with Harrison, Meyer, and congressional leaders led to the Glass–Steagall Act in February 1932 ("to improve the facilities of the Federal reserve system [and] to provide means for meeting the needs of member banks in exceptional circumstances"[16]), which might have become as memorable as the government's letter to the Bank of England

[13] Herbert Hoover, *Memoirs*, pp. 97–100.
[14] For Hoover's relations with Congress, see his *Memoirs*, pp. 100–6, and David Burner, *Herbert Hoover*, p. 257.
[15] Hoover, *op. cit.*, p. 119.
[16] Herman Krooss, *Documentary History of Banking and Currency in the United States*, p. 2672.

in 1847 if the Fed had applied it with enthusiasm. Significant open market purchases did not begin until April, six weeks after the passage of the Act, and were accompanied by a decline in Fed discounting.

> Harrison told the executive committee of his directors on April 4 that apparently "the only way to forestall some sort of radical financial legislation by Congress is to go further and faster with our own program." When Harrison reported to a full meeting of his directors on April 7 that the executive committee of the Open Market Policy Conference was deeply divided about the wisdom of accelerating the purchase program, and had voted to continue the existing program [of $25 million a week], one of the directors asked "if a more vigorous program on the part of the Federal Reserve System would not be helpful in defeating the Thomas bonus bill [to be financed by fiat money] and other similar legislation. Governor Harrison said that Senator Thomas had indicated to him that he might be satisfied not to press for congressional action if the System would proceed more vigorously." The Bank directors accordingly voted to have the Bank, subject to the approval of the Board, buy for its own account up to $50 million of Government securities, outside the System account and before the meeting of the Conference, which was set for April 12.
>
> Friedman and Schwartz, *A Monetary History of the United States*, pp. 384–85, Harrison papers

Chairman Meyer reminded participants of a joint meeting of the Open Market Policy Conference and the Board that the Senate had before it a resolution asking the Board to state its program. Pressure also came from the administration. Treasury Secretary Ogden Mills, succeeding the cautious Andrew Mellon in February 1932, had complained, "For a great central banking system to stand by with a 70% gold reserve without taking active steps in such a situation was almost inconceivable and almost unforgivable."[17] The Fed increased its holdings of government securities from (in millions) $885 on April 6 to $1,801 on June 29, an average increase of $76 a week.[18] Then they rose about $8 a week until reaching $1,851 on August 10, where they remained until the end of the year. Congress had adjourned July 16.

...And Why

The Fed's timidity between 1929 and 1933 has been blamed on the loss of Governor Strong. Irving Fisher testified to Congress in 1935 and Friedman and Schwartz wrote in 1963 that Strong had vigorously pursued price stability in the 1920s by neutralizing gold flows, and they pointed to New

---

[17] Friedman and Schwartz, *op. cit.*, p. 385.

[18] Based on Wednesday figures as reported in *Banking and Monetary Statistics*, p. 386.

York's aggressive open market purchases in the recessions of 1924 and 1927.[19] They believed that Strong's death had removed the intellectual architect and the driving personality behind the pursuit of stability in the 1920s.

Wicker and Karl Brunner and Allan Meltzer argued that these views of Strong and Fed policy in the 1920s were too simple.[20] Price and economic stability were desired, but policy responded to other factors as well. The general outline of the Fed's actions during the Great Depression differed little from those of the 1920s. The Fed continued to neutralize gold flows through open market operations (Fig. 7.2) and took the price level into account. That its actions were not sufficient to offset the tremendous internal drain is obvious, but this suggests continuity, albeit unfortunate, rather than the opposite. The "period between 1922 and 1933," Wicker wrote, "reveals a record of fundamental consistency and harmony with no sharp breaks in either the logic or interpretation of monetary policy."[21] That consistency is found in what Wicker called the "Strong rule," which was expressed at a Governors' Conference in April 1926:

As a guide to the timing and extent of any purchases which might appear desirable, one of the best guides would be the amount of borrowing by member banks in principal centers, and particularly in New York and Chicago. Our experience has shown that when New York City banks are borrowing in the neighborhood of $100 million or more, there is then some real pressure for reducing loans, and money rates tend to be markedly higher than the discount rate. On the other hand, when borrowings of these banks are negligible, as in 1924, the money situation tends to be less elastic and if gold imports take place, there is liable to be some credit inflation.... In the event of business liquidation now appearing it would seem advisable to keep the New York City banks out of debt beyond something in the neighborhood of $50 million. It would probably be well if some similar rule could be applied to the Chicago banks, although the amount would, of course, be smaller and the difficulties greater because of the influence of the New York market.[22]

---

[19] U.S. House of Representatives, *Banking Act of 1935*, p. 534; Friedman and Schwartz, *op. cit.*, pp. 407–19. See David Wheelock, "Monetary Policy in the Great Depression," for a summary.

[20] Karl Brunner and Allan Meltzer, "What Did We Learn from the Monetary Experience of the U.S. in the Great Depression?," and Wicker, "Brunner and Meltzer on Federal Reserve Monetary Policy during the Great Depression."

[21] Wicker, "Brunner and Meltzer on the Federal Reserve." Wicker and Brunner and Meltzer part company over the latter's claim that the "Strong rule" was the only policy guide. Wicker believed that gold also played a part.

[22] Wicker, "Brunner and Meltzer on the Federal Reserve" and *Federal Reserve*, p. 330; Lester Chandler, *Benjamin Strong, Central Banker*, p. 240.

The Strong rule was applied in 1924, 1927, and, as we have seen, 1930. It is difficult to see how Harrison could have been more faithful to Strong's legacy. The Fed came to the assistance of the money markets in the wake of the crash, and when that assistance was no longer required, that is, when the New York and Chicago banks were out of debt to the Fed, it was ended. Of the other occasions of the Fed's arousal, late 1931 was a traditional response to an external gold drain and the spring of 1932 was under political duress.

That the Federal Reserve was not unaware of the wider economy is clear from the Board's 1923 *Annual Report* and Governor Strong's discussions of price levels. Continuity in policy, however, is to be found in money market conditions – in what the decision makers saw and felt. They were in behavior, if not quite in words, like the Bank of England directors a century before. Fed officials did not go as far as the Bank directors in denying the macroeconomic influences of their actions. However, when they – Strong not excepted – were pressed to take responsibility, they found so many other effects, outside their control, that their own powers seemed almost insignificant. This was not so with money market conditions. In April 1932, Congressman Thomas Jefferson Busby of Mississippi urged the Fed "to cooperate with Congress, and launch out and shake off some of its fears about what might happen" if it tried to stop the deflation.

I do not know whether you know it or not, but about one-fourth of the homes in my state have been sold for taxes during the present month.... Sixty thousand homes, 7,000,000 acres of land, one-fourth of all the property, because the people can not pay taxes; and when people get in that kind of condition, they can not ... listen to fine-spun theories of fears that might arise in the event you took some step forward.

Gov. Harrison – Of course, you know Mr. Congressman, that up until the end of February we did not have capacity to do what you wanted us to do. Now, then, if you have any criticism of us, I think it is only since the 1st of March.

Mr. Goldsborough – I do not think that is hardly fair, Governor, for this reason: That the Federal Reserve Board were urged to help Congress pass such legislation long before last February.[23]

Perhaps further legislation was needed?

Mr. Harrison – I do not think there is any necessity for further legislation at the present time, if we could assume that the provisions of the Glass–Steagall bill are permanent, rather than limited to one year. That is unavoidably a restraining influence, certainly, on some of the managers of the system.

---

[23] U.S. Congress, hearings on *Stabilization of Commodity Prices*, pp. 492–93.

Mr. Busby – If you drive right up to the time when you need it, when you need any extension, Congress will be in session next year . . .

The congressman said that, considering the large gold reserve, "I can not understand . . . the Federal Reserve Board taking such hesitant uncertain or undeclared attitudes toward tackling the economic depression with which we are overwhelmed."

Mr. Harrison – But you have got to remember one other thing, Mr. Congressman. There is always difficulty about the mechanics and the speed with which we operate. First of all, it is not always easy, over a certain number of days, to buy as many Government securities as you might want. They are most popular investments and they are sometimes hard to get, and without completely disorganizing the market you sometimes can not purchase them as rapidly as you want them.

. . . you run the risk, if you go too fast, of flooding the market or the banks with excess reserves faster than they can use them, or faster than is wise for them to use them. The proper and orderly operation of the open market, I think, is to create a volume of excess reserves gradually, gradually increasing them, and keeping it up constantly, and not have periods when you have got excess reserves one week and none another week.[24]

This focus on the money market explains the Fed's neglect of the banking crises of the Great Depression. The first three crises identified by Friedman and Schwartz occurred in late 1930, mid-1931, and following Britain's departure from gold in September 1931. They believed that "under the pre-Federal Reserve banking system, the final months of 1930 would probably have seen a restriction, of the kind that occurred in 1907, of convertibility of deposits into currency. By cutting the vicious circle set in train by the search for liquidity, restriction would almost certainly have prevented the subsequent waves of bank failures that were destined to come in 1931, 1932, and 1933." They found the Fed's neglect of these crises culpable because correct, "lender-of-last resort," actions called for "the policies outlined by the System itself in the 1920s, or for that matter by Bagehot in 1873."[25]

Wicker's study of the timing and geographical incidence of these failures in *The Banking Panics of the Great Depression* raises a problem with this analysis, specifically that the crises of the 1930s were not primarily (the first two not at all) liquidity crises; and were unrelated to the money markets. We have seen how readily the New York Fed supplied funds to the money market in October 1929 and September 1931. The

---

[24] *Ibid.*, pp. 494–95.
[25] Friedman and Schwartz, *op. cit.*, pp. 311, 407.

banking crises to which Friedman and Schwartz refer were problems of solvency, not liquidity. Banks in the interior – primarily small rural banks – failed because their borrowers failed. The prices of farm products fell 17, 27, and 25 percent in 1930, 1931, and 1932, respectively. It is misleading to point to subperiods as special "crises." The problem was ongoing. Although the failure rate was not constant, the three crises of 1930–31 accounted for just forty percent of failures during 1930–32.[26] Furthermore, they were geographically concentrated. None became national in scope or exerted significant pressure on, not to say panic in, the New York money market.

We might as well have asked the 19th-century Bank of England to pour money into Lancashire banks made insolvent by a depression in textiles. The Fed might be held accountable for the bank failures of the 1930s because of its failure to resist the deflation, but it cannot reasonably be blamed for failing to perform as lender of last resort, which is concerned with the liquidity of the money market.[27]

The 1933 Bank Holiday was a special case. Although the failure rate was still high at the beginning of the year, it was declining and there was reason to hope for stability until the governor of Michigan declared a bank holiday on February 14 to protect other banks from the run that he feared might follow the collapse of the Guardian Detroit Group, which had also been heavily invested in real estate.

Michigan banks wanted the Fed's support to reopen. However, when the First National Bank of Detroit approached the Chicago Reserve Bank for a loan that would enable it to pay 50 percent of deposits upon reopening, Chicago officials refused on the grounds that the granting of a loan to a closed bank, which might not reopen, would "establish a dangerous precedent." Resources should be conserved for active banks. Furthermore, they did not want to be associated with a plan that limited depositor claims.

The Michigan holiday quickly affected contiguous states. Cleveland banks suffered heavy withdrawals, and they began to pay out deposits on a *pro rata* basis, a practice that was legalized by the Ohio legislature on February 28. By the time Roosevelt was inaugurated on March 4, banks

---

[26] More precisely, 42 percent of the failures occurred in 29 percent of the months (11/30–1/31; 4/31–8/31; 9/31–10/31) of 1930–31. On the other hand, 60 percent of the deposits of failed banks are found in these three crisis periods. See tables 1.1, 2.2, and 3.1 in Wicker, *Banking Panics of the Great Depression.*

[27] Walter Bagehot, *Lombard Street*, pp. 43–74.

had been closed or deposits had been restricted in all 48 states. However, as Wicker writes,

[There was] no evidence of a credit squeeze in the New York money market during the 1933 crisis. New York City banks were flush with liquidity and were reluctant converts to a bank moratorium. Large Chicago banks were equally loath to request a moratorium. That is not to say that there were not considerable strains placed on the Chicago banks.... There were runs on outlying banks and huge withdrawals [from] Loop banks in anticipation of a moratorium. Credit nevertheless was available in the New York and Chicago money markets throughout the crisis at reasonable rates.

Wicker, *Banking Panics of the Great Depression*, p. 132

Short-term interest rates, which had been near 1 percent since the previous summer, jumped to 3 and 4 percent, but these were hardly panic rates. "Governor Harrison and the New York Fed deserve credit for having exercised initiative in preventing a panic in the New York money market by supplying needed reserves through the bill market when security purchases were not feasible ... "[28]

Why Didn't Somebody Do Something?

The inactivity of the Federal Reserve in the face of catastrophic deflation can be traced to the structure of the organization as it was created in 1913. The agency to which Congress had delivered its responsibility for monetary matters was true to its own interests and perceptions. The New York Fed was sensitive to its immediate surroundings, the money market, and so was the Board, but neither felt much political pressure after the end of the bond-support program in 1921.

The question remains why other branches of government did not intervene. The 71st and 72nd Congresses (1929–33) were probably no more divided on monetary matters than the 43rd (1873–75) and 53rd (1893–95), but the 19th-century bodies adopted strong monetary measures, the former by committing to a date for resumption and the latter by reversing its Democratic predilections when earlier silver legislation threatened the monetary standard. These were sound-money actions. In contrast, the Republican 39th and 40th Congresses, which favored sound money *in principle*, yielded, as we saw, to "the great hosts" of debtors and creditors "outside of banking and financial centers," to slow Secretary McCulloch's application of the Contraction Act. These actions were much different

---

[28] Wicker, *Banking Panics of the Great Depression*, p. 137.

from those of 1932, when the possibility of "disorganizing the [bond] market" prevented the Federal Reserve's relief of Mr. Busby's constituents.

Significant groups, especially in the House, sought action. Over 50 bills to increase money and prices were introduced in the 72nd Congress, and although none became law their defeats narrowed with time and deflation.[29] Senator Glass, founder and then defender of the Federal Reserve System (except when secretary of the treasury), to whom his colleagues deferred on money matters, resisted reform. He reluctantly assented to the president's initiative at the end of 1931 to relax some of the credit restrictions in the Federal Reserve Act only after Hoover brought in Chairman Meyer.[30] In the scales between sound and easy money, a significant weight in the form of the Federal Reserve Act was placed on the side of the former.

From a detached intellectual viewpoint, this outcome was not inevitable. The Federal Reserve had been assigned macroeconomic objectives, which it recognized in the 1920s. The operation of the 19th-century gold standard did not imply the sacrifice of prosperity to convertibility. Hoover's efforts to promote credit expansion by the Fed or, failing that, through new agencies, while preaching sound money, a balanced budget, and commitment to the gold standard, was in the classical tradition as applied by Grover Cleveland in 1893. We do not know what Hoover would have done when the crunch came, but his statements and actions, like the British government's in 1847, did not preclude – almost invited – suspension if required by economic and electoral pressures. In the absence of the Fed, the president and Congress might have felt a greater urgency to take charge of monetary affairs.

The Treasury Takes Charge

The End of the Gold Standard
During the Goldsborough hearings in April 1932, Congressman Busby warned Governor Harrison[31] that

the policy of the Federal Reserve Board is going to do more to pass the payment of the bonus bill, to put the currency in the field, blindly, or some other way, than any other thing that can be done to present the cause of the bonus claimants. [Y]our careful policy may be the very means of Congress passing out some other

---

[29] Krooss, *op. cit.*, pp. 2661–62.
[30] Hoover, *op. cit.*, pp. 116–17.
[31] U.S. Congress, *Stabilization*, 1932, part 2, p. 492.

kind of a command to the Treasury to do something to take the place of the inactivity of the Federal Reserve Board. I am just giving you . . . the sentiment in the House, and they have practically argued the bonus bill through and sold it to the members, who do not have one particle of concern about the payment of the bonus to the soldiers, but they are demanding, and are going to drive through the Congress, legislation which will put currency in the field, so that business can have an opportunity to have it in the future.

These careful policies do not appeal to people who are hungry, when the policies are not getting anybody anywhere.

The fundamental conditions of monetary policy are seldom determined by central banks. Choices of the monetary standard, the structure of the banking system, and the right of issue have belonged to legislatures, with central banks being charged with the day-to-day operation of the standard, until it was taken away in the 1930s. The political effects of the perceived failure of the Bank of England after World War I and the Federal Reserve's in the Great Depression were similar, both derived from their distances from the effects of their policies, and so were their punishments.

"Before the outbreak of the War," a former British Treasury official recollected in 1929, "we certainly never regarded ourselves as entitled to meddle or even ask questions" of the Bank's actions. A colleague remembered that a "change in bank rate was no more regarded as the business of the Treasury than the colour with which the Bank painted its front door."[32] This separation was eroded by World War I, but its energetic devotion to the restoration of sterling made the Bank the government's senior partner after the war. The pain associated with this policy and its collapse in the suspension of convertibility in 1931 led the Treasury to take control of monetary policy, including Bank rate, and the Bank receded from actor to adviser.

This did not happen immediately. The increase in Bank rate to 6 percent that came with the suspension was a conventional central bank response to an external drain. Six weeks later, Governor Norman told the Committee of the Treasury (the senior directors of the Bank) that the rate would have to stay at its crisis level "for some time," although his goal of *de facto* stabilization of the pound at some unstated level might be reached only in "gradual steps over a long period."[33] Conditions improved in the new

---

[32] John Bradbury and Otto Niemeyer, quoted by Peter Clarke, *The Keynesian Revolution in the Making*, p. 35.
[33] R. S. Sayers, *The Bank of England, 1891–1944*, pp. 417, 423.

year, and the reductions that began in February, reaching 2 percent on June 30, 1932, were traditional responses to a gold inflow. The outflow at the end of the year brought no increase in Bank rate, however. The era of cheap money (2 percent) had begun, and it was understood that future changes in Bank rate and other monetary policies would be decided by the chancellor. The new relationship was made clear by the chancellor, Neville Chamberlain, in the House of Commons in December 1934: "Now that we are not on the gold standard, of course, the relationship between the Treasury and the Bank of England has to be necessarily closer than ever."[34]

Recrossing the Atlantic, we see that the same withdrawal of operating authority from the American central bank was accompanied by more fireworks. As soon as he took office on March 4, 1933, President Roosevelt issued a series of proclamations that closed and reopened the banks and ended the internal circulation of gold. The first orders used emergency powers granted in World War I, and to remove doubt of the legality of the actions, the Emergency Banking Act of March 9, 1933, provided the following:

During time of war or during any other period of national emergency declared by the President, the President may, through any agency that he may designate, ... investigate, regulate, or prohibit, under such rules and regulations as he may prescribe, by means of licenses or otherwise, any transactions in foreign exchange, transfers of credit between or payments by banking institutions as defined by the President, and export, hoarding, melting, or earmarking of gold or silver coin or bullion or currency, by any person within the United States or any place subject to the jurisdiction thereof....[35]

On April 5, the president declared private gold to be "hoarding" and required its delivery to the Federal Reserve by May 1. The retention of an international gold standard that conserved reserves by forbidding their internal use was similar to Ricardo's Ingot Plan, that had been adopted temporarily by Britain in the Resumption Act of 1819 and permanently in the Gold Standard Act of 1925.

The Thomas Amendment to the Agricultural Adjustment Act of May 12, 1933, gave the president powers to issue currency, direct Federal Reserve open market operations, "fix the weights of gold and silver dollars

[34] Edward Nevin, *The Mechanism of Cheap Money*, p. 111. The relationship was confirmed by Norman at the Lord Mayor's dinner in 1936 (*Times*, October 7, Nevin, *op. cit.*, pp. 111–12) and in Parliament on November 8, 1939 (Sayers, *op. cit.*, p. 573).

[35] Krooss, *op. cit.*, p. 2697.

at such amounts as he finds necessary" (except not to reduce the gold value of the dollar more than 50 percent), and accept silver in payment of foreign government debts for a period of six months up to an aggregate of $200 million "whenever he finds [among other reasons] that an economic emergency requires an expansion of credit."[36] A Senate resolution instructed American delegates to a forthcoming London conference to "work unceasingly for an international agreement to remonetize silver on a basis of a definite fixed ratio of not to exceed 16 fine ounces of silver to one fine ounce of gold."

The dollar fell on currency markets, and in July the dollar/sterling rate reached 4.86\frac{1}{2}$, the traditional level that had prevailed before the British suspension of 1931, compared with $3.40 in early March. Commodity prices crept upward from their trough in February, but both the exchange rate and prices faltered as the summer progressed, and the administration decided to intervene in the gold market. Instead of leaving this traditional central banking function to the Federal Reserve, the Reconstruction Finance Corporation was assigned to manipulate the price of gold "after consultation with the Secretary of the Treasury and the President."[37]

In a Fireside Chat on October 22, 1933, the President said that the government's gold operations were part of a policy "to restore" commodity price levels. "The object has been the attainment of such a level as will enable agriculture and industry once more to give work to the unemployed.... This is a policy and not an expedient. It is not to be used merely to offset a temporary fall in prices. We are thus continuing to move toward a managed currency." A permanent revaluation of the dollar would wait until "we have restored the price level," after which "we shall seek to establish and maintain a dollar which will not change its purchasing and debt-paying power during the succeeding generation." In fact, the "permanent revaluation" came soon thereafter in the president's proclamation of January 31, 1934, that fixed the value of gold at $35 an ounce, compared with the traditional $20.67.

The president had scuttled the main agenda of the World Monetary and Economic Conference held in London in June and July 1933 to consider ways of restoring international trade and finance. Midway through the conference he sent a wire reflecting his paramount concern for domestic reflation: "The sound internal economic system of a nation is a greater

---

[36] *Ibid.*, pp. 2719–22.
[37] G. G. Johnson, *The Treasury and Monetary Policy, 1933–38*, p. 23.

factor in its well being than the price of its currency in . . . terms of the currencies of other nations."[38] However, the American delegation led by Senator Key Pittman of Nevada procured a "silver pact" by which the principal silver-producing countries agreed to absorb 140 million ounces of silver during the next four years, at least 70 percent by the United States.

The president's bold proclamations notwithstanding, the administration was more conservative than Congress. The authors of the unsuccessful inflationary bills of 1932 had returned, and they pressed Roosevelt for action. They took his campaign promises seriously, especially the promise to do something for silver. The bloc of 16 senators from the silver-producing states had enough support from agriculture and other inflationists to pass the Silver Purchase Act of June 1934 by majorities of 263–77 and 55–25 in the House and Senate, respectively. "It is hereby declared," the Act stated, "to be the policy of the United States that the proportion of silver to gold in the monetary stocks of the United States should be increased, with the ultimate objective of having and maintaining one-fourth of the monetary value of such stocks in silver." Its setbacks the last century had not killed the silver movement. When Secretary of the Treasury Henry Morgenthau, Jr., himself a farmer and publisher of the *American Agriculturist* and originally brought to Washington to develop the Farm Credit Administraton, asked Senator Henry Ashurst why silver was so important to him, the Arizona Democrat replied, "My boy, I was brought up from my mother's knee on silver, and I can't discuss that any more with you than you can discuss your religion with me."[39]

Morgenthau was an early advocate of reflation, but within limits, and he wanted Treasury control. The administration negotiated with congressional leaders to make the silver-purchase provisions in the Act permissive instead of prescriptive, although the Treasury found it politically necessary to buy 1.6 billion ounces of silver at prices substantially above those prevailing in world markets during the next four years, adding $1 billion to the monetary base. The program was not ended by Congress until 1963, but purchases after 1937 were small, and the Treasury's silver never approached the ratio to gold required by the Act.[40]

---

[38] *New York Times*, July 4, 1933, p. 1; Esther Taus, *Central Banking Functions of the U.S. Treasury*, p. 201.

[39] John Blum, *Roosevelt and Morgenthau*, p. 92.

[40] See Friedman and Schwartz, *op. cit.*, pp. 483–91, for a history of the silver purchase program; and Blum, *op. cit.*, chap. 4, for Morgenthau's role.

The administration became less strident in the international arena. The Exchange Stabilization Fund had been created with a good deal of nationalistic bombast about the need for protection against British designs on "driving the dollar up" and so retarding American recovery.[41] However, international cooperation became more important with war on the horizon. The sterling rate of exchange reached $5 at the end of 1933 and was kept within 4 percent of that value until late 1938, when it began to fall toward the $4.03 level that would be maintained from 1940 to 1949.

The unimportance of the Federal Reserve after the coming of the New Deal is indicated by the fact that only 1 percent of the more than threefold increase in the monetary base between 1932 and 1941 was supplied by Fed credit. The rest came from silver (5 percent) and gold (94 percent).

The Abrogation of Contracts and the Unconstitutionality of Government Commitments

Reflation had considerable intellectual support. Irving Fisher argued in "The Debt-Deflation Theory of Great Depressions" that the increased burden of debts due to falling prices brought bankruptcies, unemployment, loss of confidence, and money hoarding, which brought more deflation. He applauded the New Deal's efforts to reverse this process through monetary expansion, but Congress was not content to wait for inflation when quicker and more direct relief was available.

Since the silver scares of the late 19th century, most corporate and government bonds had been indexed to the price of gold. For example, Norman C. Norman had invested in a 30-year $1,000 bond of the Baltimore and Ohio (B&O) Railroad issued in 1930 with annual interest of $4\frac{1}{2}$ percent payable semiannually "in gold coin of the United States of America of or equal to the standard weight and fineness existing on February 1, 1930." This and other gold clauses were abrogated on June 5, 1933, when Congress resolved the following:

That every provision contained in . . . any obligation which purports to give the obligee a right to require payment in gold or a particular kind of coin or currency, or in an amount in money of the United States measured thereby, is declared to be against public policy . . . Every obligation, heretofore or hereafter incurred, whether or not any such provision is contained therein . . . shall be discharged upon payment, dollar for dollar, in any coin or currency which at the time of payment is legal tender for public and private debts.

---

[41] Johnson, *op. cit.*, p. 96.

When, following the devaluation of the dollar in January 1934, the B&O sent Mr. Norman $22.50 for his coupon, he sued for the contracted value of gold, now $38.10. The Supreme Court upheld the congressional resolution by a 5–4 vote in spite of the fact that, as Justice James McReynolds pointed out in his dissent, "Over and over again [the United States] have enjoyed the added value which [the gold clause] gave to their obligations. So late as May 2, 1933, they issued to the public more than $550,000,000 of their notes each of which carried a solemn promise to pay in standard coin."

Writing for the majority, Chief Justice Charles Evans Hughes acknowledged that the resolution was part of a government policy of redistribution through inflation. However, the Court was bound by "the constitutional power of the Congress over the monetary system," specifically the power "to coin money and regulate the value thereof" under Article I, Section 8. Congress had been entitled in the exercise of that power, Hughes decreed, "to establish a uniform currency, and parity between kinds of currency, and to make that currency, dollar for dollar, legal tender for the payment of debts."

The contention that these gold clauses are valid contracts and cannot be struck down proceeds upon the assumption that private parties, and States and municipalities, may make and enforce contracts which may limit that authority. Dismissing that untenable assumption, the facts must be faced. We think that it is clearly shown that these clauses interfere with the exertion of the power granted to the Congress and certainly it is not established that the Congress arbitrarily or capriciously decided that such an interference existed.

The gold clause cases present problems for the credibility of public monetary policy. If legislatures cannot make binding agreements, the so-called contracts for central bankers recently adopted in New Zealand, Britain, and elsewhere have less status than that of private contracts. Governments cannot commit to resist the political incentives for opportunistic inflation offered by, for example, fixed money coupons. That was well known. "Parliament can do anything that is not naturally impossible," Blackstone's *Commentaries* pronounced.[42] The possibility of an exception under the United States Constitution was eliminated by the Supreme Court's decision that Congress's monetary powers were unlimited. The decision might have been self-defeating. For example, an original purpose of the Bank of England was to act as a source of government finance that was credible because it was private and enforceable. A hundred years

---

[42] Book I, chap. 2.

later, unlike its adversary across the channel, the revolutionary French government could not avail itself of a credibly temporary suspension nor borrow at reasonable interest rates. Any reputation that might have survived the Bourbons was lost by the revolutionary government's paper money (the *assignats*) and Napoleon's efforts were constrained by the necessity of establishing the government's credit. He was forced to run fiscal surpluses, restore convertibility, and pay gold whereas Britain suspended and ran deficits in the knowledge that the Bank of England could be made to honor its promises after the emergency.[43]

Riding the Tiger: Marriner Eccles, the Federal Reserve, and the Executive

The relations between Roosevelt and Marriner Eccles, who was chairman of the Federal Reserve during most of his administration, seemed to include freedom for Mr. Eccles to argue and advise on all kinds of matters and ultimate authority for the president on everything.

Herbert Stein, *The Fiscal Revolution in America*, p. 42

Reorganization of the Federal Reserve: The Banking Act of 1935
Marriner Eccles was appointed chairman of the Federal Reserve Board in November 1934[44] to succeed Eugene Black, who had resigned after 15 months to return to the Federal Reserve Bank of Atlanta. Eccles relates in his memoirs that he accepted the post

only if fundamental changes were made in the Federal Reserve System. Over the years, practices had grown up inside the System which had reduced the Reserve Board in Washington to impotence. The System had originally been designed to represent a blend of private and public interests and of decentralized and centralized authorities, but this arrangement had become unbalanced. Private interests, acting through the Reserve banks, had made the System an effective instrument by which private interests alone could be served. The Board in Washington, on the other hand, which was supposed to represent and safeguard the public interest, was powerless to do so under the existing law and in the face of the opposition offered by the men who ran the Reserve banks throughout the country.

Marriner Eccles, *Beckoning Frontiers*, p. 166

---

[43] Michael Bordo and Eugene White, "British and French Finance during the Napoleonic Wars."

[44] *Marriner Eccles* was attracted to Washington by the New Deal, serving in the Treasury (1934) and on the Federal Reserve Board (1934–51, chairman 1934–48).

The Utah businessman and banker was appalled by Roosevelt's fiscal conservatism, which he equated to Hoover's, and throughout the decade waged a war with Morgenthau for the president's fiscal soul. When the Federal Reserve tax bill was sent to Congress in May 1936, the *New York Herald Tribune* observed, "This was the first time the head of the nation's banking system assumed the responsibilities of the Secretary of the Treasury."[45] Eccles felt that his efforts were justified when the president sent a message to Congress in April 1938, near the bottom of the 1937–38 recession, asking for a resumption of large-scale spending. "Equal in importance to his request," Eccles wrote, "were the reasons he advanced for it. They were drawn from the principles of a compensatory economy, which some of us had been urging with only variable success for many years."[46]

Eccles saw monetary policy as an instrument to support fiscal policy under the direction of the president. To play its part effectively, however, the monetary authority would have to be made more efficient. Eccles believed that

under the prevailing Reserve setup a group of private individuals in the Reserve banks had the latent power to block the program by damming needed funds or by withholding the sort of action in Federal Reserve operations that could maximize in the economy the benefits sought through a resumption of large-scale spending.

Eccles, *Beckoning Frontiers*, p. 187

It would do no good to change the Federal Reserve's structure, however, unless new blood was brought in to run it. Eccles compared Roosevelt's problems with the Supreme Court to the "four old men" of the Federal Reserve Board:

[T]hroughout 1935 Roosevelt became progressively more irritated by the decisions of the Supreme Court, the character of which he attributed to the fact that so many of the justices were in their seventies. His general mood of annoyance with the "Nine Old Men" communicated itself to other quarters of the Government, and for similar reasons. The new currents in the land created by the depression seemed not to have touched many of the aged men who held key posts in various administrative bodies where long tenure was the rule.

This was as true of the Federal Reserve Board as of other administrative agencies. Four out of the six [appointed] members of the Board were approaching seventy or were in their seventies.

Eccles, *Beckoning Frontiers*, pp. 235–36

---

[45] Eccles, *Beckoning Frontiers*, p. 258.
[46] *Ibid.*, p. 311.

The purpose of the Banking Act of 1935 was to reorganize the Federal Reserve such that monetary policy would be conducted "in the public interest" along the lines just described. This meant centralization of control in the Board. Nowhere in his writings does Eccles consider the specifics or causes of past conflicts over monetary policy, including the Board's resistance to action by the Reserve Banks. Adolph Miller had complained in a Board meeting in May 1930 that "the Federal Reserve Bank of New York was obsessed with the idea that easy money would help the business recession."[47] However, the next year, in asking for full authority by the Board over open market operations, he was able to tell a Senate committee that

In my judgment, the safety of the Federal reserve system for the country depends very largely upon ... the men who constitute the Federal Reserve Board.... [A] group of conscientious men, of high character and good intelligence, sitting constantly with these problems, somewhat remote from the atmosphere of the great centers, is capable of an objective and detached view, such as the ablest of men are seldom capable of when they are right in the atmosphere of the large centers and engrossed in their own affairs.[48]

Eccles refuted the charge that the Act would make the Federal Reserve an engine of inflation.[49] He would learn that presidential attitudes toward interest rates and inflation are asymmetric, although he did not refer to his 1935 statement in the chapter of his memoirs on the "Engine of Inflation" that he claimed the administration made of the Fed in the 1940s.[50]

The main features of the Act affecting the structure and powers of the Federal Reserve may be summarized as follows:

1. *Membership of the Board*: The number of regular Board members (appointed by the president subject to Senate approval) was raised from six to seven, with terms of 14 years, a term expiring every other year. The *ex officio* members – secretary of the treasury and the comptroller of the currency – were dropped, the former at the insistence of Glass, who said that his experience had taught him that the secretary "has had too much influence upon the Board."[51]

---

[47] Hamlin *Diary*, May 9, 1930, quoted by Friedman and Schwartz, *op. cit.*, p. 341n.
[48] U.S. Congress, Senate Committee on Banking and Currency, *Operation of the National and Federal Reserve Banking Systems*, p. 131; from David Wheelock, *The Strategy and Consistency of Federal Reserve Monetary Policy*, p. 71.
[49] Eccles, *Writings*, p. 18.
[50] Eccles, *Beckoning Frontiers*, pp. 415–25.
[51] *Ibid.*, p. 216n.

The House (Eccles) version provided that members who had served at least five years should be retired at age 70. This did not survive the House–Senate conference committee, but the Act ended the terms of existing members effective February 1936. Only the relatively young Roosevelt appointees (Eccles and M. S. Szymczak) were appointed to the new Board.

2. *The chief executive officers of the Reserve Banks*, henceforth to be called presidents, were to be appointed by their directors for five-year terms, subject to the Board's approval (which had not been necessary under the 1913 Act).

3. *The Federal Open Market Committee* (FOMC), composed of representatives of all 12 Reserve Banks meeting in Washington and operating under regulations determined by the Board, had been recognized in law in 1933. The new Act prescribed a 12-member FOMC consisting of the Board, the president of the New York Fed, and four other Reserve Bank presidents on a rotating basis. The chairman of the Board was also chairman of the FOMC. Eccles had wanted voting members to be limited to the Board, but he was satisfied that "the new law at least established the principle that open-market operations would henceforth be initiated in Washington."[52]

4. *Reserve requirements* had been fixed beyond the discretion of the Federal Reserve in the 1913 Act. The Fed asked for control of them, and in May 1933 the Thomas Amendment to the Agricultural Adjustment Act authorized the Board to make unlimited changes in "emergencies" subject to the president's approval. The 1935 Act removed this condition but limited the Board's discretion to a doubling of existing ratios.

It is worth noting what the Act did not include, most obviously a statement of goals toward which the new powers would be directed. Eccles had proposed that the Board be required "to promote conditions conducive to business stability and to mitigate by its influence unstabilizing fluctuations in the general level of production, trade, prices, and employment. . . . The present objective – the accommodation of commerce, agriculture, and industry – is vague to the point of meaninglessness and in effect is no objective." However, "Glass successfully resisted the proposed

---

[52] *Ibid.*, p. 225.

change in the mandate," which did not come until the Employment Act of 1946.[53]

Another omission from the 1935 Act, indeed from the administration's program, striking in light of thousands of bank failures before and during the Great Depression and the shutdown of the system in 1933, was any attempt to treat the structure of the banking system. The Act's weakness and an obvious solution were evident in the 100-percent survival rate of Canadian banks, which had extensive branching systems.

In that most famous of inaugural addresses, the president blamed the depression on the "stubbornness and . . . incompetence . . . of the unscrupulous money changers . . . , [who] stand indicted in the court of public opinion, [and faced] by the failure of credit . . . have proposed only the lending of more money." But he would not touch the banking structure. When Eccles urged a uniform system of bank regulation in place of the existing separation between national and state regulation, he discovered that

[the current structure] was held in nostalgic affection by Roosevelt. In his view, the state nonmember banks represented the small, democratically controlled institution, responsive to local needs, with officers who had the welfare of the home folks at heart. For some curious reason the Federal Reserve, on the other hand, represented for him the banking giants, and in a way, he saw the Banking Act of 1935 as a means of curbing the giants. To unify the whole banking system, however, implied two things in Roosevelt's mind. First, it implied the end of the state banking system. And second, by forcing the small banks into the Reserve System, it implied a condition favorable to their destruction by the giants.

Eccles, *Beckoning Frontiers*, p. 269

Roosevelt doubtless also recognized the political power of the small town banker that had been demonstrated several times in the 19th century and had defeated Wilson's attempt to corral them into the Federal Reserve. Whether he was nostalgic or pragmatic, Helen Burns noted in her study of *The American Banking Community and New Deal Banking Reforms* that the bankers who "feared the radical tendencies of his recovery program . . . failed to recognize that the president, no less than they, was intent on preserving the existing banking structure."[54]

---

[53] *Ibid.*, pp. 212, 228.
[54] P. xii.

The Federal Reserve Board Acts

By mid-1937, the economy had climbed a long way from the bottom of the depression. Production and income had grown 60 percent, nearly regaining their 1929 levels. (See Fig. 8.1.) In other respects, however, recovery was far from complete. Unemployment exceeded 7 million, and prices were still 10 percent less and fixed investment a third less than in 1929. The banking system's contribution to recovery was disappointing. After falling from $42 to $22 (in billions) between June 1929 and June 1933, bank loans had stuck at the latter level. Annual failures now counted in the dozens instead of the thousands as in 1930–33 or the hundreds as in the 1920s. Nonetheless, bankers' caution was extreme. Their loans were four-fifths of investments in government securities in 1937, even less than in 1933. Loans had been more than investments throughout the 1920s.

More evidence of their caution was the high level of excess reserves. We must realize that "excess" is a legal and not an economic modifier. A bank's cash is a choice, based on considerations of profit and prudence, and "excess" reserves are simply cash in excess of legal requirements. The reserves in Fig. 8.2 are member bank deposits (claims on cash) with Federal Reserve Banks. Cash on bank premises did not count as legal reserves between 1917 and 1959, although it performed a reserve function.

In June 1929, member-bank excess reserves were an almost imperceptible $42 million, barely more than 1/10 of 1 percent of deposits and less than 2 percent of reserves. In October 1935, they were $2.8 billion, 8 percent of deposits and 53 percent of reserves. In view of the runs and failures of 1930–33, the rise in excess reserves is not surprising.

Bank reserves rose rapidly after 1933 with the "golden avalanche" of increased world production and exports of gold from Europe.[55] They had little effect on bank credit, however, as two-thirds went to "excess." The aversion to loans is understandable from the demand as well as the supply side given the excess capacities and dismal prospects of potential borrowers. Explanations of bank reluctance to invest in government securities are less straightforward. Then low returns hardly met transaction costs. Furthermore, secondary reserves – "liquid" short-term securities – might not be an effective way of recovering cash in the face of a general decline in reserves due to an increase in the public's desire for cash, tightening by the Federal Reserve, or a reversal of gold flows. In any

---

[55] Frank Graham and Charles Whittlesey, *The Golden Avalanche*.

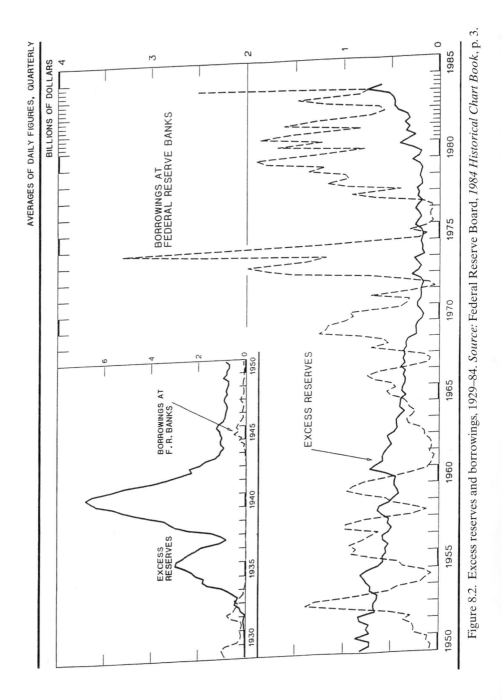

Figure 8.2. Excess reserves and borrowings, 1929–84. *Source:* Federal Reserve Board, *1984 Historical Chart Book*, p. 3.

case, these securities were in short supply and banks already held most of them.[56]

Long-term Treasury bond yields fell from 3.5 percent to 2.8 percent during 1934, and remained near that level until mid-1937, when the decline resumed. Banks might have feared a return to normal levels – long-term governments had averaged 4 percent in the 1920s – and consequent capital losses. This reason is given force by the observation that bank investments in long-term governments rose and excess reserves fell during World War II after the Fed committed to stable interest rates.

Excess reserves posed a "dilemma" – the word is used by a Fed official 25 years later – for monetary policy.[57] The Fed did not wish to hinder the recovery, but it wanted to control credit. The potential for speculative and inflationary finance was huge in case banks decided to lend their excess reserves. They needed to be "mopped up." Raising discount rates would be useless because banks had no reason to borrow from the Fed, as Fig. 8.2 shows. Nor would open market operations do the job because excess reserves exceeded the Fed's portfolio of securities. The only feasible option seemed to be an exercise of the Board's new power to raise reserve requirements, and in three steps – on August 15, 1936, and on March 1 and May 1, 1937 – they were doubled. The Board noted the following:

The part of the excess reserves thus eliminated is superfluous for all present or prospective needs of commerce, industry, and agriculture and can be absorbed at this time without affecting money rates and without restrictive influence upon member banks, practically all of which now have far more than sufficient reserves and balances with other banks to meet the increases.[58]

Unfortunately, it turned out that banks wanted their excess reserves, and they recovered them by cutting loans during the severe economic decline that lasted from May 1937 to June 1938.

Fed officials saw no connection between the increase in reserve requirements and the ensuing contraction. They never accepted that the excess reserves were bank choices. They preferred to join those who blamed the recession on a restrictive fiscal policy. Social security payments, effectively an employment tax, had been initiated in January 1937, and "improved

---

[56] George Cloos, "Monetary Conditions from the 1937–38 Recession to Pearl Harbor."
[57] Clay Anderson, *A Half-Century of Federal Reserve Policymaking, 1914–64*, p. 77.
[58] *Ibid.*, pp. 78–79.

economic conditions through the first part of 1937 seemed to offer an opportunity at last to bring the budget into balance." Relief programs were cut and a tax was levied on undistributed profits.[59] The Treasury saw in retained earnings an evasion of taxes on dividends, and Eccles pushed for the tax because he thought it would stimulate demand by inducing firms to invest their earnings or pay dividends.[60]

On April 14, 1938, after unemployment had climbed from 7 to 10 million, halfway back to the peak of 1933, the president announced a recovery plan in which federal spending was to be increased and reserve requirements were reduced.[61]

This episode can be explained as an application of the Strong rule. The legal excess reserves of New York and Chicago banks relative to their requirements were even greater than for banks as a whole. Borrowing from the Fed was almost nonexistent. Quoting from Strong's 1926 statement in the first section of this chapter, his desire to keep the borrowing of city banks within bounds to alleviate "pressure for reducing loans" was matched by a determination to avoid situations in which borrowings were "negligible, as in 1924," so that "if gold imports take place, there is liable to be some credit inflation." The situation in 1935 presented this danger in an unprecedented degree, and the Fed acted accordingly. By taking away their excess reserves, the Fed hoped to force banks to the discount window.

Engine of Inflation

The Federal Reserve monetized wartime deficits by offering to buy unlimited quantities of Treasury securities at 3/8 of 1 percent for 3-month bills and between 2 and $2\frac{1}{2}$ percent for long-term bonds. The rise in federal debt from $48 billion to $235 billion between June 1941 and June 1945 was accompanied by increases in Federal Reserve credit from $2 billion to $22 billion and in the money stock from $63 billion to $127 billion. The reported rise in prices was only 20 percent, however, because of rationing and price controls. Most of the price effect came in 1946 and 1947, after the removal of controls.

---

[59] Margaret Myers, *A Financial History of the United States*, p. 326.

[60] Eccles, *Beckoning Frontiers*, pp. 257–65. A history of the tax and its antecedents is in George Lent, *The Impact of the Undistributed Profits Tax, 1936–37*.

[61] *Federal Reserve Bulletin*, May 1938, p. 343. The arguments and maneuvering within the administration leading up to this program are discussed by Stein, *The Fiscal Revolution in America*, pp. 109–12.

Table 8.1. *Yields and Ownership (in billions of dollars) of U.S. Securities, June 1942 to June 1947*

	T Bills		Bonds	
Ownership	6/42	6/47	6/42	6/47
Private	2.3	1.3	12.1	54.7
Federal Reserve	0.2	14.5	0.4	0.1
% held by Fed	8.0	91.8	3.2	0.2
Yields	0.38	0.38	2.43	2.22

Source: Federal Reserve Board, *Banking and Monetary Statistics, 1941–70*, pp. 693–94, 720–21, 884–87.

The guarantee of different returns on short-term and long-term securities was impractical. The search by investors for high expected returns tends to produce equality between yields, possibly with risk premiums for long-term securities. The official promise of significantly higher long-term rates removed the risk, and private investors left the low-yielding bills to the Fed, as indicated in Table 8.1.[62]

Moving to the end of the war, Eccles continued to see monetary policy as a cooperative venture with fiscal tools, with the challenge shifted from unemployment to inflation. He had been dropped from the team, however. The administration thought in terms not of coordination but of support, the kind of unqualified support that the Fed gave the Treasury in the war and was expected to keep giving. Eccles urged the continuation of controls and a restrictive fiscal policy, specifically a penalty capital gains tax to discourage inflationary speculation, but his advice was dismissed and his communications went unanswered.

The greatest inflationary danger lay in the increases in bank credit and money implied by the commitment to keep interest rates low in the face of high inflation. In July 1945, a month before the end of the war, the Fed wrote to the Treasury that it was considering the elimination of the preferential discount rate on loans secured by Treasury bills and other short-term government securities. "The instance involved was a trivial one," Eccles recollected. "For that reason alone the sharp response it brought from Treasury circles speaks all the more of the frame of mind that prevailed there." Fred Vinson, who had replaced Morgenthau, objected to the Fed's proposal because it "might be interpreted by the market as

---

[62] For the formulation and implementation of this policy, see Wicker, "The World War II Policy of Fixing a Pattern of Interest Rates."

an indication that the Government had abandoned its low-interest rate policy and was veering in the direction of higher rates."[63]

The preferential rate remained. Eccles raised the issue again in December, with the same result. He was informed by Vinson "that the proposed action would increase the already large interest charge on the public debt. This was the dead-end position we were to reach in many other discussions."[64] In a tense meeting on January 31, 1946, the secretary "implied that we were proposing to stage a sit-down strike in refusing to carry out Treasury policy." However, "it was clear that if we carried out Treasury policy," Eccles recorded, "we would default on the obligations Congress imposed on the Reserve System in the field of money and credit."[65]

This skirmish in the six-year (1945–51) war between the Fed and the Treasury ended in April 1946 with the Board's approval of a unanimous recommendation by the Reserve Banks that the preferential discount rate be discontinued. "Though we were aware of the Treasury's opposition, we could not honestly veto a proposal that we fully believed was in the public interest."[66] The following statement was issued at the time of the Board's action:

The Board does not favor a higher level of interest rates on U.S. Securities than the Government is now paying. Discontinuance of the special rate will not involve any increase in the cost to the Government of carrying the public debt.[67]

"Such statements were to accompany each step in the move to higher rates," Herbert Stein noted.

The process by which the Federal Reserve achieved its freedom consisted of a number of small steps from 1946 through 1949, each step resisted by the Treasury but none big enough to provoke a showdown, and one dramatic showdown in 1950–51 when the Treasury was not strong enough to brave an open fight in Congress.

Stein, *The Fiscal Revolution in America*, p. 250

The strongest fighter for an independent monetary policy, with fewer inhibitions about discussing higher interest rates, was Allan Sproul, president of the New York Reserve Bank from 1941 to 1956. He had pushed for a higher peg – 3 percent on long-term – at the beginning of the war,

---

[63] Eccles, *Beckoning Frontiers*, pp. 422–23.

[64] *Ibid.*, p. 423; also Stein, *op. cit.*, p. 251.

[65] Eccles, *op. cit.*, p. 424.

[66] *Loc. cit.*

[67] *Federal Reserve Bulletin*, May 1946, p. 462.

and after the war, the idea of flexible interest rates, higher if necessary, was called the "New York" position.[68] The Board wanted legislation to allow it to impose special reserve requirements in the form of short-term government securities or cash, but it got little support.[69] Sproul was opposed because he did not want to be lured into inaction while waiting for legislation that might not (and did not) come. Furthermore, he did not want to give the impression that the Fed did not already have sufficient powers to fight inflation. He told a congressional committee that the best course was simply to let interest rates rise.[70]

Tensions between the Federal Reserve and the Treasury following World War II were to be expected and were also present after World War I. The same interests (price stability versus the interest cost of the government debt) and ideas (the Treasury convinced that credit controls can take the place of high interest rates) were involved in the two episodes. Another similarity was the lead taken by the New York Bank in the Federal Reserve's fight with the Treasury. But why did the second episode last so long and end so acrimoniously, with the Federal Reserve finally forcing the issue, instead of, as in 1921, waiting for the Treasury to flash the green light?

An important reason for the extended duration of the low-interest program – for the strength of the Treasury's conviction, its support in Congress, and the Federal Reserve's timidity – was undoubtedly fear of the return of depression. Eccles admitted that "the basic long-range problem was to avoid deflation by providing a flow of necessary purchasing power. . . . For both political and economic reasons we could never go back to the 1939 levels of production."[71]

Military purchases took 40 percent of the national product, and the wartime federal deficit of $45 billion would soon turn to a peacetime surplus. Investment prospects were thought to be weak, and projections of the Keynesian consumption function indicated that less than half of increases in disposable income would be spent. Economists feared that "full employment levels of GNP cannot be achieved or even approached, year after year, without positive government programs directed to that end" – primarily by "giving the maximum stimulus to private investment."[72]

[68] Eccles, *Beckoning Frontiers*, p. 245.

[69] *Ibid.*, pp. 426–33.

[70] The Joint Committee on the Economic Report, chaired by Senator Robert Taft, 1947. See Eccles, *Beckoning Frontiers*, p. 432.

[71] Eccles, *Beckoning Frontiers*, pp. 399–400.

[72] Arthur Smithies, "Forecasting Postwar Demand: I."

This position was undermined first by booming consumption and investment, and then relief that the inevitable downturn, when it came in 1948–49, was so mild.[73] The '50s' generation was underway with hardly a thought of the Great Depression. Moreover, the Treasury could no longer count on Congress. The Fed got a boost in December 1949 from the hearings and report of the Subcommittee on Monetary Credit and Fiscal Policies chaired by Senator Paul Douglas of Illinois, a noted liberal but also a Chicago economist with classical views of the relations among interest rates, money, and prices. The Subcommittee recommended the following:

As a long run matter, we favor interest rates as low as they can be without inducing inflation, for low interest rates stimulate capital investment. But we believe that the advantages of avoiding inflation are so great and that a restrictive monetary policy can contribute so much to this end that the freedom of the Federal Reserve to restrict credit and raise interest rates for general stabilization purposes should be restored even if the cost should be a significant increase in service charges on the Federal debt and a greater inconvenience to the Treasury in its sale of securities for new financing and refunding purposes.[74]

Presenting the Committee's report to the Senate, Douglas said,

Now, we all have good reason to believe that while the Federal Reserve has done this guilty thing [caused inflation], it has done so protestingly and unwillingly. It has wanted to lead a virtuous life. But over the shoulder of the Federal Reserve System has stood the Treasury, making threatening passes and gestures and from time to time cracking its whip.... The costs to the Government and to the people have been far greater than the gains which we have made from a lower interest rate. The increases in prices since Korea are probably already adding to the Federal Government costs at the approximate rate of six billion a year... I suggest simply that the Federal Reserve, which has had many years of practical experience in its open market operations, permit the Government securities market to reflect the underlying factors of supply and demand.[75]

We remember Lord Althorp's analysis of the Bank of England in 1832. The Douglas Committee brought no legislation, but its sympathetic reception strengthened the Fed's position.[76] Yet it remained

---

[73] Friedman and Schwartz, *op. cit.*, p. 597.

[74] U.S. Congress, Joint Committee on the Economic Report, *Hearings*, 1949, p. 471. See also Stein, *op. cit.*, pp. 259–60.

[75] *Congressional Record*, December 1949, p. 1518.

[76] Not everyone approved, particularly the Texas populist, Wright Patman, who had dissented from the Committee's recommendation as not making "the Federal Reserve System sufficiently responsible to the executive department" (Stein, *op. cit.*, p. 1).

more timid than in 1919–21, and the Treasury's intransigence continued. Why?

Part of the explanation might be found in the Banking Act of 1935. The Board was stronger and, more than the Reserve Banks, under the Treasury's thumb. Perhaps as important as the Act was the thinking behind it still present in its author. Marriner Eccles, unlike Benjamin Strong or Allan Sproul, could not think of monetary policy except as an adjunct of fiscal policy. Money and credit could do nothing in themselves. The famous comparison of monetary policy in a depression to "pushing on a string" originated in Eccles's testimony on the Act of 1935:[77]

Governor Eccles: Under present circumstances there is very little, if anything, that can be done.

Congressman Goldsborough: You mean you cannot push on a string.

Eccles: That is a good way to put it, one cannot push on a string. We are in the depths of a depression and . . . beyond creating an easy money situation through reduction of discount rates, and through creation of excess reserves, there is very little, if anything, that the reserve organization can do toward bringing about recovery.

On the administration's side, the president's economic views were ambiguous. Harry Truman might for his time and place be the most fiscally conservative of American presidents. Even Andrew Jackson might not have pushed for the tax increases necessary to balance the budget during the Korean War. There has been nothing like it. Receipts rose only 70 percent as much as expenditures during the Spanish–American War, and much less in major wars. However, the increase in federal spending, all for the military, from $40 to $65 billion between the fiscal years ending June 1950 and June 1952, was more than matched by the rise in receipts from $41 to $68 billion. Truman's reputation as a spender is derived entirely from the resonance of the ambitious social programs that filled his speeches, but he would not borrow. His programs were to be paid for by taxes on the ill-gotten gains of the rich grown fat on the interest ground out of Missouri farmers.[78]

Truman's position that low interest rates were not inflationary was probably genuine. There is no record of his engagement in macroeconomic argument, but the policy was consistent with the populist cost-push conviction that high interest rates cause inflation because they must be

---

[77] U.S. Congress, House Banking and Currency Committee, *Hearings, Banking Act of 1935*, March 18, 1935, p. 377.

[78] U.S. Bureau of the Census, *Historical Statistics of the United States*, Series Y412–29, Income tax rates.

incorporated in product prices. This is politically the best of both worlds because it enables one to be in favor of both low interest rates and stable prices – and if one is responsible for debt management, a small national debt and low taxes as well. The inconsistencies in the argument are discussed in Chap. 11.

The Treasury expected the outbreak of the Korean War in June 1950 to reinforce the Federal Reserve's subservience, but the renewed threat of inflation and the president's unpopularity strengthened the Fed's resolve. The New York Reserve Bank renewed its request for an increase in the discount rate in July, and in the FOMC meeting of August 18, Sproul said,

The question today is what we are going to do in our sphere of primary responsibility, not what we are going to recommend to the Treasury that it do in its primary sphere. It is not a question of the long-term bond issue or of refunding the September-October maturities, but what we are going to do about making further reserve funds available to the banking system in a dangerously inflationary situation. . . .

We can't do the whole job with general credit measures but in view of our responsibility and the national program I think that general credit measures should now be used. . . . We have marched up the hill several times and then marched down again. This time I think we should act on the basis of our unwillingness to continue to supply reserves to the market by supporting the existing rate structure and should advise the Treasury that this is what we intend to do – not seek instructions.

The Committee agreed, and later that day the Board announced an increase in the discount rate from $1\frac{1}{4}$ to $1\frac{1}{2}$ percent. On December 4, disturbed by reports of rising interest (the bill rate rose from 1.16 to 1.38 percent between mid-August and early December, although the long-term bond rate was virtually unchanged at 2.45 percent, and would fall during the 1948–49 recession), the president wrote the following to Board Chairman Thomas McCabe:

It seems to me that this situation is a very dangerous one and that the Federal Reserve Board should make it perfectly clear to the Open Market Committee and to the New York bankers that the peg is stabilized.

I hope the Board will realize its responsibilities and not allow the bottom to drop from under our securities. If that happens that is exactly what Mr. Stalin wants.[79]

---

[79] Stein, *op. cit.*, p. 269.

Truman thus stood on its head the dictum attributed to Lenin that "the best way to destroy the capitalist system is to debauch the currency."[80]

McCabe had been appointed chairman in April 1948 to succeed Eccles, whose four-year term expired on February 1. Eccles was told of the president's decision not to reappoint him in January, but no reason was given.[81] He suspected that he was an election-year sacrifice to the Bank of America, whose expansion was contested by the Board. Press speculations also touched on the Board's lack of cooperation with the Treasury and Eccles's popularity with the financial community and Republican legislators. Privately Truman told an associate that higher interest rates amounted to "a first-class doublecrossing" by Eccles.[82] A biographer suggests that Truman regarded Eccles as "yet another of those troublesome human monuments" left over from the New Deal.[83] The former monetary reformer had been washed aside by the "new currents in the land."

Eccles's term as a Board member did not end until 1958, and Truman asked him to stay on, which he did until July 1951, four months after the Fed's victory over the administration. As time wore on following his demotion, Eccles increasingly felt released from the obligation to cooperate with the administration or to refrain from public criticism. He was a key player in the last days of the Treasury–Fed dispute.

The president's letter of December 4 induced a reply by Chairman McCabe in which he reminded the president that the Fed had supported Treasury securities by purchases in excess of $1 billion the preceding 17 days, adding, "It is our view that moderate fluctuations in price in response to market forces serve a useful purpose and help to maintain public confidence."[84] In a January 3 meeting of McCabe, Sproul, and John Snyder, Missouri banker and secretary of the treasury, Sproul broached the subject of "a slightly higher rate than $2^{1}/_{2}$ percent for long term financing," thus violating, in Stein's phrase, "the holy of holies."[85] Two weeks

---

[80] By J. M. Keynes, *Economic Consequences of the Peace*, p. 148, although it has not been verified; Frank Fetter, "Lenin, Keynes and Inflation."

[81] The Federal Reserve Act of 1913 prescribed that one member of the Board "be designated by the President as Governor and one as Vice Governor," with no indication of terms. The Banking Act of 1935 changed the titles to Chairman and Vice Chairman and gave them four-year terms but without specific beginning and ending dates.

[82] Alonzo Hamby, *Man of the People*, p. 427.

[83] *Ibid.*, p. 426.

[84] Stein, *op. cit.*, p. 269.

[85] FOMC Minutes, 1951, p. 6; Stein, *op. cit.*, p. 269.

later, on January 17, McCabe was summoned before Truman and Snyder, and the latter said that the Treasury was considering a new long-term issue at $2\frac{1}{2}$ percent, which he hoped the Fed would support. McCabe was noncommittal, but the next day in a speech to the New York Board of Trade, Snyder announced,

In the firm belief after long consideration, that the $2\frac{1}{2}$ percent long-term rate is fair and equitable to the investor, and that the market stability is essential, the Treasury Department had concluded, after a joint conference with President Truman and Chairman McCabe of the Federal Reserve Board, that the refunding and new money issues will be financed within the pattern of that rate.[86]

The Fed felt betrayed. Snyder had publicly committed it to a policy without its consent. McCabe complained to the president. On January 22, Sproul "made a delicately-worded but nonetheless clear speech disapproving the support policy."[87] On January 29, the Fed permitted a slight fall in long-term bond prices. On January 30, in an unprecedented action, the president summoned the entire FOMC to the White House the next day.

In fairness, it should be noted that the story of the meeting is told almost entirely from the side of the Federal Reserve. The Board and FOMC provided more documentation of their meetings than the president and the secretary, and were more concerned to defend their integrity and patriotism. Snyder settled for a reference to "confusion about what was agreed" at the January 31 meeting, and Truman, for whom this must have been a minor issue, treated it briefly in his *Memoirs* as "one of the problems that arose in the monetary field," when he was "taken by surprise" by the Fed's failure "to support the [Treasury] program" after having "entirely voluntarily" promised to cooperate.[88]

The following account of the president's meeting with the FOMC, which had decided that the chairman would be its sole spokesman, is taken from notes prepared later in the day by Board member

---

[86] *Annual Report of the Secretary of the Treasury for the Fiscal Year Ended June 30, 1951*, p. 616; Stein, *op. cit.*, *p. 270*.

[87] "I was less guarded," Eccles wrote of his statement to the Joint Economic Committee on January 25 (*Beckoning Frontiers*, p. 486). Stein reported that the statement "involved him in a wrangle with Senator O'Mahoney and Congressman Patman" because it criticized the support program (*op. cit.*, p. 270). McCabe had excused himself from appearing because, in Eccles's words, "He could not defend the Treasury's position; as Chairman, it would be difficult for him to oppose it publicly without resigning."

[88] *Annual Report of the Secretary of the Treasury for 1951*, p. 270; Truman, *Memoirs*, ii, pp. 44–45.

R. M. Evans and approved with minor corrections by the Committee. Truman opened with a reminder "that the present emergency is the greatest this country has ever faced, including the two World Wars and all the preceding wars. . . . The President emphasized that we must combat Communist influence on many fronts. He said one way to do this is to maintain confidence in the Government's credit and in Government securities."

McCabe assured the president of the Committee's concern for the government's credit as well as its responsibility for economic stability, and promised to consult with the secretary of the treasury. If they failed to agree, McCabe hoped to be able "to discuss the matter with the President. The President said this was entirely satisfactory and closed the meeting on the same note as it was opened – namely, that he wanted us to do everything possible to maintain confidence in the credit of the Government and in the Government securities markets and to support the president of the United States in achieving this end."[89]

The FOMC returned to their headquarters and defeated a motion to support the bond market at present levels by a vote of eight to four.[90] The next day, they were shocked by a White House statement that "The Federal Reserve Board has pledged its support to President Truman to maintain the stability of Government securities as long as the emergency lasts." The purpose of the statement, the spokesman said, was to quiet rumors of a difference between the Treasury and the Federal Reserve. The same day, February 1, McCabe received a letter from Truman:[91]

Dear Tom,

I want the members of the Federal Reserve Board and the members of the Federal Open Market Committee to know how deeply I appreciate their expression of full cooperation given to me yesterday in our meeting. . . .

Your assurance that you would fully support the Treasury defense financing program, both as to refunding and new issues, is of vital importance to me. As I understand it, I have your assurance that the market on Government securities will be stabilized and maintained at present levels in order to assure the successful financing requirements and to establish in the minds of the people confidence concerning government credit.

I wish you would convey to all the members of your group my warm appreciation of their cooperative attitude.

Sincerely yours,
Harry Truman

---

[89] *FOMC Minutes*, 1951, pp. 39–41; Stein, *op. cit.*, pp. 271–72.
[90] Stein, *op. cit.*, p. 495.
[91] *Ibid.*, pp. 273–74.

The story now belongs to Eccles.[92] Responding to calls from reporters asking if the Fed had in fact capitulated to the Treasury, Eccles told them that the meeting had been misrepresented by the White House. When the Board met Friday morning (February 2) to discuss its course of action, there was some criticism of Eccles's disclosure of privileged communications with the president. He replied that the record needed to be set straight. The Board turned to the president's letter to the chairman and decided "to have McCabe see the President as soon as possible, show him the memorandum Governor Evans had prepared . . . , and then request that the letter be withdrawn. . . . "

That evening, Eccles learned that the president's letter had been released to the press. He interpreted this as "a final move in a Treasury attempt to impose its will on the Federal Reserve. If swift action was not taken to offset the effect of the move, the Federal Reserve would no longer have a voice in deciding monetary and credit policies. It would lose the independent status Congress meant it to have and . . . would be reduced to the status of a Treasury bureau." McCabe had gone to his home in Pennsylvania for the weekend, and it would be impossible to get the FOMC together in time for the prompt response that Eccles believed was needed. He gave a copy of Evans's memo to a reporter on Saturday morning along with a statement of his "astonishment" at the "confusion" caused by the president. "It was front-page news on Sunday."

In August and again in September 1950, Snyder had threatened to take the issue to Congress, but the November elections weakened an already doubtful source of support. The Democratic majorities were slender in both houses of Congress, and on most economic issues the coalition of Republicans and southern Democrats with whom Roosevelt had had to contend was still important. Truman's stature had fallen with scandals in the administration, setbacks in the Korean War, and his conflict with the popular General Douglas McArthur. The eruption of the disagreement into public view produced an outpouring of support for the Fed.[93]

When the FOMC proposed discussions with the Treasury to develop an agreed policy, it did so from a position of strength. The Treasury–Federal Reserve Accord was announced on March 4, 1951:

The Treasury and the Federal Reserve System have reached full accord with respect to debt-management and monetary policies to be pursued in furthering

---

[92] *Beckoning Frontiers*, pp. 490–98.
[93] Stein, *op. cit.*, p. 274; e.g., *New York Times*, February 6, 1951.

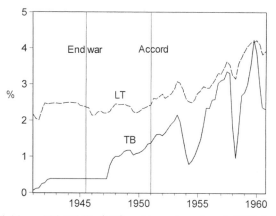

Figure 8.3. Yields on U.S. T bills (TB) and long-term bonds (LT) (quarterly averages, 1941–60). *Source:* Federal Reserve Board, *Banking and Monetary Statistics, 1941–70*, pp. 693–724.

their common purpose to assure the successful financing of the Government's requirements and, at the same time, to minimize monetization of the public debt.[94]

Some thought the Accord too weak, and half a dozen senators from both sides of the aisle wanted to give the Fed "added courage" by means of a resolution to free the Federal Reserve of any obligation to support the bond market. The infusion was not needed. On March 8, after consultation with the Treasury, for the first time in 10 years, the Fed let the market stand on its own. It promised to preserve an orderly market for government securities, which meant smoothing interest rates by being ready to take portions of Treasury issues and selling them at opportune times. However, this is the sort of thing that bankers and central bankers have always done, and it does not permanently affect credit.

An earlier *quid pro quo* undertaken by the Fed in 1947 to induce Treasury acceptance of higher interest rates had been a voluntary 90-percent tax on its interest earnings to soften the impact of higher interest rates (see Fig. 8.3) on the federal budget. The "franchise tax" on Fed earnings in the original Federal Reserve Act had been eliminated by the Banking Act of 1933. The Fed pays no interest on its liabilities, and its expenses are small relative to its earnings, which are mainly interest from its holdings of government debt. In 1951, for example, earnings, expenses, and dividends to member banks were $395, $98, and $14 million, respectively.

[94] *Federal Reserve Bulletin*, March 1951, p. 267.

Of the remaining \$283 million, \$255 million was paid (returned) to the Treasury. The Fed's 1947 action was taken unilaterally after conferring with members of Congress rather than risk the vagaries of legislation.[95]

The Accord was followed by the resignation of McCabe, whose efforts to bring the combatants together had irritated both sides.[96] He was succeeded by William McChesney Martin, Jr., assistant secretary of the treasury, who had led the Treasury's side of the negotiations for the accord. "Boy wonder of Wall Street" and president of the New York Stock Exchange at age 31, he was a Missouri Democrat whose father had been president of the St. Louis Reserve Bank from 1929 to 1941. Martin later told of Truman's final efforts to salvage bond supports:

The president called me in and said he wanted to make me chairman of the Fed. He told me a story. He said that when he was in the Army in World War I he had bought Liberty Bonds, and when he got back to Kansas City the bonds were down to 82. "You wouldn't let that happen again, would you, Bill?" he asked.

Martin could give no guarantee and the interview ended.

Later he called me back and said it just made him sick to think of the bonds going down. He said: "You will do the very best you can to see that doesn't happen, won't you?" I said I would do my best but they might go down anyway. So I got the job.[97]

---

[95] Anderson, *op. cit.*, pp. 102, 149. For Federal Reserve earnings, expenses, and payments to the Treasury, see the Board's *Annual Reports*.

[96] Stein, *op. cit.*, p. 496n74. In another account of his departure, "An unhappy and angry McCabe resigned March 9, after having exacted the right of approval over his successor. All sides settled on William McChesney Martin, an assistant secretary of the Treasury, well liked by Snyder but in agreement with the Federal Reserve position and determined to be independent" (Hamby, *op. cit.*, p. 583).

[97] Interview with Lindley Clark, *Wall Street Journal*, March 4, 1978, p. 22.

Plate I. The Old Lady of Threadneedle Street, 1797.

Plate II. The downfall of Mother Bank. *Source:* Courtesy of the New York Historical Society.

"SAME OLD GAME!"

Old Lady of Threadneedle Street. "YOU'VE GOT YOURSELVES INTO A NICE MESS WITH YOUR PRECIOUS 'SPECULATION!' WELL—I'LL HELP YOU OUT OF IT,—FOR THIS ONCE!!"

Plate III. Old lady (Punch).

Plate IV. Deliverance at Hand. Ehrhart in "Puck."

Plate V. Uncle Sam. *Source:* Courtesy of the *Philadelphia Record*.

241

Plate VIa–b. Secretary of the Treasury Fred Vinson makes the case for multilateralism in congressional hearings on the Anglo-American Financial Agreement. *Source:* AP/Wide World Photos.

Plate VII. Federal Reserve Board Chairman William McChesney Martin discusses the Board's increase in the discount rate, which President Lyndon B. Johnson had criticized at a news briefing. *Source:* AP/World Wide Photo.

NINE

Central Banking in the United States after the Great Depression, 1951 to the 1960s

> The Congress hereby declares that it is the continuing policy and responsibility of the Federal Government to use all practicable means consistent with its needs and obligations and other considerations of national policy... to coordinate and utilize all its plans, functions, and resources... to promote maximum employment, production, and purchasing power.
>
> *Employment Act of 1946*, Sec. 2

> Our purpose is to lean against the winds of deflation or inflation, whichever way they are blowing....
>
> William McChesney Martin, Jr., U.S. Senate Committee on Banking and Currency, *Nomination Hearings*, 1956, p. 15

The end of the peg required the Federal Reserve to reconsider its relations with free markets, especially the effects of open market operations, which had succeeded the discount window as the principal means of regulating bank reserves. In 1929, the Fed held an average of $449 million of U.S. securities compared with its total credit of $1,459 million, mostly in discounted private bills. In 1950, U.S. securities made up $18,410 million of Fed credit of $19,062 million.[1]

The Federal Open Market Committee wanted efficient financial markets, with healthy institutions, for its own purposes and for the efficient credit system necessary to a vigorous capitalist society. Looking for ways in which it might have a flexible influence on reserves (by buying and selling large and variable quantities) without damaging market liquidity,

---

[1] Federal Reserve Board, *Banking and Monetary Statistics, 1941* (table 100), *1970* (table 10.1).

Background: People and Events

1931: British suspension of the gold standard.
1934: U.S. devaluation.
1936: Tripartite exchange rate agreement between France, the United Kingdom, and the United States.
1944: Bretton Woods Agreement.
1947: Marshall Plan.
1951–53: Korean War; wage and price controls.
1951: Treasury–Federal Reserve Accord.
1952: Bills only.
1958: Industrial countries achieve fixed exchange rates with few exchange controls.
1961: Operation Twist; Berlin Wall.
1963: Interest-equalization tax on foreign investments.
1966, 1969: Credit crunches (discussed in chap. 12).
1968: Tax surcharge.
1971: Nixon package: wage and price controls and end of fixed exchange rates.

	President of the United States	Secretary of the Treasury	Chairman of the Council of Economic Advisors	Chairman of the Federal Reserve Board
1951	Harry Truman	John Snyder	Leon Keyserling	William Mc Chesrey Martin, Jr.
1953	Dwight Eisenhower	George Humphrey	Arthur Burns	
1957		Robert Anderson	Raymond Saulnier	
1961	John Kennedy	Douglas Dillon	Walter Heller	
1963	Lyndon Johnson			

the Committee decided on *bills only*. The FOMC's studies are described in the first section, followed by the criticisms of those who believed that the Fed focused too much on the financial markets to the neglect of macroeconomic goals.

These studies give insight into the monetary policies that are condemned for myopia and secrecy.[2] The Fed's actions are not secret, of

---

[2] For complaints see Milton Friedman, "A Tale of Fed Transcripts," and Thomas Mayer, "Minimizing Regret: Cognitive Dissonance as an Explanation of FOMC Behavior"; and for explanations see Marvin Goodfriend, "Monetary Mystique: Secrecy and Central

course. Open market operations are known immediately to the market, and soon to the public. Not known, however, and these must be the causes of the complaints, are reasons (theories) or plans of action. The Fed is like other dealers in these respects. Practitioners do not engage in abstract reasoning or make commitments except for the very short term. Securities dealers are obligated to make firm offers for minimum quantities,[3] but none makes a long, not to say unlimited, commitment. The dangers are all too obvious in an uncertain world for the Fed as well as for private dealers.

We will explore the interplay between central bankers' traditional concern for financial stability and the less traditional long-term pressures of government deficits and inflation. The policy environment had changed. The nation was determined to prevent the recurrence of depression – to maintain aggregate demand and employment even at the expense of inflation and the monetary standard – and many believed that the Keynesian Revolution had shown how to do it. For the first time, in the *Employment Act of 1946*, the government had taken responsibility for the state of the economy, as had the British government in the 1944 *White Paper on Employment Policy*. Both stopped short of guarantees of full employment, which might be traded off for "other considerations" (see the opening quotation). However, these qualifications were popularly shunted aside by the belief that governments were committed to full employment, reinforced by the confidence among economists that all (or more) good things were possible.[4]

Discussions of demand management focused on fiscal policy, specifically the taxing and spending powers of the federal government, with monetary policy relegated to a supporting role. Because the effects of money and interest rates on spending were slight, Keynesian economists believed, deficient demand was best remedied by government spending and/or reduced taxes, that is, fiscal policy. The central bank's job (monetary policy) was to assure the necessary finance on easy terms.

The Federal Reserve had a different view of its role, and a significant part of the story of central banking in the 1950s and 1960s involves the conflict between expansive governments and a conservative Fed trying

---

Banking," and Goodfriend and Jeffrey Lacker, "Limited Commitment and Central Bank Lending."

[3] For example, see the *National Association of Securities Dealers Manual*, Rule 4613.

[4] G. C. Peden, *British Economic and Social Policy*, pp. 142–43; Herbert Stein, *The Fiscal Revolution in America*, p. 197.

to hold back inflation. A silver lining from the Fed's standpoint, though unacknowledged, was that the softening of the gold constraint (ready to be cut if it should bind) eased the pain of credit restrictions. Like the Bank directors after 1797, although the Fed was concerned with inflation, it was not compelled (by the standard) or allowed (by the government) to impose tight money.

The New Economists that came to power with President Kennedy in 1961 pressed for more active monetary policies, although still subordinate to fiscal policy. The Fed side-stepped this pressure when it could, which in any case involved the impossible policies discussed in the second section.

The third section treats the international framework of central banking that was decided at Bretton Woods, New Hampshire, in 1944, and ended with President Nixon's closing of the gold window in 1971. A version of the gold standard that aimed at its benefits without its costs, the Bretton Woods Agreement, foundered on the contradictions involved in the attempt to secure simultaneously the discipline of fixed exchange rates and the freedom of flexible rates, with the added inconsistency of permanent inflation and the gold standard. The chapter concludes with a discussion of the failure of the 1944 agreement, like that of 1844, to overcome market realities.

Bills Only

As far as monetary theory and the textbooks are concerned, money might as well be dropped from helicopters or handed out on street corners by John D. Rockefeller. The Federal Reserve might as well buy cabbages as government securities. The mechanics of the financial and other markets behind supply-and-demand diagrams are presumed irrelevant to their price and quantity outcomes. This might be true in a long run, fundamental sense, but the Federal Reserve, like other agents, is sensitive to the characteristics of the markets in which it buys and sells.

The return to a more-or-less free market led the FOMC to form an Ad Hoc Subcommittee on the Government Securities Market "to study and report on the operations and functioning of the Open Market Committee, in relation to the Government securities market." The Subcommittee's Report, submitted and approved in November 1952, was made public two years later in the course of Chairman Martin's appearance before Senator Ralph Flanders's Committee on Economic Stabilization.[5]

---

[5] U.S. Congress, *U.S. Monetary Policy: Recent Thinking and Experience*, hearings.

The Ad Hoc Subcommittee's recommendations and the reasons given for them deserve study not least because they reflect the thinking of Martin, who was the most influential member of the FOMC, author of the phrase if not the practice of "leaning against the wind," and a target of criticism from the full spectrum of macroeconomists during his tenure as chairman from 1951 to 1970. Martin instigated and chaired the Ad Hoc Subcommittee and was its chief advocate in the Federal Reserve System and to Congress and the public.

The Subcommittee's Report had four parts: the importance of open market operations to the Fed's goals as prescribed by the Federal Reserve Act, the sensitivity of the financial markets to open market operations and the characteristics to be sought in those markets, the absence of some of these characteristics in the conditions then prevailing, and the improvements that might be secured by a change in Federal Reserve procedures.

Other instruments of monetary policy, the discount rate and reserve requirements, although sometimes useful, received little attention because they lacked the "precision" of open market operations. The initiative in borrowing from the Fed rests with the banks, and reserve requirements are "much too blunt . . . to maintain member-bank borrowing from week to week or month to month at an appropriate level. In short," the Report's preface continued,

open market operations are not simply another instrument of Federal Reserve policy, equivalent or alternative to changes in discount rates or in reserve requirements. They provide a continuously available and flexible instrument of monetary policy for which there is no substitute, an instrument which affects the liquidity of the whole economy. They permit the Federal Reserve System to maintain continuously a tone of restraint in the market when financial and economic conditions call for restraint, or a tone of ease when that is appropriate. They constitute the only effective means by which the elasticity that was built into our monetary and credit structure by the Federal Reserve Act can be made to serve constructively the needs of the economy.

FOMC Ad Hoc Subcommittee, *U.S. Monetary Policy*, p. 259

To be effective, open market operations "require an efficiently functioning Government's securities market characterized by depth, breadth, and resiliency. It is with these characteristics of the market that this report is mainly concerned." The government securities market is the focus of the economy's management of its money balances. The "daily turnover of securities in the market is enormous. It reflects the transactions by which thousands of individual financial institutions and business organizations keep their funds fully employed at interest, without sacrifice of their ability to meet the changing financial requirements of their more basic business operations."

The sensitivity of agents to even small changes in interest rates is great. "Arbitrage transactions" are enormous. "The relative prices at which different issues trade . . . reflect predominantly changes in the demand for and the supply of loanable funds in the money market as a whole and also as between the various short-term, intermediate, and long-term sectors of the market. Since trading is done at commissions or spreads as small as one sixty-fourth [of $1 per $100 trade] and even smaller in very short issues, there are constant opportunities for arbitrage of small differentials in prices when the impact of buying or selling is especially heavy in some particular sector of the market.". . .

It is necessary to keep these basic features of the money market in mind. . . . They help to explain why relatively small operations, sometimes even rumors of operations, by the Federal Open Market Committee may give rise to such quick and pervasive response not only throughout the money market and the investment markets generally but also in business psychology. . . . A relatively small injection of funds through the purchase of bills will ordinarily find a response in the market for long-term securities. Large purchases of bills could scarcely fail to elicit such a response.

FOMC Ad Hoc Committee, pp. 257–58

The Report noted "that the continued maintenance of a relatively fixed pattern of prices and yields in the market for Government securities was inconsistent with its primary monetary and credit responsibilities . . . – that a freer market . . . would lessen inflationary pressures and better promote the *proper* accommodation of commerce, industry, and agriculture. [A] securities market, in which market forces of supply and demand and of savings and investment were permitted to express themselves in market prices and market yields, was indispensable to the effective execution of monetary policies directed toward financial equilibrium and economic stability at a high level of activity without detriment to the *long-run* purchasing power of the dollar"[6] (emphasis added to call attention to qualifications of the Fed's assignments in the Federal Reserve and Employment Acts[7]).

The Subcommittee questioned whether the market for government securities possessed the "depth, breadth, and resiliency to the full degree that would be desirable for the efficient conduct of effective and responsive open market operations." The reference was not to price fluctuations since the Accord, which had been "moderate," but "to the psychology that still pervades the market, to the confusion among professional operators

---

[6] *Ibid.*, p. 259.
[7] In Section 14(d) of the Federal Reserve Act.

in the market with respect to the elements they should take into consideration in the evaluation of future market trends, and to their apprehension over the attitude toward prices in the market on the part of the Federal Open Market Committee and of its representatives on the trading desk."[8]

In strictly market terms, the inside market, i.e., the market that is reflected on the order books of specialists and dealers, possesses depth when there are orders, either actual orders or orders that can be readily uncovered, both above and below the market. The market has breadth when these orders are in volume and come from widely divergent investor groups. It is resilient when new orders pour promptly into the market to take advantage of sharp and unexpected fluctuations in prices.

    These conditions do not now prevail completely in any sector of the market. They are most nearly characteristic of the market for Treasury bills, but even in that market reactions have been sluggish on more than one occasion since the accord. They are least characteristic of the market for restricted bonds. In these issues, there has prevailed persistently since the accord a wide gap between the prices at which the least firm holders are willing to sell and potential buyers are willing to purchase. Within this gap, quotations have fluctuated widely, either in response to relatively small buy or sell orders, or, more frequently, as a result of professional efforts to stimulate interest by marking quotations up or down.[9]

Martin was new to the Fed and free to criticize its procedures. The market's problems were the fault of the FOMC, in particular its confusion about what was meant by a free market for government securities. Officials had stated publicly that the FOMC "contemplates operating in a free market . . . , but at the same time [its] policy record . . . shows that it is still committed to the 'maintenance of orderly markets,' which clearly implies intervention."

"This inconsistency has not added to dealer or customer confidence," the Report continued. "To take positions in volume and make markets, dealers must be confident that a really free market exists in fact, i.e., that the FOMC will permit prices to equate demand and supply without direct intervention other than such as would normally be made to release or absorb reserve funds."[10] What was the remedy? The Subcommittee put itself in the dealers' shoes:

It is in the nature of a dealer's business that he is constantly exposed to market risk from both sides of the market. One test of his professional skill and, indeed, of his fitness to be in the market at all is the ability to judge the factors in a free

[8] FOMC Ad Hoc Subcommittee, p. 265.
[9] *Ibid.*, pp. 265–66.
[10] *Ibid.*, p. 266.

market with sufficient foresight and prudence to preserve or even augment his relatively thin margin of capital, whichever way the market turns. He does this by reversing or covering his positions at times or by alert arbitrage of markets for particular issues that are out of line. Thus he is able to function continuously and to make markets. He cannot do this, however, with anything like the same degree of skill in a market that is subject to unpredictable and overpowering intervention by the Federal Open Market Committee. The Committee, with practically unlimited resources to back up its intervention, is not guided in its operations by considerations of profit, and unlike other investors, is not forced to cover its operations to minimize loss. Such intervention can impose drastic risks on a dealer or other holders, particularly if the intervention is in intermediate or long securities where the dollar impact on the capital position of modest changes in yields is large.[11]

This explained "why dealers, with their lack of confidence in the Committee's intentions to restore a free market, would be reluctant to go very far in taking positions" that would enhance the depth, breadth, and resiliency of the market.[12] The Subcommittee concluded the following:

When intervention by the Federal Open Market Committee is necessary to carry out the System's monetary policies, the market is least likely to be seriously disturbed if the intervention takes the form of purchases or sales of very short-term Government securities. The dealers now have no confidence that transactions will, in fact, be so limited. In the judgment of the subcommittee, an assurance to that effect, if it could be made, would be reflected in greater depth, breadth, and resiliency in all sectors of the market.[13]

This meant "bills only," because 13-week Treasury bills were the shortest term government securities. As many reserves as needed could be added to or taken from the system by purchases and sales of bills as by long-term bonds. The policy

would simply guarantee that the first impact of such purchases and sales would fall on the prices of very short-term issues where dollar prices react least in response to a change in yield, and where the asset value of a portfolio is least affected. A dealer organization, even though it operates on thin margins of capital, can live with impacts such as these and consider them a part of its normal market risks.

Open market operations "initiated in the short-term sector [would spread] to other sectors of the market" through the arbitrage activities of the market professionals "who are constantly balancing their investments

[11] *Ibid.*, pp. 266–67.
[12] *Loc. cit.*
[13] *Ibid.*, p. 267.

to take advantage of shifts in prices and yields between the different sectors of the market." The Federal Reserve's assurance that it "would limit its intervention to the very short-term market" would not, in general, limit its effectiveness. The assurance was within "the best central banking traditions. . . . In fact, most effective central banks have operated within this restriction, imposed either by tradition or by law. Traditional principles of central banking made no provision for operations in the intermediate or long maturities of any borrower."

The recommended assurance was subject to two exceptions. First, the FOMC was bound in its pursuit of orderly conditions to support Treasury borrowing. Even after the Accord it routinely bought portions of new issues, to be sold off slowly in succeeding weeks.[14] Second, although the Subcommittee believed that price fluctuations "in a really free market" were normally "self-correcting . . . without the necessity for intervention," it recognized the occasional occurrence of "disorderly conditions." It considered "a declining market really disorderly in the sense that it requires intervention to meet it when selling feeds on itself so rapidly and so menacingly that it discourages both short covering and the placement of offsetting new orders by investors who ordinarily would seek to profit from purchases made in weak markets." Such "disorderly reactions . . . may lead, if left unchecked, to the development of panic conditions."

In the judgment of the Subcommittee, it is in these circumstances, and these circumstances only, that the Federal Open Market Committee would be impelled, by *its basic responsibility for the maintenance of sound monetary conditions*, to intervene, and intervene decisively, in other than the very short-term sector of the Government securities market.[15]

The Subcommittee proposed that the wording of the FOMC's directive to the Manager of the System account "be changed to provide for the 'correction of disorderly conditions' rather than the 'maintenance of orderly conditions' in the market for Government securities." Emphasis was added above to call attention to the gulf between the Subcommittee's view of the Federal Reserve's *basic responsibility* and those of most economists and probably the framers of the Employment Act of 1946.

---

[14] For an estimate of the response of Fed purchases to Treasury issues in the years following the Accord, see John Wood, "A Model of Federal Reserve Behavior."

[15] FOMC, *op. cit.* p. 268.

Most economists thought that monetary policy included the willing-ness to force sudden and substantial changes in interest rates, especially long-term rates. This followed from the importance of capital goods (plant and equipment financed by long-term obligations) for growth in the long term as well as stabilization in the short term. J. M. Keynes had written in 1930,

The main direct influence of the Banking System is over the short-term rate of interest. But when it is a question of controlling the rate of investment, not in working capital but in fixed capital, it is the long-term rate of interest which chiefly matters.
A Treatise on Money, ii, p. 352

Under slump conditions, it becomes necessary to "impose on the Cen-tral Bank the duty of purchasing bonds up to a price far beyond what it considers to be the long-period norm."[16] He later expanded on this theme:

Perhaps a complex offer by the central bank to buy and sell at stated prices gilt-edged bonds of all maturities, in place of the single bank rate for short-term bills, is the most important practical improvement that can be made in the technique of monetary management.... The monetary authority often tends in practice to concentrate on short-term debts and to leave the price of long-term debts to be influenced by belated and imperfect reactions from the price of short-term debts.
The General Theory of Employment, Interest and Money, p. 206

Other students of the yield curve were skeptical of Keynes's position on two grounds. R. G. Hawtrey took the position, probably in the mi-nority, that economic fluctuations were driven primarily by inventory demands, which were sensitive to short-term interest rates. More im-portant, perhaps, and consistent with the FOMC's position, was that long-term rates were determined by long-term investment projects and resisted short-term monetary policies. The way to affect long rates was to operate on short-term rates and their expectations because rates on long-term investments are averages of expected rates on short-term investments.[17]

Keynes had not neglected these relations, and he urged that policy attacks on long-term rates be sharp and credibly persistent. The FOMC wished to avoid such attacks. The Fed's critics associated smoothness with

---

[16] J. M. Keynes, *A Treatise on Money*, ii, p. 373.

[17] R. G. Hawtrey, *A Century of Bank Rate*, pp. 195–202. The argument was surveyed by John Wood, "The Expectations Hypothesis, the Yield Curve, and Monetary Policy."

ineffectiveness, and in any case, they did not wish to relinquish monetary policy's freedom of action. A review of economists' critiques of "bills only" concluded the following:

Sizeable price changes and difficulty in selling securities – both conditions which would not exist in a market with depth, breadth, and resiliency – may at times be of great help in achieving credit policy objectives.... Difficulties in completing security transactions and in financing dealer positions – in a word, impairment of the bond market's ability to function, temporarily at least – are an essential part of a restrictive credit policy. Thus the "bills only" policy was not only poorly designed to achieve its purpose; its very purpose was wrong.
    Daniel Ahearn, *Federal Reserve Policy Reappraised, 1951–59*, pp. 65–66, 69

It seemed to economists that the FOMC was more interested in the welfare of securities dealers than effective policy. This attitude was similar to the "paternalistic support accorded to the bankers' acceptance market" in the 1920s, when, according to Seymour Harris, "credit policy [was] jeopardized by the assumed need of protecting" that market.[18] His Harvard colleague, Alvin Hansen, thought that the FOMC's concern was misplaced. "The notion that Fed intervention in the market has the effect of increasing risk and uncertainty is certainly one of the most curious arguments I have ever encountered."[19] Supporting Hansen's "rightful dismay," Sidney Weintraub of the University of Pennsylvania wrote,

Economic stabilization would suffer a sharp setback if the view took root that the central banking mechanism was designed to protect bondholders from changes in capital values rather than reserved for broader conceptions of economic policy.[20]

He derided as "cajoling oratory" Martin's statement "that 'the credit and money of this country is at the grass roots,' and that 'the composite judgments which come up through...groups in various towns and hamlets...has [sic] more to do with the credit basis of this country than the influence of the Treasury and the Federal Reserve put together'; but the job of controlling monetary phenomena still remains with the Reserve System and cannot be farmed out to the mythical 'grass-roots'."

---

[18] Seymour Harris, *Twenty Years of Federal Reserve Policy*, i, p. 428; also Lawrence Clark, *Central Banking under the Federal Reserve System*, p. 378.

[19] "Monetary Policy."

[20] " 'Monetary Policy': A Comment." The quotation is from Martin's speech to the Bond Club of New York on December 15, 1954, reported in *The Commercial and Financial Chronicle*, December 23, 1954.

New York Fed President Allan Sproul also disagreed with "bills only" because it restricted the Fed's freedom of action, although he hastened to add that he shared the Subcommittee's objectives.[21] An unspoken reason for Martin's advocacy of the policy, felt more in Washington than in New York, was that it provided some protection from Treasury pressures to control the rate structure.[22]

Explaining the Postdepression Inflation

The "bills-only" controversy tells us a lot about Federal Reserve thinking and monetary policy in the 1950s, but not everything because orderly rates leave their level and trend unsettled. The FOMC had decided that the injections of reserves, given the amounts decided, should have as little effect on interest rates as possible, especially long-term rates. But what determines the quantities of reserves injected?

The nearly continuous inflation after 1933 is usually explained as a symptom of the government's determination to avoid a recurrence of the deflation of the 1930s. On the surface, monetary policy was consistent with this determination. It was also consistent with a combination of the traditional desire for orderly financial markets and the untraditionally soft constraint. This is where the presumption comes in that the gold standard would be suspended if it got in the way of domestic goals. Although bankers like to make loans, and dislike calling them in, they tighten if necessary to defend their reserves. The suspension of its reserve restraint helps to explain the Bank of England's behavior after 1797, and it may apply to the Federal Reserve after its operational independence from the Treasury in 1951.

The Fed knew that it was "too easy." Near the end of the 1954–57 boom, Martin told the Joint Economic Committee,

If we had the whole period to go through again, I think I would be inclined toward having a little more restriction in monetary policy from the latter part of 1954 to date. If we had been more restrictive, we would have had more influence, not that monetary and credit policy is the only thing, but it would have been a more stabilizing force in the economy.[23]

---

[21] Testimony to the Flanders Committee, December 7, 1954; reprinted in L. S. Ritter, ed., *Selected Papers of Allan Sproul.*

[22] I am indebted to a reviewer for this insight.

[23] U.S. Congress, *Hearings on the January 1957 Economic Report of the President*, 1957, p. 257; also see Daniel Ahearn, *Federal Reserve Policy*, p. 119, for this and the next quotation.

This could have been Benjamin Strong in the 1920s. After the 1957–58 recession, Martin responded to criticisms of insufficient ease before the House Ways and Means Committee:

I do want to point out that in eight years of experience in the Federal Reserve System, I am convinced that our bias, if anything, has been on the side of too much money rather than too little.[24]

When its attempt to limit credit in 1966 in the face of the Vietnam buildup led to a "credit crunch" involving high interest rates and problems for the money center banks, the Fed relented again. (This episode is related in Chap. 12.) Even in the 1990s, after the reaction to the high inflation of the 1970s, cutbacks in military spending, and the advent of independent central banks avowedly dedicated to price stability, inflation was significant compared with that under the gold standard. The shift in monetary standards/restraints was signified by New York Fed President William McDonough when he said of reported inflation of 1.9 percent, "If that isn't price stability, I don't know what is."[25] Such an inflation doubles prices every 37 years, compared with their near identity in 1824 and 1914.

Operation Twist

"Bills only" was terminated in 1961 under pressure from an administration that wanted fewer restrictions on policy instruments. Not everyone thought the Fed had been too easy. "No one but Mr. Martin knows," wrote James Tobin, soon to be a member of the Council of Economic Advisers, "how much slack the Federal Reserve is willing to force upon the economy in the effort to stop inflation."[26] The 1960 Democratic platform promised "an end to the present high-interest, tight-money policy" that had produced "two recessions within five years" and had "bankrupted many of our families."[27] Much had to be done to fulfill the promise "to get the country moving again." Among the problems awaiting the ambitious new administration were slow economic growth and a deteriorating balance of payments.

The "dollar shortage" following the war had turned to a glut that foreigners were converting to gold. At its peak in 1949, the United States

---

[24] *Public Debt Ceiling and Interest Rate Ceiling on Bonds, Hearings*, 1960, p. 185.
[25] *New York Times*, October 1, 1999, p. 5.
[26] "Defense, Dollars, and Doctrines."
[27] Donald Kettl, *Leadership at the Fed*, p. 97.

owned $25 billion of the world's monetary gold stock of $35 billion. By the end of 1957, U.S. gold was falling nearly $2 billion a year, and by early 1961 it was just over $17 billion – on its way to $11 billion at the end of the decade. Net short-term foreign investments in the United States (which were readily convertible into gold) exceeded the gold reserve by a substantial margin.

President Kennedy's advisors preferred fiscal policy but came up with a challenging program for the Fed that aimed at the triple objectives of growth, balance of payments surplus, and price stability by twisting the yield curve. The Fed would stimulate long-term investment by buying long-term securities whereas helping the balance of payments by attracting short-term investments through the higher short-term yields that would result from sales of short-term securities. The program would not be inflationary because the added reserves from the purchases of long-term investments would be offset by the sales of short-terms. Operation Twist was a compromise between the president's social goals and his conservative fiscal and monetary outlook, an advisor wrote, and

the outflow of gold rose to proportions which could not continue without disaster. The need for world confidence in the dollar, and the danger of a "run on the bank" by dollar-holders turning them in for gold, dominated several of his conversations as president-elect. They were the decisive influence in his choice of a secretary of the Treasury [Republican investment banker Douglas Dillon, who had been undersecretary of state under Eisenhower and might have been Nixon's secretary of the treasury]. They started us working on the balance of payments program he presented in February. In his State of the Union Message he emphasized the priority he was giving the problem, his refusal to devalue the dollar by raising the price of gold and his determination to do whatever had to be done "to make certain that . . . the dollar is sound."

Theodore Sorenson, *Kennedy*, p. 406

Secretary Dillon thought that what the president had in mind might not be enough, and he warned that the budget deficits implied by the programs under consideration might raise doubts about the dollar and "cause foreign bankers . . . to take more American gold."[28]

Outside the Treasury, "Almost to a man," the president's advisers "thought he was excessively concerned about the problem. . . . [M]ore concerned with the domestic economy, [they] pointed out that the totals owed this nation by others far exceeded the claims upon our reserves, and that the wealthiest nation in history, possessing two-fifths of the free

[28] Theodore Sorenson, *Kennedy*, p. 407.

world's gold stocks, was hardly in dire straits."[29] Some advisers thought that devaluation was "not unthinkable," but Kennedy did not like even the mention of "that weapon of last resort." He was at once more pessimistic and more optimistic than his advisers.

> "I know everyone else thinks I worry about this too much," he said to me one day as we pored over what seemed like the millionth report on the subject. "But if there's ever a run on the bank, and I have to devalue the dollar or bring home our troops, as the British did, I'm the one who will take the heat. Besides it's a club that De Gaulle and all the others hang over my head. Any time there's a crisis or a quarrel, they can cash in all their dollars and where are we?" He also had some evidence to back his suspicions that the gloomy rumors which triggered the gold withdrawals of 1960 had been deliberately spread by American bankers to embarrass him politically, and he did not want to be vulnerable to the same tactic in 1964.
>
> Sorenson, *Kennedy*, p. 408

However, Kennedy, was also readier to try expedients. "He refused to believe," Sorenson wrote, "that he had to choose between a weaker economy at home or a weaker dollar abroad." The president persuaded Congress to levy a tax on foreign bond issues floated in the United States, although he found the Treasury "very skillful at shooting down every balloon floated elsewhere in the administration" to fix the balance of payments. He regretted that there were not more restrictions on American investments abroad. "Sure they bring more in earnings in the long run, but by then this problem will be over. It's a ridiculous situation for us to be squeezing down essential public activities in order not to touch private investment and tourist spending – but apparently that's life."[30]

The candidate had promised: "I have no doubt that any new Democratic president will find the Federal Reserve pursuing a somewhat different policy." He reminded voters that "The president has great influence" and hinted that Martin might be replaced.[31] After the election, when the chairman-designate of the president's Council of Economic Advisers (CEA), Walter Heller, called on Martin, the latter warned, "I'm not going to give up the independence of the Fed." But he added, "There's plenty of room for cooperation."[32]

---

[29] *Ibid.*, p. 408.
[30] *Ibid.*, p. 409.
[31] Herbert Brattner, "The Federal Reserve's Independence."
[32] Heller interview, Erwin Hargrove and Samuel Morley, *The President and the Council of Economic Advisers*, p. 189.

The administration got Martin's agreement to nudge short-term rates up while keeping long-term rates low. Operation Nudge turned into Operation Twist, which would involve vigorous actions to reduce long rates. "This is an historic reversal of policy," Heller wrote the president, "for which Chairman Martin deserves our appreciation."[33]

Heller's satisfaction turned out to be premature. Several members of the FOMC "were strongly opposed to the end of 'bills only' [as] a step back toward political interference in monetary policy and a pegged bond market," and Martin managed to obtain and keep the majority's support for Operation Twist only by an execution that bordered on the imperceptible.[34] The administration was disappointed in the Fed's "team spirit." Heller recalled that

we'd have a meeting with Kennedy... and before the meeting Bill would be out there buying those long-term securities, but afterwards his buying would flag. ... Jim Tobin would keep track of this and he'd say, "Walter, you'd better ... arrange another meeting ... because Martin isn't buying enough long-term bonds." So I'd call a meeting and sure enough the purchases would rise again, and Martin would be able to tell Kennedy, "We're doing everything we can."[35]

We are reminded of the Fed's security purchases while Congress was in session in 1932. A later CEA chairman, Arthur Okun (1968–69), remembered that "the change in the federal funds rate in the week preceding [meetings with President Johnson] was almost always negative ... Martin was always bringing the president the present of a little lower interest rate than he'd run in the interim" – a present to "a boy from Texas," who could not "see high interest rates as a lesser evil than anything else."[36]

Kennedy's advisers opposed the Fed chairman's reappointment in 1963 at first. "They discovered, however, that Martin had a formidable reputation in the domestic business community, and internationally he was a symbol of the fight to maintain the dollar's value." Dillon told the president that Martin "can be a tower of strength." Dillon's team spirit was also suspect as Heller saw Treasury financing operations unwind the twist.[37]

---

[33] Memo, Council of Economic Advisers to the president, February 16, 1961, Heller Papers, "Monetary Policy," Kennedy Library, in Kettl, *op. cit.*, p. 98.

[34] Kettl, *op. cit.*, pp. 98–99.

[35] Hargrove and Morley, *op. cit.*, p. 191.

[36] *Ibid.*, pp. 293, 274.

[37] Kettl, *op. cit.*, p. 100.

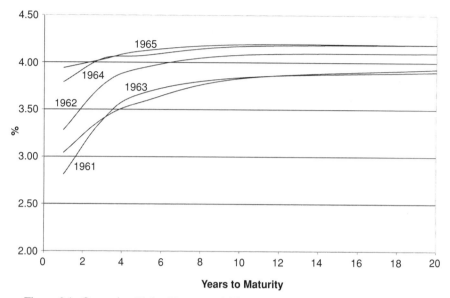

Figure 9.1. Operation Twist: Treasury yield curves, January averages, 1961–65.
Source: Federal Reserve Board release: constant-maturity yields.

The yield curve twisted the desired direction during the period that it was proclaimed policy (1961–64), as we see in Fig. 9.1. The Council of Economic Advisors pointed to the "remarkable stability" of long-term rates during a period of generally rising rates.[38] In fact, the movements in long- and short rates had not differed from tradition. Smaller rises in long than short rates are characteristic of economic expansions, as could have been checked as recently as 1949–53, 1954–57, and 1958–60 (see Fig. 8.3). Such movements are consistent with the expectations theory of the term structure of interest rates, for which long rates are averages of current and expected short rates that approach a normal level.[39]

A good deal of evidence pointed to the futility of attempts to control more than one price of substitutable assets in the face of the "alert arbitrage of markets for issues that are out of line" (to repeat a phrase of the Ad Hoc Subcommittee). The dislocations caused by the World War II bond support program (see Table 8.1) were among the most obvious. Subsequent research, much of it stimulated by Operation Twist, have reinforced these observations. Changes in the relative quantities of

[38] *Economic Report of the President*, January 1966, p. 50.
[39] John and Norma Wood, *Financial Markets*, pp. 629–36.

short- and long-term Treasury debt have no perceptible effect on the yield curve; "price adjustments in the markets for securities are very rapid."[40]

Operation Twist could not have worked and was hardly tried. Heller's fears were realized in the "half-hearted" and "timid" efforts of the Fed, notwithstanding its protestations in the Board's *Annual Reports*.[41] Furthermore, the Treasury acted contrary to declared policy by issuing more long than short debt, a natural step when interest rates are expected to rise. "As a result, the maturity of the debt lengthened appreciably, instead of shortened as the policy would require," Chicago economist Harry Johnson noted.[42]

Bretton Woods

In Place of the Gold Standard

The international monetary agreement among 44 countries at Bretton Woods, New Hampshire, in July 1944, intended to restore the advantages of the pre-1914 gold standard without its disadvantages. In that system as it came to be idealized after the disruptions of the interwar period, international money flows had been unrestricted. Importers, exporters, and investors could pay, receive, and maintain bank accounts and other investments in the currencies of their choice. National defaults were not unknown, and fears of them produced currency runs. However, in normal times an importer could buy anywhere and pay in any of the several national currencies that exporters could be confident of exchanging for other currencies or gold at fixed rates. Its best features were free exchange, efficiency (as funds were free to flow to the areas of highest return), and long-run price stability.

Many believed that these benefits had been purchased at the cost of the short-term instability of money, prices, and employment. The costs, like the benefits, arose from the system's automatic nature. Domestic inflation set opposing forces in motion. High prices encouraged imports and discouraged exports, leading to gold losses that forced restrictions on a country's money and credit until its prices were brought into line

---

[40] G. O. Bierwag and M. A. Grove, "A Model of the Structure of Prices of Marketable U.S. Treasury Securities."

[41] Heller's appraisals of the Fed's efforts are from Kettl, *op. cit.*, p. 99. See pp. 12–13 of the 1963 and 1964 Federal Reserve Board *Annual Reports*.

[42] "An Overview of Price Levels, Employment, and the U.S. Balance of Payments." For the maturity structure of the federal debt, see Federal Reserve Board, *Banking and Monetary Statistics, 1941–70*, table 13.5.

with prices elsewhere and equilibrium in its balance of payments was restored. That was good. Not so good was the transmission of inflation across national boundaries by the same process. This international business cycle was bad enough, but central banks were thought to have reinforced it by the "rules of the gold standard game," that is, by restricting or expanding their credit as they lost or acquired gold. This belief exaggerated actual policies. Most central banks, most of the time, had moderated rather than reinforced gold flows.[43] Policies, however, are governed by beliefs.

The gold standard was not automatic. We have seen that there was considerable scope for discretion on both sides of the Atlantic. Nevertheless, the concern for gold reserves had inhibited domestic responses to the Great Depression. The system collapsed when governments broke with the restrictive policies necessary to maintain convertibility at fixed rates. They suspended convertibility or devalued their currencies, imposed controls on the export of gold and foreign exchange, and restricted imports. "Beggar-my-neighbor measures had aimed to reverse deflation and promote domestic demands at the expense of others."[44] Countries felt that they had no other choice in the face of the volatility of gold flows as investors sought safe havens. They had to ration gold and foreign exchange to ensure the essentials of industry and life.

The global payments system broke into bilateral agreements that sometimes amounted to barter. Country A might license imports from country B less on the grounds of cost than because B reciprocated. Officially controlled multiple exchange rates discriminated in favor of exporters and against the importers of "nonessential" goods.

Attempts to reconstruct the old system began as early as 1933 at the London Monetary Conference. The United States at first refused to participate because of its preoccupation with internal conditions, but it soon joined British and French consultations about exchange rates and stabilization funds. These procedures, highlighted by the British and American announcements that they would not react to the French devaluation of September 1936, was called the "tripartite monetary agreement," although it was extended to Belgium, the Netherlands, and Switzerland.

---

[43] For example, Arthur Bloomfield, *Monetary Policy under the International Gold Standard, 1890–1914*.

[44] See Joan Robinson, "Beggar-My-Neighbour Remedies for Unemployment" and the bibliography (VI) at the end of Howard Ellis and Lloyd Metzler, *Readings in the Theory of International Trade*.

By the end of the decade, three major systems of multilateral payments had been assembled.[45] The "dollar area" that covered North America, the Caribbean, and northern South America pegged their currencies to the U.S. dollar and tended to pay and receive dollars. In the "sterling area," consisting of Britain and its colonies and dominions except Canada, tariff concessions were made to members (Imperial Preference), and payments to nonmembers were restricted. The third group, with fewer payment restrictions, consisted of France, Belgium, Luxembourg, Switzerland, and the Netherlands. The rest of the world relied on bilateralism.

Planning for Peace

War renewed fragmentation, but planning for the return to unrestricted multilateral payments continued, with the United States as the driving force. This was a little surprising in light of its history of tariffs and diplomatic noninvolvement, but the politics of American foreign policy had changed. Isolationism was in retreat and the new political consensus regarding military alliances and international peace-keeping organizations extended to trade and finance. The traditionally high-tariff country had become the world's leading advocate of free trade.

The postwar international economic agreements, "taken together," Raymond Mikesell, war-time Treasury researcher and negotiator, wrote in 1947, "constitute an American program for the restitution of multilateral world trade. They are in large measure postulated on the existence of a world in which trade is conducted by unregimented private enterprise and are designed to assure its successful operation by correcting the sources of international maladjustment which characterized the 1920s and 1930s."[46] It had not started out that way. Secretary Henry Morgenthau and his staff "were not believers in *laissez-faire*; they shared the belief of most New Deal planners that government had an important responsibility for the successful direction of economic life," we are reminded in Richard Gardner's *Sterling–Dollar Diplomacy*. By 1943, however, "the balance of power on economic issues was shifting to a conservative coalition of Republicans and Southern Democrats." The Democratic Party had lost ground in the 1942 congressional elections, and within the administration "some unrepentant New Dealers were being ousted by more conservative

---

[45] See Raymond Mikesell, *Foreign Exchange in the Postwar World*, chap. 1.
[46] Mikesell, "The Role of the International Monetary Agreements in a World of Planned Economies."

leaders recruited from the ranks of finance and industry."[47] Mikesell did not object to their goal but wondered about its feasibility in the face of the world trend toward the "socialization of production and distribution and the growing adherence to the philosophy of economic planning...."[48]

Most surprising of all, perhaps, was America's determination to return to a form of the gold standard. The Federal Reserve had neutralized gold flows in the interests of stable domestic money and prices. Its refusal to play by "the rules of the game" had made life difficult for those striving for convertibility in the 1920s, and New Deal officials had been notable for their attacks on traditional institutions and their declarations of the priority of national over international interests.

Notwithstanding this record, the system that the U.S. Treasury proposed to the conference at Bretton Woods was as close to the classical gold standard as its understanding of conditions permitted. The key elements of the American, or White Plan (after the Treasury's chief author and negotiator, Harry Dexter White), are listed in the following:[49]

The purposes of the proposed International Stabilization Fund were to help stabilize exchange rates, shorten the periods and lessen the degree of disequilibrium in balances of payments, and create favorable conditions for the smooth international flow of trade and productive capital, including the elimination of foreign exchange restrictions.

The Fund would consist of contributions of gold and foreign exchange, with member quotas dependent on national incomes, the size and fluctuations of the balance of payments, and other "relevant factors." Quotas would be 30 to 50 percent in gold.

The monetary unit of the Fund would be the *unitas*, worth 137 1/7 grains of fine gold (equivalent to $10), which could not be changed except by 85 percent of member votes (with country votes related to their quotas, but none with more than one-fifth of the total).

Exchange rates for initial members would be based on the values of their currencies in terms of the U.S. dollar on July 1, 1943. Others, including the Axis powers and occupied countries would be determined in consultation with the governing Board of the Fund. The Fund would determine the range within which rates would be permitted to fluctuate, and changes in rates would be considered only when essential to the correction of fundamental disequilibrium in its balance of payments, and would be made only with the approval of three-fourths of member votes.

---

[47] Richard Gardner, *Sterling–Dollar Diplomacy*, pp. 76–77.

[48] Mikesell, "The Role of International Monetary Agreements in a World of Planned Economics."

[49] The White and Keynes plans are reproduced in John Williams, *Postwar Monetary Plans and Other Essays*, appendices.

The Fund would have the power to buy the currency and government securities of a member up to twice its quota if (i) in the judgment of the Fund satisfactory measures were being taken or would be taken by the member to correct the disequilibrium in its balance of payments, and (ii) it was believed that the excess currency holdings of the Fund could be disposed of within a reasonable time.

The rival to the American Plan was the British proposal for an International Clearing Union. The Keynes Plan, named after White's counterpart in the British Treasury, differed from White's in two important aspects relating to the immediate and long-term futures. The Americans expected a rapid return to trade and exchange between solvent and vigorous peoples; it looked at the world through the eyes of a production powerhouse seeking markets. Keynes was more attuned to the devastations of war and the difficulties of the recovery that would have to precede normal relations. For the long run, unsurprising in his experience and as author of *The General Theory*, Keynes was as concerned with depression as expansion. He thought that creditor nations should share the burdens of adjustment rather than forcing deflation on debtors.

Keynes's Clearing Union was addressed to flexibility in currency arrangements. It differed from the White Plan in placing support ahead of discipline. It was "a means of reassurance to a troubled world, by which any country whose own affairs are conducted with due prudence is relieved of anxiety, for causes which are not of its own making, concerning its ability to meet its international liabilities, and which will, therefore, make unnecessary those methods of restriction and discrimination which countries have adopted hitherto...." An "instrument of international currency having general acceptability between nations" would be provided in an amount not "determined in an unpredictable and irrelevant manner as, for example, by the technical progress of the gold industry, nor subject to large variations depending on the gold reserve policies of individual countries; but...governed by the actual current requirements of world commerce and...capable of deliberate expansion and contraction to offset deflationary and inflationary tendencies in effective world demand."[50]

Keynes's wish for half the rules of the game – expansion by creditors without contraction by debtors – was unacceptable to the United States. As a safe haven and supplier of goods to a war-torn world, it had accumulated most of the world's monetary gold, and its undamaged productive

---

[50] "Proposals for an International Clearing Union" (the Keynes plan), HM Government, April 7, 1943, in Williams, *op. cit.*

capacity assured that it would be a creditor country for the foreseeable future. Keynes had cooked up a scheme, it seemed to the Americans, by which a financially strapped Britain might pick their pockets. He proposed a quota of $25 to $30 billion, compared with White's $5 billion, and no special prescience was required to foretell a rapid accumulation of overdrafts by countries short of productive capacity, foreign exchange, and financial discipline. Congress later showed its willingness to give aid; but it would have to be in line with American interests as it saw them. "If we are big enough suckers to swallow the Keynes plan," exclaimed the Council Bluffs *Nonpareil*, "we shall be swindled out of everything we have left from the war – and we shall deserve to be swindled."[51] The idea of taxing credit balances seemed "utterly grotesque" to another observer. Some preferred the old system. The *New York Times* declared the following on March 30, 1943:

If...each nation were fully convinced that it would best serve its own interest by maintaining the integrity of its currency unit, no elaborate arrangements or clearing houses would be needed. Every nation, rich or poor, is free to stabilize its own currency system with respect to gold...provided that it abstains from domestic credit expansion and inflation. The gold standard was, without international agreements, the most satisfactory international standard that has ever been devised.... It is often said that the gold standard "failed." The truth is that governments sabotaged it deliberately because it interfered with the nationalistic "planning" that governments preferred to stability of exchange rates.

American negotiators disliked the leisurely pace toward the new system envisioned by the British, who expected trade and exchange restrictions to be necessary for some time, until recovery permitted their dismantlement. The United States was impatient to be underway. Its exporters wanted access to British markets. The White Plan was aimed as much as anything at Imperial Preference, which Secretary of State Cordell Hull called "the greatest injury, in a commercial way, that has been inflicted on this country since I have been in public life."[52] Assistant Secretary of State Dean Acheson assured congressional committees not only that access to the proposed Fund's credit would not be too easy but that the new arrangements "would eliminate the use of some of the most flagrant devices for discriminating against the trade of the United States by

---

[51] Gardner, *op. cit.*, pp. 97, 99.
[52] U.S. Congress, House Committee on Ways and Means, *Hearings on Extension of Reciprocal Trade Agreements Act* (Gardner, *op. cit.*, p. 19).

other countries."[53] Trade liberalization, access to foreign markets, was a persistent thread running through American foreign policy. The American "gift" of over $20 billion of lend-lease materials to Britain during the war, called by Churchill "the most unsordid act in history," had a *quid pro quo* in the promise of postwar multilateral trade and payments that the Americans understood as the opening of the British Empire. "I have not become the King's first minister in order to preside over the liquidation of the British Empire," Churchill had said.[54] Neither had the Americans fought to preserve it.

The United States got what it wanted at Bretton Woods, and so in a way did the British, because their agreement to the White Plan brought a desperately needed loan. The International Monetary Fund was ready to operate from its headquarters in Washington, in the spring of 1947, but to little avail because it had been overtaken by events. By that time, the Americans realized that they had been too optimistic about the speed of recovery of the international economy, and spurred by the communist threat, they turned their emphasis to reconstruction. Secretary of State George Marshall announced his plan on June 5, 1947. The Fund's implementation would have to wait . . . and wait.

Where Were the Central Banks?

One might be tempted to conclude that British planning for the postwar monetary system bypassed the Bank because of its low repute after the debacle of the 1920s and that the Federal Reserve Board wandered in the wilderness because of the failure of Marriner Eccles's bid to be the president's chief economic adviser. Governments, however, have nearly always taken the lead in changing the monetary regime. Consider the various suspensions and resumptions, the Act of 1844, silver purchase acts, the Gold Standard Act of 1900, the dollar devaluation of 1934, and, as we will see, the British resumption of 1947 and the American suspension of 1971. These were political decisions affecting important interests. The British return to gold in 1925 was an exception that later governments were determined not to repeat. The job of central banks is to facilitate regimes established by governments.

The Bank of England also looked forward, some day, to free trade and unrestricted convertibility, but it distrusted the methods contemplated by its own and the U.S. governments. The Bank was afraid of

---

[53] Hearings before committees of the Senate and House, Gardner, *op. cit.*, pp. 135–36.
[54] Speech at the Lord Mayor's Day Luncheon, November 10, 1942.

moving too quickly and thought that the grandiose Keynes and White schemes would "be regarded as painless cures, diverting national attention from fundamental problems," John Fforde wrote in his history of the Bank between 1941 and 1958. "Above all, the Bank was seemingly haunted by its own bitter experience of 1925–31 and fearful lest the British authorities should again undertake external monetary commitments, in particular the early resumption of external convertibility at a fixed rate of exchange, which they would find that they were unable to honour."[55] Its attitude toward resumption was more like that taken in 1819 than in 1925.

Norman set up a committee in 1941 to study postwar arrangements. It was led by Cameron Cobbold, later the second-longest-serving governor (1949–61), who like Keynes was educated at Eton and King's College, Cambridge, although unlike Keynes but like Norman, he left Cambridge after a year for the City. He and most of the rest of the committee were career Bank operating officials. Their opposition to Keynes's plan stemmed in good part from an "instinctive dislike, even resentment," as Fforde put it, of "grand international . . schemes dreamt up by economists who may seem, if only because of terminological differences, to be giving insufficient attention to the practicalities of the market-place."

[They] proposed instead a much more step-by-step and try-it-and-see procedure. Its ultimate international monetary component would have been a development of the 1936 Tripartite Agreement for mutual co-operation between the exchange stabilisation funds of the US, the UK, and France. This set of ideas was not confined to the Bank and became known as the "key-currency approach" to distinguish it from the new-institution approach of Keynes and others. A prominent American exponent was Professor J. H. Williams, economic adviser to the FRBNY, the Bank of England's principal contact in the US.[56]

Williams described his "key countries, or central countries, approach" as "less elaborate" and "closer in conception than either the Keynes or the White plan to the way the gold standard actually worked, around England as the central country, in the nineteenth century." The first order of business, after the necessary transition period of recovery from the war, was to stabilize "the truly international currencies whose behavior dominates and determines what happens to all the others."[57] The "younger countries,

---

[55] John Fforde, *The Bank of England and Public Policy, 1941–58*, p. 33.

[56] Fforde, *op. cit.*, p. 39.

[57] "Currency Stabilization: The Keynes and White Plans," *Foreign Affairs*, July 1943 (reprinted in *Postwar Monetary Plans*).

whose economic conditions primarily reflect the conditions existing in the great world markets, for which they are only secondarily responsible, should be permitted to vary their currencies. It might help them somewhat, without too seriously affecting the larger economies." The proposed international organizations would not have the "sharp teeth" to impose their rules, anyway. These countries might come on board a system of fixed exchange rates as their situations permitted, but the first emphasis of postwar monetary planners should be on the countries whose currencies dominated international trade.

In a letter prepared for presentation by His Majesty's government to the U.S. government, the Bank argued as follows:

The discussions throughout have tended to assume two entirely different phases: (i) a transitional period and (ii) the final post-war period ("when things have settled down") when it may or may not be possible to introduce a completely new economic plan.

This is, it seems to us, a somewhat misleading picture both for our own working and for presentation to others. The cardinal mistake and the greatest admission of defeat which we can make is to put up as a final objective something which we do not believe has a reasonable chance of coming about. We must set ourselves aims in which we believe and our policy must from the start be directed towards bringing them about. Progress can only be by trial and error but we must constantly strive to form and adapt our controls and our international economic relations with the ultimate goal always in view. We must never allow ourselves to contemplate a static transitional period and hope that on a given date one, two or three years after the war the heavens will open and our problems be solved.

It has come to be believed that exchange controls and trade controls are inevitably destructive and restrictive. On the contrary we believe that their intelligent use in co-operation with other countries is the only possible alternative to a regime of fluctuating exchange rates and speculative movements of funds, far more destructive of trade, and that if properly used they can be constructive and expansive: in fact, that without them the post-war world would inevitably fall back into the chaos of the Thirties.[58]

The Bank's approach found no favor among those in charge, Fforde reports, especially Keynes "and his supporting cast of like-minded economists." Dennis Robertson expressed to Keynes "a glowing hope that the spirit of Burke and Adam Smith is on earth again to prevent the affairs of a Great Empire from being settled by the little minds of a gang of bank clerks who have tasted blood...."[59]

[58] Fforde, *op. cit.*, p. 42.

[59] November 27, 1941, quoted in Fforde, *op. cit.*, p. 43.

Keynes reacted to Lord Beaverbrook's concern that his plan looked like the system that had caused so much damage:

It is, indeed, quite the opposite. Instead of setting out, as the gold standard does, from the assumption of rigidity, it sets out from the assumption of appropriate changes to meet circumstances.... Surely it is not plausible to cast *me* for the role of a defender of the gold standard and the Bank for the role of pointing out what a shocking affair it is. You cannot have forgotten back history so much as to think that that makes sense!...

You speak of the Bank having a plan. I have never seen anything from them which deserves this name. They could be described as having a prejudice in favour of an atmosphere. But as for a plan, it has never been produced.... The Bank is engaged in a desperate gamble in the interests of old arrangements and old-fashioned ideas, which there is no possibility of sustaining. Their plan, or rather their lack of plan would, in my firm belief, lead us into yet another smash.... The whole thing is sheer rubbish from beginning to end. For God's sake have nothing to do with it![60]

Notwithstanding their histories, Keynes had become readier than the Bank to leap to a form of the gold standard, and he was more willing to commit to a course of action. Negotiations between the Treasuries proceeded, and the Bank's representative was little more than an observer at Bretton Woods.

The International Monetary Fund (IMF) never got off the ground. In his 1954 account of *Foreign Exchange in the Postwar World*, Mikesell reported that the Fund had not been able to perform its task "of making exchange rates a matter of international deliberation and judgment. Even the general realignment of exchange rates in September 1949 which accompanied the devaluation of sterling [from $4.20 to $2.80] was undertaken with little more than token consultations with the Monetary Fund." As before the war, changes were made after consultations among the major countries concerned or unilaterally. When Chancellor Sir Stafford Cripps announced sterling's devaluation in 1949, he said that the decision "had to do with matters that were entirely our own concern and upon which there was no question of consulting others, even our best friends."[61]

---

[60] Keynes, *Collected Writings*, xxv, pp. 410–13; Robert Skidelsky, *John Maynard Keynes*, iii, pp. 330–32; Fforde, *op. cit.*, pp. 59–61. Beaverbrook was a member of the ministerial group (chaired by the chancellor) to whom Keynes reported and had written with the chancellor's approval.

[61] Mikesell, *Foreign Exchange*, p. 24.

The transition period was taking longer than expected. Production had recovered in the industrial world, but "with the exception of the United States, Canada and a few Central American republics all members of the Monetary Fund have availed themselves of the right to continue their exchange and trade restrictions under the escape clause covering the transitional period." The explanation, wrote Mikesell, lay in "the fact that the nations whose representatives formulated the liberal trading policies underlying [the Fund and other agreements] were unable to accept the disciplines necessary to permit these policies to work."[62]

The most generous estimate of the life of the IMF as designed at Bretton Woods is from the end of 1958, when most of the industrial powers began current account convertibility, to 1968, when under American pressure they refrained from redeeming dollars. The link with gold was severed and the world had embarked on a dollar standard. It was understood that an attempted conversion of dollars on a significant scale would result in suspension by the United States, which happened in 1971. Even after 1958, Japan and the European members maintained various capital controls and were joined by the United States in the early 1960s.[63]

The decade following 1958 was less like the system envisioned by Morgenthau, White, and Keynes, in which adjustments would be negotiated, financed, and supervised by an international agency, than the arrangements between the major powers that had developed before the war. "There never was a 'Bretton Woods *system*,'" Robert Mundell observed.[64] "The Bretton Woods Agreement accommodated the rest of the world to an international monetary system that already existed. After the Tripartite Agreement among the United States, Britain, and France in 1936, the essential structure of the gold-dollar standard was already determined." The Bank of England and the Federal Reserve Bank of New York got their monetary system, or "atmosphere," after all.

Whatever its name – Bretton Woods, key currency, or gold–dollar exchange standard – we are entitled to wonder whether it "worked" better than the classical gold standard that it was supposed to replace and why it collapsed in 1971. Answers require an understanding of the gold standard, which was neither as automatic nor as rigid as its post-1914 critics and

---

[62] *Ibid.*, p. 29, referring to Art. XIV of the Fund Agreement, and p. 32.

[63] Such as the Interest Equalization Tax on the purchase of foreign securities in 1963; Harold James, *International Monetary Cooperation since Bretton Woods*, p. 161.

[64] "Discussion," in Michael Bordo and Barry Eichengreen, eds., *Retrospective on the Bretton Woods System*, p. 605; also see Martin Feldstein, "Lessons of the Bretton Woods Experience," with a section on, "A system that never was," pp. 613–18.

defenders claimed. The causes of the IMF's breakdown were foreseen, and its evolution is a story of the neutralization of the forces that made the gold standard work.

How the Gold Standard Worked

The pre-1914 gold standard has been called a contingent rule that was effective because the commitments of central banks and governments to convertibility under all but exceptional circumstances made it credible.[65] The policies pursued during the half-century before 1914 show that participants did not play by the "rules of the game." We saw the neutralization of gold flows by the Federal Reserve during the 1920s. No one before 1914 had the luxurious gold reserves of the United States after the war, but Arthur Bloomfield found that European central banks moderated flows of gold and foreign exchange reserves two-thirds of the time between 1880 and 1913.[66]

How was convertibility maintained in the face of reserve losses that might have inspired runs and suspension? The answer lay in the credit that goes with credibility. Countries that were believed to be committed were able to weather adverse trade movements with minimum monetary restrictions.[67]

The monetary regime leading up to 1914 has been called fortuitous in the vibrancy of its key countries and their acceptance of free trade and exchange. When he pleaded against the reparations imposed at Versailles, Keynes warned that the prewar system was "unusual, unstable, complicated, unreliable, temporary...."[68] However, there are strong arguments for the opposite view. Keynes's stress on the fragility of the prewar system was part of his case against reparations. The stability and growth of the western economy could have been as much a consequence as a cause of the gold standard. Gold was one of the supports of the system. Any system would have been disrupted by the Great War. The worldwide organization that had been developing since 1815 was as strong and performed as well as any the world had seen. The difficulties facing the gold standard after 1918 were great, but the 19th century "was not as quiet a world as the next generation came to imagine," R. S. Sayers wrote. "[T]he international

---

[65] Michael Bordo and Finn Kydland, "The Gold Standard as a Commitment Mechanism."

[66] Bloomfield, *op. cit.*, chap. v.

[67] Robert Triffin, *Our International Monetary System: Yesterday, Today and Tomorrow*; M. Panić, *European Monetary Union: Lessons from the Gold Standard*.

[68] Keynes, *Economic Consequences of the Peace*, p. 1.

gold standard had worked under disadvantages of the same kind, though not the same degree, as those of the post-war years. Tariff policies, war debts, reparations, political insecurity – all were present in the pre-war world."[69] Nonetheless, Keynes's appraisal of the growing social pressures for government intervention, in money as well as other markets, was on the mark. A large portion of the failure of the gold standard must be attributed to the decline in commitment arising from its conflict with other goals.

As the short-run flexibility of the gold standard was underrated, so was its generation of price stability in the long run. Rather than coincidental, it followed from forces inherent in the system. The value of gold relative to other commodities is governed by their relative costs of production. Lags were sometimes painfully long, but increases in the relative price of gold, as after the long deflations of 1820–48 and 1873–96, attracted resources to its exploration and production. Figure 9.2 illustrates the adjustment of gold production to relative prices so as to preserve their long-run ratio. The increases in the demand for gold as the major countries shifted to the gold standard in the last third of the 19th century induced production in South Africa and the Yukon, just as the earlier price decline had been followed by the California and Australia gold rushes. In the 20th century, inflation caused by fiat money during and after World War I discouraged gold production in the 1920s. This was reversed by the deflation and devaluations of the 1930s, bringing the Golden Avalanche discussed in Chap. 8. No similar reversal occurred after World War II until the $35 gold price was abandoned in the 1970s.

The End of Bretton Woods

The IMF was primarily a rule with an escape clause that could be invoked with the institution's agreement that a "fundamental disequilibrium" warranted a revision of a country's exchange rate.[70] It was supposed to possess an advantage over the pre-1914 gold standard in the explicit commitment of the international community to provide the finance necessary to preserve convertibility at the existing rate, subject to a country's consent to policies consistent with that rate. However, the open-ended nature of the escape clause undermined the traditional commitment. There was no understanding that after revision the original rate would be resumed.

---

[69] *The Bank of England, 1891–1914*, p. 9; *Bank of England Operations, 1890–1914*, p. xx.
[70] Alberto Giovannini, "Bretton Woods and Its Precusors."

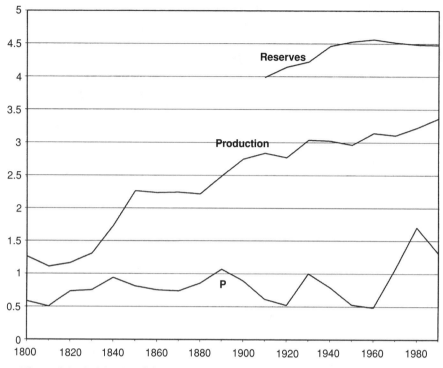

Figure 9.2. Gold value (p), production, and official reserves (decade averages, 1800–1999). Ratio of gold price to wholesale price index (1930 base), logs of annual production and reserves (metric tons). *Sources:* Federal Reserve Board, *Banking and Monetary Statistics*, and IMF, *International Financial Statistics*, linked to Roy Jastram, *The Golden Constant*.

Furthermore, the Bretton Woods Agreement did not anticipate the sources of most of the "fundamental disequilibria" that would occur in the postwar world. The term was not defined, possibly, according to Ragnar Nurkse, for "tactical" reasons to give discretion to the "managers of the Fund or to the member countries concerned in each particular case."[71] This was Peel's 1844 position that a statement of the conditions sufficient for suspension (or devaluation) might induce the event. Nurkse attempted to give the term operational meaning by stating that a country should be considered in "fundamental equilibrium" if its international payments

[71] "Conditions of International Monetary Equilibrium." This is consistent with the account of negotiations surrounding "fundamental equilibrium" in Kenneth Dam, *The Rules of the Game*, pp. 88–93.

were in balance without trade or exchange controls over a period long enough for cyclical fluctuations to be ironed out, probably 5–10 years. "Beggar-my-neighbor" devaluations should not be allowed, and resorting to them as a buffer against deflations originating from abroad would be made unnecessary by IMF assistance. Exchange rate adjustments were "appropriate mainly in cases of chronic or structural disequilibria in the balance of payments." He gave no examples. As it turned out, most of the pressure for devaluation arose from divergent monetary policies.[72]

In 1960, Robert Triffin predicted the breakdown of Bretton Woods because of the inconsistency between the increasing liquidity demand for U.S. dollars to compensate for a virtually constant monetary gold stock and the inevitable collapse of confidence in the dollar as its supply eclipsed American gold reserves.[73] The pre-1914 gold standard was confronted by the same problem when the widespread adoption of gold during the 1870s raised its demand as production was falling.[74] The result in the earlier period was an increase in the relative value of gold unopposed by the monetary authorities, an increased production of gold, and the restoration of price levels. Under Bretton Woods, in contrast, the $35 price of gold was accompanied by government full-employment policies and inflation. Rising costs discouraged production, and no gold was added to reserves, as Fig. 9.2 shows. The fundamental contradiction that led to the end of Bretton Woods was the refusal to encourage the supply of reserves by letting the price level fall.

Markets Have Their Way

In 1993, Rudiger Dornbusch wrote that "the Bretton Woods system may not have come to an end in 1971 – it is alive and well. If we think of it as a narrowly defined system of fixed exchange rates and current account convertibility,... it lasted only from 1958 to 1971. But if we take the broader purpose of an exchange rate system that supports open trade and the financing of imbalances, the system is still functioning. We do have open trade, and, flexible exchange rates not withstanding, current

---

[72] The major devaluations (relative to the dollar) in the late 1960s were France (12%), India (58%), Spain (14%), and the United Kingdom (14%), whose domestic prices had risen at annual rates of 3.9%, 8.0%, 9.0%, and 3.7%, respectively, since 1960, compared with 2.5% for the United States.

[73] *Gold and the Dollar Crisis.*

[74] Giulio Gallarotti, "The Scramble for Gold: Monetary Regime Transformation in the 1870s."

account imbalances are financed with substantial ease."[75] Jacob Viner stated in 1944 that "American objectives with respect to the pattern of postwar international economic relations are in their general outlines clear": low and nondiscriminatory trade barriers, freely convertible currencies at stable exchange rates, easy movement of long-term capital for long-term growth, ways of international collaboration for high employment, and abundant scope for competitive enterprise.[76] "If we take this to be the agenda of Bretton Woods, and not the narrow issue of the IMF and fixed parities," Dornbusch wrote, it succeeded, and "continues functioning quite well.... One might well argue that the system has evolved to cope with the challenges."[77]

This in effect says that the system as conceived at Bretton Woods never operated. It is like Whale's statement that the Act of 1844 "worked satisfactorily because it did not work in the way designed." In the simplest terms, the latter's goal of financial stability was achieved because it was not permitted to interfere with the operation of other political and economic forces: repeal of the corn laws, advances in government finance, consolidation of the banking structure, and the evolution of Bank rate.

Similarly with Bretton Woods, there was hardly a pretense of abandoning the procedures of the Tripartite Agreement to an international organization. The central banks had wanted to continue this approach, with adjustments as conditions dictated, and they got it, not by deliberately undermining the system, but because there was no other way. When Bretton Woods got in the way, it was suspended, like the Act of 1844.

---

[75] Rudiger Dornbusch, "Comment."
[76] "The Views of Jacob Viner."
[77] Dornbusch, *op. cit.*

TEN

The Bank of England after 1914

> Onto a permanent staff mostly devoted to the efficient performance of reg-
> ular tasks, Norman had superimposed an entourage or Cabinet of his own,
> either by special recruitment or by selection from the career staff... some
> chosen for a combination of intellectual distinction and special experience,
> others for their knowledge and experience of financial markets, others still
> for a combination of administrative ability and some particular aptitude
> that the Governor wanted to harness. Their numbers were not large, per-
> haps no more than fifteen or twenty. They were more numerous on the
> overseas and foreign side.... The numbers concerned with domestic mon-
> etary policy were tiny, not more than five at most. Economic advice was
> available as required, from two members of the profession.
>
> J. S. Fforde, *The Bank of England and Public Policy, 1941–58*, pp. 1–2

Central banks were different after 1914. This was obvious in the United
States, where the newly created Federal Reserve System assumed most of
the monetary functions of the Independent Treasury and the New York
Clearing House. It was no less true in Britain, where, without benefit
of law, the rotating, part-time, amateur company of merchants that had
managed the Bank of England since 1694 was replaced by a full-time
bureaucracy. The first section of this chapter tells the story of how the new
institution, with an altered structure of information and incentives, approached an old problem – the resumption of convertibility at the prewar par.

One of our goals in this chapter is to understand the Bank's role in
monetary policy in the postdepression, post-Keynesian, post–World War
II political environment dominated by the government's commitment to
full employment before the events of the 1980s and 1990s restored much
of the power of the old Bank. The road passes through the interwar period

Background: People and Events

1914–18: World War I.
1918, 1919: Cunliffe Reports on Currency and Foreign Exchanges.
1924–25: Chamberlain–Bradbury Committee.
1925: Resumption of convertibility at prewar rate of $4.86.
1931: Suspension of convertibility.
1932–51: Bank rate 2% (except 4% then 3% August to October 1939).
1936: Tripartite Declaration.
1939–45: World War II.
1944: Bretton Woods conference.
1946: American loan.
1947: Marshall Plan.
1949: Devaluation from $4.03 to $2.80.
1951: Reintroduction of flexible Bank rate; consideration of ROBOT.
1958: End of most exchange controls.
1957: Radcliffe Report.
1967: Devaluation to $2.40.
1971: End of Bretton Woods.
1972–74: Oil price shocks and miners strikes.

	Prime Minister	Chancellor of the Exchequer	Governor of the Bank of England	Party
1916	David Lloyd George	Bonar Law	Walter Cunliffe	Coalition War Cabinet
1918			Sir Brien Cockayne	
1919	Lloyd George	Austin Chamberlain		Coalition
1920			Montagu Norman	
1922	Law	Stanley Baldwin		Conservative
1923	Baldwin	Neville Chamberlain		
1924	Ramsay Macdonald	Philip Snowden		Labour
1924	Baldwin	Winston Churchill		Conservative
1929	Macdonald	Snowden		Labour
1931		Neville Chamberlain		National Government
1935	Baldwin			
1937	Neville Chamberlain	Sir John Simon		

	Prime Minister	Chancellor of the Exchequer	Governor of the Bank of England	Party
1939				Coalition War Cabinet
1940	Churchill	Sir Kingsley Wood		
1944		Sir John Anderson	Lord Catto	
1945	Clement Attlee	Hugh Dalton		Labour
1947		Sir Stafford Cripps		
1949			Cameron Cobbold	
1950		Hugh Gaitskill		
1951	Churchill	R. A. Butler		Conservative
1955	Sir Anthony Eden	Harold Macmillan		
1957	Macmillan	Peter Thorneycroft		
1958		Heathcoat Amory		
1960		Selwyn Lloyd		
1961			Earl of Cromer	
1962		Reginald Maudling		
1963	Sir Alec Home			
1964	Harold Wilson	James Callaghan		Labour
1966			Leslie O'Brien	
1968		Roy Jenkins		
1970	Edward Heath	Anthony Barber		Conservative
1973			Gordon Richardson	
1974	Wilson	Denis Healey		Labour
1976	Callaghan			

Note: Baldwin was chancellor May–August 1923; Anderson succeeded after Wood's death in September 1943; Iain Macleod served a month in 1970.

because the Bank's attitudes and place in later policies were strongly influenced by its actions and their perceived consequences after World War I. The deflation and unemployment that went with the attempt to recover the prewar system changed attitudes toward monetary policy in general and the Bank's role in particular, both inside and outside the Bank, in ways that persisted to the end of the century.

The second section examines the Bank's part in another aborted resumption. Britain was even weaker in 1945 than in 1918. In desperate straits, broke and unable to feed itself, the country depended on American aid, which, as we saw in the previous chapter, came at the price of a quick return to free trade and exchange, including convertibility in 1947. The Bank resisted early resumption on this occasion, but its former influence had been lost. It made something of a comeback in the 1950s but was still an adviser against the tides of political and economic opinion. The third section describes monetary policies and the Bank's checkered influence from Labour's "cheap money" to the Tories' "stop–go."

Emphasis shifts to the foreign position of the pound in the fourth section, especially the steps toward convertibility that were proposed and sometimes pursued in the 1950s and Labour's defense of the exchange rate from 1964 to 1967. The last section explores the intellectual background of the inflation of the 1970s, beginning with the Radcliffe Committee's endorsement of the futility of monetary control in 1959.

Norman's Bank and the Return to Gold in 1925

The New Breed

No one could say after 1914 that the Bank of England was like any other bank. The government had always been the Bank's most important customer, but after 1914 its business was dominant. The Bank in effect became a government department with a permanent professional staff, and governors served at the pleasure of governments instead of their stockholders. Although the Bank was still privately owned, its stockholders had less influence on policy than the member banks of the Federal Reserve System. The Bank's nationalization in 1946 did no more than "bring the law into accord with the facts of the situation as they have developed," the chancellor of the exchequer told the House of Commons, nor did it, said the leader of the opposition, Winston Churchill, raise a matter of principle.[1]

---

[1] J. S. Fforde, *The Bank of England and Public Policy, 1941–58*, p. 7.

Much was made of Norman's professionalization of the Bank. He was dissatisfied with its concentration of "City men" and wanted a "new breed" of full-time professionals without ties to their own businesses.[2] A grandson of George Warde Norman, Bank director from 1821 to 1872, and Sir Mark Collet, governor from 1887 to 1889, Norman began a merchant banking career in Collet's firm of Brown Shipley in 1894, becoming a Bank director in the traditional way in 1907. He departed from tradition when he severed relations with Brown Shipley to serve as a full-time, unpaid assistant to the deputy governor and then the governor during the war. He became deputy governor in 1918 and governor two years later.

As the longest serving governor, Norman was able to put his stamp on the Bank. Members of staff were made directors, eclipsing those from outside. The collection and analysis of statistics was organized in a new section in 1921, and in 1925 the addition of an economist was considered. "A man chosen from the Cambridge School, if under the influence of Mr. Keynes, might perhaps have acquired this desirable aptitude [of applying economics to practice]; but if he had also followed this Economist in his progressive decline and fall, dating from the *Tract on Monetary Reform*, he would be worse than useless."[3] No permanent economist was hired until Humphrey Mynors came from Cambridge to the renamed Economics and Statistical Section in 1933, but some of the governor's advisors, a post initiated in 1926, were economists. These included Walter Stewart, on loan from the Federal Reserve Bank of New York (1927–30; "a kindred spirit" to Benjamin Strong as well as Norman, "a man of instinctive judgments, not given to writing lengthy memoranda but at his most effective in the Governor's parlour," R. S. Sayers wrote in his history of the Bank[4]), and Harvard's O. M. W. Sprague (1930–33).

Deputy governors continued to be elected on the old system of rotation until the end of the 1920s, when the increased workload made it "clear ... that what was needed was a full-time Deputy Governor, without ties to his own business elsewhere," Elizabeth Hennessey wrote in her history of the Bank's management.[5] Ernest Harvey, who served in

---

[2] Elizabeth Hennessy, "The Governors, Directors and Management of the Bank of England"; Fforde, *op. cit.*, chap. 1; Henry Clay, *Montagu Norman*, p. 310; R. S. Sayers, *The Bank of England, 1891–1944*, chap. 22.

[3] From an internal communication, Hennessy, *A Domestic History of the Bank of England*, p. 314.

[4] Sayers, *op. cit.*, p. 621.

[5] Hennessy, *op. cit.*

that capacity from 1929 to 1936, was promoted from the Bank's full-time staff, as was his successor, B. G. Catterns (1936–45). Executive directors were initiated in 1932. Gone were the days when the senior committee of the Bank consisted of part-timers linked to the City and trade who had become directors as young men to serve 20-year apprenticeships on their way to four years as deputy governor and governor.

Governments had always been disinclined to let the Bank fail, and any question of such an event was ended by the war. It was unthinkable that the monetary authority be altered except by Parliament. Finally – and this is where the Bank grasped the power that had been given to the Fed – through its prestige and single-minded purpose in contrast to uncertainty in government and the public, the Bank was able to secure and then maintain convertibility until 1931 almost without regard to its economic effects, including those on the profits of the private customers upon whom its survival had once depended.

Paul Einzig wrote in 1932 that "more has been done to bring the Bank of England up to date during the twelve years of Mr. Norman's regime than during the hundred years between the Bullion Committee and the Cunliffe Committee [1918]. . . . Incredible as it may sound, a few years ago the Bank of England did not possess either a statistical department or even a foreign exchange department."[6] During and after the Great War, J. H. Clapham wrote,

Central Banking was everywhere developing into a thing distinct from banking; and the advice and authority of the Bank of England, in whose half-unconscious and sometimes rather unwilling hands the practices of central banking had originally been worked out, were respected, extended and sought.[7]

Respect there may have been, for awhile, but the effects of these changes were not all positive. Professionalism did not make up for the Bank's remoteness from the economy. At the end of his examination of *British Monetary Policy, 1924–31: The Norman Conquest of $4.86*, Donald Moggridge wrote,

To a considerable extent, the root of the policy problem in 1924–5 and thereafter lay in a lack of knowledge. Policy-making depended almost exclusively on the use of rules of thumb, often disguised as general principles, derived from an earlier, less complicated and more benign age. It rested on instinct rather than analysis.

[6] Paul Einzig, *Montagu Norman*, pp. 32–33.
[7] J. H. Clapham, *The Bank of England*, ii, pp. 416, 421.

"Reasons, Mr. Chairman? I don't have reasons. I have instincts," Norman responded to Lord Macmillan's question about the establishment of the Bankers' Industrial Development Company.[8]

We understand that, of course, Mr. Governor, nevertheless you must have had *some* reasons. – Well, if I had I have forgotten them.

Its critics believed the new Bank lacked knowledge even of the earlier age, which had been less benign than Norman seemed to think. In "The Economic Consequences of Mr. Churchill," referring to the chancellor of the exchequer, Keynes declared that the decision to resume and then maintain the convertibility of sterling at prewar rates could be attained "*In no other way than by the deliberate intensification of unemployment.*" The object of the Bank's credit restriction was

to withdraw from employers the financial means to employ labour at the existing level of prices and wages. The policy can only attain its end by intensifying unemployment without limit, until the workers are ready to accept the necessary reduction of money wages under the pressure of hard facts.

Keynes accused the Bank of holding the extreme form of the quantity theory in which the only effect of monetary change is on prices, without disturbing production or employment. Although this may be true in the long run, the interval is painful, he wrote, and "in the long run we are all dead."[9] Ricardo had condemned the Bank for its rejection of the quantity theory, but he would not have pushed that theory as far as the new management seemed willing to go. Keynes quoted Ricardo's 1822 speech in the House of Commons: "If in the year 1819 the value of the currency had stood at 14s for the pound note [par 20 shillings], which was the case in the year 1813..., on the balance of all the advantages and disadvantages of the case, it would have been as well to fix the currency at the then value, according to which most of the existing contracts had been made...."[10] The pound – now customarily quoted in dollars – had a par of $4.86, and it traded at about $4.40 when Keynes wrote, although it had averaged $3.75 in 1920–21. Norman's predecessors had recognized the effects of monetary policy. As we saw in Chap. 5, a former governor told a parliamentary committee after the crisis of 1847 that an increase

---

[8] This exchange is not in the published minutes of the Macmillan Committee but was reported by Edward Boyle, *Montagu Norman*, p. 327, based on Norman's papers.

[9] *The Tract on Monetary Reform*, p. 65.

[10] *Op. cit.*, p. 125. Ricardo expressed the same view in 1821 in the letter to John Wheatley quoted in the second section of Chap. 3.

in Bank rate "causes the stoppage of trade." These concerns were now suppressed. R. G. Hawtrey's message in *A Century of Bank Rate* was that the Bank and government of the 1920s had forgotten the effects of credit restrictions on domestic activity. Bank rate was an effective defense of the gold standard in the years before 1914, he argued, primarily through its effects on the internal demand for gold; a rise in interest rates restrained the internal demand for coin by retarding transactions. Effects on international gold flows were secondary. Norman gave the impression that he thought only of the latter. When he told the Macmillan Committee that Bank rate was "effective" in "preserving the stock of gold," the Chairman wondered about side effects:[11]

One of the problems to which we have been addressing ourselves is whether the use of the instrument of Bank Rate, effective it may be in achieving the purpose you have indicated, may not be accompanied internally with unhappy consequences. You may be effecting an operation of great value from the financial point of view which has nevertheless unfortunate repercussions internally by restricting credit and enterprise. Your instrument may be doing good in one direction and harm in another. I should like to have from you your conception of the internal effect of the alteration of the Bank Rate....

Norman: Well I should think that its internal effect was as a rule greatly exaggerated – that its actual ill effects were greatly exaggerated and that they are much more psychological than real....

Chairman: But even if it has psychological consequences they may be depressing consequences, and may be serious?

Norman: Yes, but not so serious as they are usually made out to be, and I think that the benefit on the whole of the maintenance of the international position is so great an advantage at home, for industry, for commerce, for [interrupted]

Chairman: You take the large view. In your opinion, I gather, the advantages of maintaining the international position outweigh in the public interest the internal disadvantages which may accrue from the use of the means at your disposal?

Norman: Yes, I think that the disadvantages of the internal position are relatively small compared with the advantages to the external position.

Chairman: What is the benefit to industry of the maintenance of the international position?

Norman: This is a very technical question which is not easy to explain, but the whole international position has preserved for us in this country the wonderful position which we have inherited, which was for a while thought perhaps to be in jeopardy, which to a large extent, though not to the full extent, has been re-established. We are still to a large

---

[11] Committee on the Finance and Industry (Macmillan), *Evidence*, Q3328–33.

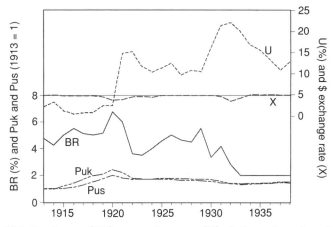

Figure 10.1. Bank rate (BR), unemployment (U), dollar value of sterling (X), and U.K. and U.S. price levels (1913 base), 1913–38. Horizontal line at $4.866 par. *Source:* B. R. Mitchell, *British Historical Statistics*; U.S. Dept. of Commerce, Historical Statistics of the United States.

> extent international bankers. We have great international trade and commerce, out of which I believe considerable profit accrues to the country;...a free gold market...and all of those things, and the confidence and credit which go with them are in the long run greatly to the interest of finance and commerce.

This exchange resembled that between Congressman Busby and Governor Harrison two years later. Although the central bankers were able to fend off their inquisitors at the time, they were soon toppled.

The Return to Gold

The war effort depended heavily on borrowing. The public debt increased from £620 to £7,414, in millions, between 1914 and 1919. Much of it was financed by Treasury currency and Bank credit, and both money and prices doubled. Monetary expansion continued after the war, and prices rose 25 percent during the two years after the Armistice in November 1918.[12] American inflation was also high, though less than in Britain (Fig. 10.1), and with the loss of overseas markets and much of the workforce, it was feared that the recovery of prewar conditions, including the gold standard, would take time.

[12] Forrest Capie and Alan Webber, *A Monetary History of the United Kingdom*, v. iii, table III(11); B. R. Mitchell, *British Historical Statistics*, 1st ed., Public Finance, abstract, table 5.

Work in that direction began at an early stage. In January 1918, the Committee on Currency and Foreign Exchanges after the War (the Cunliffe Committee, after Chairman Walter, Lord Cunliffe, governor of the Bank, 1913–18) was appointed "to examine the problems of the transition from war to peace and to suggest appropriate policies," with members from the Treasury, the City, and the universities.[13] Its Interim Report, in August 1918, noted the following: "During the war the conditions necessary to the maintenance of [the gold] standard have ceased to exist. The main cause has been the growth of credit due to Government borrowing from the Bank of England and other banks for war needs." The Committee's solution was straightforward:[14]

In our opinion it is imperative that after the war the conditions necessary to the maintenance of an effective gold standard should be restored without delay. Unless the machinery [especially Bank Rate] which long experience has shown to be the only effective remedy for an adverse balance of trade and an undue growth of credit is once more brought into play, there will be grave danger of a progressive credit expansion which will result in a foreign drain of gold menacing the convertibility of our note issue and so jeopardizing the international trading position of the country.

Sec. 47

As a hundred years before, resumption at a different par than before the war was rejected while the timing was hotly debated. This was partly because some were less than eager to return to gold, but most wanted to wait until it could be reinstated without deflation. They would have liked to see the pound rise to its old value freely on the basis of the American inflation that ought to follow its accumulation of gold. The return to gold on prewar terms is a story of the triumph of a policy, with considerable reason and experience on its side, pursued by dedicated officials with a clear goal, over the more diffuse population that would bear the brunt of the policy but lacked an affirmative program.[15]

---

[13] Donald Moggridge, *The Return to Gold, 1925*, p. 12.

[14] The Cunliffe Reports are in T. E. Gregory, *Select Statutes & Reports Relating to British Banking, 1832–1928*, ii, pp. 334–70.

[15] Leading characters in the debate included R. G. Hawtrey, of the Treasury (1904–45), who was economist more than advisor; Reginald McKenna, who was chancellor of the exchequer (1915–16), and Chairman, Midland Bank (1919–43), and served on the Macmillan Committee; Otto Niemeyer, of the Treasury (1906–27; serving as controller of finance from 1922 to 1927), Bank of England (1927–52), and Chamberlain–Bradbury Committee; and A. C. Pigou, Cambridge professor of economics (1908–43), who served on the Cunliffe and Chamberlain–Bradbury Committees.

The moderate stance of Professor A. C. Pigou on the Cunliffe Committee and afterward was shared by the majority of economists and businessmen.[16] However, their preference for return at an opportune time in the possibly distant future was too hesitant for the hawks. Sir John Bradbury, joint-permanent secretary of the treasury and a member of the Cunliffe and Chamberlain–Bradbury Committees wrote the following to an associate:[17]

The general impression... which [Pigou's written testimony to the latter Committee] leaves in my mind is rather flabby. "For the moment we propose to wait and see which way the cat jumps [American inflation and European exchange rate policies]. If she jumps one way, and we can avoid jumping after her – and whether we can or not remains to be seen – everything will probably be all right. If it isn't, we shall be prepared to be a good deal braver than we are at the moment."

I think that we ought to make it perfectly clear that we regard a return to a free gold market at the pre-war parity without long delay as of vital importance....

The return was delayed by volatile conditions. Controls had kept the exchange rate near the $4.86 par during the war to assure American creditors of the dollar value of their British investments, but it was turned loose in March 1919 and fell to $3.38 a year later (monthly averages). The postwar inflation was followed by deflation and recession in 1920–21, after which prices were fairly stable and the pound hovered around $4.50 most of 1922–23. Unemployment stubbornly stayed above 10 percent, but officials were tired of waiting, and when the pound slipped in early 1924, a committee was appointed to plan resumption. This committee was chaired by the former Conservative Chancellor Austin Chamberlain, who was succeeded by Bradbury after he joined the new government in October. Norman asked for "a fixed and immutable date beyond all possibility of change" and to [be left] to work toward it, but when the committee reported in September it recommended the continuation of "wait-and-see."[18] Noting the deflationary "inconveniences" that would be involved in closing a 10- to 12-percent gap in the exchange rate, it suggested that

---

[16] "Industrialists were perfectly well aware of the probable consequences of a return to the pre-war parity in 1925," Robert Skidelsky wrote, "but their warnings were brushed aside" (*Politicians and the Slump*, p. 26). For the go-slow preferences of bank and industrial witnesses before the Chamberlain–Bradbury Committee, see Moggridge, *The Return to Gold*, pp. 25–34.

[17] N. E. Young, assistant principal, HM Treasury, secretary of Chamberlain–Bradbury Committee, September 11, 1924; Moggridge, *Return*, pp. 33–34.

[18] Pigou Papers, Moggridge, *The Return to Gold*, pp. 26–27.

the government wait up to 12 months for American prices to rise. There should be another look at the situation "not later than the early autumn of 1925."[19]

The pace was quickened in October by the fall of the government. A shaky Labour/Liberal coalition was replaced by a large Conservative majority that set the political landscape for the next five years. Norman saw it as a green light, and he visited the United States to negotiate a credit to support a fixed rate. Critics still called attention to high unemployment and an already tighter, monetary policy than had been normal in depression before 1914, although the Bank and the Treasury played them down and argued that the undesirable consequences, if any, were worth the long-term benefits of the gold standard.[20] They also assumed that its accumulation of gold would induce a rise in American prices.

When the new chancellor tried to allay fears by declaring that unemployment and falling wages had no more to do with the gold standard than the Gulf Stream, Keynes charged that he had been misled by his advisers and was helpless because he had "no instinctive judgment."[21]

> The Bank of England is *compelled* to curtail credit by all the rules of the gold standard game. It is acting conscientiously and "soundly" in doing so. But this does not alter the fact that to keep a tight hold on credit – and no one will deny that the bank is doing that – necessarily involves intensifying unemployment in the present circumstances of this country. What we need to restore prosperity today is an easy credit policy. We want to encourage business men to enter on new enterprises, not, as we are doing, to discourage them. Deflation does not reduce wages "automatically." It reduces them by causing unemployment. The proper object of dear money is to check an incipient boom. Woe to those whose faith leads them to use it to aggravate a depression!

Notwithstanding his public statements, Churchill was sympathetic to Keynes's position, and he later adopted it completely. A quarter of a century later, debating another resumption and no doubt thinking of his former advice from Norman and the Treasury, he complained from the opposition front bench that "[t]here is no sphere of human thought in which it is easier for a man to show superficial cleverness and the appearance of superior wisdom than in discussing questions of currency and exchange."[22]

---

[19] Chamberlain–Bradbury Committee, third draft report, Treasury Papers, Moggridge, *British Monetary Policy*, p. 50.
[20] Pigou Papers, Moggridge, *The Return to Gold*, p. 30.
[21] Keynes, "The Economic Consequences of Mr. Churchill."
[22] House of Commons, September 28, 1949, *Hansard*, col. 160.

The records show that Churchill deserved a better light than he was given at the time.[23] The decision was his responsibility, and he defended it publicly. Nonetheless, he was skeptical and resisted as much as was possible for a politician surrounded by experts all of one mind – and his instincts were sound. He asked the questions and raised the objections that might have been expected of an intelligent layman. His memorandum to his Treasury advisers and Norman in February 1925 appears in the Treasury files as "Mr. Churchill's Exercise." His questions and points – probably a combination of genuine doubts and solicitations of arguments to strengthen the case that he would have to make – can be summarized as follows:[24]

1. Gold was a survival of rudimentary and transitional stages in the evolution of finance. (Keynes and Ricardo had called it a "relic" of "a less-enlightened period.") The nation was showing that stable money and credit could be managed without the gold standard.
2. Why is the United States so anxious that we return to gold? Is it in our interests that we share the costs of maintaining the value of gold?
3. What about the wider economic effects of the proposed return to gold? The high interest rates that seem to be required by resumption would administer "a very serious check" to industry, and leave the government open to charges that it "favoured the special interests of finance at the expense of the special interests of production."
4. What's the hurry?

Churchill got little satisfaction from his advisers. Businessmen and labor leaders were dismissed as selfish and shortsighted inflationists. Norman declaimed from the moral high ground:

In connection with a golden 1925, the merchant, manufacturer, workman, etc., should be considered (but not consulted any more than about the design of battleships).

Cheap money is important because 9 people out of 10 think so: more for psychological than for fundamental reasons.... The cry of "cheap money" is the Industrialists' big stick and should be treated accordingly.

The restoration of Free Gold *will* require a high Bank Rate: the Government cannot avoid a decision for or against Restoration: the Chancellor will surely be charged with a sin of omission or of commission. In the former case (Gold) he

---

[23] Moggridge, *Return*, pp. 66–68, 87–88.
[24] Moggridge, *British Monetary Policy*, appendix 5.

will be abused by the ignorant, the gamblers and the antiquated Industrialists; in the latter case (not Gold) he will be abused by the instructed and by posterity.[25]

Still looking for a way out, Churchill referred his chief advisor Otto Niemeyer to Keynes's criticisms:[26]

The Treasury have never, it seems to me, faced the profound significance of what Mr. Keynes calls "the paradox of unemployment amidst dearth." The Governor shows himself perfectly happy in the spectacle of Britain possessing the finest credit in the world simultaneously with a million and a quarter unemployed . . .

It may be of course that you will argue that the unemployment would have been much greater but for the financial policy pursued; that there is no sufficient demand for commodities either internally or externally to require the services of this million and a quarter people; that there is nothing for them but to hang like a millstone round the neck of industry and on the public revenue until they become permanently demoralised. You may be right, but if so, it is one of the most sombre conclusions ever reached. . . . I would rather see Finance less proud and Industry more content.

Niemeyer responded that it was too late to reverse the engines.[27] Since 1918, governments had advocated for a return to gold as soon as conditions warranted, and the pound was trading at $4.80 on the foreign exchange markets, up from $4.30 the previous summer. A loss of nerve now would convince the world that Britain had never meant business, and no one could tell when another such opportunity would come. We saw that Lord Liverpool took a similar position in 1825, although in defense of a resumption already undertaken.

A good part of the rise in sterling from November 1924 was speculative in light of the hawks' strengthened position following the election. With no important change in the country's domestic or international situations, "imminent" resumption became a foregone conclusion. In its final report, submitted to the government in early February 1925, the Chamberlain–Bradbury Committee assumed convertibility in the near future. The timing of the decision had become a matter of circular reasoning: The price of the pound, which anticipated resumption at $4.86 (and the policies necessary to make it effective), was evidence that justified resumption.

---

[25] Reply to the Chancellor, Treasury papers, February 2, 1925, Moggridge, *British Monetary Policy*, pp. 69–70, 271.

[26] Especially Keynes's evidence to the Chamberlain–Bradbury Committee, discussed by Moggridge, *British Monetary Policy*, pp. 42–43.

[27] See the end of Chap. 3.

The decision was made on March 20. Norman's diary records the following:

Chancellor for lunch in Downing Street. Gold return to be announced April 6th or 8th. Cushion to be meanwhile arranged by Bank. I warn him of 6% Bank rate next month. [It had been raised to 5% on March 5.]

The announcement actually came as part of the Budget Speech on April 28. The governor undertook not to raise the Bank rate for at least a week. As it happened, the markets showed confidence in the government's commitment, there was no immediate loss of gold, and the rate was not raised to 6 percent until October 1929.

The rate was cut to $4\frac{1}{2}$ and 4 percent in August and October, respectively, but when it returned to 5 percent in December, Churchill rang Norman in protest. The governor stuck by his guns, but the incident prompted a Treasury review of its relations with the Bank. A survey of former Treasury civil servants supported Norman's position that rate decisions belonged to the Bank. The chancellor's wartime claim on the Bank's subservience had lapsed.[28]

The pound and the Bank's gold reserve did well until 1929, but the economy did not fare as well. The responsible politician and symbol of the increasingly unpopular decision was bitter. After another agonizing Budget Speech in April 1927, Churchill wrote Niemeyer,

We have assumed since the war, largely under the guidance of the Bank of England, a policy of deflation, debt repayment, high taxation, large sinking funds and Gold Standard. This has raised our credit, restored our exchange and lowered the cost of living. On the other hand it has produced bad trade, hard times, an immense increase in unemployment involving costly and unwise remedial measures, attempts to reduce wages in conformity with the cost of living and so increase the competitive power, fierce labour disputes arising therefrom, with expense to the State and community measured by hundreds of millions....

... the financial policy of Great Britain since the war has been directed by the Governor of the Bank of England and distinguished Treasury permanent officials who, amid the repeated changes of Government and of Chancellors, have pursued inflexibly a strict, rigid, highly particularist line of action, entirely satisfactory when judged from within the sphere in which they move and for which they are responsible, and almost entirely unsatisfactory in its reactions upon the wider social, industrial, and political spheres.

---

[28] For this and a similar episode in 1929, see Moggridge, *British Monetary Policy*, pp. 162–63; Stephen Clarke, *Central Bank Cooperation, 1924–31*, p. 102; Susan Howson, *Domestic Monetary Management in Britain, 1919–38*, p. 35.

The hoped-for American inflation never came. Notwithstanding Benjamin Strong's pep talks and promises of support for the pound, the Federal Reserve prevented America's gold from affecting its price level. American consumer and wholesale prices fell 2 and 6 percent, respectively, between 1925 and 1929. British prices fell even more, and unemployment stayed above 10 percent. Churchill felt betrayed by the experts, and his Treasury private secretary remembered the venting of his anger on Norman:

> The events of 1925 and 1926 undoubtedly led to something very like an estrangement between the Chancellor and the Governor of the Bank of England. These two had some things in common – a profound sense of public duty, great vision, a pronounced obstinacy and desire to have their own way, jealous pride of position and so on. But they were totally unlike in others. Winston was a magnificent rhetorician. He also had a sense of mischief which kept creeping into his rhetoric. Norman was no talker. He found it difficult to assign reasons for the faith that was in him and he was not a believer in admitting anything in the nature of levity into the serious subject of public finance. Of course they met frequently – they had to – and this gave the Chancellor of the Exchequer abundant opportunity to make speeches about the evil effects of the gold standard – partly abusive, partly derisory and not entirely unmeant. The Governor retired more and more into his carapace, and the so necessary relations of confidence and candour ceased to exist.
>
> P. J. Grigg, *Prejudice and Judgment*, p. 193

The Tories were defeated in 1929, and the new Labour government under Ramsey McDonald promised to defend the pound. In July 1930, Keynes responded to McDonald's questions about depression remedies:[29]

> [T]he peculiarity of my position lies, perhaps, in the fact that I am in favour of practically all the remedies which have been suggested in any quarter. Some of them are better than others. But nearly all of them seem to me to tend in the right direction. The unforgivable attitude is, therefore for me the negative one – the repelling of each of these remedies in turn.
>
> Accordingly, I favour an eclectic programme, making use of suggestions from all quarters, not expecting too much from the application of any one of them, but hoping that they may do something in the aggregate. . . .
>
> I am afraid of "principle." Ever since 1918 we, alone amongst the nations of the world, have been the slaves of "sound" general principles regardless of particular circumstances. We have behaved as though the intermediate "short periods" of the economist between one position of equilibrium and another were short, whereas they can be long enough – and have been before now – to encompass the

---

[29] Keynes, *Writings*, xx, pp. 370–84; also quoted at the end of Moggridge, *The Return to Gold*.

decline and downfall of nations. Nearly all our difficulties have been traceable to an unaltering service to the principles of "sound finance" which all our neighbours have neglected.... Wasn't it Lord Melbourne who said that "No statesman ever does anything really foolish except on principle"?

In February 1932, three years out of office and five months after Britain had given up on the exchange rate, Churchill wrote the following to his former parliamentary private secretary, Robert Boothby:

I have gone the whole hog against gold. To hell with it! It has been used as a vile trap to destroy us. I would pay the rest of the American Debt in gold as long as the gold lasted, and then say – "Hence-forward, we will only pay in goods. Pray specify what goods you desire."

Surely it will become a public necessity to get rid of Montagu Norman. No man has ever been stultified as he has been in his fourteen years' policy.[30]

The American Loan and the Resumption of 1947

Britain emerged from World War II as "the greatest debtor in the history of the world."[31] Its overseas liabilities had increased fivefold between 1939 and 1945, to $14 billion compared with gold and dollar reserves of $2 billion. Most of its foreign assets had been liquidated. Even with "considerable austerity" enforced by "strict controls" on imports, a trade deficit of $3.2 billion was projected for 1946 according to Keynes's paper for the cabinet in August 1945.[32]

Keynes's position as chief negotiator for Bretton Woods and the American loan may have owed as much to the Treasury's low status as to his talents. "Churchill had a fixed antipathy to the 'Treasury view'," Skidelsky wrote, "which he believed had misled him as Chancellor in the 1920s and postponed rearmament in the 1930s.... On the other hand, Churchill had considerable respect for Keynes, whom he judged to have been right over the gold standard.... The Treasury's incorporation of Keynes can be seen as a shrewd move in its longer-term effort to gain control over economic policy."[33]

Britain's war deficits had been financed by sterling credits in the Empire and American lend-lease, of which $2 billion per annum was for nonmunitions, for the necessities of life. This was to continue for the duration of the

[30] Martin Gilbert, *Winston S. Churchill*, v, p. 425.
[31] R. S. Sayers, *Financial Policy, 1939–45*, p. 486.
[32] "Proposals for Financial Arrangements in the Sterling Area and between the U.S. and the U.K. to Follow after Lend Lease," *Writings*, xxv, pp. 427–51.
[33] Skidelsky, *John Maynard Keynes*, iii, p. 158.

war and would provide "breathing space" to "allow some rebuilding of our export trade" because the war in the Pacific was expected to last a year or two after Germany's surrender in April 1945.[34] However, because Japan surrendered in less than four months, pursuant to the terms of the agreement, lend-lease was terminated immediately. The people faced lower living standards than in wartime. They had a debt "which no one else will be expected to carry," Keynes said, "not even the defeated enemy."

"There seemed no alternative but to seek a loan from the United States," recalled government economist, J. C. R. Dow.[35] "But three months 'of very intricate discussions and some very hard bargaining' [quoting Chancellor Hugh Dalton's defense of the agreement in the House of Commons in December 1945] showed that a loan could only be had at a price; and the price aroused the deepest misgiving."

Misgiving was due less to the financial terms of the loan than to the other conditions attached. It was a condition, first, that the United Kingdom should accept the Bretton Woods proposals for the International Monetary Fund and the International Bank. These would undoubtedly have been accepted in any case, though far less abruptly....

Even more onerous was the required undertaking to restore convertibility almost immediately. In the Bretton Woods negotiations the United Kingdom had insisted on remaining free to maintain exchange controls on current transactions for a transition period of five years.... But under the Loan Agreement, she had to agree to restore the convertibility of sterling within one year of the agreement coming into operation.

Britain was slated to have, within 18 months, the only convertible currency in an inconvertible world. "The debate in the House was therefore a scene of gloom and disillusion." A former chancellor who had suffered a less precipitate resumption observed that the agreement was "so doubtful and perilous that the best hope is that in practice it will defeat itself, and that it is in fact too bad to be true."[36] "We are sitting here today as the representatives of a victorious people, discussing the consequences of victory," said Tory M. P. Oliver Stanley. "If a visitor were to come ... from Mars ... he might well be pardoned for thinking that he was listening to the representatives of a vanquished people discussing the economic penalties of defeat."[37]

---

[34] J. C. R. Dow, *The Management of the British Economy, 1945–60*," p. 17.

[35] *Loc. cit.*

[36] Churchill in the House of Commons, December 13, 1945, Richard Gardner, *Sterling–Dollar Diplomacy*, p. 230.

[37] Dow, *op. cit.*, p. 18.

Keynes defended his postwar plans as part of

an ideal system which would solve the problem on multilateral lines by international agreement. This is an ambitious scheme. But the post-war world must not be content with patchwork.[38]

Although the Bank "expressed support for Keynes' ultimate international objectives," Fforde records, it was "a consistent and determined critic of almost all his practical proposals for attaining them."[39] It was skeptical of the early restoration of convertibility and free trade "that was passionately advocated by the U.S. Treasury and the State Department." The Bank and his critics in the Treasury felt that Keynes had succumbed to the Washington atmosphere of grand designs. Investment banker Robert (later Lord) Brand, the Treasury's representative in Washington, thought Keynes's approach "a great leap in the dark, . . . a gamble, even if the world goes moderately well."[40]

Convinced that Britain had to conform to American wishes, Keynes rejected these cautions: "[T]his is not a case where we can muddle through without a drastic solution, grasping no nettles and just hoping it will be all right on the day."[41] He had exchanged positions with the Bank since 1930, and this time the government was on his side.

Keynes took this approach into his negotiations with the Americans, who had yet to recognize the problems of the postwar "transition." His negotiating strategy seems naïve to us now – and must have seemed so to the hard-headed Americans. He "sought to conjure up a vision of a grand financial settlement between the U.S., Canada, and the Sterling Area based upon a just division, among victors, of the burdens left behind by the war."[42] The American public had a different view of "Justice." They had been injured by the British, and by Europeans in general, who had dragged them into two foreign wars and failed to pay their debts after the first. If "just" payments were owed by anyone, it was not the United States. There were ugly scenes between Keynes and the American negotiators, especially the former congressman and now Treasury Secretary Fred Vinson.[43] Keynes did not seem to appreciate that Congress would

---

[38] Treasury memorandum, September 8, 1941, Dow, *op. cit.*, p. 37; Keynes, *Writings*, xxv, p. 26.

[39] Fforde, *op. cit.*, p. 33.

[40] *Ibid.*, p. 70.

[41] *Ibid.*, p. 93.

[42] *Ibid.*, p. 65.

[43] Recorded by several observers, including Roy Harrod, who dwelt on Vinson's lack of deference to Keynes (*The Life of John Maynard Keynes*, chap. 15).

scrutinize the payments to be exacted from their constituents. President Truman noticed that the United States was cartooned as Santa Claus as well as Shylock.[44]

With no backup plan, Keynes and the government that had given itself into his hands were at the mercy of the Americans, who wanted something for their money. The "consideration" for lend-lease (Britain's acceptance of multilateral free trade and exchange) was called in.[45] The terms of the loan were generous: $3,750 million (with an additional $650 million in final settlement of lend-lease) for 50 years at 2 percent, with no payments before 1951, and forgiveness of interest in any year in which exports were insufficient to pay for the prewar volume of imports. The string attached to the loan that most concerned the Bank of England was the convertibility of sterling in little more than a year, on July 15, 1947, at the existing exchange rate of $4.03.

Britain ended the war with an extensive payments network, and the Bank had developed plans "for a strengthened and integrated Sterling Area, a fixed sterling/dollar rate, the continued centralisation of foreign exchange and gold transactions through the Bank, the continued elaborate control of outward capital movements long and short, and the development of bilateral monetary agreements with non-sterling countries and currency areas."[46] It hoped that the recovery of exports, combined with import controls, would remedy the balance of trade and allow the gradual liberalization of trade and payments.

Instead, it had to deal with an end to controls even earlier than agreed at Bretton Woods. This seemed possible, at first. Exports grew rapidly

---

[44] Truman, *Memoirs*, i, p. 480.

[45] Gardner, *op. cit.* p. 209. Section 3(b) of *The Lend-Lease Act* of March 1941 stated, "The terms and conditions upon which any such foreign government receives any aid . . . shall be those which the President deems satisfactory, and the benefit to the United States may be payment or repayment in kind or property, or any other direct or indirect benefit which the President deems satisfactory." Article VII of *The Master Lend-Lease Agreement* of July 1942 was more specific: "In the final determination of the benefits to be provided to the United States of America . . . , the terms and conditions shall be such as not to burden commerce between the two countries. . . . To that end, they shall include provision for agreed action . . . to the elimination of all forms of discriminatory treatment in international commerce, and to the reduction of tariffs and other trade barriers . . . " (Edward Stettinius, *Lend-Lease: Weapon for Victory*, pp. 335–43; William McNeill, *America, Britain, & Russia: Their Co-operation and Conflict, 1941–46*, pp. 137–49). See McNeill for Britain's "half-hearted acceptance." British "stubbornness" was remembered by Undersecretary of State for Economic Affairs Dean Acheson, *Present at the Creation*, pp. 27–33.

[46] Fforde, *Bank of England*, pp. 40–41.

and the Bank and the Treasury made progress in getting the holders of sterling to agree to limits on conversions to gold and dollars. However, in 1947, the dollar shortage became severe as a hard winter meant a fuel shortage, and other imports also grew faster than expected, because, according to the chancellor's critics, the American loan was dissipated to put off the inevitable belt tightening, or according to Dalton, a rise in U.S. prices worth $1 billion of the loan. "The Loan, upon which all other plans depended, negotiated with difficulty and intended to last three years or so, in fact lasted only one year and a half."[47]

The drain on reserves accelerated as the date for full convertibility approached, and the process was suspended on August 20. The crisis followed the Loan Agreement "as night follows the day," the Bank's Deputy Governor Cameron Cobbold recalled. This was more than hindsight. He had told a colleague,[48]

I have always personally believed that the whole pack of cards of Bretton Woods, Washington Loan, ITO etc., was unsoundly or at any rate prematurely built and that it would collapse under "transitional period" stresses. I agree therefore that convertibility in the Loan Agreement (by which our hands are tied and which precludes us from using our trade, etc., negotiating weapons) must be modified.

The international payments system was to be managed as the Bank had planned, after all – under the negotiable system that had been evolving since the 1930s. Convertibility would wait until 1958.

In conclusion, although resumption failed in 1947, the attempt was not very costly because it was half-hearted. The drain would have to be paid for, but the loan was needed and resumption was not permitted to constrain domestic activity as in 1819 and 1925. When it came, resumption was more like that in the United States in 1879, the other case in our history in which it was the direct responsibility of politicians sharing the pain of the electorate instead of remote experts or independent or scapegoat central banks. However, it would be less durable.

Monetary Policy, 1945–1960: From Cheap Money to Stop–Go

My purpose [in the first edition] was to show that the reliance on Bank rate as an instrument of monetary policy had been evolved through a century of experience, and that despite changes this experience was applicable to the problems of monetary policy in 1937.

[47] Dow, *op. cit.*, p. 23.
[48] *Ibid.*, pp. 162, 151.

[T]he skepticism of the monetary authorities as to their power so to regulate credit as to maintain monetary stability . . . has, I think, increased. At any rate they seem always unwilling to trust to Bank rate alone as a regulator. For example the resort to the "credit squeeze" in 1955, and to "special deposits" in 1961 to reduce the liquid resources of the banks. Yet the decisive effect of 7 percent in 1957 and 1961 is hardly to be denied.

R. G. Hawtrey, *A Century of Bank Rate*, 2nd ed., xi–xii, xxii

Cheap Money

The new Labour chancellor "converted a cheap money policy into a cheap money campaign."[49] Britain shared America's desire for low interest rates to stimulate demand, but for Dalton, the redistributional effects were paramount. "The Chancellor of the Exchequer must be on the side of the borrowers of money as against the money lenders, on the side of the active producer as against the passive *rentier*," Dalton said in his Budget Speech in April 1947. His monetary policy rested on exhortation. He called on Keynes's argument that the rate of interest is a psychological phenomenon, "largely governed by the prevailing view as to what its value is expected to be." This meant, for Dalton, that it could be kept low by persuasion (and controls) in the face of demand-stimulating budgets.[50] The American administration's rationale for low interest rates – the preservation of wealth – was the opposite of Dalton's, but they amounted to the same thing in practice.

Dalton thought he could avoid inflation and was successful for a while. The end of the war, sales of war materials, the last of the lend-lease payments, and the American loan allowed cuts in both taxes and internal debt. Bank rate was kept at 2 percent, and the bond rate was brought down from 3 to $2\frac{1}{2}$ percent between 1945 and 1947. Trouble came the latter year, which Dalton called *annus horrendus*, compared with the *annus mirabilis* of 1946. Inflation burst through controls, a bond conversion failed to hold at $2\frac{1}{2}$ percent, a fuel crisis led to power cuts, the balance of payments worsened, the chancellor was unable to persuade his cabinet colleagues to cooperate in budget cuts, and the resumption ended in a run on the pound.

Dalton was succeeded by Sir Stafford Cripps, whose name is linked to austerity. There was still no monetary policy except cheap money. Chancellors continued to hope that controls on wages, prices, and bank loans

---

[49] *Ibid.*, pp. 223–24.
[50] Keynes, *The General Theory of Employment, Interest and Money*, p. 203; Dow, *op. cit.*, p. 225.

would hold back inflation. The Bank of England was relegated to technical tasks: operations in securities to enforce the Treasury's interest targets, supervision of an inconvertible currency, and controls on bank advances (private loans). The first was routine, but the second and third were complicated, time consuming, and, in the end, impossible.[51]

Official goals during most of the quarter-century after the war included full employment, low inflation, a fixed exchange rate, and government access to low interest rates. The Bank's principal domestic assignment was to serve as the government's agent of credit control, principally by suppressing private consumption and investment. It was a reluctant agent. When the Treasury asked the Bank to look into ways of limiting bank loans (without raising their cost), the Old Lady responded that qualitative guidelines would not prevent loans from increasing in line with prices. "As long as the price-weapon, i.e., the rate of interest, is forsworn, there is no other criterion."[52]

Was the Bank trying hard enough? Gaitskell, who succeeded an ailing Cripps in October 1950 for the last year of the Labour government, thought it would "be simpler merely to give [banks] direct instructions about the level of advances, with perhaps some guidance as to the particular borrowers who should be cut," always subject to the condition "that there should be no increase in the rate at which the Government borrows short-term." Cobbold, governor since 1949, replied,

The main thought in our mind is that having gone a long distance, with considerable success, in keeping down advances by co-operation with the banking system, what is needed is something which will also influence the attitude of the potential borrower. It is true that no action will bite heavily and violently, short of a rise of a point or two in interest rates generally which would appear impolitic on general grounds at the moment. The effect of a smaller firming up of interest rates on the general mentality of the commercial community cannot be assessed by any rule of thumb and must be a matter of judgment. It is certainly possible that we are wrong but the consensus of opinion at the Bank is definitely that a small firming up on the lines proposed would have a material effect and would well justify the increased charge on the Exchequer.[53]

The new breed of central bankers disliked credit restrictions as much as the old, and the government's power to force their hand had, oddly, been restricted by nationalization. "If ever there was anything done for show,

---

[51] Fforde, *op. cit.*, pp. 360–96, 695–703.

[52] *Ibid.*, p. 362.

[53] Governor to chancellor, June 21, 1951, Fforde, *op. cit.*, p. 392.

not for effect, this is it," Robert Hall, the government's frustrated economic adviser, complained.[54] The Bank of England Act of 1946 reserved banking supervision to the Bank:

The Bank of England may, if they think it necessary in the public interest, request information from and make recommendations to banks and may, if so authorised by the Treasury, issue directions to any banker.

The "Bank disliked this idea," Fforde tells us, because it "already possessed, or mostly thought it possessed, an authority over the banking system that was quite sufficient for all reasonable purposes." Furthermore, it believed that "its prestige and standing in the financial community quite largely depended on the exercise of informal authority, often in private, by established custom. On this view, resort to statutory power would look like a clearly altered and actually diminished status, inconsistent with the underlying spirit of the Bill. . . . Informal methods that are effective when dependent upon powers inherent in central banking and upon the persuasive strength of leadership . . . from within the private sector can become weaker if they are seen to be simply a means whereby Treasury authority can be made effective without statutory powers of enforcement." The Bank did not object too strenuously to its new statutory powers, however, for fear the Treasury might "take the powers the Bank did not want." The effect was that the Treasury, although "deemed the ultimate authority in matters of monetary policy, could neither issue directives to commercial banks nor direct the Bank to do so." On the other hand, the Bank could not issue directives without the Treasury's approval.[55]

The head of the Economic Section and chief economic adviser to the government from 1947 to 1961 had a low opinion of the Bank's intelligence and suspected its loyalty.[56] After an angry meeting, Hall wrote, "It is hard not to get the impression that the Bank, and the banks generally, do not think at all about credit control as economists do, and indeed that they don't quite understand what it is all about." He later complained to his diary that "all we are asking is that the Bank should be neutral and not act against us in our struggle, as they must have been doing."[57]

[54] *The Robert Hall Diaries, 1947–53*, p. 38.

[55] Fforde, *op. cit.*, pp. 10–12, 697–98.

[56] The Economic Section was in the Cabinet Office from its inception until it moved to the Treasury in 1953. Its history is told by Alec Cairncross and Nita Watts, *The Economic Section, 1939–61*.

[57] *Hall, op. cit.*, September 11 and November 18, 1948; January 18 and February 2, 1949.

Norman's modernization and expert advisers notwithstanding, the Bank was still in the City, and if its fortunes were not as tightly linked to the community's as formerly, it still saw among its primary goals the health and stability of finance. We might get a picture of how it saw itself, and of its relations with the Treasury, through the impressions that the institutions made on journalists. "The relationship between the Bank and the Treasury," Anthony Sampson wrote in 1961 in *Anatomy of Britain*, "is one of the most peculiar of all, complicated by the personal contrast between bankers and Treasury men, two miles away. [M]en who have never been to boarding-school often feel they are dealing with men who never left it. The Bank embodies the unquestioning regimental spirit" and reverence for traditions "of the public school proletariat.... Their spirit is at odds both with the introspective musicians of the Treasury and the blasé graduates of the Foreign Office. The men in Threadneedle Street are on top of the day-to-day abrasive mechanism of the city, in the midst of sixty-fourths, fine rates, moneyness, etc. They are inarticulate but confident, tilling the financial fields with an almost agricultural rhythm, and their senior men are held in some awe by Great George Street where the mandarins work in their ivory tower surrounded by abstractions." These are the people of whose infrequent and obscure reports a banker said, "It isn't so much that they don't *want* to tell you what's going on, it's more that they don't know how to explain it: they're like a Northumbrian farmer." Sampson thought the Treasury looked on the Bank "as a foreign tribe, who must not be interferred with.... " Even Labour governments "dreaded any kind of outright clash with Threadneedle Street" and the "city opinion" it represents.[58]

The Bank was even more distant from the government's economists than its civil servants, and its contacts with the former were as unsatisfactory as in the United States. "In a meeting [the Bank] seem to agree and when it comes to the final draft they water it down so much that it is worthless," Hall wrote. They are "as obstructive as possible."[59] He shared Ricardo's opinion that the Bank understood nothing of monetary theory or policy, although that is the end of intellectual comparisons between the two. Hall was far from a classical economist and was skeptical of prices and markets as rationing devices. His major research project at Oxford involved a questionnaire circulated in the mid-1930s to which businesses responded that (a) interest rates played no role in their investment

[58] Anthony Sampson, *Anatomy of Britain*, pp. 356, 366–67.
[59] *Hall, op. cit.*, August 26 and September 4, 1949.

decisions and (b) they did not set prices to clear markets or maximize profits, but charged "fair" markups over costs.[60]

The role of monetary policy in cost-push theories of inflation is accommodative so that wage demands do not cause unemployment through high real wages. The fight against inflation has to rest on controls. A political effect of this reasoning was the demonization of labor that would bring down governments of both parties, but that would come in the 1970s. The wage freeze of 1948–50 was half-hearted, and Hall could not persuade his superiors to repeat the attempt. Not until near the end of his career did he get a chancellor, Selwyn Lloyd, "who took inflation seriously and was a believer in incomes policy."[61] Previous Tory chancellors had looked on wage and price controls as impolitic and impractical, encouraged, thought Hall's staff, by Treasury officials who were "market men" at heart.[62]

There was an exchange crisis in the summer of 1949, followed by the sterling's devaluation from $4.03 to $2.80. The new exchange rate was to be supported by wage controls and tighter fiscal and monetary policies, but these intentions were derailed by a massive increase in spending for the Korean War.[63] A deteriorating balance of payments and dollar drain in the summer of 1951 brought fears of another devaluation, and the *Economist* saw "the beginning of a new period of economic stringency."[64] Labour had been returned with a slim majority in February 1950, to see its popularity fall with inflation, domestic budget cuts, and the war. Gaitskell was forced to bring bad economic news and the necessity of cuts in imports just before the election in October 1951.

Stop-Go

Cobbold gave chancellors little respite from his plea for flexible interest rates, and he and his staff continued to search for new tactics. After another rebuff from Gaitskell, who nevertheless wanted banks to help restrict private investment, Humphrey Mynors (now an executive director) wrote to a colleague,[65]

It is difficult to think of any novel arguments for dearer money. The familiar arguments must be mobilised, after studying where the opposition appears to

---

[60] Hall and C. J. Hitch, "Price Theory and Business Behavior."
[61] Kit Jones, *An Economist among Mandarins*, p. 153.
[62] *Loc. cit.*
[63] Dow, *op. cit.*, pp. 41–45.
[64] July 7, 1951, p. 7; Dow, *op. cit.*, p. 62.
[65] Susan Howson, *British Monetary Policy, 1945–51*, p. 295.

be concentrated, and bearing in mind any change in the terrain since the last engagement.

They might try "pointing out that you could not control both quantity and price of any commodity, including money."[66] Perhaps the "out of line and unreal" rate structure will "break down." The long-term rate had been allowed to rise to 4 percent (which Mynors saw as a "crack" in Gaitskell's armor), whereas the discount rate remained below 1 percent. The government had been able to maintain low interest rates on Treasury bills since the 1930s by "recommended" bank demands for them as part of their "liquidity ratio," combined with short supplies sometimes approaching bill "famines." As in the United States, the government could have low short-term rates if it did not take advantage of them.[67]

Cobbold asked Niemeyer if they could get around the Treasury's aversion to the budgetary effects of interest-rate hikes by segmenting the market for short-term debt so that Treasury bills would still bear interest of 1/2 percent whereas others paid more. The long-time Treasury and Bank adviser responded with the obvious:[68]

The Treasury always lay too much stress on the purely Budgetary aspects of the question. (No doubt short-financing generates short views!) [exclaimed the man who with Norman had tried to impress the long view on Churchill] The importance (and effects) of the problem are far wider. Its neglect may easily produce economic results far more costly to the nation than any Budget cost of a remedy. People abroad mistrust Sterling. They know that we continue to inflate, and are well aware where this will lead us, particularly when Marshall Aid ceases. We cannot counter this want of confidence by arguments about Budget cost – indeed that line only intensifies doubts about our resolution to secure sound finance; and these doubts are very expensive to us.

I see nothing to be gained by clever tricks to avoid the natural course. They will not carry conviction either at home or abroad. I believe they will even do us more harm than having to wait until we can carry the right policy.

On November 7, 1951, thirteen days after the election, the new Conservative chancellor, R. A. Butler, announced, "After the most careful consultation with the governor of the Bank of England," that it was "necessary to depart from the arrangements in force.... The Bank of England are today, with my approval, raising the Bank Rate by 1/2% to 2½%."[69]

---

[66] The words are Howson's, *loc. cit.*
[67] Sayers, *Financial Policy*, p. 148; Edward Nevin, *The Mechanism of Cheap Money*, p. 126.
[68] Fforde, *op. cit.*, p. 384.
[69] *Ibid.*, p. 405.

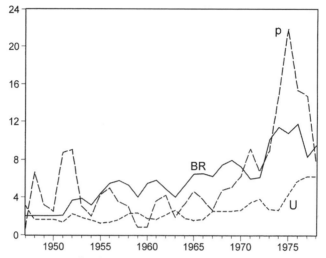

Figure 10.2. Bank rate (BR), inflation (p), and unemployment (U), 1947–78 (annual averages). *Sources:* B. R. Mitchell, *British Historical Statistics*; U.S. Dept. of Commerce, *Historical Statistics of the United States.*

Butler and Cobbold had had a long discussion on October 30, and they had arranged for regular weekly meetings. For some time, relations between governors and chancellors had been "cordial, correct, but slightly distant. The Governor had been treated more like a senior Civil Servant than some special being who could be treated more like a colleague."[70]

The Bank was not back in charge, but it had gotten the ear of those who were. Hall resented this arrangement, which interfered with his efforts to coordinate economic policy. He complained in his diary at the time of the Radcliffe hearings in 1957 that the Bank wanted independence, which modern society would not permit. "The thing that I find most irritating . . . is that the central fact is not being brought out and I do not suppose it can be brought out, which is that the Bank hardly collaborate with the Treasury at all in internal policy matters – the Chancellor talks to the Governor in private and the Bank neither give us their assessment of the situation, nor of the part they expect monetary policy to play in it."[71]

The policies of the period, which came to be known as "stop–go," may be summarized as expansive government budgets and cheap money until

[70] *Ibid.*, p. 404.
[71] *Hall, op. cit.*, December 18, 1957.

a threatened or actual exchange crisis forced a fiscal retreat or tight money, after which the process would be repeated. Figure 10.2 shows the relationship between Bank rate and domestic variables, with the rate tending to rise and fall with inflation and employment – until 1967, after which unemployment and inflation tended to move in the same direction.

Samuel Brittan included among "stop–go" highlights "the deflationary crisis measures of Thorneycroft in 1957, Selwyn Lloyd in 1961, Wilson in 1966 and the reflationary Budgets of Heathcoat Amory in 1959 and Maudling in 1963."[72] We look at the first episode in detail because it tells us something of the Bank's thinking in the post-Keynesian era (not as changed as some had hoped) and its relations with Conservative governments (not as different from its relations with Labour as might have been expected from the first signals), and it is a good story in its own right.

The fiscal expansion of 1953–54, including Housing Minister Harold Macmillan's "crusade," brought wage and price inflation and a deficit in the balance of payments. Bank rate was raised from 3 to $3\frac{1}{2}$ percent in January 1955, and than to $4\frac{1}{2}$ percent in February. This was a high rate, the Bank pointed out in a letter to the chancellor,

a rate which they would not wish, in the monetary conditions at present ruling in the world, to exceed except in moments of crisis, and which they would not wish to maintain for too long. A rate at this level, if continued for a long period, is bound to have undesirable as well as desirable effects. It is the Court's hope that the results of the general economic policy of HM Government will make possible some relaxation in credit policy at a fairly early date.[73]

The chancellor thanked the Bank and went the other way. An election was looming (and would be held in May, giving an increased Conservative majority), and in the April budget speech he announced a plan to boost the expansion with a cut in the income tax and relying on "the resources of a flexible monetary policy" to check inflation. Unfortunately, reported the Treasury's *Economic Survey*, "By the summer," it was evident "that the pressure of demand persisted and that monetary policy was not operating as rapidly as had been expected."[74]

---

[72] Samuel Brittan, *Steering the Economy*, p. 450.
[73] Fforde, *op. cit.*, pp. 631–32.
[74] Dow, *op. cit.*, pp. 78–79.

Policies the next two years were deflationary, marked by Butler's take-backs in the October 1955 budget and the 7-percent Bank rate in September 1957. The government, Treasury, and Bank all dance around credit controls. The Tory acceptance of changes in Bank rate had not carried with it a forswearing of controls. "Hire-purchase" restrictions on consumer credit were introduced in 1952, and Butler and his successors continued to press the Bank to "request" the banks to restrict their loans.

There was little evidence in the spring of 1955 of any effect of the recent increases in Bank rate on advances, and the Treasury, "sharply on the lookout for such evidence," Fforde writes, suggested that the Bank ask the banks to provide monthly instead of quarterly data; "not worth the extra work," responded the deputy governor.[75] Governor Cobbold wanted to hold back advances to mollify the chancellor, but he disliked strong-arm tactics. He "was not keen to write letters" and avoided directives, preferring oblique signals in polite conversation. The bankers were less polite, complaining "that it was difficult to select the victims of restriction and they grumbled about the lack of restraint by nationalised industries."[76] Lord Aldenham, Chairman of the Westminster Bank, was not disturbed by his customers "and bank managers" lack of cooperation.

The Bank was caught in the middle. Irritated by the banks' stubbornness, an executive director warned, "If they want HMG (present and future) to run their business, this is the way to go about it. The banks should read the signals themselves and act accordingly."[77] Cobbold thought the interest rate increases would yet be effective without much rise in unemployment if, he told Butler, the public sector cooperated. At the request of the Committee of London Clearing Banks and in furtherance of his own desire to get an agreement on principles, Cobbold gave a lunch at the Bank on July 5 for the chancellor and bank representatives.

The bankers told the chancellor they needed a more helpful climate. Adverse responses to their letter in the *Times* (see the box) showed that customers saw no reason why their business should be curtailed when public expenditure showed no signs of economy and ministers made optimistic speeches about investing in prosperity. The governor supported them, arguing for a government statement about the need for

---

[75] Fforde, *op. cit.*, p. 632.
[76] *Ibid.*, p. 633.
[77] Kenneth Peppiatt, Fforde, *op. cit.*, pp. 237, 633.

all-around restraint. The chancellor remarked disarmingly that the majority of his advisers had placed exaggerated faith in the efficacy of monetary measures and were correspondingly disappointed. He then suggested that Treasury officials might meet the bankers for enlightenment, and it was agreed that the Bank should arrange this.[78]

Restrictions on Credit: An Appeal to Bank Customers

TO THE EDITOR OF THE TIMES: Sir, – It is by now well known that it is the policy of her Majesty's Government to restrict the total volume of credit in order to curtail internal demand in the interests of the national balance of payments.

Such a policy makes it necessary for the banks to restrict their advances, and they have had to be, and must continue to be, more stringent in their attitude in regard to advances to customers, large and small alike, however reasonable those advances would be in normal times.

The banks therefore hope that their customers will understand that the present stringency is a matter of public policy and will cooperate with the banks by keeping their credit requirements as small as possible. Yours faithfully,

Aldenham, Chairman, D. J. Roberts, Deputy Chairman,
Committee of London Clearing Bankers. 10 Lombard Street, June 28, 1955.

Aldenham told Cobbold that "he did not find the lunch party reassuring." "Nor was it," Fforde notes, "for the Chancellor said nothing specific about action in the public sector." The Bank was also disturbed by the prospect of direct contacts between the Treasury and the banks, which would displace the Bank as intermediary and make "a mess" of monetary policy.[79]

In negotiations over the government's directive, the Bank and the banks fought against an official quantitative limit on advances. They escaped with a letter in which the chancellor told the governor that "the necessary reduction in demand is unlikely to be achieved unless the total of bank advances is reduced below its present level." The governor told the banks that he expected to see a material reduction in advances by

[78] *Ibid.*, p. 637.
[79] *Loc. cit.*

October and a further cut in December. They acted "decisively and without delay [and] agreed that the aim should be to cut advances by 10% by the end of the year...." They were, however, "Having obeyed the authorities with such alacrity,... distinctly nettled to read that the Chancellor had assured [shadow chancellor] Gaitskell in the House that existing investment [public] programmes would not be affected."[80]

The course of policy was set for the next two years. Advances remained below their mid-1955 level, Bank rate was raised to $5\frac{1}{2}$ percent and hire-purchase restrictions were tightened in 1956, and public spending was maintained. Meanwhile total bank credit, money, wages, and prices continued to rise, leading to more meetings of chancellors with bankers and more complaints that monetary policy was too slow, if effective at all. There was parliamentary pressure on Macmillan, who had succeeded Butler as chancellor in December 1955, to conduct an inquiry into monetary policy and the monetary system.[81]

The government's authority was weakened by the country's poor economic performance compared with the "miracles" elsewhere, "a weakening intensified by the Suez affair and the fall of Eden." (The British–French–Israeli attack on Egypt in October 1956 after the nationalization of the Suez Canal was aborted under American and Soviet pressure.) The Bank stepped up its efforts to shift the focus of monetary policy from controls to interest rates. Cobbold wrote the chancellor the following:

Whatever longer-term effects Suez may prove to have on the economy, it has certainly had the immediate effect of laying bare to the public eye, both at home and abroad, some of the weakness of which we have long been conscious.

You and I have, I think, both felt that the measures of the last few years, including the credit squeeze and various fiscal adjustments made by your predecessor and yourself, have helped to move the economy towards an uneasy equilibrium but have left some basic problems untouched. We have over the last five years been able to maintain our position on a see-saw, retaining just adequate confidence in the currency by a slender margin. After the events of the past few months I do not believe this is good enough.

Macmillan, who was shortly to succeed Anthony Eden as prime minister, should have understood. The outflow of foreign exchange reserves had been a significant factor in the decision to halt the Suez adventure in

---

[80] *Ibid.*, pp. 639–40.
[81] *Ibid.*, p. 659.

November 1956, and it might have explained his sudden switch from "the warmest cheerleader of the operation" to a strong supporter of those who wanted to abandon it, although he denied saying "we can't afford it."[82] This does not mean, as we will see, that the experience would override earlier and deeper lessons.

Peter Thorneycroft, who succeeded Macmillan as chancellor in January 1957, proved after an initial hard line toward the Bank to be more malleable. An increase in advances led him to write "a curt letter" to the governor in March expressing his concern that they might be losing control of the economy: "It is not so much that I think we ought to apply the brake any harder at the moment; but I do want to know that we have a brake that works."[83]

Cobbold's reply, after defending the banks and their judgments in accommodating "priority needs," shifted to the attack. The banks had been made restless by the continued denial of competition. "A credit squeeze might be all right as a short-term instrument, but if it was necessary to prolong it for a long period something fundamental must have gone wrong elsewhere."[84]

The new chancellor's personality contributed to the faster pace of policy review. Fforde wrote that Thorneycroft "was unlike Macmillan or Butler. Intellectual subtlety and persuasive charm were not his style. He preferred clarity, simplicity and the issue of clear instructions rather than carefully phrased requests. He preferred statutory authority to less formal methods of getting his way and was frightened rather than encouraged by a long-standing credit squeeze that relied more upon co-operation than compulsion. He was rightly nervous about losing control of events, a nervousness that was by no means misplaced after the unimpressive record of economic policy since the winter of 1954–55."[85]

The issue was forced by an exchange crisis in August 1957 after the devaluation of the French franc. Pressure on the pound might have been increased by a signal from Thorneycroft that he was unlikely to do anything about inflation. In announcing a Council on Prices, Productivity and Incomes to "keep under review changes in prices, productivity and the level of incomes... and to report thereon from time to time," he told the House, "There is clearly no simple act of policy which

---

[82] Brittan, *op. cit.*, p. 207.
[83] *Ibid.*, pp. 670, 673.
[84] Fforde's summary, *op. cit.*, p. 673.
[85] *Ibid.*, p. 670.

is a remedy for inflation.... The Government, the private employers, the trade unions and the nationalized industries all have a part to play."[86]

Nevertheless, something had to be done. The banks threatened to end their voluntary compliance whereas Thorneycroft wanted tighter and more explicit restrictions on advances. "The Bank was truly boxed in and an attempt had to be made to get out, by violence if need be."[87] On August 22, just before going on holiday, Cobbold sent the chancellor a letter outlining his proposals. The tune was unchanged. Credit restrictions were "played out" and other nonprice measures were similarly ineffective. If the signs of inflation were confirmed in September, measures would have to be taken: "They should be sharp and comprehensive, and (bearing in mind various doubts on the international horizon and possibilities that the tide may turn) they should so far as possible be easily reversible." The only viable monetary candidate "is a drastic increase in Bank Rate either in one move or in quick stages. The objections are obvious and by itself further Bank Rate action could well do more harm than good [presumably referring to the possibility that the government might take the opportunity to increase spending, counting on tighter monetary policy to restrain inflation]. We should, however, consider it seriously if we judged that in conjunction with a general programme it would have quick effects and the very high rates need not be maintained too long."[88]

After three weeks of negotiations between Cobbold's staff and the Treasury, Thorneycroft accepted the need for fiscal measures and a rise in Bank rate on condition that the banks agreed to hold average advances in the coming year to the average of the last 12 months. The Bank dissuaded the chancellor from including a threat of statutory authority over advances in his statement, but he got more than "their best endeavours" initially offered by the banks. The Bank proposed at least a 2-percent increase in Bank rate, to 7 percent, and would have liked more. Thorneycroft thought he might go as high as 7 but asked for the Bank's case in writing before making a decision and probably as ammunition for the case that he would have to make to the prime minister. Macmillan had not been encouraging about the new direction of policy. His economic views were "coloured by his acquaintance with mass unemployment at his old constituency of Stockton-on-Tees in the interwar period." Whitehall officials

---

[86] *Hansard*, July 25, 1957, col. 643–50; Dow, *op. cit.*, p. 99.
[87] Fforde, *op. cit.*, p. 677.
[88] *Loc. cit.*

"were said to keep a mental tally of the number of times he mentioned Stockton-on-Tees in any one week."[89] "He always feared," added Richard Chapman in his study of the decision to raise Bank rate, "that prosperity and full employment could be too easily sacrificed by a one-sided devotion to 'sound money' at the expense of other objectives." Portions of the Bank's argument follow:[90]

It would show determination to take strong action in this field in support of objectives....

It would give a jolt, show that the exchange position is serious ... but that the Bank propose to fight for the pound by determined use of their weapons.

A rise of this sort would have a considerable effect on borrowers, and is likely to cause deferment of spending plans. It would, in our view, be at this stage the most effective contribution on the monetary side to restriction of spending in the private sector – much more effective than any pressures or directives on the banks....

The statement finished by pointing out that "a smaller move ... would be regarded as routine ... without much significance.... In our view, it would involve additional cost for little advantage." This recalls Keynes's prescription for inflation: "a sharp dose of Dear Money." If you wish to stop an inflation embedded in people's expectations, you had better convince them that you mean business.

The chancellor accepted the lower end of the Bank's proposals, and after sleeping on them, the prime minister went along. It is interesting to speculate about whether Thorneycroft's acceptance of 7 percent was influenced by Professor Lionel Robbins, to whom it was said the chancellor turned when he found his Treasury advisers bereft of ideas. Shortly after this incident, Robbins wrote of the "controversial" issue of inflation that more weight was given "to the push of costs, less to the pull of demand, than I find appropriate. But on one point I hope we should all be agreed; namely, *that none of this could happen if there was a sufficiently strong control of the supply of money....* "[91] Cobbold expressed the same idea more picturesquely at the Lord Mayor's dinner on August 10, 1957, when he put aside "learned discussion" of cost versus demand inflation and talked of "the push-me-pull-you" – "a fascinating creature of one of the

[89] Brittan, *op. cit.*, p. 203.
[90] *Ibid.*, pp. 684–85.
[91] Robbins, "Thoughts on the Crisis."

nursery books.... If we can shoot one end of that animal, the other end will not long survive."[92]

Whether because of events, arguments, or company, the chancellor's conversion was complete. "The speeches Thorneycroft made in his first six months in the Treasury were so different from those he made in his second six months," Brittan wrote, "that it is difficult to credit them with the same authorship." The April 1957 Budget Speech went as follows:

There are those who say that the answer lies in savage deflationary policies, resulting in high levels of unemployment. They say that we should depress demand to a point at which employers cannot afford to pay and workers are in no position to ask for higher wages. If this be the only way in which to contain the wage-price spiral it is indeed a sorry reflection upon our modern society.

By July, he was instructing the Treasury "to consider possibilities of checking inflation by taking firmer control of the money supply," and on August 7 he directed that "a study should be made in the Treasury of the possibility of bringing about a measure of deflation in the economy."[93] He had been quietly moving toward the Bank's position before the September negotiations without giving away his ability to bargain for a politically viable package. Announcement of his "September Measures" to an IMF meeting in Washington included, along with a commitment to hold government spending in check, the following sentences:

The Government are determined to maintain the internal and external value of the pound....
There can be no remedy for inflation ... which does not include, and indeed is not founded upon, a control of the money supply. So long as it is generally believed that the Government are prepared to see the necessary finance produced to match the upward spiral of costs, inflation will continue....[94]

Inflation slowed in 1958, although probably due as much to the international recession as to the new policy, and Bank rate was cut to 6 percent in March. By November it was 4 percent. Advances and consumer credit were decontrolled.

What was learned from this episode? Probably nothing. At least, nothing changed. The institutions and ideas of the mid-1950s prevailed until

---

[92] Dow, *op. cit.*, p. 100.
[93] Brittan, *op. cit.*, pp. 209–13.
[94] Dow, *op. cit.*, p. 101.

they were shocked by similar but larger forces two decades later. Monetary policy would continue to be implemented by an institution (the Bank of England) at cross-purposes with the responsible body (Parliament). This point has been made more positively by describing central banks as the sound-money consciences of the politicians, the Jiminy Crickets who remind them that they can't have everything but are attended to only when things go wrong. However the process is pictured, the stop–go policies implied by the inconsistent goals of continuous full employment and price stability continued.

Thorneycroft thought there had been a change. However, what he had intended to be a new policy, based on a new (or neglected) intellectual framework, not just a tactical move within an existing policy, was shortly rejected. Labour's criticism was to be expected. Patrick Gordon Walker said that one of the chancellor's main objects "was really to declare war on the trade unions." "The whole trouble," Harold Wilson said, "is that the chancellor is trying to fight what is a cost-push inflation . . . with the crude techniques which classical theory considers appropriate to a demand inflation. [M]erely to freeze the supply of money does not of itself freeze prices."[95]

Thorneycroft was more surprised by the lack of support from his own party and resigned over the budget four months later when the cabinet backed out of his pledge to hold down government spending. His junior ministers, Enoch Powell and Nigel Birch, who had been "largely responsible for turning the anti-inflationary policies into a crusade," resigned with him. Their colleagues, who thought the £50 million involved a minor issue, were puzzled. The group's belief that there had been a genuine shift to a policy in which price stability had first priority was not an accurate reading of the minds of their colleagues. The cabinet regarded the September measures as a tactical reaction to a crisis, to be reversed as soon as possible.[96]

The revolving door of chancellors under Macmillan (four in less than seven years) reflected the unsettled policy. Heathcoat Amory, who succeeded Thorneycroft and lasted the longest, presented a preelection "tax relief" budget in April 1959, and in the next 15 months brought back controls, raised Bank rate, and resigned in favor of Selwyn Lloyd, whose experience was similar. His successor, Reginald Maudling, was luckier

---

[95] *Hansard*, October 29, 1957, col. 72; Dow, *op. cit.*, p. 102.
[96] Brittan, *op. cit.*, p. 213; Andrew Shonfield, *British Economic Policy since the War*, pp. 248–49.

in being able to pass the consequences of his "reflation" to the Labour government elected in October 1964.

The Bank, Prime Ministers, and the Pound: From One Unmentionable to Another, 1951–1967

Although the Bank had opposed unrestricted convertibility immediately after the war, it never lost sight of the pound's return to its former primacy. This section relates two episodes in the history of the Bank's efforts to achieve and preserve convertibility.

Robot

The sterling crisis in the winter of 1951–52 following the Korean War rearmament boom was another of a series of blows to sterling that had seen the failure of the 1947 resumption and the 1949 devaluation, with little prospect of improvement. "It is not therefore surprising," Fforde wrote, "that the Bank then finally abandoned the whole evolutionary approach to convertibility that it had pursued since 1941." There seemed nothing left but "to make a virtue of necessity" and take a leap in the dark.[97] The Bank joined the Overseas Finance Division of the Treasury in advocating a jump to convertibility, which would have to be done with a floating rate.

From a commitment to fixed rates, the governor had shifted to the view that "there was no advantage in sitting still and waiting for the deluge" in the form of another crisis suspension or devaluation.[98] The proposal was given the code name Robot after its chief protagonists, Thomas ROwan, George BOlton, and OTto Clarke, the second from the Bank and the others from the Treasury.[99] Details were not filled in, but the basic idea was to allow the pound to float within wide limits, say, \$3.20 to \$2.40, instead of the prevailing \$2.84 to \$2.76, and to unblock sterling balances in stages as conditions allowed.

The chancellor was persuaded, and he brought Robot to the cabinet at the end of February 1952. Churchill liked the idea of "setting the pound free," but the proposal soon foundered on fundamental differences.[100] The goals of the Treasury's proponents differed from the Bank's. The former

[97] Fforde, *op. cit.*, pp. 169, 430.
[98] *Ibid.*, p. 431.
[99] Anthony Seldon, *Churchill's Indian Summer: The Conservative Government, 1951–55*, p. 171.
[100] Churchill statement recollected by Cobbold, Fforde, *op. cit.*, p. 435n.

made the standard macrostabilization case that a floating rate would take the pressure of the balance of payments off the domestic economy.

This is not what the Bank had in mind. It had thought of the wider band as insurance, in place of a large stock of reserves, that would permit greater convertibility. "I told the chancellor that I thought the argumentation good," Cobbold said of a paper by Clarke, "but that there was much too much 'floating.'" He wrote to Butler,[101]

The wider limits...must be supported by every possible measure to strengthen the real and psychological position of the currency. If not so regarded and so supported, a "floating rate" is a polite name for progressive devaluation and would be even worse than devaluation to a new fixed rate.... An international currency must have a high degree of stability.... It is most important that a decision to float the rate should be presented in this way, both for home opinion...and foreign opinion generally, and not least for the Sterling Area, who will not be attracted by a currency which looks likely to fluctuate all over the place and to "take on the rate" any absence of necessary action in other fields.

"So much for the benign equilibrating force that" some of Robot's proponents "had found so alluring," Fforde comments.[102] It had begun to look like another Bank scheme for tighter money, enforced by convertibility.

Four months earlier, as he was putting the new government together, Churchill told Oliver Lyttleton (later Viscount Chandos), Butler's rival for the Exchequer, "I have seen a Treasury Minute and already I know that the financial position is almost irretrievable: the country has lost its way. In the worst of the war I could always see how to do it. Today's problems are elusive and intangible, and it would be a bold man who could look forward to certain success."[103] The clear objective of the war – "Victory at all costs"[104] – had been replaced by a mixture of complicated and sometimes conflicting economic goals. The prime minister's course with respect to Robot, however, was made clear by his trusted adviser in matters of economics as well as the physical sciences. Lord Cherwell (F. A. Lindemann, "the Prof") generally favored the elimination of controls, including the restoration of convertibility – as conditions allowed. However, he argued that the freeing of the pound would have to wait

---

[101] Fforde, *op. cit*, p. 438.
[102] *Loc. cit.*
[103] Lord Chandos, *Memoirs*, p. 343.
[104] From Churchill's first speech in the House of Commons as prime minister, May 13, 1940, *Hansard*, col. 1502.

for improved export performance. Convertibility without severe devaluation in the current situation of small reserves and an uncertain future of the balance of payments might force a policy of deflation, leading to unemployment. The government would not survive a departure from the postwar consensus in which full employment held first priority.[105] Robot was set aside.

The Defense of Sterling, 1964–67

Convertibility was made possible in Western Europe, including Britain, in 1958 by American payment deficits, a shift in the terms of trade away from primary producers, and the restrictive monetary policies begun in the summer of 1955.[106] Foreign positions were assisted by the European Payments Union, which allowed members, helped by Marshall aid, to run larger deficits than with the IMF. The negotiating machinery also enabled debtors to raise trade barriers. It was more like the Keynes Plan or the pre-1939 system than Bretton Woods.[107]

Even so, Britain's international position remained tenuous. Its reserves were erratic, and in the 1960s it would have covered two months' imports, on average, compared with six months for the United States, West Germany, France, and Italy. A comparison with West Germany is given in Table 10.1. Moreover, Bank rate, now reserved for emergencies, and not always utilized then, was not the powerful protector of the "thin film" of reserves that it had been before 1914.

This was the background against which "Mr. Maudling's reflation" yielded "Mr. Callaghan's bitter harvest" when the latter succeeded to the exchequer on Labour's narrow victory in the October 1964 election. The popular Harold Macmillan had retired and been succeeded the previous October by the lackluster Sir Alec Douglas Home through a procedure much criticized in his own party. An election would have to be held within 12 months, and polls and by-elections were going against the Conservatives. The government decided to go for 4-percent growth.

Employment was full and the Treasury thought the rate of increase in capacity was closer to 3 percent, but neither governments nor economists have liked the Treasury's arithmetic. The National Economic Development Council was established in 1962 as an expert body,

---

[105] Earl of Birkenhead, *The Professor and the Prime Minister*, chap. 10.

[106] For policy adjustments sparked by currency crises, see Samuel Katz, *Sterling Speculation and European Convertibility, 1955–58*.

[107] Alan Milward, *The European Rescue of the Nation-State*, pp. 348–51.

Table 10.1. *Official Reserves (at Year End in Millions of Dollars) 1949–58*

	United Kingdom	German Federal Republic
1949	1,688	—
1950	3,300	274
1951	2,335	518
1952	1,846	1,190
1953	2,518	1,956
1954	2,762	2,636
1955	2,120	3,076
1956	2,133	4,291
1957	2,273	5,644
1958	3,069	6,321

Sources: U.K. Central Statistical Office, *Economic Trends;* IMF, *International Financial Statistics;* Alan Milward, *The European Rescue of the Nation-State,* tables 7.2 and 7.3.

independent of the Treasury, to advise on policies for growth. Its purpose was to find a steady-growth path in place of the "stop–go" crises of the 1950s, hopefully at the enviable rates across the Channel. It would give the chancellor an alternative to the Treasury's sombre notes. Neddy's staff "jocularly referred to the Treasury as 'the other side.'"[108]

They were persuaded that the productivity speedup had been hidden by the 1961–62 recession. The high investment of 1960–61 "had not yet found expression in the output figures because demand had been held down."[109] Taxes were cut, government spending was increased, and when prices rose and the balance of payments worsened, Maudling was praised for refusing to panic. When his April 1964 budget took back only a small part of the benefits of the preceding two years, Professor E. A. G. Robinson wrote,

It has been courageous (some critics would say foolhardy) in allowing the economy the chance of another year's expansion above the 4 percent rate without anything more than a delicate lightening of the pressure on the accelerator.[110]

[108] Brittan, *op. cit.,* p. 244.
[109] *Ibid.,* p. 278.
[110] *London and Cambridge Economic Bulletin,* p. v (*Times Review of Industry*), June 1964. This and the next quotation are from T. W. Hutchison, *Economics and Economic Policy in Britain, 1946–66,* pp. 224, 227.

The Spectator, edited by Iain Macleod (who would be Heath's first chancellor until his death after a month), told Maudling that he

must drive straight through fluctuations in the balance of payments.... If Mr. Maudling is really hoping to win the election he will have to show the public that he is up to date and "with it."[111]

Growth averaged 2.6 percent in the 1950s and never reached 3 percent in the 1960s or attained that average in any decade the rest of the century. This is hindsight, but Maudling's reflation was no different from the policies of his postwar predecessors, and it had the same effects: inflation, balance of payment difficulties, and exchange crises.

The possibility of devaluation had circulated before the election, but the new Labour government was surprised by the size of the problem. The EEC Monetary Committee advised that sterling was in fundamental disequilibrium and should be devalued 10 to 15 percent, a step also urged by the economic "left," including the new advisors brought to Whitehall from the universities. The Bank and the City opposed devaluation.[112] However, the decision not to devalue seems to have been taken independently of these views, on political grounds, immediately after the new government took office. Prime Minister Harold Wilson feared that another devaluation, after that of 1949 by the last Labour government, would be an admission that Labour was unfit to manage the economy.

Given this mindset, devaluation would have to be done quickly or not at all, and the option soon expired. Wilson told the Economic Club of New York on April 14, 1965,

If an incoming government were at any time likely to consider devaluing the nation's currency, political considerations would have dictated doing it on that first day, when the fault would clearly and unequivocally lie with those who had charge of the nation's affairs for 13 years. So that decision, once taken, was a decision for good.

Devaluation became "the great unmentionable" in the government and the civil service and even, "to a large extent, by tacit and patriotic agreement, in the Press." Looking back, Professor Alan Day wrote in the *Observer* that "open advocacy of devaluation was ... the next worse thing

---

[111] June 5, 1964, p. 771.
[112] Brittan, *op. cit.*, pp. 291–92; Peter Browning, *The Treasury and Economic Policy, 1964–85*, p. 4.

to publishing obscene literature."[113] The subject was hardly discussed by officials, and then only in whispers behind closed doors. Deputy Prime Minister George Brown remembered that the prime minister and chancellor were "terrified lest talking, or even thinking, about devaluation should alert the world to what was going on."[114]

The foreign exchange markets were not always convinced, especially when, after Wilson had announced the severity of the problem and "in Churchillian terms, his determination to take whatever measures were necessary for the defence of sterling," the government did not follow through.[115] There were the usual gimmicks – import surcharges, tax rebates on exports, and talk of wage and price restraint – but the budget was not tightened significantly and the traditional call to quarters in these circumstances, a rise in Bank rate, was not seen. A return to stop–go policies was rejected.[116] The aspiration to 4-percent growth had survived the change of government.

Wilson's statement on November 16, 1964, was followed by a run on the pound that accelerated when Bank rate was raised from 5 to 7 percent on the 23rd. This perverse reaction has been attributed to investors' interpretation of the unusual handling of the rise as a sign of panic, as well as to official statements that it was merely a technical adjustment that was not intended to deflate demand.[117] On the 25th there was "a dramatic announcement from the Bank of England that eleven central banks, together with the Bank for International Settlements and the U.S. Export-Import Bank, had arranged a further $3,000m. of short-term credits which Britain could draw upon to protect the pound."[118] This did no more than slow the outflow of funds, and further credits had to be arranged – and used – before devaluation from $2.80 to $2.40 in November 1967.

Macroeconomic "policy" during these years (if such a word can be used) was inconsistent over time and among members of the government. Budgets alternated between restrictive and expansionary, accompanied by verbal commitments to faster growth and the parity of the pound, apparently to be reconciled by price, wage, and credit controls. One of

---

[113] November 26, 1967, Browning, *op. cit.*, p. 5.
[114] Brown, *In My Way*, p. 194; Browning, *op. cit.*, p. 6.
[115] Browning, *op. cit.*, p. 7.
[116] White Paper on *The Economic Situation*, October 26, 1964.
[117] Brittan, *op. cit.*, p. 303; see p. 298 for a chronology of the crisis.
[118] *Ibid.*, pp. 303–4.

the sharpest inconsistencies was between the stated objectives of growth in total output, especially in exports, and the rising share of resources taken by public programs.

The ambiguity of government policy was institutionalized in a new Department of Economic Affairs (DEA), under George Brown, to plan macroeconomic policy, especially growth, whereas the Treasury looked after short-term finance. Its first task was to produce a National Plan for the economy that, in Brown's words, "would break the ancient Treasury tradition of making economic policy and industrial activity subject to all the inhibitions of orthodox monetary control."[119]

The last phrase was a knock at the "Treasury view," which was the name given to the positions of budget-minded officials who denied that government spending improved employment because it diverted resources from other areas:

"It is the orthodox Treasury dogma, steadfastly held," [Chancellor Churchill] told the House of Commons, "that whatever might be the political or social advantages, very little additional employment and no permanent additional employment, can, in fact, and as a general rule, be created by State borrowing and State expenditure."

When Keynes and Hubert Henderson wrote this in support of Lloyd George's 1929 campaign to promote demand by public works (*Can Lloyd George Do It?*), unemployment was above 10 percent.[120] If this view is valid, Keynes and Henderson said, it must apply

to any new enterprise entailing capital expenditure. If it were announced that some of our leading captains of industry had decided to launch out boldly, and were about to sink capital in new industrial plant to the tune, between them, of £100 millions, we should all expect to see a great improvement in employment. And of course, we should be right.

When Brown made his statement, however, unemployment was $1\frac{1}{2}$ percent. Even in the most favorable conditions for the employment benefits of government spending, there is likely to be some inflation and possibly devaluation. The last was part of Keynes's prescription.

Brown's sums failed as completely for political institutions as for economics. No coherent policy could be gotten from accounts that were determined to conflict. As long as budgets and monetary policy were managed by the Treasury, the DEA could only present minority proposals

---

[119] Brown, *op. cit.*, p. 104.

[120] Pigou had criticized what came to be called the Treasury View in *Wealth and Welfare*, p. 485, and *Industrial Fluctuations*, pp. 290–91.

that led to increased workloads, dissension, and finally arbitration by the prime minister.[121] The DEA was terminated and economic management reverted wholly to the Treasury before the 1970 election.

Wilson was also unlucky in his governor, George Rowland Stanley Baring, the Earl of Cromer, who had succeeded Cobbold in 1961. Relations between the Bank and the government, never smooth, had deteriorated the last years of Cobbold's term. He received "a strong protest" from the new chancellor, Selwyn Lloyd, in July 1960 when bank advances showed a large rise in spite of his predecessor's calls to restrict credit in the face of an "overheating" economy. The protest was suggested by Robert Hall, who "was especially annoyed because only a month earlier the governor had claimed that he had everything under control."[122] Hall wrote in his diary,[123]

It is one of the great disadvantages of monetary policy, compared to fiscal policy, that if you change taxes the revenue departments will go out and collect the money and be very unpleasant to the taxpayer if they do not get it. But if you try to tighten up on the money side, you get the Bank of England falling over themselves to soften the blow and to make all sorts of excuses for the bankers that they probably would be ashamed to make for themselves.

The prime minister was also dissatisfied and sought the chancellor's reassurance that Cobbold would leave at the end of the year as promised.[124]

The desire for new and more compliant blood was heightened by the recent insinuations of the Radcliffe Committee (see the next section) touching on the Bank's competence and cooperation. It is not surprising that the call was to someone from outside the Bank. Cromer had not been a director, nor had he held any other position in the Bank, and was one of the few governors who had not been deputy governor. At 43, he was the youngest governor in 200 years. He was a new kind of governor in these ways. On the other hand, he was a throwback to the pre-Norman governors who had not (before their deputy-governor service) been full-time in the Bank, and he was a merchant banker who would return to his firm. Like Governor Whitmore and Deputy Governor Pearse encountered in Chap. 2, Cromer had not been softened by the bureaucratic give and take between the Bank and the government that had developed since

---

[121] Browning, *op. cit.*, p. 12, from Brown, *op. cit.*, p. 105, and Richard Crossman, *Diaries*, pp. 58, 219.

[122] Kit Jones, *Economist among Mandarins*, p. 141.

[123] *Hall, op. cit.*, p. 243.

[124] Jones, *op. cit.*, p. 142.

1914. He did not see why he had to pretend that Maudling's or Brown's sums added up. This may be why Peter Browning, who was sympathetic to the "third-way," through controls, between devaluation and deflation, thought that "Cromer's grasp of macroeconomic policy had never been of the strongest."[125]

Odd as it was in some respects, the choice of a Baring for the new broom seemed necessary to give assurance to the markets. Nevertheless, conflict was inevitable regardless of personalities when the government wanted an accommodative governor who would at the same time instill confidence in the currency. These conflicts were heightened by Cromer's confrontational and public style. For one reporter, he "emerged as the keeper of his country's financial conscience . . . when he sounded solemn warnings against 'indulging ourselves' by 'an enlargement of governmental spending.'"[126] When in their "meeting of the minds" on November 24, 1964, Cromer demanded an about-face in the government's economic and social programs to restore confidence in sterling, Wilson threatened to go to the country in defense of the government's constitutional rights.[127]

Wilson recalled that "we had to listen night after night to demands that there should be immediate cuts in Government expenditure, and particularly in those parts of Government expenditure which related to the social services. It was not long before we were being asked, almost at pistol-point, to cut back on expenditure, even to the point of stopping the road-building programme, or schools which were only half-constructed. . . . "

Indeed, in January, 1965, at a private lunch at No. 10, . . . I told [Cromer] that Government expenditure was committed far ahead; schools which were being built, roads which were part-way to completion, had been programmed by our Conservative predecessors in 1962–63. Was it in his view, I asked him, that we should cut them off half-finished – roads left as an eyesore on the countryside, schools left without a roof, in order to satisfy foreign financial fetishism? This question was difficult for him, but he answered, "Yes."[128]

Cromer returned to Barings after a single term at the Bank, and relations improved with the accession of Leslie O'Brien in 1966. A career bank employee, Callaghan found O'Brien "Modest, quiet, considerate of the views of others but firm in his own beliefs, . . . technically

---

[125] Browning, *op. cit.*, p. 27.

[126] Joseph Wechsberg, *The Merchant Bankers*, p. 163.

[127] Harold Wilson, *A Personal Record: The Labour Government, 1964–70*, pp. 37–38; David Kynaston, "The Bank and the Government."

[128] Wilson, *op. cit.*, p. 34.

proficient."[129] Gordon Richardson, governor from 1973 to 1983, also had "generally good, constructive working relationships" with Labour governments. Chancellor Denis Healey (1974–79) enjoyed the "creative tension."[130] However, O'Brien and Richardson delivered even less financial stability than Cobbold and Cromer. The average annual rates of inflation during the tenures of the four governors – 1949–61, 1961–66, 1966–73, and 1973–83 – were 3.9, 3.6, 6.4, and 13.6 percent, respectively.

From Radcliffe to Competition and Credit Control

Governor O'Brien addressed the Lord Mayor's Dinner in October 1972:[131]

To all these efforts to improve the efficiency of the system, our critics tend to say: certainly we are getting the competition in the provision of financial services, but where is the credit control?

A Conservative government had come to office in June 1970, and it terminated wage, price, and credit controls to promote competition and efficiency. In the interests of monetary control, the *Act for Competition and Credit Control* (CCC) replaced the cash reserve requirement by a redefined liquidity ratio.[132] O'Brien's question was addressed to the surges in money and inflation since CCC's adoption. Most of the answer lay in government deficits, as usual, but inflation was also facilitated by changes that had been suggested by the 1959 *Radcliffe Report*. The *Report* deserves our attention partly for its meteoric appearance on the stage of monetary theory but mainly for its influence on policy.

Thorneycroft had been spurred by complaints of the ineffectiveness of monetary policy to appoint the Committee on the Working of the Monetary System, chaired by Lord Radcliffe, in May 1957. The monetary theory upon which the *Report* was based had faded by the time of its issue two years later, but it received a great deal of attention at the time and influenced policy more than a decade later. Bank rate proved to be effective in 1957 (see Hawtrey's statement at the head of the third section), but the Committee was already set to support the political preference for

---

[129] James Callaghan, *Time and Chance*, p. 195.

[130] Kynaston, *op. cit.*; Denis Healey, *The Time of My Life*, p. 375.

[131] Bank of England *Quarterly Bulletin*, December 1972; reprinted in Bank of England, *The Development and Operation of Monetary Policy, 1960–83*. The speech was delivered by the deputy governor in the governor's absence.

[132] Maximilian Hall, *Monetary Policy since 1971*, pp. 7–13.

controls. It took a firm position against the argument that demand and prices were governed by interest rates and money.

The limited effectiveness of interest rates made it necessary, the *Report* argued, "to strike directly at the banks." Controls should not be aimed at bank deposits, however, but at advances.[133] This was the preconversion-Thorneycroft position. Radcliffe's theory posited that money

> was only part of the wider structure of liquidity in the economy. It is the whole liquidity position that is relevant to spending decisions.... A decision to spend depends not simply on whether the would-be spender has cash.... There is the alternative of raising funds either by selling an asset or by borrowing; ...
>
> The decision to spend thus depends upon liquidity in the broad sense, not upon immediate access to the money.... The spending is not limited by the amount of money in existence; but it is related to the amount of money people think they can get hold of....
>
> Paragraph 389–90

This *liquidity theory* that minimized the power of monetary policy was soon overtaken by the resurgence of the *quantity theory of money* under the leadership of Milton Friedman and the monetarists discussed in the next chapter.[134] The Bank's contributions to this debate were less than straightforward. It did not counter with an explicit model of its own but at one point suggested a money target. The context suggests a diversionary tactic. O'Brien, then chief cashier, wrote in April 1957, at the height of the chancellor's pressure for limits on advances, "The principal object of credit policy at the present time is, as a brake on an undue growth of money incomes, stockpiling and exuberant spending generally, to restrain as far as possible any further expansion in the supply of money and perhaps even, in case of need, to achieve some contraction in it." He left no doubt that the way to achieve this was "by pushing up interest rates."[135]

More attention to money, and by implication the monetary effects of government borrowing, would have undeceived officials of the belief that restrictions on specific categories of credit such as bank advances were sufficient. O'Brien was less interested in money targets than in ending controls. Radcliffe's endorsement of the liquidity movement was a refutation of the Bank.

---

[133] Radcliffe Report, paragraphs 395–97.

[134] For the *liquidity theory*, or *new orthodoxy* as some versions were called, see W. T. C. King, "Should Liquidity Ratios Be Prescribed?" and Sayers, "The Determination of the Volume of Bank Deposits: England 1955–56." Sayers and Alec Cairncross were the two economists on the Committee.

[135] Fforde, *op. cit.*, p. 634.

In the spring of 1971, Governor O'Brien looked forward to the new system. Earlier procedures had not recognized that "financial systems are infinitely adaptable and the channels whereby money and credit end up as spending are many and various" and had suffered from the delusion "that if we do succeed in restraining bank lending we have necessarily and to the same extent been operating a restrictive credit policy." Glossing over a quarter-century of conflict with governments, he said that the Bank had "increasingly shifted [its] emphasis" away from loans to the private sector "towards the broader monetary aggregates . . . the money supply under one or more of its many definitions, . . . or domestic credit expansion." The end of direct controls would allow the return to an indirect market-control system "under which the allocation of credit is primarily determined by its cost."[136] O'Brien's position had not changed since 1957, and he seemed to have found a government that he could work with.

The priority of the 1970 Conservative Party manifesto had been inflation, and speaking to a Party conference in October, four months after the election, Prime Minister Edward Heath renewed the promises to cut taxes, public spending, and inflation and to end wage, price, and credit controls. His ambition was to end Britain's economic malaise by replacing socialist technocracy with free-market efficiencies:

We were returned to office to change the course and the history of this nation. . . . The free society which we aim to create must also be a responsible society. . . . Free from intervention, free from interference, but responsible. Free to make your own decisions, but responsible for your mistakes. . . .

However, "the quiet revolution" soon made one of the "U-turns" for which Heath is remembered. Inflation exceeded 8 percent at the time of his speech, and unemployment, which had been growing with inflation, was nearly 3 percent, more than the public had grown accustomed to, or, the government feared, would stand for. Its policy, named for the chancellor of the exchequer, was "Barber's dash for growth," a more ambitious version of Maudling's reflation. In the 44 months of the Heath government, until its efforts to enforce wage controls on the miners brought it down in February 1974, inflation averaged 9.3 percent, and at the end it was running at 18 percent.

---

[136] "Key Issues in Monetary and Credit Policy," speech to the International Banking Conference in Munich, May 28, 1971; reprinted in *Bank of England Quarterly Bulletin*, June 1971, and Bank of England, *Development*. Discussed by Dorothy Christelow, "Britain's New Monetary Control System."

Where *was* credit control? The government's spending and borrowing and its refusal to let the Bank restrict credit would have produced rampant money growth and inflation under any system, but the process was spurred by Competition and Credit Control. The 8-percent cash ratio had been binding, after all. The end of its requirement was followed by a drop almost to 4 percent. Bank credit was the main factor, but a good part of the increase in money was made possible by the fall in the cash reserve ratio.

O'Brien found the answer to the question that he posed at the beginning of this section in political pressures. He began by defending Bank rate:

I have stressed on a number of occasions that in a system free of direct intervention . . . credit control requires the flexible adjustment of interest rates both up and down. . . .

In the last few months there have indeed been periods when prices in financial markets moved very sharply. Naturally this has proved an uncomfortable experience. But the rejection of reliance on direct controls implies the corollary of living with considerably more flexible interest rates. It follows that we must not temper our approach so as to protect whatever soft spots there may be at any particular time. . . .

However, we hear the refrains of financial stability:

[A]nd the emergency help which we extended to banks in the sterling crisis this summer is in no way inconsistent with that approach. This help arose rather from our proper concern to avoid an exceptional event having too disruptive an effect.

And political pressure:

My opinion now is that late last year [1971] we [meaning the Government?] should have resisted the downward movement in interest rates more strongly than we did; or failing that, we should have moved earlier this year . . . to establish a higher level of interest rates. [We] underestimated the strength and persistence of the surge in lending. . . . Moreover the state of the property and housing market had become unruly with prices moving wildly ahead. . . .

Yet the objections at the time to higher interest rates were very powerful. Unemployment was still rising to new peaks. . . . Output was then barely rising. . . . For all these reasons it was the Government's expressed policy to encourage by all means the expansion of activity. And perhaps I may be forgiven for recalling that over these months the whole tenor of press comment was that we should get interest rates lower still.

He pointed to more pressures in the months ahead, particularly

the sharply rising deficit in the public sector, the revival of borrowing by manufacturing companies, which could lead to a renewed acceleration in monetary expansion. We will need to be vigilant and active to prevent this . . . and that is why

I pin so much hope on the current initiatives of the prime minister and chancellor, the successful outcome of which means so much to us all.

The governor was whistling in the dark. Controls continued, the restraint of fixed exchange rates had been jettisoned with the Bretton Woods system, and the next three years saw sterling fall more than 25 percent on international markets.

ELEVEN

Rules versus Authorities

The monetary problem stands out today as the great intellectual challenge to the liberal faith. For generations we have been developing financial practices, financial institutions, and financial structures which are incompatible with the orderly functioning of a system based on economic freedom and political liberty.... The liberal creed demands the organization of our economic life largely through individual participation in a game *with definite rules....*

There are, of course, many special responsibilities which may wisely be delegated to administrative authorities with substantial discretionary power; health authorities, for example, cannot well be limited narrowly in their activities by legislative prescriptions. The expedient must be invoked sparingly, however, if democratic institutions are to be preserved; and it is utterly inappropriate in the money field. An enterprise system cannot function effectively in the face of extreme uncertainty as to the action of monetary authorities or, for that matter, as to monetary legislation.

Henry Simons, "Rules versus Authorities in Monetary Policy"

It seems that monetary policy is always too inflationary or too tight. This is no small wonder when we consider that it is decided by "companies of merchants" with perverse incentives and insufficient knowledge. Wouldn't we be better off if policy was governed by a rule based on the best available theory, free of meddling by self-interested and uninformed groups? The following pages examine the rules that have received the most attention and have sometimes been followed. The first two sections present the rules, aimed at price stability, that have been favored by economists: Wicksell's interest-rate rule that is much like the current policies of the Bank of England and the Federal Reserve, and Chicago's constant-money-growth rule that bears some resemblance to

---

Background: People and Events

Summary of actual rules of monetary policy

Gold standard: The underlying rule that set the standard for the United Kingdom until 1931 and the United States until 1934. Gold contents of the pound and dollar became variable in the 1930s, effectively suspending the gold standard, although they did not float freely until 1971.

Prudential policy rules for convertibility without panics

Resumption Act of 1819: Directed the Bank of England to increase the gold value of the pound at a regular rate until par was restored.

Bank Charter Act of 1844: Separated the Bank into two departments and tied the Issue Department's legal-tender currency to its gold reserve.

Reserve ratios: The U.S. Treasury was directed to hold specified levels of gold from 1846 to 1913; the Federal Reserve was directed to hold gold in specified ratios of its currency from 1913 to 1968. The gold reserve of the Bank of England was left to its discretion.

Money and inflation guides/objectives: Money objectives were reported by the Federal Reserve to Congress but not enforced, 1975–2001. Required inflation targets were set for the Bank by the Chancellor in the 1990s, and approximately adopted by the Fed without legislation.

Rules proposed by economists

David Ricardo and Samuel Jones Loyd (Currency School) proposed the Acts of 1819 and 1844, based on the quantity theory of money.

Later money–growth rules were proposed less successfully by Irving Fisher, the Chicago School, and the monetarists.

The interest rule proposed by Knut Wicksell (and often applied, especially at the end of the 20th century) was also based on the quantity theory.

Opposition to money rules

Thomas Tooke (Banking School), with J. W. Gilbart and later supported by J. S. Mill and Walter Bagehot, contended that monetary stability would follow normally prudent banking practices with ample discretionary reserves, preferably with competitive note issues.

Central bankers wanted discretion to carry out what they have seen as multiple responsibilities for the monetary standard and financial stability.

Keynesians (New Economists) wanted central banks to pursue multiple goals within the framework of the government's macropolicies.

---

the 1844 Bank Act. The third and fourth sections examine the leading discretionary policies advocated for or pursued by the "authorities." The first, preferred by most economists from World War II to the 1970s, is the Keynesian/econometric theory of policy that in combination with other instruments, aimed at multiple objectives. The second is the "free reserves" approach that underlay many of the Fed's actions and statements that were described in Chapters 7–9.

Who will make the rules, and if there are rules, who will enforce them? If rules are unattainable or too restrictive, who will exercise and oversee discretion? Monetary policy is a political activity, and in a democracy it depends on the people. The last two sections look at the democracies of alternative monetary arrangements and their implications for the structure of the Federal Reserve.

Interest Rules: Tooke, Wicksell, and the Quantity Theory

The Quantity Theory versus Cost–Push
Increases in money are often depicted as independent events that temporarily depress interest rates on the way to inflation.

> I do not dispute that if the Bank were to bring a large additional sum of notes into the market and offer them on loan, but that they would for a time affect the rate of interest. The same effects would follow from the discovery of a hidden treasure of gold or silver coin. If the amount were large, the Bank, or the owner of the treasure, might not be able to lend the notes or the money at four, nor perhaps above three percent; but having done so, neither the notes nor the money would be retained unemployed by the borrowers; they would be sent into every market, and would every where raise the prices of commodities till they were absorbed in the general circulation. It is only during the interval of the issues of the Bank, and their effect on prices that we should be sensible of an abundance of money; interest would during that interval be under its natural level; but as soon as the additional sum of notes or of money became absorbed in the general circulation, the rate of interest would be as high, and new loans would be demanded with as much eagerness as before the additional issues.
>
> David Ricardo, *The High Price of Bullion*

A change in money ultimately changes the prices of goods and services in the same proportion, leaving the real stock (purchasing power) of money and therefore the rate of interest as before. This is the quantity theory of money. Changes in the quantity of money have no lasting real effects; they do not permanently alter production, consumption, relative prices, or the rate of interest. "There cannot ... be intrinsically a more insignificant thing, in the economy of society, than money; except in the character of a contrivance for sparing time and labour," John Stuart Mill stated in the leading text of the 19th century – *Principles of Political Economy*, first published in 1848. "It is a machine for doing quickly and commodiously what would be done, though less quickly and commodiously, without it: and like many other kinds of machinery, it only exerts a distinct and independent influence of its own when it gets out of order."[1]

---

[1] Mill, Book III, chap. 7, p. 488.

Money had gotten out of order several times, however, even after the Act of 1844 provided an impersonal mechanism to regulate it. This is where Thomas Tooke came in. He contended that the Ricardian Currency Principle, upon which the Act was based, failed because its conceptual framework – the quantity theory – corresponded neither with reasonable behavior by borrowers and lenders nor with the facts. His guns were directed specifically at J. W. Bosanquet's "theory of high prices as a consequence of a low rate of interest," which supposed, Tooke wrote, "that a facility of borrowing at a low rate of interest not only confers the power of purchasing, but affords the inducement – applies *the stimulus* to speculation in commodities. If by facility of borrowing [Bosanquet] meant a laxity of regard to security for repayment on the part of the lender, there is every probability that money so borrowed will be hazardously, if not recklessly employed.... But to suppose that persons entitled to credit are likely to be induced – *stimulated* is the favourite term – by the mere circumstance of a low rate of interest to enter into speculations in commodities ... argues a want of knowledge of the motives which lead to such speculations."[2] Anticipating the argument used by the U.S. Treasury and the Federal Reserve Board to oppose interest rate increases after World War I (Chap. 7), Tooke wrote that speculations "are seldom if ever entered into with borrowed capital except with a view to so great an advance of price, and to be realized within so moderate a space of time, as to render the rate of interest or discount a matter of comparatively trifling consideration."[3]

Tooke also observed that the data contradicted the quantity theory. Money and interest were positively instead of negatively correlated. If the increases in Bank rate during 1836 "had a considerable influence in depressing prices," as Bosanquet suggested, "how was it," Tooke asked, that an increase "in 1839 to 6 percent had not any such depressing effect?" Furthermore, "the progressive fall in the rate of interest from the commencement of 1840 to the close of 1842 ... was accompanied by a marked fall in most of the leading articles of consumption (the greatest depression of prices coinciding with the lowest rate of interest, viz. $1\frac{1}{2}$ percent)...."[4]

It is not easy, indeed, to imagine evidence of facts more decisive than those which can be adduced of the negative of the direct influence ascribed to a low rate of

---

[2] Tooke, *An Inquiry into the Currency Principle*, pp. 81–82; Bosanquet, *Metallic, Paper and Credit Currency, and the Means of Regulating Their Quantity and Value.*

[3] Tooke, *op. cit.*, p. 82.

[4] *Ibid.*, p. 84.

interest in raising the prices of commodities, and *vice versa*. The theory is not only not true, but the reverse of the truth.

Thomas Tooke, *An Inquiry into the Currency Principle*, p. 84

His explanation was a cost-push theory of prices. "A general reduction in the rate of interest is equivalent to or rather constitutes a diminution of the cost of production," especially "where much fixed capital is employed, as in the case of manufactures . . .; the diminished cost of production hence arising would by the competition of the producers inevitably cause a fall of prices of all the articles into the cost of which the interest of money entered as an ingredient."[5] This is a popular theory of inflation. It is convenient to be able to advocate low interest rates and low inflation simultaneously. Populists like Texas Congressman Wright Patman have enjoyed it, and it may explain President Truman's attachment to bond supports.[6]

A Reconciliation: Wicksell's Interest Rule
Tooke's facts were robust. John Locke had criticized Josiah Child a century and a half earlier for seeking to stimulate the economy by reducing the legal ceiling on interest rates.

High *Interest* is thought by some a Prejudice to Trade: But if we look back, we shall find that *England* never throve so well, nor was there ever brought into *England* so great an increase of Wealth since, as in Queen *Elizabeth's* and King *James* I, and King *Charles* I time, when Money was at Ten and Eight *per Cent*. I will not say high *Interest* was the cause of it. For I rather think that our thriving Trade was the Cause of high *Interest*, every one craving Money to employ in a profitable Commerce.

John Locke, *Some Considerations of the Consequences of the Lowering of Interest and Raising the Value of Money*, pp. 106–7

Wesley Mitchell and his successors at the National Bureau of Economic Research later recorded the procyclical tendencies of interest and prices in the United States, and monetary theories of the business cycle put forth by Irving Fisher and Ralph Hawtrey (as we will see later), among others, were founded on the co-movements of money, prices, investment, interest rates, and wages, with the last two variables being less volatile and tending to lag behind the others.[7]

---

[5] *Ibid.*, p. 82.

[6] The low-interest, low-inflation cost-push arguments of Patman and Senator William Proxmire were examined by George Horwich, "Tight Money, Monetary Restraint, and the Price Level."

[7] For example, see D. H. Robertson, *A Study of Industrial Fluctuation*, and the survey by F. Lavington, *The Trade Cycle*.

The Swedish economist Knut Wicksell accepted these data, but he disagreed with Tooke's explanation. Beginning in 1898, he reconciled them with the quantity theory by observing that general economic movements were often initiated by shifts in the demands for consumption or investment goods, especially the latter. Ricardo's "natural" rate of interest was determined by the propensities to save and invest, by thrift and productivity, and the price level adapted to these real forces.

Wicksell's framework was the quantity theory taking into account the disturbances. If an increase in money changes prices in the same proportion, it leaves the real economy, including savings and investments, unchanged. However, a rise in productivity with no change in money raises interest and causes prices to rise sufficiently to reduce the real quantity of money, M/P, commensurate with the higher rate of interest. In this case, the money market adapts to real forces.

The real economy is simply depicted as in Fig. 11.1, where S denotes desired saving (and lending) and I is desired investment (and borrowing). If an initial equilibrium of S and I_o at R_m is disturbed by an increase in investment to I', we normally expect the rate of interest to rise to the new intersection at R_n.

So Wicksell found the data to be consistent with the quantity theory. Observed relations are governed by disturbances to the system. A change in money imposed on the system from outside – an exogenous increase as assumed by Ricardo in the passage quoted earlier – produces for a time opposite movements in interest and prices. On the other hand, commodity demands produce the positive relation that is shown in the figure and is most often observed. Tooke's error as Wicksell saw it was in the logic of cost-push inflation that confuses the price level with relative prices. Increases in the costs of particular inputs, whether interest or oil, raise the prices of products especially dependent on those inputs. But if the supply and demand for money have not changed, neither has the price level. The prices of interest- or oil-intensive goods rise whereas others fall.

This has little meaning for monetary policy if interest-rate adjustments are rapid. However, the correspondence between interest rates and the price level is not as close as we would like. The price level is too variable if interest rates are not variable enough. Referring to Fig. 11.1, we see that if banks and other lenders are slow to adjust R, and satisfy some of the increased loan demand below the new equilibrium R_n, excess demand is financed by increased loans and money, causing inflation.

This process was central to the lesson that Ricardo and the Bullion Committee had tried to teach the Bank of England, that is, that lending

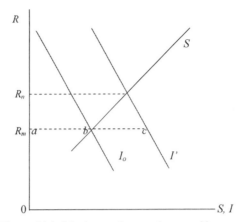

Figure 11.1. Market and natural rates of interest.

below the natural rate produced inflation notwithstanding "real bills" collateral. "Whilst the bank is willing to lend, borrowers will exist," Ricardo wrote.[8]

Irving Fisher and Ralph Hawtrey agreed that the typically slow response of interest to inflation encouraged excessive demands for goods and finance in the early stages of inflation and excessive rates of liquidation later when prices fell faster than interest. Hawtrey blamed the slow interest adjustments on central banks:

Professor Fisher in his *Purchasing Power of Money* held that the fluctuations of the trade cycle were due to the adjustment of the market rate of interest to the real rate being incomplete. When prices were rising, the market rate rose, but not enough to make the real rate normal; when prices were falling, it fell, but not low enough....

Professor Fisher, perhaps, laid too much stress on the tendency to overlook the effect of rising or falling prices when determining the rate of interest. For Bank rate was settled by a method of trial and error, which allowed automatically for all the factors at work. The delay in adjusting it, to which Professor Fisher quite rightly attributes the fluctuations, was really due to the practice of using the Bank of England's reserve as a criterion. The reserve responded very tardily to an expansive or contractive movement, so that there were long periods in which the Bank acquiesced in such movements without attempting to counteract them.

R. G. Hawtrey, *A Century of Bank Rate*, pp. 213–14

---

[8] *Morning Chronicle, Works*, iii, p. 17 (see Chap. 2). Henry Thornton's natural rate was the expected rate of profit on borrowed money (*Paper Credit*, pp. 236–59). The history of this idea was surveyed by Friedrich Hayek, *Prices and Production*, lecture I.

The reluctance of central bankers to revise interest rates as often as economists would like has been encountered several times in our story and is still with us.[9] Hawtrey's explanation was incomplete, however, Fisher's data were American, and the United States had no central bank during the period to which Hawtrey referred. *Bankers*, not just *central* bankers, adapt to changing circumstances slowly and deliberately, perhaps too slowly for price stability.

Even a small difference between the natural and market rates of interest can generate significant inflation. If excess demand is not eliminated by a rise in market rates of interest, it is rationed by price increases and delays in delivery. Would-be spenders find that their loans do not command as many goods as they had expected. These price increases are taken into account in new loan requests, so that the same real excess demand for goods generates ever greater increases in money as long as interest remains below the natural rate. This is Wicksell's "cumulative process":

It is possible in this way to picture a steady, and more or less uniform, rise in all wages, rents, and prices (as expressed in money). But once the entrepreneurs begin to rely on this process continuing – as soon, that is to say, as they start reckoning on a future rise in prices – the actual rise will become more and more rapid. In the extreme case in which the expected rise in prices is each time fully discounted, the annual rise in prices will be indefinitely great.

Knut Wicksell, Interest and Prices, p. 148

This "extreme state" was restated in 1975 by Thomas Sargent and Neil Wallace, who showed that under rational expectations, where people know the economic structure, the central bank's imposition of an interest rule engenders immediate unlimited demands in anticipation of the prices rising.[10] For example, an interest rule at the market rate (the old natural rate), R_m, implies funds supplied in the dollar amount $P_0(c - b)$ when P_0 is the initial price level. Borrowers get the real amount b from private lenders and $c - b$ from the banking system. Borrower/investors will be disappointed (and know that they will be disappointed) because only $b - a$ of output is unconsumed. Attempted $c - a$ of investment will drive up prices, so that their loans must be more than at P_0, which means even higher expected prices, and so forth. The price level is undefined.

---

[9] See Brian Sack and Volcker Wieland, "Interest-Rate Smoothing and Optimal Policy: A Review of Recent Empirical Evidence."

[10] Sargent and Wallace, " 'Rational' Expectations, the Optimal Monetary Instrument and the Optimal Money Supply Rule."

A qualification of this critique of interest rules is that central bank offers, like those of private dealers, are for limited amounts that are revised in the face of unforeseen responses.[11] What is a central bank to do? Wicksell proposed the following rule:

So long as prices remain unaltered the banks' rate of interest is to remain unaltered. If prices rise, the rate of interest is to be raised; and if prices fall, the rate of interest is to be lowered; and the rate of interest is henceforth to be maintained at its new level until a further movement of prices calls for a further change in one direction or the other.

Knut Wicksell, *Interest and Prices*, p. 189

"The more promptly these changes are undertaken," he suggested, "the smaller is the possibility of considerable fluctuations of the general level of prices; and the smaller and less frequent will have to be the changes in the rate of interest." Interest smoothing is still with us, although changes have often been resisted for the purpose of stimulating output, or for political reasons, as we saw after the World Wars in the United States, in Britain after World War II, and as we will see in the next chapter, in both countries in the 1970s.

Money Rules

The Chicago School

Money rules grew from the conviction that discretionary monetary policy is a major source of instability. Continuing the quotation at the beginning of this chapter, Simons urged, "We must avoid a situation where every business venture becomes largely a matter of speculation," which could be achieved only by withdrawing the central bank's freedom of action. Previous proposals, including interest rate rules, which were loose *guides*, would not accomplish this. Price changes are recognized too late, the targeted price index is arbitrary, and who knows the interest rate that will stabilize it?

What was needed, Simons argued, was "a simple mechanical rule of monetary policy," preferably "the fixing of the quantity of circulating media." This rule was "definite and simple" and "clear enough and reasonable enough to provide the basis for a new 'religion of money,' around which might be regimented strong sentiments against tinkering with the currency." Most of all, it avoided the discretion of a monetary authority.

---

[11] Bennett McCallum, "Price Level Determinacy with an Interest Policy Rule and Rational Expectations."

The time was not ripe for a money rule, partly because of "the abundance of what we may call 'near-moneys' – with the difficulty of defining money in such a manner as to give practical significance to the conception of quantity," and partly because, however money might be defined, the central bank did not have complete control. Some reformers had seen a partial solution in 100-percent reserves. Under fractional reserve banking where banks keep cash in small proportions of deposits, cash withdrawals by depositors force large contractions of bank credit and deposits. Between 1929 and 1933, the public raised its ratio of cash to bank deposits from 9 to 23 percent, and the average reserve ratio of banks rose from 8 to 12 percent, a combination that reduced the money stock from $48 billion to $30 billion despite an increase in the monetary base (bank reserves and the public's cash) from $7.3 billion to $8.4 billion.[12]

On March 16, 1933, eight Chicago economists, including Simons and Paul Douglas (later a senator from Illinois), wrote a public letter to the new administration advocating the replacement of banks by institutions subject to 100-percent reserves.[13] If money issuers held cash equal to their deposits, the public's conversion of deposits to cash would not affect the quantity of money. The plan separated banks into two departments, one simply an exchanger of checks and cash, the other a nonmonetary financial intermediary, raising funds, like other firms, by issues of stock and nonmonetary debt. "To get a sound currency it is absolutely necessary to cut this tie between our chief currency and loans and investments," Irving Fisher wrote in support of the plan.[14] It resembled Britain's Bank Act of 1844 but went further by tying all bank monetary liabilities (now deposits, because the note issue had been taken over by the government) to their cash. Roosevelt and Morgenthau were said to have looked at the proposal, but nothing came of it.[15]

In any case, it was not enough for Simons. He feared that "The fixing of the quantity of circulating media might merely serve to increase the perverse variability in the amounts of 'near-moneys' and in the degree of their general acceptability, just as the restrictions on the issue of bank notes served to hasten the development of deposit (checking-account) banking." The danger was "clearest in the case of savings accounts (time deposits), where one faces a real difficulty of preventing and even of

---

[12] Friedman and Schwartz, *A Monetary History of the United States*, table B-3.
[13] Ronnie Phillips, *The Chicago Plan and New Deal Banking Reform*, chap. 4.
[14] Letter to the *New York Times*, February 21, 1939, Phillips, *op. cit.*, p. 157.
[15] Phillips, *op. cit.*, pp. 49, 158.

defining, effective circulation." He wanted not only to stabilize the supply of money by ending the money-creating powers of banks but to stabilize the demand for money by eliminating money substitutes.

Friedman's Rule

Milton Friedman believed that these institutional changes were unnecessary. He agreed with Simons's objectives, but he thought that too much blame for the Great Depression was laid on the private sector. "The monetary authorities, not the private economy, were the major source of deflationary pressure," he wrote.[16]

In the most complete statement of his rule, in the last chapter of his Fordham Lectures published in 1960, *A Program for Monetary Stability*, Friedman agreed that "Relying on the discretion of authorities in so important an area of policy is highly objectionable on political grounds in a free society. Experience has demonstrated that it has also had unfortunate monetary consequences." The "continual and unpredictable shifts" in monetary growth and even in the apparent objectives of policy suggest that the Federal Reserve is not to be trusted with the selection of goals, and in any case it has repeatedly demonstrated its inability to hit its targets.

What were the authorities to do? The goal is stable prices, but the central bank does not control prices. It controls money – or could if it wished, Friedman argued. However, there is a long and variable lag in the effect of money on prices, and Wicksell's rule would find the Fed leaning against an inflationary wind only to reinforce a future deflation, when it would reverse policy to worsen the next inflation. A satisfactory performance would be difficult even for a more committed and knowledgeable group than the Fed.

> We seldom in fact know which way the economic wind is blowing until several months after the event, yet to be effective, we need to know which way the wind is going to be blowing when the measures we take now will be effective, itself a variable date that may be a half year or a year or two years from now. Leaning against next year's wind is hardly an easy task in the present state of meteorology.
>
> Milton Friedman, *A Program for Monetary Stability*, p. 93

It is better "to stand straight upright whichever way the wind is blowing" and to adopt the "rule that the stock of money be increased at a fixed rate year-in and year-out without any variation in the rate of increase to

---

[16] Friedman, "The Monetary Theory and Policy of Henry Simons."

meet cyclical needs." "Money" and its "rate of increase" were left unspecified. Friedman preferred the sum of commercial bank deposits and currency as money, but he wrote later that "the precise definition of money adopted, or the precise rate of growth chosen, makes far less difference than the choice of a particular definition and a particular rate of growth."[17]

Friedman recognized that the Fed does not have complete control of money. It controls its own assets: government securities and loans to banks. Between these and money are the currency/deposit and reserve/deposit ratios already discussed, public preferences between types of deposits with different reserve requirements, and international reserve flows. Nevertheless,

the links between Reserve action and the money supply are sufficiently close, the effects occur sufficiently rapidly, and the connections are sufficiently well understood, so that reasonably close control over the money supply is feasible, given the will. I do not mean to say that the process would not involve much trial and some error but only that the errors need not be cumulative and could be corrected fairly promptly.

Milton Friedman, *A Program for Monetary Stability*, p. 89

Monetarism is the larger school, in the spirit of the Chicago School, which believes "that changes in the money stock are the predominant factor explaining changes in money income."[18] Monetarists are also like the classical economists in accepting the free-market economy as efficient and stable. They first fought to reverse the Keynesian Revolution's minimization of money's role in inflation, and second, in the 1960s when the New Economists advocated inflation to promote employment, to show that it could not be done – that the historically positive relationship between employment and inflation represented by the Phillips Curve could not be reproduced by monetary policy.[19]

Monetarism implies the control of money, although sometimes more flexibly than Friedman's constant growth. Alan Meltzer would set the quarterly growth rate of money equal to the 12-quarter moving average of real gross domestic product minus the 12-quarter moving average of velocity, which would enhance price stability if the changes in velocity and output persisted.[20] This is an explicit form of Chairman Martin's policy

[17] Friedman, *Capitalism and Freedom*, p. 54.
[18] Thomas Mayer, "The Structure of Monetarism."
[19] A. W. Phillips, "The Relation between Unemployment and the Rate of Change of Money Wage Rates in the UK, 1851–1967."
[20] Meltzer, "Commentary."

of "leaning against the wind." It is similar to the "Taylor rule," which is a version of Wicksell's rule that would tie the federal funds rate to a moving average of inflation, that is, in adapting to change without discretion by policymakers.[21]

Monetarism triumphed in gaining acceptance of its primary principles: the importance of money for inflation but not its manipulation for growth.[22] There is no longer a distinct monetarist school, however, nor has its policy been adopted. Regarding the former, monetarism was partly a victim of its own success. "We are all monetarists, now." The rejection of its policy may be due to technical problems such as the difficulty of finding a stable definition of money. Another reason may be the resistance of central bankers to thinking in terms of monetary control, preferring interest rates and credit, as we have seen throughout our study.

Econometrics and the Theory of Economic Policy

Whereas in the nineteenth century governmental behavior was perhaps almost restricted to a fiscal activity, since then the development has ever been more into the direction of an attempt at looking after the *general interest*, in whatever sense that may be taken. We shall indicate this entity by the symbol Ω. It is a function of a certain number of variables which we will call target variables, [indicated] in vector form by z. These targets will be chosen so as to make $\Omega(z)$ a maximum. Acts meant to attain this maximum may also be referred to as the optimum policy....
Jan Tinbergen, *On the Theory of Economic Policy*, p. 1

If policymakers know how the economy works, Chairman Martin's caution and Friedman's rule are both mistaken, and we can go directly to the correct interest rate without Wicksell's partial adjustments. Interest rates, tax rates, spending, and other instruments can be chosen with knowledge of their effects. These relations are expressed by econometric models. "Econometrics" was defined by a founder as the unification of statistics, economic theory, and mathematics, and large macroeconometric models arose in the 1960s with computers that reduced their costs of estimation and manipulation.[23] Keynesian economics and econometrics grew up together.[24]

---

[21] John Taylor, "Discretion Versus Policy Rules in Practice."
[22] Meltzer, "Monetarism: The Issues and the Outcome."
[23] Ragnar Frisch, "Editorial" foreword to the first issue of *Econometrica*.
[24] Although Keynes was skeptical of the policy uses of econometrics; Letters to Roy Harrod and R. Tyler, *Collected Writings*, xiv, pp. 287, 295–97; Robert Skidelsky, *John Maynard Keynes*, ii, pp. 610–21.

They may be illustrated by a small model in which the targets, x and y, are jointly explained by the following equations:

$$ax + by + (c + dM + \upsilon) = 0, \tag{1}$$

$$ex + fy + (g + hS + \xi) = 0. \tag{2}$$

The parameters fall into three categories: $a, b, \ldots, h$ are fixed parameters to be estimated, M and S are policy instruments, and υ and ξ are random variables. The policymaker controls M (money) and S (government spending) in the interests target values x^* and y^* (the vector z in the quotation at the top of this section), which might be *inflation* and *unemployment*. The mathematical problem is the solution of the equations for M^o and S^o given x^* and y^*. An ambitious income objective might call for a high level of government spending; however, this might mean too much inflation and call for tight money.

The model can be expanded to include dynamic relations and the maximization of functions of goals rather than aiming at specific values.[25] They are used by the staffs of central banks to lay out the probable effects of alternative policies, although central bankers do not use the language of econometrics.[26] There are several possible reasons for this. First, goals often conflict, and central bankers refuse to commit publicly to their violation. It is asking a lot of a political body to commit to an explicit trade-off between prices and employment. Second, the models are not always completely believed. Central bankers often decide to wait for more information before committing to a change in course even when it is implied by the model. A good example of this is the Bank of England's Monetary Policy Committee (introduced in the first chapter).

Finally, economists' models sometimes arise from agendas that conflict with the less explicit views of policymakers. In the 1960s, models were used to advance the interventionist program of the New Economics. One of the uses of models is their exposure of conflicts. A model of supply and demand makes it clear that price and quantity are not chosen independently, a benefit that is even greater in macroeconomic systems with complicated relationships. It is somewhat surprising that the number of supposedly attainable, though formerly conflicting, goals grew in the 1960s with the development of econometrics. However, it is the scientific approach of Keynesian economics, which lends itself to econometric

---

[25] Henri Theil, "On the Theory of Economic Policy."
[26] An early example of such a model was provided by Frank de Leeuw and Edward Gramlich, "The Federal Reserve–MIT Econometric Model."

relations, that has been credited with the demonstration that many of the relations that had been asserted were unattainable.[27] The ambitious claims of econometricians have conformed to the more modest aspirations of central bankers rather than the other way around. The new contracts in the last chapter seek to restore a unique goal to central banks (except it is low inflation rather than convertibility) although leaving financial stability to their discretion.

We saw the futility of Operation Twist when curves were moved without regard to likely investor responses. A more general example was the inconsistency of the large models that government economists used to justify their multiple goals. In 1964, Warren Smith pointed out that high employment, stable prices, satisfactory long-term economic growth, free international movement of goods and capital, and free currency convertibility with fixed exchange rates rested on a single instrument, monetary policy (central bank credit).[28] "Fiscal policy is, as a practical matter, a relatively inflexible instrument, partly because of unsatisfactory administrative arrangements and in some cases also because of outmoded and unenlightened views about budget deficits." Wage and price controls and other forms of compulsion were excluded as inconsistent with the goal of freedom. A consequence of these conflicts, he thought, would be the abandonment of a fixed exchange rate, which happened seven years later, only to reveal that other trade-offs such as the Phillips Curve were beyond the powers of the instruments at hand.

Free Reserves

For short-term operating purposes, the essential immediate guide is the volume of total bank reserves that is adequate to meet the current needs of member banks for required reserves against their deposits plus some volume of excess reserves. The volume of reserves supplied relative to minimum needs or desires of banks represents the degree of restraint on or encouragement to credit expansion. The figure of "free reserves" or its negative counterpart "net borrowed reserves" provides a convenient and significant working measure of the posture of policy at the time.

Federal Reserve Board, "Processes and Procedures Involved in the Formulation and Execution of Monetary Policy"

The Federal Reserve Board's answers to questions from the Commission on Money and Credit in 1963 indicated that monetary policy had continued the attention to the financial markets that we saw in the 1923 *Annual*

---

[27] Robert Lucas and Sargent, "After Keynesian Macroeconomics."
[28] Smith, "Are There Enough Policy Tools?"

Report, the interpretation of excess reserves as easy money during the Great Depression, the resistance to disturbing the bond market in 1932, increases in reserve requirements to "mop up" excess reserves in 1936–37, and "bills only" in the 1950s. *The Federal Reserve's Attachment to the Free Reserve Concept* was heavily criticized by economists, especially Karl Brunner and Allan Meltzer, who argued that its focus on "very short-run considerations," "money-market myopia," reduced its awareness of the underlying causes of inflation.[29] The *Record of Policy Actions* in 1967 is an example of this approach (see the box).

Record of Policy Actions of the FOMC, February 7, 1967

The pace of economic expansion continued to moderate in early 1967.... Layoffs and short workweeks continued to be reported in the automobile and in some consumer appliance industries, but the labor market as a whole apparently remained strong.... In December the wholesale price index was stable and the consumer price index again rose by only one–tenth of 1 percent.... The deficit in the U.S. balance of payments ... was estimated to have been at an annual rate of about $2 billion in the fourth quarter....

Abroad, interest rates had declined substantially from their recent peaks....

On January 25 the Treasury announced that it would refund se-curities maturing in mid–February with a cash offering of two new securities.

The rate of increase in total bank credit between late December and late January was the highest since mid–1966....

As a result of the marked increase in time deposits ... which was offset in part by a decline in private demand deposits ... bank credit ... rose more than had been expected, even in the light of the easing of money market conditions that had occurred....

Open market operations since the last meeting of the Committee had been directed at attaining somewhat easier conditions in the money market. Net borrowed reserves averaged about $60 million in January and member bank borrowings about $475 million, compared with

---

[29] Brunner and Meltzer traced the intellectual sources of free reserves to Winfield Riefler (1930) and Emanuel Goldenweiser (1941) of the Board's staff and to Randolph Burgess (1927, 1936) of the New York Reserve Bank. Charles Calomiris and David Wheelock saw free reserves as a guide to policy up to the 1960s: "Was the Great Depression a Watershed for American Monetary Policy?"

$190 million and $530 million, respectively, in December. Rates on Federal funds moved generally lower. . . .

The following current economic policy directive was issued to the Federal Reserve Bank of New York:

> . . . it is the Federal Open Market Committee's policy to foster money and credit conditions, including bank credit growth, conducive to noninflationary economic expansion and progress toward reasonable equilibrium in the country's balance of payments.
>
> To implement this policy and taking account of the current Treasury financing System, open market operations until the next meeting of the Committee shall be conducted with a view to maintaining the prevailing conditions of ease in the money market, but operations shall be modified as necessary to moderate any apparently significant deviations of bank credit from current expectations.
>
> Votes for this action: Mssrs. Martin, Hayes, Brimmer, Clay, Daane, Hickman, Irons, Maisel, Robertson, Shepardson, and Wayne. Votes against this action: Mr. Mitchell
>
> Mr. Mitchell dissented . . . because he favored moving somewhat further toward ease. He was inclined to give more credence to the present expectations for a weaker economic performance in the first half of the year than to those for a stronger performance in the second half.
>
> *Federal Reserve Bulletin*, July 1967, pp. 1131–36

This brief section is inserted to bring the Fed into the 1960s. We will see in later chapters that the free-reserves guide was supplanted by various measures of money and interest rates in the 1970s, and the 1990s saw interest policy along the lines suggested by Wicksell. However, financial-market conditions have kept their place in policy considerations.

Democratic Central Banking

Since it is the nature of a democracy that the people determine monetary policy, the government is concerned with promoting the system that best exercises the people's will. Advocates of their systems all claim superior "democracy." The New Economists called the Federal Reserve "undemocratic" because it was not fully answerable to elected representatives, the president, in particular. Simons would have thought this condition "too answerable" to passions, and a further step away from the "rule of law." The House Banking Committee under chairman Wright Patman provided an extensive collection of these positions in its hearings on *The Federal Reserve System after Fifty Years* in 1964. After pointing to a half-century in which the Fed had "throttled" the economy, Patman looked forward to "answers to our questions on the Federal Reserve's past and present policies, and on how much independence it needs."[30]

The answer to the latter question by economists and other academics among the witnesses was "None." According to MIT's Paul Samuelson,

> Whatever may have been true in a few countries for a few decades in the 19th century, there can never be a place in American life for a central bank that is like a Supreme Court . . . – truly independent, dedicated to the public weal but answerable for its decisions and conduct only to its own discretion, and to the consciences of its men in authority as they each envisage their duty.
>
> Lack of coordination between monetary, fiscal, and debt policies, as determined by the Executive and Congress, with monetary credit, interest, and debt-management policies, as determined by Federal Reserve policy, can lead to short-run crises and to costly long-run ineffectiveness. Yet, at this stage of Federal Reserve evolution, there is nothing to prevent tragic recurrence of such undesirable conflicts. It has been more of a lucky accident than an inherent feature of present legislation and practice that the United States has been able to avoid costly friction: but, not even with our lucky combination of personalities and events has our economy been spared some cost attributable to lack of unified monetary policy.
>
> A central bank that is not responsible is irresponsible, rather than independent. To be responsible means to be responsive. It need not mean being responsive to each month's 50.001 percent of democratic opinion; or being responsive to the articulate minority. . . .
>
> But it does mean being responsive to the changing values, views, moods, and even fads of the American citizenry. It does mean a definite relinquishment of an adherence to certain thought-to-be-eternally sound doctrines, dogmas, and principles. Neither Governor Strong, nor Montagu Norman, nor even Chairman Martin can perform the role of Peter, holding a thumb in the dike against the floods of what is considered temporary unreason.[31]

Samuelson recommended a Federal Reserve essentially like the Bank of England (although he did not mention the Bank by name or give examples of its performance) to conduct "day-to-day operations" but "be responsible to the Executive," who "should have the power to ask for their resignations. . . ." Even within these constraints, the terms of the board of governors should be shortened, the chairman should be appointed by and serve at the pleasure of the president, and the influence of the regional Fed Banks should be reduced or eliminated.

John Gurley of Stanford said that Fed independence

> is like having two managers for the same baseball team, each manager independent of the other. The managers could get together for lunches once a week – that

---

[30] U.S. Congress, *The Federal Reserve System after Fifty Years*, p. 926.
[31] *Ibid.*, p. 1105.

might help. Or one of them could try to offset the actions of the other – that might work a bit. Nothing of this sort, really, would correct the basic situation – the intolerable arrangement of having two managers.[32]

An independent Fed means that the president must "design overall economic policy in the face of unnecessary uncertainty."

The manner of paying for expenditures – by taxes, newly created money, or new Government debt – is a decision for the administration; it is a decision that is part and parcel of the overall economic program.

Of the 23 professors (17 in economics, 3 in law, and 3 in political science) who testified before the Patman Committee, all opposed Fed discretion. Four, including Milton Friedman, favored money rules, and the rest joined Samuelson and Gurley in recommending the subordination of monetary policy to the president. It was unthinkable, even "ludicrous," that monetary policy did not conform to the program of elected officials.[33]

Bankers, on the other hand, were content with the current structure and policies. They were rebuked by Patman.

The question before us, gentlemen, of course, is to consider these bills strictly from the standpoint of the public, the people. Although I am sure you keep in mind the public interest, you have a special interest. . . . It disturbs me to think that you gentlemen think that the private banks, with an ax to grind, with a special interest in money, the volume of money and interest rates, should be represented on boards to determine these questions for the whole country.[34]

When investment banker and Secretary of the Treasury Douglas Dillon warned against tinkering with a complicated, evolving institution that was performing satisfactorily and said that there was a good working relationship between the Treasury and the Fed, Patman dismissed their "buddy-buddy" luncheons as ineffectual because the administration was powerless to enforce its views.[35]

Patman's attacks on the Federal Reserve got nowhere. Parts of his program to change the Fed's structure and limit its powers were brought before Congress every session from 1964 to 1977, all without success except for a limited annual audit enacted in 1977. Thomas Havrilesky, who studied the effects of a wide variety of influences on the Fed, thought that Patman's efforts might have been self-defeating; "his extremism, fed by

[32] *Ibid.*, p. 1309.
[33] Dudley Johnson said; *ibid.*, p. 1444.
[34] *Ibid.*, p. 1184.
[35] *Ibid.*, p. 1266.

ancient populist fear of private banking influence, lost him considerable collegial support. Patman's infatuation with big-banker-versus-little-man imagery prevented other members of Congress, who were interested in policing monetary policy, from criticizing the monetary authority for fear of association."[36]

The about-turn of economists' attitudes toward central bank independence during the next three decades was due to a combination of events and intellectual developments, none of which involved democratic ideals: the inflation of the 1970s, the government surpluses of the 1990s, and the breakdown of the Phillips Curve. Neither in the 1970s, when inflation was high and growth was poor, nor in the 1990s, when both were improved, was the Fed's structure seriously threatened. We saw that its alterations were modest even in 1935. Nevertheless, Patman's ideals are alive today.

The Structure of the Federal Reserve

In 1993, a later House Banking Committee chaired by Henry Gonzalez unsuccessfully introduced a bill "to make the Federal Reserve a stronger and more efficient central bank" by increasing its "accountability" and assuring that "decision-makers reflect the diversity of our population." It proposed that Bank presidents be appointed, like the board of governors, by the president of the United States, and that Bank directors conform with the requirement of the Federal Reserve Reform Act of 1977 that they be chosen "without discrimination on the basis of race, creed, color, sex, or national origin." The Committee's staff reported that in 1990, "among the 72 class A and B directors who are chosen by private member banks in the 12 Federal Reserve districts there was one African American, no Hispanic Americans, and only three women. Of the 36 class C directors chosen by the members of the Board of Governors – who are supposed to represent the public, 50 percent were former bank directors and none worked for consumer or labor organizations."[37]

Another bill would have eliminated Reserve Bank presidents' votes on the FOMC. The federal structure of the American central bank is unusual and, although necessary to the Fed's acceptance in 1913, it has been a frequent target of the System's opponents, who focus on its undemocratic nature. An examination of the role played by the Reserve Banks in monetary policy against the background of these complaints is interesting.

[36] Havrilesky, *The Pressures on American Monetary Policy*, p. 109.
[37] *Congressional Record*, 103rd Congr., 1st sess., January 5, 1993, pp. H64–65.

Fed Chairman Greenspan defended the current structure on the grounds of the information brought to bear on decisions by policymakers from throughout the country. He dismissed questions of the relative democracy of appointment procedures. Regardless of whether the presidents "are viewed as more public than private or more private than public, the real question remains: Does their participation on the FOMC make for better monetary policy?" Answering in the affirmative, he said,

The input of Reserve Bank presidents who reside in and represent the various regions of the country has been an extremely useful element in the deliberations of the FOMC. By virtue of their day-to-day location and their ongoing ties to regions and communities outside of the nation's capital, the presidents see and understand developments that we in Washington can overlook. They consult routinely with a wide variety of sources within their districts, drawing information from manufacturing concerns, retail establishments, agricultural interests, financial institutions, consumer groups, labor and community leaders, and others.[38]

Although not mentioned by Greenspan, the presidents might also be supported or opposed for their preferences and policy stances. They have preferred to work for price stability by operating on the market. We saw that they were in advance of the governors in resisting the Treasury's bond-support pressures after the world wars, and the little that the Fed did after the 1929 crash was on the presidents' initiative in opposition to the Board. The next chapter shows that they provided most of the support for Chairman Paul Volcker (who had just come from the New York Fed) in 1979. They were more willing to work through interest rates as opposed to the persuasion and credit controls that were preferred by Washington.

Bank presidents have been the most opposed to inflation in the FOMC. Their interest-rate preferences compared with the governors were estimated from FOMC votes for 1966–96 as shown in Table 11.1. The presidents were more willing to extinguish inflationary demands by high interest rates. They also dissented more often from the majority on the side of tightness. These differences are not affected by limiting the sample to those with experience as academic economists.[39] Either the

---

[38] Greenspan, Statement to House Committee on Banking, Finance, and Urban Affairs, October 13, 1993, *Federal Reserve Bulletin*, December 1993, p. 1103.

[39] The Board's economists in ascending order of interest preferences were Seger, Yellen, Phillips, Lindsey, Blinder, Mullins, Maisel, Angell, Brimmer, Wallich, and Shepardson; economist presidents were Jordan, Winn, and Willis.

Table 11.1. *Average Preferred Interest Rates Estimated from FOMC Votes*

	Governors	Presidents
Desired interest rate		
All	6.35%	7.05%
Economists	6.38%	7.27%
Net dissents for ease		
All	1	−8
Economists	−3	−20

Source: Henry Chappell and Rob McGregor, "A Long History of FOMC Voting Behavior."

proximity to markets and the public affect economists as much as others or Bank directors choose congenial presidents.

Bank presidents have also been "democratically responsive" by supporting policies addressed to conditions in their regions. Regional unemployment has been correlated with votes for ease.[40] "Accountability" may depend on local interests. The most democratic part of the Wilson/Glass creation may be the Reserve Banks.

We should not forget Congressional oversight. It has not always seemed careful or effective, such as when the Senate stood in the way of the House's efforts for monetary expansion during the Great Depression, but it has come into play on other occasions. Congress backed the Fed in its fight against the Executive's domination of monetary policy in 1921–22 and 1948–51, and the imposition of money rules and frequent visits to Capitol Hill since the mid-1970s were in part reactions to the apparent subordination of monetary policy to President Nixon's political interests.[41] During hearings on the renewal of Chairman Martin's term in 1956, Senator Paul Douglas told him,

I have had typed out this little sentence which is a quotation from you: "The Federal Reserve Board is an agency of Congress." I will furnish you with scotch tape and ask you to place it on your mirror where you can see it as you shave each morning."[42]

[40] John Gildea, "The Regional Representation of Federal Reserve Bank Presidents."

[41] Havrilesky, *op. cit.*, chap. 3; Sanford Rose, "The Agony of the Federal Reserve."

[42] U.S. Congress, Senate Banking Committee, *Nomination* (1956 hearings), pp. 24–25. From Donald Kettl, *Leadership at the Fed*, p. 84.

TWELVE

Permanent Suspension

The time has come for a new economic policy for the United States. Its targets are unemployment, inflation and international speculation. . . .

I will propose to provide the strongest short-term incentive in our history to invest in new machinery and equipment that will create new jobs for Americans: a ten per cent [tax] credit . . .

The time has come for decisive action . . . that will break the vicious circle of spiraling prices and costs. I am today ordering a freeze on all prices and wages throughout the United States for a period of 90 days.

In recent weeks, the speculators have been waging an all-out war on the American dollar. . . . I have directed the Secretary of the Treasury . . . to suspend temporarily the convertibility of the dollar into gold or other reserve assets except in amounts and conditions determined to be in the interest of monetary stability and the best interests of the United States.

President Richard Nixon, August 15, 1971

The environment of central banking was changed by the severance of the last tie with gold in the early 1970s. The breakdown of Bretton Woods was described in Chap. 9. The present chapter relates the steps leading to the breakdown, specifically the subordination of international arrangements to domestic goals. The first section describes the interactions between central bankers and presidents in the run-up to the closing of the gold window. It details how our fiat system was brought about by frustrated policymakers who wanted an expanding government and easy money without inflation and who (some cynically, some naively) turned to seductive wage and price controls without the necessary accompaniment of monetary control. The last section is about the early years of a central bank and exchange rate cut loose from its gold-standard moorings.

Background: People and Events

After averaging 1.3% per annum between 1952 and 1963 (1958 was the highest at 2.7%), the rate of increase in the consumer price index accelerated during the Vietnam War to 4.6% in 1968.

The buildup of U.S. troops in Vietnam reached 184,000 at the end of 1965 and peaked at 543,000 in 1969.

The unemployment rate averaged 4.3% during 1946–50, 4% in the mid-1950s, and 5.5% during 1962–64, falling to 3.6% in 1968.

1957, Sputnik; 1961, Berlin Wall; 1963, Martin Luther King, Jr., march on Washington; 1965, Watts riots; 1968, Johnson decides not to run; 1971, gold window closed; 1971–74, wage and price controls; 1973, first oil-price shock; 1974, Nixon resigns; 1975, Fed required to announce money targets to Congress.

	President of the United States	Secretary of the Treasury	Chairman of the Council of Economic Advisors	Chairman of the Federal Reserve Board
1963	Lyndon Johnson	Douglas Dillon	Walter Heller	Wm. Martin, Jr.
1964			Gardner Ackley	
1965		Henry Fowler		
1968			Arthur Okun	
1969	Richard Nixon	David Kennedy	Paul McCracken	
1970		John Connally		Arthur Burns
1973		George Schultz	Herbert Stein	
1974	Gerald Ford	William Simon	Alan Greenspan	

The Economics of Frustration

President Nixon

"Mr. Nixon 'believed' in the free enterprise system," Herbert Stein of his Council of Economic Advisors observed.[1] "Government" was a bad word – and not a whole word, at that. To Nixon "the whole word was 'damngovernment,' and the people who ran it contrary to his policies were the 'damnbureaucrats.'"[2] This section tells the story of how these principles were overridden by the president's political priorities and the conditions he inherited. He wanted an end to inflation but feared that tight money would raise unemployment.

---

[1] *Presidential Economics*, p. 136.
[2] William Safire, *Before the Fall*, p. 246.

Presidential speechwriters had to change their tune. "Circumstances change," Nixon told his advisers two days before the speech quoted at the head of this chapter. "In this discussion, nobody is bound by past positions." "Least of all, he might have added, himself," William Safire observed. "One past position was a fierce opposition to wage and price controls; in every economic speech I had ever worked on with him, there was a boilerplate paragraph on the horrors of wage and price controls, how they would lead to rationing and black markets and a stultifying government domination of the economy." Other positions had been "free trade" (except for textiles and steel, where campaign promises had been made) and "'protecting the value of the dollar,' a general term that included a hearty pooh-poohing of changes in the price of gold."[3]

We follow the administration and the Federal Reserve down the path to the suspensions of convertibility and the price system in August 1971. It is another tale of central bankers overcome by the politically powerful forces of inflation, although Martin gave them a run for their money before his replacement by a more cooperative chairman, who, however, had a price.

Nixon and Martin

The president and his Council of Economic Advisers wanted to reduce inflation without raising unemployment, at least not by much. Council Chairman Paul McCracken referred to their plan as "gradualism," which Paul Volcker called a "comforting word meaning that nothing very drastic is going to happen."[4] The Council was attracted to a mixture of monetarism and Keynesianism and thought that money might be managed with "delicacy," using Stein's term, to bring "a successful transition to price stability," that is, without a politically unacceptable rise in unemployment.

The administration had an ideal picture of the way in which the situation might develop. Unemployment would rise to a little over 4 percent, which was thought to be the rate of unemployment at which inflation would be stable. With a slight excess of unemployment above the 4 percent level the inflation would decline. This would occur gradually, but with increasing momentum as the expectation of a return to price stability gained force. When the inflation rate had declined sufficiently, and the expectation of price stability had become sufficiently strong, the economy would return to full employment (4 percent unemployment). But

---

[3] *Ibid.*, p. 509.
[4] William Neikirk, *Volcker*, p. 98.

to accomplish all this required getting the monetary policy just right – tight enough to slow down the economy to just below 4 percent unemployment but not tighter.

Herbert Stein, *Presidential Economics*, pp. 149–50

Four percent was ambitious considering the 5-percent average unemployment rate the last half of the 1950s and $5\frac{1}{2}$ percent the first half of the 1960s. It was also understood to be sensitive to inflationary expectations. This was recognized by the Council, and as we have seen, their plan included the manipulation of expectations. Unfortunately, prices were in other hands, and the Federal Reserve did not share the Council's views on the best way to attack inflationary expectations. Nor was the Fed convinced of the power of money, even if it could be controlled, which was also doubted. The Council tried to be both monetarist and Keynesian; the Fed was neither.

The Fed had not waited for the new administration to attack inflation; it had raised its discount rate from $5\frac{1}{4}$ to $5\frac{1}{2}$ percent in December 1968. In April, after inflation had jumped to 6.9 percent in the first quarter, with unemployment steady near 4 percent, the Fed raised the discount rate to 6 percent, its highest since 1929, and increased reserve requirements. The Fed was trying to tell the markets something. Martin was not a gradualist. He believed that the prevailing inflationary psychology needed shock treatment. The financial markets had to be persuaded of the Fed's commitment.

The Council of Economic Advisors had a different understanding of the dynamics of market expectations. It still accepted "adaptive" expectations, according to which expected inflation would fall in line with experience. The failure of the temporary tax surcharge of 1968 to make a dent in aggregate demand had not been translated by economists into the knowledge that a little monetary tightening might fail for the same reasons.[5] The activities of economic agents are ongoing. In the presence of developed capital markets, temporary losses of revenue or increases in costs (including interest rates) have limited effects on plans. We saw in Chap. 9, in connection with "bills only," that Martin's reluctance to disturb the financial markets was criticized by economists, who wanted interest rates to be manipulated freely in the interests of economic stability. Positions were reversed in 1969. Martin was convinced of the necessity

---

[5] See Robert Eisner's analysis of the ineffectiveness of the temporary tax surcharge because of life-cycle consumption plans, "Fiscal and Monetary Policy Reconsidered."

of a demonstration that the Fed meant business: "[T]here is no gadgetry in monetary mechanisms and no device that will save us from our sins," he told an audience of bankers in June. "We're going to have a good deal of pain and suffering before we can solve these things."[6]

We are not sure of the effects of the Fed's actions on market expectations, but they shocked the president. "Nixon always believed that William McChesney Martin would try to ruin him," the chronicler of *Nixon's Economy* wrote "and in the second half of 1969, he almost did."[7] Nixon blamed Martin for the fall in money growth and the recession that had cost him the 1960 election. He wanted to replace Martin with Arthur Burns as soon as he assumed office, but Martin chose to complete his term that ran through January 1970. Things started well enough. Money growth fell from an annual rate of 11 percent in the fourth quarter of 1968 (9 percent for the year) to 6 percent the first half of 1969, and the gradualists were hopeful (see Fig. 12.1)[8]. Then it stalled the next several months. Nixon had never been comfortable with the idea of controlled disinflation. "I remember 1958," he told Stein. "We cooled off the economy and cooled off 15 senators and 60 congressmen at the same time."[9] In face-to-face meetings and through his aides, Nixon unsuccessfully tried to prod Martin into a more expansive policy. Inflation had not been licked, however. Prices were rising at an annual rate of $6\frac{1}{2}$ percent at the end of the year. Furthermore, unemployment was rising. The unthinkable had happened, stagflation – high inflation *and* unemployment – with congressional elections coming up.

Martin's Fed

We may have paid too much attention to Martin, who was not the autocrat the White House assumed. It is true that he leaned toward sound money. However, he was not the foremost anti-inflation hawk in a divided Federal Open Market Committee, and he could not move without the majority. The restrictive policy of 1969 had been building, with intermittent rests and retreats for eight years, and a review will throw some

[6] Allen Matusow, *Nixon's Economy*, p. 25.
[7] *Loc. cit.*
[8] The money used here is M2, currency and all commercial bank deposits, although the story using M1, which excludes time deposits, is similar.
[9] Matusow, *op. cit.*, p. 22.

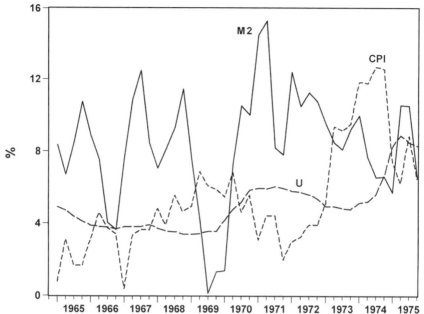

Figure 12.1. Rate of unemployment (U) and annual rates of change of money (M2) and consumer prices (CPI), 1965–75 (quarterly averages). *Sources:* Federal Reserve Board, *Banking and Monetary Statistics, 1941–70*, and *Annual Statistical Digest, 1971–75*; Department of Commerce, *Business Statistics*, 1963–91.

light on central bankers' thinking and decisions during the last years of Bretton Woods.

"For four years there had been a widening difference of opinion within the Federal Reserve Board and the Open Market Committee over the issue of how soon and how much to tighten monetary policy," new Board member Sherman Maisel observed in 1965.[10] "This was a contrast to the situation which had prevailed during the Eisenhower Administration when, even on most of the critical votes, there had never been more than one dissenting member, and even that had been rare. Recent appointees of the Kennedy and Johnson Administrations, however, had brought new value judgments and theories to the Board.…" Much of the following account of the FOMC and monetary policy during the last five years of Martin's chairmanship, from the conflict with Lyndon Johnson in 1965 to

[10] Maisel, *Managing the Dollar*, p. 69.

that with Nixon in 1969, is drawn from Maisel's autobiographical *Managing the Dollar*. Coming from the University of California at Berkeley at age 46, with a Ph.D. in economics from Harvard, he was the Board's first academic New Economist. The two Kennedy appointees who preceded him were also economists, and they shared a considerable part of Maisel's belief that monetary policy should be more active on the side of economic growth and more supportive of administration economic policies. However, George Mitchell and Dewey Daane had come from long tenures at the Federal Reserve Banks of Chicago and Richmond, and they shared the System's collegial approach. Although Maisel had company in the general pursuit of goals, he felt alone on the path toward them. "I had spent nearly twenty years studying and teaching monetary economics. I thought I understood what the Fed did and how it affected the economy. I soon discovered how little I knew."[11] Although informing us of Fed decision processes, Maisel's description of monetary policy as an insider and critic gives another illustration of the gulf between central bankers and economic theory.

The other Board members were James Robertson, who had been a lawyer for the comptroller of the currency and was appointed by Truman in 1952, and two college deans born in the 19th century and appointed in Eisenhower's first term: Canby Balderston from the University of Pennsylvania's Wharton School of Finance and Commerce and Charles Shepardson from Texas A&M's College of Agriculture. The vice chairman of the FOMC was New York Fed President Alfred Hayes. Maisel reported that Hayes, Balderston, and Shepardson were anti-inflationists who "based their votes primarily on the price and balance of payments doctrine.... They were usually joined by two of the rotating Bank presidents," whereas Robertson, Mitchell, Maisel, and two presidents "favored a policy of furnishing the funds necessary for full employment." This "basic five-to-five split" left the deciding votes to Martin and Daane, who also leaned toward "the price and balance of payments goals." So decisions "generally favored the more restrictive targets. However, because a strong minority stressed broader objectives, as did the administration, moves to restrict credit were less frequent and more moderate; those in the middle had to be sure of themselves before they joined the restrictivists."[12]

[11] *Ibid.*, p. ix.
[12] *Ibid.*, pp. 69–70.

Other disagreements arose over "the question of coordination with other government agencies versus the independence of the Fed, and the method of tightening money to be used." Those who favored "coordination" (their opponents would have said "subordination") were undermined by the unreliability of the administration. Maisel, operating on his own, was heartened by offers of the Treasury and the Council "to coordinate monetary and fiscal policies." Council Chairman Gardner Ackley "told me that he too was becoming convinced that increases in demand ought to be slowed up. And he had also concluded that it would be preferable to use fiscal rather than monetary policy." Ackley and the secretary of the Treasury made the offer that "if fiscal policy were not tightened, they would urge President Johnson to call for a tighter monetary policy in his State of the Union message."[13] Neither action was forthcoming, but the FOMC went ahead with restraint.

How should it be applied? As quietly as possible: "No announcement effect," urged Daane, Robertson, and Maisel. A quiet slowdown in open market purchases would do the job. The majority, however, felt that the announcement of a discount rate increase would have a favorable impact on foreign central banks, slowing their exchange of dollars for gold.[14]

"But a more critical factor," Maisel added, "was the desire to aid the banks in breaking President Johnson's stranglehold on the prime rate." The president had set low-interest guideposts, and because the banks wanted to avoid a political confrontation, "some Board members felt that it was up to the Federal Reserve to oppose him in order to avoid a threatened inflationary increase in bank credit."[15] The increase in the Fed's discount rate from 4 to $4\frac{1}{2}$ percent was immediately followed by a rise in the bank prime rate from $4\frac{1}{2}$ to 5 percent.

The Board also raised the maximum rate on short-term time deposits from 4 to $5\frac{1}{2}$ percent. The Banking Act of 1933 had prohibited interest on checking accounts and gave the Board responsibility for maximum rates on time and savings accounts in commercial banks. The avowed purpose, in the wake of the failures of the Great Depression and the establishment of deposit insurance, was to protect bank profits and discourage the risk-taking that might ensue from competition for government-guaranteed

[13] *Ibid.*, pp. 74–75.
[14] *Ibid.*, pp. 75–76.
[15] *Ibid.*, p. 76.

deposits. The maximum rate was $2\frac{1}{2}$ percent from 1936 until 1957, when the Board began to raise it to allow banks to compete with rising market rates of interest. The rise in December 1965 seemed large enough "to prevent the ceilings from having any effect on the market for the present and far into the future."[16]

What was the intellectual basis for these actions? Maisel was in the dark. "By January, after the dust from the increase in discount rates and interest ceilings had settled, . . . after being on the Board for eight months and attending twelve open market meetings, I began to realize how far I was from understanding the theory the Fed used to make monetary policy. . . . When I arrived at the Federal Reserve in 1965, I was handed volumes of documents and descriptions of what the Fed did. . . . Nowhere did I find an account of how monetary policy was made or how it operated." Moreover, in policy discussions, "words took on special connotations and nuances were extremely important. Further, I was struck by surprising gaps in the arguments and presentations."[17]

He could not have referred to the staff's presentations, which offered forecasts in the context of a large-scale econometric model. When the presentation was over, however, and the FOMC got down to business, its attention turned to the money markets. The money markets were barely evident in the staff model and definitely not crucial, but Maisel found that his colleagues "used money market conditions simultaneously as a target, or measure, of monetary policy and as a guide for the manager of the Open Market Desk. This meant that the Desk operated by buying and selling securities so as to force the banks to maintain a particular net reserve position. The desired position (within a range) was set by the FOMC at each meeting, but the manager was also given some leeway depending on the tone and feel or atmosphere of the market."[18]

A 1989 "Analysis of the Policy Process" was still unable to find any influence of the staff, whose backward-based forecasts had continued to abstract from potential market responses to Fed actions.[19] Joshua Feinman and William Poole, the latter formerly of the Board's staff and later president of the Federal Reserve Bank of St. Louis, observed that Fed actions corresponded more closely with the *Manager's Report* of

---

[16] *Ibid.*, p. 77.
[17] *Loc. cit.*
[18] *Ibid.*, pp. 78–79.
[19] Nicholas Karamouzis and Raymond Lombra, "Federal Reserve Policymaking."

Table 12.1. *Monetary Policy, 1964–70 (Average of Last Month of Quarter)*

	Free Reserves (Millions of Dollars)	Discount Rate (%)	T Bill Rate (%)
1964, 4	168	4	3.84
1965, 1	−75	4	3.93
2	−182	4	3.80
3	−144	4	3.92
4	−2	4 1/2	4.38
1966, 1	−246	4 1/2	4.59
2	−352	4 1/2	4.50
3	−368	4 1/2	5.37
4	−165	4 1/2	4.96
1967, 1	236	4 1/2	4.26
2	297	4	3.54
3	268	4	4.42
4	107	4 1/2	4.97
1968, 1	−315	5	5.17
2	−341	5 1/2	5.52
3	−132	5 1/4	5.19
4	−310	5 1/2	5.96
1969, 1	−701	5 1/2	6.02
2	−1064	6	6.44
3	−831	6	7.09
4	−829	6	7.82
1970, 1	−781	6	6.63
2	−701	6	6.68
3	−335	6	6.13
4	−49	5 1/2	4.87

Source: Federal Reserve Board, *Banking and Monetary Statistics, 1941–70*, pp. 533–36, 667, 695–96.

money-market conditions and bank reserves than with its staff's macroeconomic projections.[20]

Returning to the course of policy, the Fed continued its pressure on the banks into 1966. Their increasingly negative free reserves are shown in Table 12.1. Interest rates rose during the summer, and large financial institutions experienced a "credit crunch." Increases in deposit rates threatened the solvency of those that had made long-term loans, especially the savings and loan (S&Ls) associations that financed home mortgages with

[20] "Federal Reserve Policymaking: An Overview and Analysis of the Policy Process: A Comment."

savings accounts. In addition, banks and S&Ls that competed for time deposits were unable to keep them because market rates had risen above the legal maxima on deposit rates. Investors shifted to Treasury bills and other short-term investments. President Hayes described the 1966 "credit crunch" as follows:

> The squeeze on banks . . . was quickly transmitted to the securities markets. Just as banks had stepped up their acquisitions of state and local obligations earlier in the 1960s in response to a rapid growth of CDs, they began to withdraw from this market as their competitive position in the time-deposit markets started to decline . . . to make room for intense loan demand from business borrowers. . . . The municipals sector was . . . the first to feel the impact of a gathering storm in the securities markets. Indeed, while the tone of the money and corporate bond markets remained fairly steady, the climate in the municipal market began to reflect pessimism in June, and by early July the market was disorderly and confused. . . . The selling by banks was described by one commentator as "continuously undermining the market by a heavy volume of securities that has nowhere to go even at distress prices."[21]

The Fed tried to relieve the problem by offering banks easy access to funds through the discount window if they would "cooperate in the System's efforts to hold down the rate of business loan expansion."[22] This was unsuccessful, even counterproductive. Banks were reluctant to resort to the discount window because, Hayes tells us, they feared it "might bring their portfolio decisions, and particularly their business lending policies under close scrutiny by the Federal Reserve. . . . The bond market reached frightening lows on Friday, August 26. One observer described the market psychology as 'the coldest, bleakest I have ever experienced on Wall Street.'" On September 13, Hayes told the FOMC,

> The financial markets were marked by convulsive movements and an atmosphere of great uncertainty. At the nadir of the bond market about two weeks ago there is no doubt that the financial community was experiencing growing and genuine fear of a financial panic. This fear seemed to stem mainly from the conviction that credit demands would remain very strong, . . . that fiscal policy was making no contribution toward a dampening of the economy, . . . and that the Federal Reserve System was determined to push its restrictive policy ruthlessly.

The Fed backed down and increased open market purchases. Hayes also emphasized the improvement in market psychology brought by administration promises of fiscal restraint. He thought the Fed had helped

---

[21] Alfred Hayes, "The 1966 Credit Crunch."
[22] *Federal Reserve Bulletin*, September 1966, pp. 1338–39.

the administration accept its responsibilities, but the problems facing the Fed and the economy in 1965 and 1966 were not solved. The war continued, inflation rose, and when the Fed returned to the fray in 1968, it was determined to show, this time, that it would keep its nerve. The majority was with Martin, and, as Table 12.1 shows, the FOMC kept up the pressure into 1970.

Nixon and Burns

Arthur Burns came to the Nixon administration with a distinguished record in economics and government. He studied under Wesley Mitchell at Columbia and they collaborated on *Measuring Business Cycles*, the classic work on cyclical indicators. He became active in politics, supported Eisenhower in 1952, and was chairman of the Council of Economic Advisors most of Ike's first term. Burns pushed for an active stabilization policy, including tax cuts, spending increases, and pressures on the Fed to ease credit during the 1953–54 recession. His Liberal views and forceful manner brought him into conflict with Treasury Secretary George Humphrey, who was keen to balance the budget.[23]

Burns became a Nixon advisor and tried to help him in the spring of 1960 by (unsuccessfully) advising the president to ask the Fed for easy money to moderate the recession that he saw coming.[24] He was also active in Nixon's 1968 campaign, and the new president asked Burns to join his staff as coordinator of domestic economic policy with the understanding that he would succeed Martin in 1970.

Looking toward a more pliant Fed, Nixon could hardly wait. "Eisenhower liked to talk about the independence of the Federal Reserve," Burns said at a cabinet meeting in February 1969. "Let's not make that mistake and talk about the independence of the Fed again."[25] In October, shortly after Burns's nomination to the Fed, Nixon invited him in for "a little chat."

"You see to it – no recession," the president said. Martin is "six months too late," Burns replied. "I don't like to be late." Pressing on, Nixon said, "Shultz says 'turn now'" [referring to a memo from Labor Secretary George Shultz]. This time Burns did not respond on cue. Sounding rather like William McChesney Martin, Burns said he thought easing now would be bad psychology, that it was time to "show

---

[23] Wyatt Wells, *Economist in an Uncertain World*, p. 16.

[24] *Ibid.*, p. 18.

[25] Minutes of Meeting of Cabinet Committee on Economic Policy, February 13, 1969, Safire papers; quoted by Matusow, *op. cit.*, p. 20.

backbone." In that case, said Nixon, the Fed should move in December. Burns countered that interest rates would be down by then, implying that December would not be a good time to ease either. At that moment Nixon may have glimpsed that Burns might not be his pliant tool after all, that the man who as courtier had seconded Nixon's desire to puncture the "myth of the autonomous Fed" might insist no less than Martin on the preservation of the Fed's autonomy. A day later, Burns sent his response to Schultz's memo, which had warned of a recession and urged monetary ease. He had his doubts, Burns said, and so did Paul McCracken.[26]

McCracken, who was chairman of the Council of Economic Advisers, and the other chief economic positions – the secretary and undersecretary of the treasury, David Kennedy and Charls Walker, and Budget Director Robert Mayo – had come to Martin's side. Kennedy and Mayo were from the Continental Illinois Bank of Chicago, and as executive director of the American Bankers Association, Walker had defended the Fed's independence to the Patman Committee in 1964. They were soon gone, but Nixon was stuck with Burns.

Maisel recalled Burns's swearing-in at the White House on January 31, 1970, in the presence of an assembly that included the cabinet, the senior White House staff, the Federal Reserve Board, prominent bankers, and the media.

In a news conference the preceding night, the president had indicated that he thought the immediate easing of monetary policy was necessary. At the swearing-in ceremony President Nixon publicly greeted the new chairman with some pointed, joking-in-earnest comments about easing credit and lowering interest rates: "I respect his independence," said Mr. Nixon. "However, I hope that independently he will conclude that my views are the ones that should be followed." After a burst of applause, the president added: "You see, Dr. Burns, that is a standing vote of appreciation in advance for lower interest rates and more money."[27]

"It did not take a very close observer," Maisel continued, "to see that both the incoming and the outgoing chairmen were extremely uncomfortable with the president's jokes." Even so, the easy money was forthcoming.

"After the most bitter debate I experienced in my entire service on the FOMC," Maisel wrote of Burns's first meeting the next month, monetary policy changed direction.[28] Warning of an approaching recession,

[26] Matusow, *op. cit.*, p. 31
[27] Maisel, *op. cit.*, p. 107.
[28] *Ibid.*, p. 250.

Burns cajoled and whipped the Committee into an expansive monetary policy. He was not the president's man unreservedly, however. He would do his part for economic stabilization, but he expected the administration to do its part. Credibility in the fight against inflation required fiscal discipline, Burns argued, and he made a cutback in government spending a condition of monetary ease. Among the reductions found for a small projected surplus was the postponement of a scheduled pay raise for federal employees. When New York City postal workers went on strike in March, Nixon called out the army but finally yielded to a "budget-busting wage settlement." Presidential aide John Erlichman heard Nixon say that Burns "had brought on the strike."[29]

Burns had much in common with Marriner Eccles. Neither was a central banker in market outlook, and, unlike Martin and Benjamin Strong, neither saw his primary goal in finance. Like Eccles, Burns wanted to help the president run the country. George Shultz felt that "Arthur has a way of holding the money supply as a hostage – saying that 'if you don't behave, I'll tighten up on money,' and in fact in that way he's trying to run the whole executive branch with the Federal Reserve." To economists worried about inflation, however, Burns was shirking his duty, blaming everyone and everything – government fiscal policy, union wage demands, business mark-up pricing, and consumer spending – for an inflation that could be traced to a single cause over which the Fed had complete control: too much money. "Burns seems to have a model," Raymond Lombra wrote, "where there are n causes of inflation, and monetary policy is the nth. Within this model monetary policy is totally endogenous; the nation must first deal successfully with the $n - 1$ causes of inflation and only then can the nth – that is, monetary policy – be formulated and executed in a manner consistent with long-run price stability."[30]

To those who said that the way to reduce inflation is to reduce money growth, Burns replied, "The rules of economics are not working the way they used to." He told the Joint Economic Committee in July 1971 that "Despite extensive unemployment in our country, wage rate increases have not moderated. Despite much idle industrial capacity, commodity prices continue to rise rapidly."[31] Throughout his time at the Fed, he blamed inflation on the economic structure. "In recent decades, a new pattern of wage and price behavior has emerged," he told

---

[29] *Ibid.*, p. 59.
[30] "Reflections on Burn's Reflections."
[31] Reprinted as "The Economy in Mid-1971," in Burns, *Reflections*.

a university audience in 1975.[32] "The average level of prices...hardly ever declines.... Wage reductions are nowadays rare even in severely depressed industries.... Lenders...expect to be paid back in cheaper dollars, and therefore hold out for higher interest rates," which they are able to obtain "because the resistance of borrowers to high interest rates is weakened by their anticipation of rising prices.... Structural reforms of our economy...deserve more attention...than they are receiving," especially from economists, who "have tended to concentrate excessively on over-all fiscal and monetary policies...."

Newly inflexible wages, prices, and interest rates are an old story. The continued high interest rates during the long deflation of the late 19th century were a source of farmers' and William Jennings Bryan's attack on the "cross of gold" in the 1896 Democratic Convention. Irving Fisher wrote extensively of the sluggishness of interest rates.[33] In Britain, William Ashley and others urged a "sliding scale" (an application of later escalator clauses to deflation) to overcome the rigidity of wages.[34] British officials blamed the unemployment of the 1920s on the failure of wages to fall. Moving forward to Burns's time, it was unlikely that wages, prices, and interest would fall quickly in the environment of inflation and expected inflation that had persisted since the 1930s.

Burns was not the first economist or policymaker to deny this history. The belief in a "golden age" of competition and flexibility seems to have been built into the human psyche along with honesty, good workmanship, and respectful youth. British economist and Bank of England adviser Henry Clay wrote in 1929, "Before the war..., in the absence of any general unemployment relief, it was impossible to maintain wage-rates generally at a level that restricted unemployment throughout industry."[35] William Beveridge expressed the same view in the second (1930) edition of *Unemployment*, apparently forgetting his complaints of the inflexibility of wages in the first (1909) edition.[36] Thomas Tooke (1838) and A. L. Bowley (1900) attributed the rigidity of wages in the face of unemployment to the recent development of worker combinations even though Adam Smith had observed that "in many places

---

[32] "The Real Issues of Inflation and Unemployment," in Burns, *Reflections*.
[33] *Appreciation and Interest* and *The Theory of Interest*, chap. 19.
[34] *The Adjustment of Wages*.
[35] "The Public Regulation of Wages in Great Britain."
[36] Pp. 9–11, 231 in the first edition, pp. 359–72 in the second.

the money price of labour remains uniformly the same for half a century together."[37] Similar inflexibilities were documented for the United States.[38]

We saw in the last chapter that several theories of the business cycle were based on the rigidities documented by Burns and Mitchell. Mitchell's *Business Cycles and Their Causes*, published in 1913, was among them. Burns "knew" the history of wages, prices, production, and interest rates, but his intellectual activity was in a separate compartment from his politics. He was surprised and overwhelmed by the forces that he had studied all his adult life.

Probably none of this mattered. The administration was in no position to force the structural changes that Burns advocated, even if the president had wished, and he would not risk the economic or political costs of tight money.

Belief that there would have to be a resort to controls was spreading. Some, including McCracken, became resigned. Others were more eager, including Maisel, who wanted nothing to interfere with easy money; Congress; the cabinet; and, most outspoken of all, the new Fed chairman. Among the advantages of controls that Maisel saw was the elimination of conflict between the administration and the Fed.[39] Postmaster William Blount and Secretaries John Volpe, George Romney, and Maurice Stans of the Transportation, Housing and Urban Development, and Commerce Departments, respectively, all businessmen, pressed for wage–price (with the emphasis on "wage") guideposts at least from early 1970.[40]

At a cabinet meeting on February 18, Romney shattered the usual false harmony by challenging the "lack of policy in the wage–price field" at a time when "some very inflationary wage settlements" were looming. McCracken responded with the argument most likely to impress the president: "If we set guidelines, they will be broken and then the question will be asked: Mr. President, what are you going to do about that? . . . When Romney pressed his point, Nixon shot back, "What wage–price policy ever worked?" "The British Plan," Romney replied. "Oh, no.

---

[37] Tooke, *History of Prices*, ii, pp. 70–74; Bowley, *Wages in the United Kingdom in the 19th Century*, p. 125; Smith, *Wealth of Nations*, book I, chap. 8. Also see Arthur Gayer et al., *Growth and Fluctuation of the British Economy*, pp. 137, 167–70.

[38] Edgar Furniss, *Labor Problems*, chap. IV.2; Albert Rees, "Patterns of Wages, Prices, and Productivity."

[39] See, for example, Maisel, *op. cit.*, pp. 165–66.

[40] Matusow, *op. cit.*, pp. 66–67.

Now, George," said Nixon..., "don't tell me about British wage–price policy. I know about that. It didn't work."

Gallup polls showed a majority for controls, and in August 1970 Congress attempted to force the president's hand, or embarrass him, by giving him discretion to impose mandatory controls on wages and prices for up to six months.[41]

If the Fed's price for monetary accommodation was an incomes policy, "I think we should pay the price," Herb Stein advised.[42] The president held out and was irritated when Burns publicly challenged the administration. Nixon told Ehrlichman to "freeze" Burns out for telling a group of bankers that an incomes policy should be an option.[43] Nixon's view of the appropriate policy did not change. His *Memoirs* stated that the "August 15, 1971, decision to impose [controls] was politically necessary and immensely popular in the short run. But in the long run I believe that it was wrong... and there was an unquestionably high price for tampering with the orthodox economic mechanisms." He regretted that "the *politics* of economics has come to dictate action more than the *economics* of economics."[44]

Burns's campaign for controls was supported in Congress and the press. Referring to the chairman's "old-rules-not-working" statement, Democratic Senator William Proxmire said, "The administration's do-nothing attitude with respect to incomes policy is a costly mistake.... Dr. Burns's testimony... makes the administration's position on incomes policy inexcusable." The *Des Moines Register* of July 6, 1971, noted that Burns "has again recommended that stronger action is needed to stop inflation, and he favors a wage–price review board to establish an 'incomes policy.'... It is hard to see how the Administration can reduce unemployment without spurring inflation to a new high rate, unless it is willing to use its power in some way to check soaring wage rates." Bills introduced by Proxmire and Republican Senator Edward Brooke requiring the president to act on wages and prices had considerable support.[45]

---

[41] Polls indicated that the public favored controls for almost four years before their adoption, wanted them to be made "stricter while they were in effect, and has wanted to see them reenacted ever since they lapsed in May 1974," Alan Blinder wrote in 1979 (*Economic Policy and the Great Stagflation*, p. 111).

[42] Matusow, *op. cit.*, p. 90.

[43] *Ibid.*, p. 70.

[44] Nixon, *Memoirs*, p. 521.

[45] Wells, *op. cit.*, pp. 72–73.

Connolly and Volcker

In the meantime, the dollar was under attack in international markets, and the end of Bretton Woods appeared to be near at hand. The administration was not unprepared. Nixon was aware of these problems when he assumed office, and believed that a new system would be necessary. He "regarded gold as a monetary anachronism," Allen Matusow recorded, and "periodically expressed a desire for an entirely new system that would avoid annoying crises, and insisted that international economic issues remain subordinate to his domestic economic objectives."[46]

Burns was bereft of ideas, but a Treasury task force headed by Under secretary for Monetary Affairs Paul Volcker had been assigned to study the problem. Its report to the president in June 1969 laid out three options, none of which it considered viable. The first was to close the gold window. The dollar was effectively inconvertible, anyway, except with American consent. This option was shunned because of the benefits that the current system conveyed on the United States by making it the world's banker. International trade was conducted in dollars that were in principle claims on gold. It was in the country's interest to keep up the pretence as long as possible. Moreover, other countries, although unhappy with the "exorbitant privileges of the dollar" that were being used to transmit American inflation to the world, were not eager for radical change.[47]

Another option was the devaluation of the dollar to improve America's international competitiveness. This would be ineffective, however, because others would follow suit. The increase in the price of gold that might follow would increase the world's liquidity, but that step involved too many uncertainties.[48]

The third option, recommended half-heartedly, was "evolutionary reform," by which Bretton Woods was to be taken at face value: pressing countries in "fundamental disequilibrium" to devalue or revalue their currencies. This would preserve, for a while, "a major role for the dollar and monetary leadership of the United States." Frequent changes, whether actual or threatened, in exchange rates were out of the question. They were a recipe for chaos, a speculator's dream and a government's nightmare. Devaluations had been rare since 1950 and had always been denied until the last minute. A European central banker shook his fist in

---

[46] Matusow, *op. cit.*, p. 126.
[47] Volcker and Toyoo Gyohten, *Changing Fortunes.* pp. 64–67.
[48] *Ibid.*, p. 67.

Volcker's face: "If all this talk about flexible exchange rates brings down the system, the blood will be on your American head."[49]

A fourth option, bringing American inflation under control, was dismissed. It looked like nothing would be done until the issue was forced by a crisis, presumably a run on the dollar. Nixon and his new Treasury Secretary John Connolly decided to "go for a long bomb," in Nixon's words, that would turn looming economic defeat into political victory. Connolly found the sources of America's problems in foreign capitals and financial centers where restrictions on American exports were hatched and speculators plotted the destruction of the dollar. "My basic approach is that the foreigners are out to screw us," he told a group of Treasury consultants. "Our job is to screw them first."[50]

The story was told that the British precipitated the weekend meeting at Camp David and the statement at the head of this chapter by their request on August 12 that the United States "cover," or guarantee, the gold value of its dollars, implicitly threatening to start a run if it were not forthcoming. But the complex New Economic Plan had to have been ready, or nearly so, and Volcker tells us that the die was cast. The meeting had been called and its outcome was "unstoppable."[51]

Burns supported the tax cuts and of course wage and price controls, but he did not want to close the gold window. Taken in its entirety, the plan was a signal that the United States would not address inflation. This was understood by nearly everyone else at the meeting, but Burns's difficulty with the price system and trust in exhortation were such that he thought foreigners could be asked to hold their dollars until a new set of exchange rates could be negotiated. Volcker was incredulous. "I had to tell the president it was not at all a credible option to negotiate a new exchange rate while keeping the gold window open." Other countries would have "been placed in an intolerable position. How could they continue to hold and buy dollars in the market and not convert them to gold? . . . Arthur Burns had personal seniority among all of Mr. Nixon's advisers and was given the opportunity to present his case more privately to the president later. I don't know whether new points were made, but the outcome seemed to me preordained."[52] Nixon recalled in his *Memoirs* that Burns warned, "*Pravda* would write that this was a sign of the collapse of capitalism."[53]

[49] *Ibid.*, p. 68.
[50] John Odell, *U.S. International Monetary Policy*, p. 263.
[51] Volcker and Gyohten, *op. cit.*, p. 77.
[52] *Ibid.*, p. 78.
[53] Nixon, *op. cit.*, p. 519.

Monetary Policy with a Floating Exchange Rate,
August 1971 to October 1979

In 1314 university officials complained to the king that the Oxford market ran unreasonably high, so that poor scholars could hardly live. The king sent down his mandate to regulate this affair, and Parliament took the same thing with respect to the whole nation into consideration. The rates they set for provisions included the following:

	l.	*s.*	*d.*
A stalled or corn-fed ox	1	4	0
A grass-fed ox	0	16	0
A fat stall'd cow	0	12	0
An ordinary cow	0	10	0
A fat goose in the City, 3 d., elsewhere	0	0	2 1/2
A fat hen in the City, 1d. 1/2, elsewhere	0	0	1
24 eggs (20 in the City)	0	0	1

Nothwithstanding this Act of Parliament, things could not be purchased at these rates, for people would not bring them to market (and that is a thing parliaments cannot remedy), and so the king revoked the Act and left people to sell as they could (for a trade will do as it can, and never be forced, one way or other).

Bishop Fleetwood, *Chronicon Preciosum*, London, 1745 (from the back cover of the *Journal of Political Economy*, August 1983)

Controls and Inflation

More-or-less ambitious controls lasted until shortages forced their abandonment in April 1974. Lids on agricultural prices, in particular, were followed by shortages that increased the pressures to raise them, which led to cries for stricter regulation, and so forth. This pattern had been expected by those who had thought about or had experience with markets and was well known to economic historians and Richard Nixon.[54] His program produced the same results that had been petitioned and suffered by his ancestors.

The timing and relative effects of money growth and controls on inflation are controversial, but it is not disputed that prices rose throughout the

---

[54] One of the reminders published in these years was *Forty Centuries of Wage and Price Controls* by Robert Schuettinger and Eamonn Butler.

period (Fig. 12.1). Inflation had been slowing since mid-1970 but had accelerated despite a fall in money growth. Prices and money grew at annual rates of 8 and 9 percent, respectively, during the controls. A substantial part of the inflation pick-up (which was no doubt greater than reported) was probably due to an upward revision of expected prices caused by the August 1971 announcement, accentuated by the continuation of controls three months later, which could only have been interpreted as avoidance of a serious inflation policy.

The oil-price shock two years later was itself a response to the rising industrial prices faced by oil producers. The price of crude oil had risen only 7 percent between 1963 and 1970, a quarter of the increase in U.S. prices, and the Organization of Petroleum Exporting Countries (OPEC) stepped up its plans to coordinate prices and take over production from the western oil companies. In February 1971, noting industrial inflation, OPEC raised the price of Arabian light from $1.75 to $2.18 a barrel and provided for a 2.5-percent annual inflation adjustment. In the month after the Nixon package was announced, it resolved to offset adverse effects of the dollar's *de facto* devaluation, and it was poised for the hike to $5.12 under the banner of protest against the West's assistance to Israel during the 1973 Yom Kippur War.[55]

In addition to the Price Commission and the Pay Board, a third arm of the bureaucracy of controls was the Committee on Interest and Dividends. It had seemed logical that the latter be headed by the Fed chairman, and the uncomfortable Burns was divided between explaining to a skeptical Congress that interest rates were different from prices and wages – that raising them was necessary to fight inflation – and using the Fed's authority to pressure bankers into not raising their loan rates in line with money market rates. "To a large degree, we are chasing shadows here," he told the Joint Economic Committee.[56] The president was unsympathetic: "What an ugly tree has grown from your seeds," he told Burns.[57]

Money Control

Burns was not a monetarist in the sense of wanting a rule for the money supply. He was an activist who looked for the appropriate countercyclical action implied by forecasts. This meant to him, as a macroeconomist in charge of monetary policy, the control of money. Maisel had been pushing

---

[55] See www.OPEC.com.

[56] Joint Economic Committee, *1973 Economic Report of the President*, p. 429.

[57] John Erlichman, "Notes of Meetings with the President," April 18, 1973; Wells, *op. cit.*, p. 113.

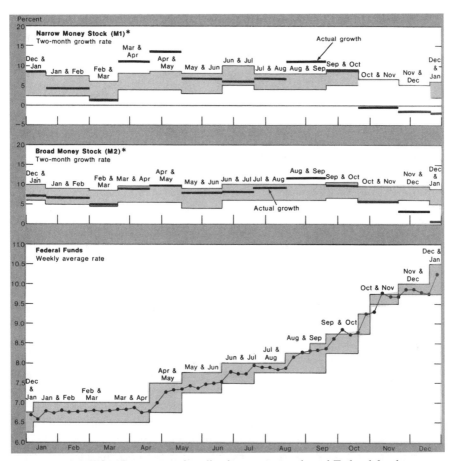

Figure 12.2. FOMC ranges and realized money growth and Federal funds rate, 1978. *Source:* Fred Levin and Ann-Marie Meulendyke, "Monetary Policy and Open Market Operations in 1978."

for a more quantitative approach before Burn's arrival, and he had gotten the FOMC to expand its Directive beyond money market conditions. "The question at issue," he wrote, "was whether the Federal Reserve could adopt a monetary target that would enable the System to control monetary policy instead of merely influencing the money market."[58] With Burns's support, the Directive began to give money targets equal billing with interest rates.

There were problems, however. Specifications of money were unstable in their relations with interest and prices. Figure 12.2 shows M1 and M2,

[58] Maisel, *op. cit.*, p. 248.

but several other versions were presented to the FOMC. Congress was unhappy with the fall in money growth as the economy went into recession, and Concurrent Resolution 133 of 1975 required the Fed to present quarterly reports of its money-growth plans to the House or Senate Banking Committee. The requirement was repeated with modifications in the *Federal Reserve Reform Act of 1977* and the *Full Employment and Balanced Growth (Humphrey–Hawkins) Act of 1978.* The reporting process was less enlightening than obfuscating, a member of the Fed's staff and former student of Maisel, reported. Representatives of the Fed "appeared before the banking committees armed with growth rate ranges for five different measures of money and credit aggregates," enabling them "to create confusion and to direct attention away from policy objectives and toward the technical question of who has the best M. Furthermore, the growth rate ranges for each aggregate were sufficiently wide to be virtually assured of having at least one of the aggregates within its range 12 months ahead."[59] The breakdown of one money–income relationship could be replaced by the discovery of another.

Congress eventually tired of an exercise that looked like harassment of an institution whose reputation was restored by low inflation and prosperity (see the box).

At its June meeting, the FOMC did not establish ranges for growth of money and debt in 2000 and 2001. The legal requirement to establish and to announce such ranges had expired, and owing to uncertainties about the behavior of the velocities of debt and money, these ranges for many years have not provided useful benchmarks for the conduct of monetary policy. Nevertheless, the FOMC believes that the behavior of money and credit will continue to have value for gauging economic and financial conditions.

Monetary Policy Objectives 2000, Executive Summary of the Board's Monetary Policy Report to the Congress, July 20, 2000, p. 12

Not So Different

Poole observed that monetary policy under Burns (1970–78) was about as procyclical as that under Martin. "It is widely understood that a major reason for procyclical money growth is the Federal Reserve's effort to

---

[59] James Pierce, "The Myth of Congressional Supervision of Monetary Policy."

Table 12.2. *FOMC Directives before and after October 6, 1979*

September 18, 1979: Early in the period before the next regular meeting, System open market operations are to be directed at attaining a weekly average federal funds rate slightly above the current level. Subsequently, operations shall be directed at maintaining the weekly average federal funds rate within the range of 11.25 to 11.75 percent. In deciding on the specific objective for the federal funds rate, the Manager for Domestic Operations shall be guided mainly by the relationship between the latest estimates of annual rates of growth in the September–October period of M1 and M2 and the following ranges of tolerance: 3 to 8 percent for M1 and 6.5 to 10.5 percent for M2. If rates of growth of M1 and M2, given approximately equal weight, appear to be close to or beyond the upper or lower limits of the indicated ranges, the objective for the funds rate is to be raised or lowered in an orderly fashion within its range.

April 22, 1980: In the short run, the Committee seeks expansion of reserve aggregates consistent with growth over the first half of 1980 at an annual rate of 4.5 percent for M1A and 5 percent for M1B, or somewhat less, provided that in the period before the next regular meeting the weekly average federal funds rate remains within a range of 13 to 19 percent.

If it appears during the period before the next meeting that the constraint on the federal funds rate is inconsistent with the objective for the expansion of reserves, the Manager for Domestic Operations is promptly to notify the Chairman, who will then decide whether the situation calls for supplementary instructions from the Committee.

Note: M1A and M1B were new monetary aggregates, the first being currency and checking accounts in all depository institutions, the second limited to commercial banks.
Sources: Federal Reserve Bulletin, Nov. 1979, pp. 912–13; June 1980, p. 488.

control interest rates in the short-run. This situation did not change under Arthur Burns."[60] A staff member thought that the Fed's focus on interest-rate stability increased after Congress directed it to target money.[61] The FOMC's stated targets and accuracy in hitting them in 1978 are depicted in Fig. 12.2. Similar stair steps can be drawn for previous years and for 1979 through September (which would not have surprised Wicksell).

The figure shows a central bank responding to inflationary pressures with increases – too little and too late – in its target federal funds rate. Excerpts from FOMC directives to the manager of the Open Market Desk in New York are shown in Table 12.2. The first, on September 18, 1979, directed the manager to conduct open market purchases and/or sale of

---

[60] "Burnsian Monetary Policy."
[61] Pierce, *op. cit.*

securities in such a way as to keep the federal funds rate between 11.25 and 11.75 percent and the annual rate of growth of the narrow money supply (M1) between 3 and 8 percent. The narrow interest and the wide money range suggest that, because of its importance or attainability, the former was the preferred target. In fact, directives before October 1979 suggest infinite ranges for money. The federal funds rate was "to be raised or lowered in an orderly fashion within its range" even at the cost of violating the money ranges. Figure 12.2 indicates that the Desk followed this direction, sometimes allowing large deviations from money "targets," but never from interest targets.

The priority of targets was reversed on October 6, 1979, with the dramatic announcement by Volcker, recently named Fed chairman, of a shift in policy toward the monetary aggregates and away from the control of interest rates. The lower half of Table 12.2 shows an excerpt from one of the new directives, which indicated a willingness to depart from the interest target if necessary to meet the money targets.

THIRTEEN

Back to the Beginning? New Contracts for New Companies

It all came about quite unexpectedly. With oil prices and inflation rising, the economy looking stagnant and administration credibility low, Jimmy Carter had gone up to his Camp David mountain to think things out. There he fired some of his cabinet, including his secretary of the Treasury, and came down again to give what came to be known as his "malaise" speech. [T]he change that moved Fed chairman G. William Miller into the job of Treasury secretary left a vacancy at the top of the agency that would have to do something about inflation, if anybody could.

I was a little surprised when I got a call in New York [Volcker had been president of the New York Fed since 1975] from Bill Miller asking me to see the president. He didn't give a reason, but of course I could guess. . . . I went to Washington without any particular expectation, mainly concerned that the president not be under any misunderstanding of my own concern about the importance of an independent central bank and the need for tighter money – tighter than Bill Miller had wanted. . . . As I recall it, I did most of the talking. I remember . . . a certain sense of relief that, after my performance, I surely wouldn't be asked to pull up stakes to return to Washington . . .

Paul Volcker, *Changing Fortunes*, pp. 163–64

The tolerance of rising prices that had brought down Bretton Woods proved to be limited. The increase in inflation to double digits produced political reactions throughout the industrial world. This chapter is devoted to those actions, which were makeshift at first, and then more lasting. The first two sections describe the measures undertaken in 1979 by Paul Volcker, the new chairman of the Federal Reserve, and Margaret Thatcher, the new British prime minister. (The Bank of England's operational independence was in the future.) Stable money requires confidence

Background: People and Events
1979–84: British and American experiments with money targets.
1989: Fall of the Berlin Wall; New Zealand Reserve Bank Act.
1990–92: Britain on the Exchange Rate Mechanism.
1992: Chancellor announces inflation targeting.
1998: Bank of England Act.
1998: First U.S. budget surplus since 1969.
2001: 9/11 attack on the World Trade Center.
2002: U.S. budget deficit.

	President of the United States	Secretary of the Treasury	Chairman of the Council of Economic Advisors	Chairman of the Federal Reserve Board
1979	Jimmy Carter	G. Wm. Miller	Charles Schultze	Paul Volcker
1981	Ronald Reagan	Donald Regan	Murray Weidenbaum	
1982			Martin Feldstein	
1985		James Baker	Beryl Sprinkel	
1987				Alan Greenspan
1989	George H. W. Bush	Nicholas Brady	Michael Boskin	
1993	William Clinton	Lloyd Bentson	Laura Tyson	
1995		William Rubin	Joseph Stiglitz	
1997			Janet Yellen	
1998		Lawrence Summers		
1999			Martin Bailey	
2001	George W. Bush	Paul O'Neill	Glenn Hubbard	
2003		John Snow	Gregory Mankiw	

	Prime Minister	Chancellor of the Exchequer	Governor of the Bank of England
1979	Margaret Thatcher	Geoffrey Howe	Gordon Richardson
1983		Nigel Lawson	Robin Leigh-Pemberton
1989		John Major	
1990	Major	Norman Lamont	
1993		Kenneth Clarke	Edward George
1997	Tony Blair	Gordon Brown	
2003			Mervyn King

in its producers, and lacking institutional restraints, they leaned on verbal assurances.

After their initial successes at great economic and political costs, the authorities looked for more reliable disciplines, which in some cases turned out to be formal contracts similar to earlier times. The last three sections examine the new contracts, compare them with the old, and speculate on their future. We can make guesses of parts of the future because the new contracts will, like the old, be managed by central bankers whose ideas and actions have shown remarkable continuity.

Turning Point

Surprised or not, Volcker was given the job and was sworn in on August 6, 1979. The president needed a new monetary policy. This could only be revealed in time, but the markets wanted immediate assurance. Volcker was not the chairman the administration wanted. It already had its preference in "team player" William Miller, who had succeeded Arthur Burns in 1978. A businessman without banking experience, Miller shared the president's belief in a monetary policy at once "accommodative" and "credible." The introduction to Carter's last *Economic Report of the President* (January 1981) recognized that "Monetary policy is the responsibility of the Federal Reserve System, which is independent of the Executive. I respect that independence." He accepted that "Sustained restraint in monetary policy is a prerequisite to lowering inflation," but when he wrote that "It is very important, however, that public opinion not hold the Federal Reserve to such a rigid form of monetary targeting as to deprive it of the flexibility it needs to conduct a responsible monetary policy," inflation was running at 14 percent and money measures were growing 7 to 11 percent per annum.

A year and a half earlier, in the summer of 1979, inflation was at 12 percent, interest rates were near record highs, and the dollar was falling on international markets. Polls showed an overwhelming preference among Democrats for Ted Kennedy in next year's election. On July 15, after 10 days of reflection at Camp David, Carter urged the nation to spiritual renewal and sacrifice. Otherwise, the focus of his speech was on rising energy prices, which he proposed to attack by conservation and the development of domestic resources, and he promised to use his authority to set quotas on oil imports. Apart from the suggestion that materialism was the root of the problem, he did not address inflation.

Oil prices immediately accelerated, more than doubling during the next 18 months. They did not fall until the spring of 1981, after American inflation had slackened and under the pressure of weakening demand during the "Volcker recession."

Carter's speech boosted his standing in the polls, but "financial markets reacted negatively," the *New York Times* reported, with "Treasury bills climbing to their highest rates since early June."[1] There was no reassurance in the cabinet housecleaning later in the week that saw the replacement of Treasury Secretary Michael Blumenthal by William Miller. A financial columnist wrote,

> In turning to Mr. Miller, the President has chosen a man who, despite the vaunted independence of the Federal Reserve Board, has already demonstrated a willingness to respond closely and sympathetically to signals emanating from the Oval Office.
>
> This spring, in the face of strong pressure from conservatives in the banking and investment world to tighten money further and raise interest rates to check inflation, Mr. Miller clung to his steady-as-you-go policy, contending that the economy was already slowing down and no further tightening was needed. Secretary Blumenthal was on the other side of that issue. Mr. Miller's victory in the fight over monetary policy foreshadowed, and may well have contributed to, his succession to Mr. Blumenthal's post as the nation's chief economic policy maker.[2]

Who would replace Miller at the Fed? A deluge of calls from the financial community made it "obvious" to the director of the White House Domestic Policy Staff, Stuart Eizenstat, "that we had to quell the nervousness of the markets." The search was coordinated by Richard Moe:[3]

> It was a very intense and compressed process, very rushed. The big factor was: we've got to reassure the markets. That's all we heard. Coming in the wake of the Camp David meetings and the Cabinet changes, people were very nervous about the direction we were going. I wouldn't call it panic, but there was clearly a level of concern. We've got a problem on our hands and we have to do it right.

Friends warned the president against appointing the "strong-minded" Volcker, and a "liberal economist" called to label him "Very right-wing...not a team player." Nevertheless, Eizenstat explained, "Volcker

---

[1] July 17, 1979, p. D1.
[2] Leonard Silk, *New York Times*, July 20, 1979, p. D2. Miller, a director of the Federal Reserve Bank of Boston, was "an outspoken member of the National Alliance of Businessmen [with] a long-standing commitment to jobs programs" and "promoted good relations between Carter and the AFL–CIO" (www.ustreas.gov/curator).
[3] Interviews with William Greider, *Secrets of the Temple*, pp. 22, 34.

was selected because he was the candidate of Wall Street. That was their price, in effect."[4]

Carter's choice of Volcker was comparable to Kennedy's reappointment of Martin, whose teamwork was also suspect, and his selection of Republican investment banker Douglas Dillon for the Treasury, as well to Martin's original appointment by Truman. These presidents wanted signals to the markets that inflation would be addressed. Controls were ineffective and politicians' promises were unreliable. What was needed was someone in the inner councils of the administration or at the central bank whom the markets trusted.

The need is not special to irredeemable currencies. Even under the gold standard, governments wanting to maintain the values of their currencies had needed to assure the markets of their future good behavior. Yet the promise of convertibility inherent in the gold standard implied a commitment that in ordinary times was sufficient. The fiat system that came with the breakdown of Bretton Woods needed extra supports.

Floating exchange rates were a disappointment. They showed the disadvantages predicted by their critics without the benefits promised by their advocates. They had been favorites of economists, who assumed that they would respond proportionally to relative price levels, and so preserve real international exchange values. Under Purchasing Power Parity (PPP), if the pound trades at $4 and British prices double relative to American prices, the pound falls to $2. This is the Law of One Price applied to international trade. If it is violated, for example, if the pound falls only to $3, British goods are overvalued, its exports fall and its imports rise, the pound is a drag on the market, and its value falls.

By this process, in one of their few agreements, Milton Friedman and J. M. Keynes had argued that floating rates enable countries to manage their price levels in the face of changes abroad.[5] The abandonment of fixed exchange rates cushions the international transmission of business cycles and allows countries to pursue the monetary policies they desire, whether through Keynes's discretion or Friedman's rule.

Things did not work out that way. Currencies are more than the media of exchange. They are also investments whose values fluctuate with beliefs about future values. Economists rediscovered in the 1970s that they are as volatile and unpredictable as common stocks.

---

[4] *Ibid.*, pp. 35, 47.
[5] Milton Friedman, "The Case for Flexible Exchange Rates"; J. M. Keynes, *The General Theory*, pp. 270, 339.

Friedman wanted "a world in which exchange rates, while *free* to vary, are in fact highly stable."[6] However, Robert Roosa, who had worked at the Federal Reserve Bank of New York (1946–60) and the U.S. Treasury (1961–64) (and was Volcker's mentor in both places) before going into private banking, pointed out that theorists had not reckoned on the difficulties of making markets in a flexible-rate system. The perfectly competitive markets with automatically adjusting prices of the textbooks do not, and cannot, exist. Markets are *made*. Nothing is automatic, and dealers and other traders are reluctant "to make markets... without some benchmarks to guide them." It is "inevitable," Roosa wrote in 1967 in terms that recall the FOMC's concern for the breadth, depth, and resiliency of the government securities market, "that every central bank will always have to be a factor of some importance in the market trading of its own currency against others – if not through active intervention, then at least through the setting of a par value and buying or selling at the outer limits of the agreed margin for variation around that par value." Without such guidelines, private dealers are afraid of being "crunched between the pressures generated by central banking giants in a free-for-all." These risks would be reflected in the prices of dealer services, adding another impediment to international trade and investment in a world of uncertain exchange rates.[7]

The volume of international transactions did not suffer under flexible rates. On the other hand, they did not deliver their promised contribution to economic stability. An example of the failure of exchange rates to reflect domestic purchasing powers is presented in Fig. 13.1. The ratio of the price levels of the United States and other industrial countries varied within a narrow range – less than 10 percent – between 1975 and the 1990s. However, the real exchange value of the dollar (adjusted for relative inflations) fell 20 percent in the 1970s, more than recovered by 1985, and fell more than 60 percent over the next 10 years. For most of the period, the real exchange rate, which according to PPP ought to have been constant, tracked the nominal (actual) rate.

We have seen that the PPP explanation of exchange rates on which Ricardo relied failed during the Napoleonic Wars and the resumption that followed, as well as during and after the American Civil War. Economists had had ample opportunities to observe its failure in other floating rate periods: in France and Spain in the 16th century (because of fluctuating

[6] Friedman, *op. cit.*
[7] Robert Roosa, "Second Lecture," in Friedman and Roosa, *op. cit.*

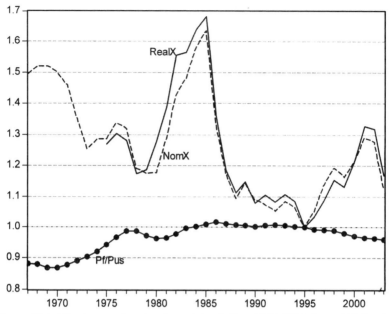

Figure 13.1. The international value of the dollar, 1967–2003 (base 1995) price level of industrial countries relative to the United States, Pf/Pus, and average nominal and real exchange rate of the U.S. dollar. *Source:* International Monetary Fund, *International Financial Statistics.*

values of gold and silver coins), in the British colonies of North America, with the assignat of the French Revolution, and in Europe after World War I (when deviations of rates from purchasing powers had been even greater than in the 1970s):[8]

[A]nd thus hordes [of Bavarians] went over [to Salzburg] with wives and children to indulge in the luxury of guzzling as much beer as their bellies could hold. . . . But the happy Bavarians did not know that a terrible revenge was approaching. For when the [Austrian] crown stabilized and the mark plummeted downward in astronomical proportions, the Austrians went over [to Bavaria] from the same railway station in their turn.

Stefan Zweig, *Die Welt von Gestern*, pp. 336–37[9]

Peter Bernholz concluded that "modern economists have only redis-covered some of the hypotheses concerning flexible exchange rates that

---

[8] Paul de Grauwe et al., *Real Exchange-Rate Variability from 1920 to 1926 and 1973 to 1982*; Peter Bernholz, *Flexible Exchange Rates in Historical Perspective.*
[9] Translated by Bernholz, *op. cit.*, p. 1.

had been stated by earlier economists once or several times." When institutions change, "experiences and theories tend to be forgotten or not transmitted because they are no longer applicable.... In the meantime, knowledge has been lost, and the same serious mistakes that were made before may be repeated again and again."[10] The problems of floating exchange rates, like those of inflation, had to be rediscovered – and for that, it seems, they had to be reexperienced.

New Operating Procedures

Volcker

The markets briefly responded to Volcker's appointment: Stocks, bonds, and the dollar rallied; but they soon resumed their declines. An appointment was not enough. The markets would have to be shown; knocked down, as it turned out. "In September 1979," Volcker recalled, "the markets seemed confident of only one thing: bet on inflation. Even if the cost to do so was rising, that cost lagged inflation, and there always seemed to be enough money to finance whatever you wanted to buy."[11]

Signals from the Fed were uncertain. Reserve Bank discount rates (nearly always a joint move by all twelve Banks) are changed on the applications of their boards of directors subject to the approval of the Federal Reserve Board (which might have requested them). Volcker had hoped that the half-percent increase in mid-September, the second in a month, would impress the markets. However, the Board's vote, which is announced with the rate, was four to three. "Ordinarily, I might have been reluctant to move with such a split Board," Volcker writes, "but I knew from the discussion the four votes were solid.... There was no reason for me to believe that further steps to tighten could not be taken when and if I was prepared to make the case for them."[12]

The press and the market did not see it that way. To them, the split vote spelled hesitation and left the impression that this would be the Board's last move to tighten money. The whole maneuver was therefore counterproductive in seeming to send a message that inflation could not, or would not, be dealt with very strongly.

The situation forced Volcker "to think hard about how we could be more effective." In the presence of excess demands for goods and loans

[10] *Ibid.*, p. 39.
[11] Paul Volcker and Tyoo Gyohten, *Changing Fortunes*, p. 166.
[12] *Ibid*, pp. 165–66.

stimulated by inflationary expectations, one cannot know what interest rates are necessary for price stability, but the greatest practical obstacle was the unpopularity of high interest rates.

Volcker wrote that the solution was suggested by Carter's question, "Why can't you control the quantity of money without raising interest rates?"[13] That could not be done, of course. The Bank of England had tried to tell the chancellor three decades earlier that one could not control price *and* quantity. Perhaps the Fed might find a use for monetarism, after all. It could fix the quantity of money and let the market find the right interest rates without incurring the blame for the high rates that might ensue.

Volcker found the Bank presidents "eager to proceed," but he wanted more support from the Board. Surprisingly, the inflation hawks who had voted with him on the last discount rate increase were the most reluctant, whereas the doves saw the New Operating Procedure as a way off the hook. As a president put it, "Everyone could say: 'Look, no hands.'"[14] The hawks went along as a way to a consensus approach to inflation.[15]

They did not know what they were in for. Interest rates reacted strongly to Volcker's announcement of the New Operating Procedure on October 6 (Treasury bill rates rose a full percentage point the first business day) and continued to climb the next six months. William Melton observed consternation among the dealer "lab rats."[16] The prime rate reached 20 percent, fell to 11 in December under the pressure of recession, and jumped to spend most of 1981 above 20. Interest rates did not return to 1960s levels until the 1990s, years after falling inflation had shown the way.

Federal Reserve Press Release, October 6, 1979

The Federal Reserve today announced a series of complementary actions that should assure better control over the expansion of money and bank credit, help curb speculative excesses in financial, foreign exchange and commodity markets and thereby serve to dampen inflationary forces.

---

[13] Greider, *op. cit.*, p. 120.
[14] *Ibid.*, p. 107.
[15] Volcker and Gyohten, *op. cit.*, p. 169; Greider, *op. cit.*, pp. 111–13.
[16] William Melton, *Inside the Fed: Making Monetary Policy*, pp. 48–49.

Actions taken are:

1. A 1 percent increase in the discount rate, approved unanimously by the Board, from 11 percent to 12 percent.
2. Establishment of an 8 percent marginal reserve requirement on increases in "managed liabilities" – liabilities that have been actively used to finance rapid expansion in bank credit. This was also approved unanimously by the Board.
3. A change in the method used to conduct monetary policy to support the objective of containing growth in the monetary aggregates over the remainder of this year within the ranges previously adopted by the Federal Reserve. These ranges are consistent with moderate growth in the aggregates over the months ahead. This action involves placing greater emphasis on day-to-day operations on the supply of bank reserves and less emphasis on confining short-term fluctuations in the federal funds rate. It was approved unanimously by the Federal Open Market Committee.

Federal Reserve *Bulletin*, October 1979, p. 830

More surprising than the volatility of interest rates, which were expected to fluctuate under the new procedure, was the increased volatility of money. The Fed missed its money targets even more than when interest rates were supposed to be the primary targets. Milton Friedman complained about the bad name the Fed was giving monetarism, which for him meant a constant rate of money growth.[17] He should have heeded the warning of the manager of the Desk, who told dealers at the beginning,

We don't plan to be rigid or mechanistic in pursuit of reserve targets. This may cause some die-hard monetarists to subdue their elation at our change in approach and recall their congratulatory messages. But we are too aware of slippages of various kinds in the short run to be really rigid.[18]

Money cannot be controlled in the manner assumed by the textbooks, where the Fed controls bank reserves by open market operations as deposits change as banks expand, or restrict loans in response to the change in reserves as interest rates adjust to the supply of money. The actual order of causation is precisely the opposite. Interest rates determine a bank's lending, which determines its deposits and reserve requirements.

[17] Friedman "The Federal Reserve and Monetary Instability."
[18] Quoted in Melton, *op. cit.*, p. 50.

The cost of a three-month loan to a bank is the cost of reserves, which is the average federal funds rate during the life of the loan. So the supply of loans depends on the spread between the loan rate and expected federal funds rates. An increase in loans and deposits calls forth the reserves necessary to support them – either voluntarily by the Fed to prevent violations of reserve requirements or involuntarily in the form of reserve deficiencies.

The Fed might discourage loan increases by accepting deficiencies and enforcing their penalties, but this would operate through interest rates. The effect of the high rates caused by bank competition for limited reserves depends on bank expectations of future interest rates. The yo-yo in money growth of which Friedman complained followed from a similar pattern in interest rates. If current rates are more or less projected into the future, a low federal funds rate induces an expansion of loans and deposits and more required reserves, and, if the Fed fails to supply them, a high federal funds rate. This induces a contraction of loans, a diminished demand for reserves, and a low federal funds rate, which induces another expansion, etc.[19]

Reasonably steady money growth might have been achieved by steady interest rates. In other words, the old operating procedure, which targeted interest rates, was more conducive to steady money growth than the new procedure that purported to target money. A way around these problems, in the spirit of monetarism, would have been a constant or at least a predictable rate of open market purchases by the Fed.[20] Although it pursued neither of these courses, it eventually reached its goal. Average money growth came down, and so did inflation, although with more variability and greater economic cost, including two short but sharp recessions, than even those who had warned of the unavoidable pain of ending inflation had counted on. The fall in interest rates to politically acceptable levels allowed a return to interest targets in 1983.

Thatcher

The United Kingdom also performed a "monetarist experiment" in 1979, with results similar to those in the United States: volatile money and interest rates, recession, and falling inflation, followed by a long economic

---

[19] These problems were increased by the lagged-reserve accounting system then in use (Robert Laurent, "Lagged Reserve Accounting and the Fed's New Operating Procedure," summarized in John and Norma Wood, *Financial Markets*, pp. 263–66) but exist in some degree in any system of average reserve accounting.

[20] The Bank of England looked at monetary base targeting but did not apply it; M. D. K. W. Foot et al., "Monetary Base Control."

expansion. The political hurdles were also similar. Like Jimmy Carter, Margaret Thatcher, prime minister from 1979 to 1990, subjected her political future to the fight against inflation, and she almost joined him in defeat. She might have owed her reelection in 1983 to the military success in the Falklands a year earlier.

J. S. Fforde, executive director of the Bank and advisor to the governors (and later historian of the Bank), explained the political economy of "setting monetary objectives" to a conference at the Federal Reserve Bank of New York in 1982:[21]

> The United Kingdom is a unitary state and a parliamentary democracy. Subject to parliamentary and ultimately electoral approval, macroeconomic policy is decided and carried out by a unified executive branch. This includes ... the Treasury and the Bank of England. The latter is institutionally and operationally separate from the Treasury but is best regarded as the central banking arm of a centralised macroeconomic executive.

Monetary targeting was not new. A form had been imposed by the International Monetary Fund as a condition of assistance after sterling's devaluation in 1967. The IMF's conditions

> obliged the borrowing country to carry out an internally consistent macroeconomic policy ... so as to restrict the fiscal deficit, restrain the provision of finance to the private sector and ... bring about control of a specially devised broad credit aggregate (DCE).

Domestic credit expansion (DCE) is the increase in commercial bank lending, including the finance of government debt. In practice, it was supplanted by a monetary aggregate on the assumption that there was a more "workable degree of stability in the relationship between money and income ... than 'credit' and income."

> The requirements of the IMF fitted readily into the established flow-of-funds accounting matrix and could thereby be made analytically consistent and visibly interrelated. It did not matter too much, for the purposes of political economy, that a set of accounting identities yielded of themselves relatively little information about causality; or that financial forecasts of the way such identities would turn out *ex post* were extremely imperfect. It sufficed that the various "intermediate" fiscal and monetary magnitudes could be presented in directly interrelated form, through the financial accounts, and directly related to externally imposed conditions (DCE) which had perforce to be met.

---

[21] Bank of England, *Quarterly Bulletin*, June 1983.

The Bank hardly qualified as monetarist, but its statements took increasing notice of money as the 1970s progressed. In spite of "the breakdown of the previously established relationships between M3 [currency and bank deposits, roughly equivalent to M2 in the United States] and interest rates and nominal income," Fforde recalled, "political and market opinion remained very sensitive to the development of the money supply." In 1976, M3's status was advanced from a "moderate" to "an overriding constraint upon policies which might otherwise fail to stop inflation reaccelerating to 20 percent per annum or more." The same year, Prime Minister James Callaghan read Keynesianism's obituary to the Labour Party Conference:

The cosy world we were told would go on forever, where full employment would be guaranteed by a stroke of the chancellor's pen, cutting taxes, deficit spending, . . . is gone. . . . We used to think that you could spend your way out of a recession. . . . I tell you in all candour that that option no longer exists, and that in so far as it ever did exist, it only worked on each occasion since the war by injecting a bigger dose of inflation into the economy, followed by a higher level of unemployment as the next step.[22]

Inflation fell from 22 percent in 1975 to 8 percent in 1978, but the government's hold on monetary policy was broken by a revolt against its wage and price restraints in the 1978–79 "winter of discontent." Inflation resurged and the general election of May 1979 brought a new government.

Mrs. Thatcher ended direct controls and brought a new determination to the reduction of inflation by monetary restraint. As in the United States, the volatility of money increased, but its average growth came down with economic activity and eventually inflation. Monetary targeting lasted until 1985, after which inflation rose, returning to double digits in 1990. This differed from the American experience, but while it lasted, British monetary targeting was rationalized on the same political grounds as in the United States.

[I]t would scarcely have been possible to mount and carry through, over several years and without direct controls of all kinds, so determined a counter-inflationary strategy if it had not been for the internal "political economy" of the firm monetary target. Though not considered at the time, it would have been possible to initiate such a strategy with a familiar "Keynesian" exposition about managing demand downwards, and with greater concentration on ultimate objectives than on intermediate targets. But this would have meant disclosing objectives for, *inter alia*,

---

[22] *Report of the Seventy-Fifth Annual Conference of the Labour Party*, p. 188; Michael Oliver, *Whatever Happened to Monetarism?*, p. 23.

output and employment. This would have been a very hazardous exercise, and the objectives would either have been unacceptable to public opinion or else inadequate to secure a substantial reduction in the rate of inflation, or both. Use of strong intermediate targets, for money supply and government borrowing, enabled the authorities to stand back from output and employment as such. . . . In short, whatever the subsequent difficulties of working with intermediate targets, they were vitally important at the outset in order to signal a decisive break with the past and enable the authorities to set out with presentational confidence upon a relatively uncharted sea.

J. S. Fforde, "Setting Monetary Objectives"

Monetary policy was buffeted by the same political conflicts as in the United States. The Lady had declared in 1980 that she was "not for turning," differentiating herself from her Tory predecessor noted for his U-turns. She could not keep her associates in line indefinitely, however, Chancellor Nigel Lawson's emphatic verbal recommitment to the fight against inflation in June 1984 raised eyebrows. Observers wondered why, in light of the government's behavior to that point, his statement was considered necessary. In fact, it was soon revealed that the new chancellor's monetarism "was not as zealous as his predecessor's" (Geoffrey Howe).[23] Unemployment was still rising, and in January 1985 a currency crisis turned Lawson's attention to the exchange rate in disregard of the prime minister's opinion, expressed in the House of Commons, that "There is no way in which one can buck the market."[24]

Mrs. Thatcher's autobiography looked back at the situation in 1988, when inflation was on the rise again. Interest rates responded, but she complained of Lawson's insistence "on raising them only half a percent at a time. I would have preferred something sharper to convince the markets how seriously we took the latest [signs] that monetary policy had been too lax." He "took a more laid-back view of" the signs of inflation than the prime minister.

It is on the face of it extraordinary that at such a time . . . Nigel should have sent me a paper proposing an independent Bank of England. My reaction was dismissive. Here we were wrestling with the consequences of his diversion from our tried and tested strategy which had worked so well in the first Parliament; and now we were expected to turn our policy upside down again. I did not believe, as Nigel argued, that it would boost the credibility of the fight against inflation. In fact, as I minuted, "it would be seen as an abdication by the Chancellor when he is at his most vulnerable . . . it would be an admission of a failure of resolve on our

---

[23] Oliver, *op. cit.*, pp. 90–91.
[24] Thatcher, *op. cit.*, p. 703.

part." I also doubted whether we had people of the right calibre to run such an institution. . . . I had thought in the late 1970s about having an independent central bank but had come down against it. I considered it more appropriate for federal states. But in any case there could be no question of setting up such a bank now. Inflation would have to be well down – to say 2 percent – for two or three years before it could be contemplated.

In fact, I do not believe that changing well-tried institutional arrangements generally provides solutions to underlying political problems – and the control of inflation is ultimately a political problem.

Margaret Thatcher, *The Downing Street Years*, pp. 706–7

New Contracts . . .

The stated objective of central banks has become "price stability," which in practice means low inflation. The progress of this program during the last decade of the 20th century needs to be explained. It is not enough to say that the revulsion against inflation was deep and broad enough for the public to accept the costs of ending it. The political will was necessary, of course, but its implementation was not automatic. Significant technical problems had to be solved.

What kinds of institutions would most efficiently bring and keep inflation within the desired range? A return to the gold standard was out of the question politically because of its unpleasant historical associations, as well as on technical grounds because of the probable lack of credibility, at least in the initial stages, that would induce runs on meager reserves. Any kind of fixed-exchange-rate system would have to follow, not precede, price stability. International declarations of good intentions like Bretton Woods, with all the qualifications and escape clauses that multiple goals and majority approval entail, had lost their appeal.

The arrangements put in place in the 1990s were ambitious in aiming at continuous low inflation, and by implication avoidance of the periodic price fluctuations of the gold standard. On the other hand, they accepted more inflation *in the long run* than had been realized under the gold standard. The new goal does not suffer the contradictions of Bretton Woods, but the obvious discipline of the gold standard is missing, and that is what the new contracts for central bankers seek to supply.

The following paragraphs describe the essential features of the new contracts. The section ends with a look at inflation before and after their adoption. It is interesting to ask whether they were the cause or effect. Did the contracts compel the Bank of England, the Reserve Bank of New Zealand, and other central banks to cut back on their money creation, or were they primarily reinforcements of the credibilities of policies already underway? And if the latter, have they been successful? We look at the experiences of New Zealand, which led the way, of Britain, which was introduced in Chap. 1, and of some – Canada, the United States, Germany, and Switzerland – that cut inflation without legislation.

Essential Features

The new contracts attempt to establish credible government promises of good behavior, specifically low inflation. It is accepted that governments are tempted to inflate, either to monetize a deficit or to play the Phillips Curve. The latter temptation is present even if the Phillips Curve is ineffective in the long run, so that inflation is suffered without a lasting benefit in employment. Because the public realizes government incentives to inflate in the short run, they set wages accordingly, and governments are forced to do what was feared (inflate) to escape unemployment. Finn Kydland and Edward Prescott described this problem as "The Time Inconsistency of Optimal Plans."

Promises are not enough. Credibility has to be paid for. Individuals secure cooperation by contracts that are enforceable at law, but governments are not so bound. Blackstone wrote that Parliament can "do everything that is not naturally impossible," and we saw in Chap. 8 that the U.S. Supreme Court found in the 1935 gold clause cases that the government's monetary powers were not limited even by the Constitution.[25] The English government addressed this problem in 1694 by establishing a source of credit, the Bank of England, which could be credible because it was subject to law. More recent governments have had to rely on hostages to political fortune. This is where *transparency* comes in. Governments legislate low inflation that may not be repealed without "good reason," that is, without political risk, and central banks reveal their actions to allay fears that the commitment is being violated.

Credible commitments are also difficult because governments do not wish to completely surrender their monetary control. An increase in the world price of lamb, for example, which significantly affects New Zealand's price level, should not force a monetary contraction to enforce deflation elsewhere. The central bank may wish to increase liquidity following a stock market crash. Governments want flexibility in the face of

---

[25] A. V. Dicey (*Introduction to the Study of the Law of the Constitution*, pp. 41–42) wrote that this view in Blackstone's *Commentaries* (i, pp. 160–61) was shared by other authorities, including Sir Edward Coke and Sir Matthew Hale.

shocks without giving up the public's confidence in low inflation over long periods. The reasons for deviations must be clear.[26]

The first country with a formal agreement between the government and the central bank for the containment of inflation, New Zealand, is representative of the new contracts. The Reserve Bank Act of 1989 required the Bank "to formulate and implement monetary policy directed to the economic objective of achieving and maintaining stability in the general level of prices." The objective was to be negotiated between the finance minister and the Bank governor and made public in a Policy Targets Agreement (PTA) that set forth "specific targets by which monetary policy performance, in relation to its statutory objective, can be assessed during the Governor's term."

The Reserve Bank Act of 1964 was standard for its time in its multiple goals for monetary policy: "the highest degree of production, trade and of employment and of maintaining a stable internal price level." However, monetary instability and the economy's dismal performance during the next two decades led to demands for reform. New Zealand fell from the top rank to near the bottom of the industrial nations in per capita income and experienced double-digit inflation in all but two years between 1974 and 1987. The Labour government elected in 1984 launched a package of reforms aimed at liberalizing (deregulating and privatizing) the economy and reducing the government deficit, supported by the Reserve Bank's promise to reduce inflation. Inflation came down from 17 to 6 percent between 1985 and early 1988 (see the top of Fig. 13.2) as the government and Bank moved toward price stability "without indicating precisely how they would go about reaching that goal."

They finally committed to the long term. The Bank's *Bulletin* of June 1988 stated the following:

[A]ccompanying the growing acceptance that much lower rates of inflation would be achieved, there was an expectation amongst some commentators that policy would be eased once inflation rates of around 5 percent had been achieved or were in prospect.... Official concern at the growing credence given to this view... prompted a more explicit statement [by the Minister of Finance] of the ultimate inflation objective than had previously been formally made... that the

---

[26] Models of credibility with flexibility include those of Matthew Canzoneri, "Monetary Policy Games and the Role of Private Information," and Michelle Garfinkel and Seongwan Oh, "Strategic Discipline in Monetary Policy with Private Information: Optimal Targeting Horizons." Surveys of the literature on monetary targeting include those by Carl Walsh, *Monetary Theory and Policy*, and Michael Woodford, *Interest and Prices*.

UNDERLYING INFLATION, HEADLINE INFLATION, AND TARGETS

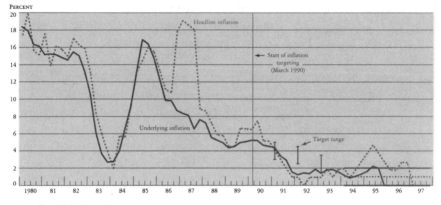

Source: Reserve Bank of New Zealand.

Note: The I-shaped bars indicate the target range for inflation in effect before the adoption of an ongoing target range of 0 to 2 percent in March 1994; a dashed horizontal line marks the midpoint of the ongoing target range.

RPIX INFLATION AND TARGETS

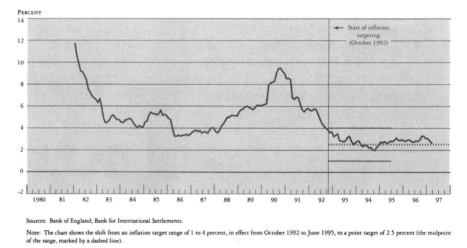

Sources: Bank of England; Bank for International Settlements.

Note: The chart shows the shift from an inflation target range of 1 to 4 percent, in effect from October 1992 to June 1995, to a point target of 2.5 percent (the midpoint of the range, marked by a dashed line).

Figure 13.2. Actual and targeted inflation in New Zealand and the United Kingdom, 1980–97. *Source:* Frederic Mishkin and Adam Posen, "Inflation Targeting: Lessons from Four Countries."

ultimate goal is to achieve price stability by the early 1990s. . . . The Bank shares the Minister's objective.

The governor could be dismissed if inflation was not on target, although exceptions were allowed. Again quoting from the *Bulletin*:

It should be emphasized, however, that the single price stability objective embodied in the Act does not mean that monetary policy is divorced from consideration of the real economy. At the technical level, the state of the real economy is an important component of any assessment of the strength of inflationary pressures. More importantly, inflation/real economy trade-offs may need to be made on occasion, particularly in the context of a decision about the pace of disinflation. . . . The main trade-offs are essentially political ones, and it is appropriate that they be made clearly at the political level. The framework allows trade-offs in areas such as the pace of disinflation, or the width of target ranges, to be reflected in the PTA with the Governor. The override provision can also be used, if required, to reflect a policy trade-off.

Reserve Bank Bulletin, September 1992

The Act permits the government to override the PTA "for a limited period, but this must be done in public and in writing."[27]

The price index is also flexible. The target is based on the "headline" consumer price index and "is the basic yardstick against which the Bank should be assessed,"[28] but "the Reserve Bank has, in practice, paid greater attention to its measure of 'underlying' or 'core' inflation; that is, inflation excluding relatively temporary influences on the price level."[29] The exclusions most often cited are "significant" first-round effects of "supply-shocks" such as changes in commodity prices and the terms of trade.

Financial stability is also an objective:

The Bank now has effective independence to implement monetary policy in pursuit of its statutory objective, without limitations on the technique except that the choices made must "have regard to the efficiency and soundness of the financial system."

Reserve Bank Bulletin, April 1992

The first PTA, signed March 2, 1990, stipulated that price stability, defined as annual inflation between 0 and 2 percent, be achieved by the end of 1992 and required the Bank to issue *Monetary Policy Statements* with five-year projections of inflation. The first *Statement*, issued the next month, projected target ranges of 3 to 5 percent for 1990, 1.5 to 3.5 percent for 1991, and 0 to 2 percent for 1992 and after. Inflation fell from 7.5 percent in 1989 to 5.5 percent in 1990, barely missing the target, and unemployment rose. The election of October 1990 gave a large majority to the National (conservative) Party, which decided that inflation was being reduced too quickly and pushed the targets back a year. In fact,

---

[27] Reserve Bank of New Zealand, "The Reserve Bank of New Zealand Act 1989: Our Accountability to New Zealanders," March 1989, p. 7.

[28] *Monetary Policy Statement*, August 1991, p. 17.

[29] Ben Bernanke, et al., *Inflation Targeting: Lessons from the International Experience*, p. 93.

inflation continued to fall, bettered the original projections, hit zero the second quarter of 1992, and remained below 2 percent until the second half of 1994.

The 1991 economic upturn had become a boom by 1994, especially in construction, and the Bank's inflation forecasts were low. Governor Donald Brash took "full responsibility" for the Bank's failure to act sooner, but as the target breach was "temporary," and the Bank's actions, though belated, were proving effective, he was supported by the minister of finance and did not resign. Inflation remained under 1.5 percent the rest of the decade.

The relationship between the Bank of England and the chancellor of the exchequer that was adopted in 1997 followed New Zealand's example, with a few exceptions that might be significant. A Monetary Policy Committee consisting of a majority from outside the Bank, mostly academic economists, was superimposed on the Bank's internal policy structure. This step was unusual. Others followed New Zealand's lead in leaving the execution of monetary policy to their central banks without changing their structures. A possible effect of the Monetary Policy Committee is that monetary policy will take less notice of financial stability because economists tend to focus on the rate of interest most likely to produce the desired rate of inflation with little regard for the financial markets. However, a separate Financial Services Committee was created to redress the balance. The New Zealand Act merely noted that the Reserve Bank would continue to have regard for financial stability. Finally, if the Monetary Policy Committee misses the assigned target, instead of being dismissed, the governor is required to write a public letter of explanation.[30] As we have seen, this has been the practice in New Zealand.

The British path to the new system was uneven. We have seen some of the tensions. Mrs. Thatcher wanted to end inflation, but she was unwilling to trust to a rule or the central bank, nor could she find a satisfactory chancellor. In 1989, she reluctantly agreed to join the Exchange Rate Mechanism (the snake) under which most of the European Union linked their currencies to the deutschemark in what was seen as a step toward a common currency. However, a run on the pound pushed it off the snake in September 1992. Shifting to a more direct approach, and signaling that the government meant business, the chancellor shortly announced

---

[30] "The Bank of England Act" (which was implemented in 1997) is described by Peter Rodgers.

an inflation target and "invited" the governor of the Bank of England to publish a quarterly *Inflation Report* of progress toward the target.

This was approximately the strategy that Mrs. Thatcher had preferred: Focus on the domestic price level and let the exchange rate take care of itself.[31] The lower portion of Fig. 13.2 shows the relationship between British inflation and its targets between 1992 and 1998. The initial range was succeeded by a point target.

Labour's transfer of operational control of monetary policy to the Bank in 1997 was called a shrewd political move to take monetary stability as a campaign issue from the Tories and their superior reputation for sound money.[32] This point might have some merit based on the rhetoric of the parties, but it has no basis in fact. The soundest and tightest chancellor between the wars, the one most committed to the gold standard, was Labour's Phillip Snowden (1924, 1929–31), and the tightest money after World War II was overseen by Labour's Roy Jenkins (1967–70) as he saw to the payment of the debt that had been accumulated to support the pound between 1964 and 1967. The Tory easy money of Reginald Maudling and Anthony Barber more than matched Hugh Dalton's.

Central bank commitments to inflation targets have not always been legislated. The joint announcement of targets by the governor of the Bank of Canada and the minister of finance in 1991 "followed a three-year campaign by the Bank of Canada to promote price stability as the objective of monetary policy." The announcement coincided with the budget to underscore "the Government's support of the Bank's commitment to the goal of price stability."[33] The initiative for targeting was even more clearly the central bank's in Sweden when the Riksbank unilaterally announced in 1993 that its objective would be to "limit the annual increase in the consumer price index from 1995 onwards to 2%, with a tolerance up or down of 1 percentage point."[34] As in the United Kingdom, and at about the same time, inflation targeting was announced after a currency crisis and abandonment of the currency's peg to the deutschemark. Sweden's approach is typical of most of the dozen or so shifts by central banks to inflation targets in the 1990s.[35] Because they are less formal than in New

[31] Thatcher, *op. cit.*, pp. 715–18.

[32] Gian Milesi-Ferratti, "The Disadvantage of Tying Their Hands: On the Political Economy of Policy Commitments," and the *Economist*, October 13, 1990.

[33] Frederic Mishkin and Adam Posen, "Inflation Targeting: Lessons from Four Countries."

[34] Bernanke et al., *op. cit.*, p. 174.

[35] For example, Australia and Spain in 1994. Israel's adoption of an inflation target in 1991, in contrast, was jointly announced by the Ministry of Finance and the central bank.

Table 13.1. *Inflation (p), Interest Rates on Long-Term Government Bonds (R), and Real Rates (r)*

	1880–1913	1953–62	1963–72	1973–82	1983–92	1993–99	2000–2003
p							
UK	−0.33	2.54	4.96	14.19	5.50	2.63	2.31
NZ		3.09	5.07	13.96	8.00	1.60	2.73
US	−0.15	1.33	3.29	8.74	3.81	2.49	2.51
Germany	−0.49	2.09*	3.24	5.37	1.85	2.00	1.70
Switzerland		1.32	4.04	4.92	3.19	1.16	0.94
R							
UK	2.76	5.61	7.53	13.39	10.01	7.07	4.73
NZ		5.09	5.37	9.68	13.19	7.74	6.19
US	2.34	3.44	5.45	9.36	9.11	6.17	4.92
Germany	3.60	6.46*	7.20	8.33	7.30	5.83	4.59
Switzerland		3.03	4.53	5.02	5.03	2.53	3.07
$r = R - p$							
UK	2.43	3.07	2.57	−0.80	4.51	4.44	2.42
NZ		2.00	0.30	−4.28	5.19	6.14	3.46
US	2.29	2.11	2.16	0.62	5.30	3.68	2.41
Germany	3.11	4.37*	3.96	2.96	5.45	1.83	2.89
Switzerland		1.71	0.49	0.10	1.84	1.37	2.13

Note: *1956–62.

Sources: International Monetary Fund, *International Financial Statistics*; Sidney Homer and Richard Sylla, *History of Interest Rates*, and B. R. Mitchell, *European Historical Statistics*.

Zealand and the United Kingdom, the new objectives may be regarded as the continuation of discretionary monetary policy. They are, however, striking rejections of former declarations of multiple objectives.

Performance

Despite the falls in inflation, contributions of the new contracts and other inflation-targeting procedures to the credibility of monetary policy were slow to take hold. They were supposed to engender trust in promises that had become a joke, but private forecasts of inflation stubbornly stayed above announced targets, and their revisions toward the targets, even as the promises were kept, were cautious. Observers noticed that the "regime change does not appear to have induced a revolution in expectations formation."[36]

Table 13.1 shows inflation and interest on long-term government bonds since the Korean War inflation and under the classical gold standard where

[36] Bernanke et al., *op. cit.*, p. 268. However, Mark Spiegel estimated that expected long-term rates fell on the May 6, 1997, announcement of enhanced independence of the Bank of England ("Central Bank Independence and Inflation Expectations").

data are available. Interest rates in the 1990s were comparable with historical standards in countries that had proved their commitments (Germany and Switzerland), without benefit of the bells and whistles, over long periods. New Zealand, the United Kingdom, and the United States finally showed signs of returning to regimes of low inflation expectations in the new millennium, although this is a small sample dominated by recession.

Another Way: The Federal Reserve

Variations in the stance of policy . . . in response to evolving forces are made in the framework of an unchanging objective – to foster as best we can those financial conditions most likely to promote sustained economic expansion at the highest rate possible. Maximum sustainable growth, as history so amply demonstrates, requires price stability. Irrespective of the complexities of economic change, our primary goal is to find those policies that best contribute to a non-inflationary environment and hence to growth.

Chairman Alan Greenspan presenting the Federal Reserve's
Report on Monetary Policy to the Senate Committee on
Banking, Housing and Urban Affairs, July 20, 2000

More and more, as the 1980s wore on, Fed spokesmen stressed the goal of price stability. The FOMC dropped the "reasonable" qualifier from "price stability" in its March 1988 Directive, telling Congress in February 1990 that it was "committed to the achievement, over time, of price stability," an "objective [which] derives from the fact that the prospects for long-run growth in the economy are brightest when inflation need no longer be a material consideration in the decisions of households and firms."[37]

Congress apparently acquiesced to the new unwritten contract, but this may not be an adequate picture of the determinants of the new monetary policy. Who was really running the show? Was the Fed leading or following? It is worth pointing out that the new American contract is like the more formal agreements elsewhere in following, rather than leading, the fall of the Phillips Curve and improved fiscal discipline by governments. We shall return to this momentarily.

. . . Compared with the Old . . .

The new commitments have famous precedents. The 1694 contract was between a government in need of finance and Bank investors in search of

---

[37] *Monetary Policy Report to the Congress*, pursuant to the Full Employment and Balanced Growth Act of 1978, February 20, 1990. Richard Timberlake notes the shift to the single goal of price stability in 1988 (*Monetary Policy in the United States*, p. 391).

profit. It was renewed several times under similar circumstances until a decade and a half after Waterloo, in a new era of peace and fiscal surpluses, the government looked coolly on the Bank – all the more so because of its ineptness in times of financial stress and because of the growing influence of competing interests. The government now wanted the Bank less for its own financial needs than as an instrument for the public welfare. The Bank was turned loose to pursue these public goals with transparency so that it and the government could be monitored. The Bank Charter Act of 1833, like the central bank contracts of the 1990s, may be understood more as a commitment to good behavior on the part of the government than as directions to the central bank. The Bank of England's independence of the government was made possible by the government's independence of the Bank.

This is also true of the new contracts, although the sources of the new independence are different. The end of belief in the capacity of monetary policy to achieve more than a single financial objective, price stability, lessened the need for government control of monetary policy. However, the promise alone was not enough. The conversion had to be validated by an end to the pressure of government deficits for monetary accommodation. The European Central Bank started on the same footing. The Maastricht Treaty of 1992 made its overriding goal "price stability" (which it has interpreted as less than 2-percent inflation). It stipulated that the Bank could not lend directly to member governments, and admission to the Euro system was made contingent on lower deficits than governments had been used to running.[38]

The ends of the Phillips Curve and Government deficits restored some of the former political strength to central banks. Governments still value the financial credibility that a conservative central bank can give, although improved taxing powers and credit ratings have dispensed with the necessity of conciliating central bank investors. With the advent of fiat money in the 1930s, central banks were more often than not treated as government departments. More recently, the desires for credible low-inflation monetary policies have led governments with profligate histories not unlike those of the Stuart kings to allow central banks degrees of independence that have given them some of the bargaining power of the Bank of

---

[38] The structure and goals of the ECB were specified in Title VI, "Economic and Monetary Policy," of the Maastricht Treaty of 1992; see Neville Hunnings and Joe Hill, *The Treaty of Rome Consolidated and the Treaty of Maastricht*, and Richard Corbett, *The Treaty of Maastricht*. The operational objective is from its 1999 *Annual Report*.

England in the 18th century. The "New Lady of Threadneedle Street," as the governor called the Bank in 1998, is a lot like the old.[39]

The new contracts almost restore the early simplicity of central bank commitments when they were only responsible for convertibility and financial stability. They are still responsible for financial stability, but the other goal has been replaced by price stability, which is tantamount to gold convertibility except into a market basket of goods.

. . . and Their Prospects

The new contracts (formal or, as in the United States, unilateral commitments) may be seen as (1) the end of the road in developing a new monetary policy that is better than the gold standard in the short run as well as for long-run price stability (or low inflation), (2) another postwar adjustment to be reversed when the government wants monetary support, or (3) a step in the transition to a monetary commitment with the credibility of the gold standard, possibly a form of that standard. Time will tell, but notable deviations from inflation targeting in the United States are suggestive.

The assurances of liquidity by substantial open market purchases at the turn of the millennium and after the 9/11 attacks of 2001 did not threaten the Fed's credibility. The occasions of such lending of last resort soon pass, the liquidity is soon withdrawn, and worries of inflation do not arise. They are similar to the seasonal variations in credit that the Fed has supplied since its beginning.

Apparent relapses to the Phillips Curve are more of a problem. Chairman Greenspan told the House Budget Committee during the 1990–91 recession,

The conduct of monetary policy . . . has involved a careful balancing of the need to respond to signs that economic activity was slowing perceptibly, on the one hand, and the need to contain inflationary pressures on the other.[40]

The same view was expressed by the FOMC during the next recession a decade later despite the unqualified commitment to price stability during the mid-1990s.[41] Do these statements mean that the Phillips Curve is still part of monetary policy? Or is it simply something to which the Fed must

---

[39] Edward George, "The New Lady of Threadneedle Street."
[40] Federal Reserve *Bulletin*, January 22, 1991.
[41] FOMC Minutes, November 15, 2000.

pay homage in times of rising unemployment? The steady rate of change of the gross domestic product deflator close to 2 percent between 1992 and 2003 bodes well for the future. The political costs of violating the new contracts could provide as much credibility as the gold standard, which itself was a political arrangement. The issue will be settled by experience. In any case, whatever the formal arrangements and stated commitments, our knowledge of the companies of merchants that will manage them tells us that much discretion will be involved. Conflicts between economists and central bankers, and between rules and discretion, will continue.

References

Acaster, E. J. "Henry Thornton – the Banker," *Three Banks Review*, December 1974, March and June 1975. (Reprinted Marc Blaug, *Pioneers in Economics*. Edward Elgar, 1991.)

Acheson, Dean. *Present at the Creation: My Years in the State Department*. W. W. Norton, 1969.

Acres, W. Marston. *The Bank of England from Within, 1694–1900*. Oxford University Press, 1931.

Acworth, A. W. *Financial Reconstruction in England, 1815–22*. P. S. King & Son, 1925.

Ahearn, Daniel S. *Federal Reserve Policy Reappraised, 1951–59*. Columbia University Press, 1963.

Anderson, Clay J. *A Half-Century of Federal Reserve Policymaking, 1914–64*. Federal Reserve Bank of Philadelphia, 1965.

Anderson, Richard G. and Thornton, Daniel L. "The FOMC's 'Considerable Period'," Federal Reserve Bank of St. Louis *Monetary Trends*, February, 2004, 1.

Andreades, A. *History of the Bank of England*. P. S. King & Son, 1909.

Andrew, A. Piatt. "Substitutes for Cash in the Panic of 1907," *Quarterly Journal of Economics*, August 1908, 497–524. (Reprinted Sprague, *History of Crises*.)

Anonymous. *Note on the Suspension of Cash Payments at the Bank of England in 1797*. (Reprinted McCulloch, *Select Collection of Scarce and Valuable Tracts on Paper Currency and Banking*.)

Ashley, W. J. *The Adjustment of Wages*. Longmans, Green, 1903.

Ashton, T. S. and Sayers, R. S., eds. *Papers in English Monetary History*. Clarendon Press, 1953.

Ashworth, William. *An Economic History of England, 1870–1939*. Methuen, 1960.

Aspinall, A., ed. *Three Early Nineteenth Century Diaries*. Williams and Norgate, 1952.

Attwood, Thomas. *Prosperity Restored, or Reflections on the Cause of the Public Distresses and on the Only Means of Relieving Them*. Baldwin, Cradock, and Jay, 1817.

——. *A Letter to the Earl of Liverpool on the Reports of the Committees of the Two Houses of Parliament on the Questions of the Bank Restriction Act*. R. Wrightson, 1819. (Reprinted Attwood, *Selected Writings*. Frank W. Fetter, ed., London School of Economics and Political Science, 1964.)

——. "Famine," *The Globe*, June 11, 1828. (Reprinted Attwood, *The Scotch Banker*, 2nd ed., James Ridgway, 1832; Capie, *History*.)

Bagehot, Walter. "What a Panic Is and How It Might Be Mitigated," *Economist*, May 12, 1866, 554–55. (Reprinted Collins, *Central Banking*.)

——. *Lombard Street*. Henry King, 1873. (Reprinted with updated examples, John Murray, 1917.)

Bank of England. *Representation by the Directors to the Chancellor of the Exchequer*, May 20, 1819. (*British Parliamentary Papers, Monetary Policy, General*, 2, 359–62.)

——. *The Development and Operation of Monetary Policy, 1960–83: A Selection of Material from the Quarterly Bulletin*. Clarendon Press, 1984.

Baring, Francis. *Observations on the Establishment of the Bank of England and on the Paper Circulation of the Country*. Minerva Press, 1797. (Reprinted with *Further Observations*, Augustus M. Kelley, 1967.)

Beard, Charles. *Economic Origins of Jeffersonian Democracy*. Macmillan, 1915.

Bernanke, Ben S. "Nonmonetary Effects of the Financial Crises in the Propagation of the Great Depression," *American Economic Review*, June 1983, 257–76.

Bernanke, Ben S., Laubach, Thomas, Mishkin, Frederic S., and Posen, Adam S. *Inflation Targeting: Lessons from the International Experience*. Princeton University Press, 1999.

Bernholz, Peter. *Flexible Exchange Rates in Historical Perspective*. Princeton Studies in International Finance 49, July 1982.

Berry, Thomas S. *Production and Employment since 1789*, Bostwick Paper 6. Bostwick Press, 1988.

Beveridge, William. *Unemployment: A Problem of Industry*. Longmans, Green, 1909, 1930.

Bierwag, G. O. and Grove, M. A. "A Model of the Structure of Prices of Marketable U.S. Treasury Securities," *Journal of Money, Credit and Banking*, August 1971, 605–29.

Birkenhead, Earl of (F. E. Smith). *The Professor and the Prime Minister: The Official Life of Professor F.A. Lindemann, Viscount Cherwell*. Houghton Mifflin, 1962.

Blackstone, William. *Commentaries on the Laws of England*. Clarendon Press, 1765–69.

Blaine, James G. *Twenty Years in Congress*. Henry Bill, 1886.

Blinder, Alan S. *Economic Policy and the Great Stagflation*. Academic Press, 1979.

——."Central Banking in a Democracy," *Federal Reserve Bank of Richmond Economic Quarterly*, Fall 1996, 1–14.

——. "What Central Bankers Could Learn from Academics – and Vice Versa," *Journal of Economic Perspectives*, Spring 1997, 3–19.

Bloomfield, Arthur I. *Monetary Policy under the International Gold Standard, 1880–1914.* Federal Reserve Bank of New York, 1959.

Blum, John M. *Roosevelt and Morgenthau: A Revision and Condensation of "From the Morgenthau Diaries."* Houghton Mifflin, 1970.

Bordo, Michael D. and Eichengreen, Barry, eds. *A Retrospective on the Bretton Woods System: Lessons for International Monetary Reform.* University of Chicago Press, 1993.

Bordo, Michael D. and Kydland, Finn E. "The Gold Standard as a Commitment Mechanism," in Tamin Bayoumi et al., eds., *Modern Perspectives on the Gold Standard.* Cambridge University Press, 1996.

Bordo, Michael D. and White, Eugene N. "A Tale of Two Currencies: British and French Finance during the Napoleonic Wars," *Journal of Economic History* 51, June 1991, 303–16.

Bosanquet, J. W. *Metallic, Paper and Credit Currency, and the Means of Regulating Their Quantity and Value.* Pelham Richardson, 1842.

Bourne, Edward G. *The History of the Surplus Revenue of 1837.* G. P. Putnam's Sons, 1885.

Bowley, A. L. *Wages in the United Kingdom in the 19th Century.* Cambridge University Press, 1900. (Reprinted A. M. Kelley, 1972.)

Boyd, Walter. *A Letter to the Right Honourable William Pitt on the Influence of the Stoppage of Issues in Specie at the Bank of England on the Prices of Provisions and Other Commodities.* J. Wright, 1801. (Reprinted O'Brien, *Foundations.*)

Boyle, Andrew. *Montagu Norman.* Cassell, 1967.

Bratter, Herbert. "The Federal Reserve's Independence," *Banking* 53, September 1960, 90–91, 124.

British Parliamentary Papers. Irish University Press, 1969.

Brittan, Samuel. *Steering the Economy.* Penguin Books, 1971.

Brown, George. *In My Way.* St. Martins, 1971.

Browning, Peter. *The Treasury and Economic Policy, 1964–85.* Longman, 1986.

Brunner, Karl and Meltzer, Allan H. *The Federal Reserve's Attachment to the Free Reserve Concept.* For the Subcommittee on Domestic Finance, *The Federal Reserve after Fifty Years.* House Committee on Banking and Currency. U.S. Government Printing Office, 1964. (Reprinted Brunner and Meltzer, *Monetary Economics.* Basil Blackwell, 1989.)

——. *Some General Features of the Federal Reserve's Approach to Policy.* For the Subcommittee on Domestic Finance, *The Federal Reserve after Fifty Years.* House Committee on Banking and Currency. U. S. Government Printing Office, 1964.

——. "What Did We Learn from the Monetary Experience of the United States in the Great Depression?" *Canadian Journal of Economics*, May 1968, 334–48.

Burgess, W. Randolph. *The Reserve Banks and the Money Market* (1927), 2nd ed. Harper, 1936.

Burner, David. *Herbert Hoover: A Public Life.* Knopf, 1979.

Burns, Arthur F. *Reflections of an Economic Policy Maker: Speeches and Congressional Statements, 1969–78.* American Enterprise Institute, 1978.

Burns, Arthur F. and Mitchell, W. C. *Measuring Business Cycles.* National Bureau of Economic Research, 1946.

Burns, Helen M. *The American Banking Community and New Deal Banking Reforms, 1933–35.* Greenwood Press, 1974.

Cairncross, Alec and Watts, Nita. *The Economic Section 1939–61: A Study in Economic Advising.* Routledge, 1989.

Callaghan, James. *Time and Chance.* Collins, 1987.

Calomiris, Charles W. and Wheelock, David C. "Was the Great Depression a Watershed for American Monetary Policy?," in Michael Bordo et al., eds., *The Defining Moment: The Great Depression and the American Economy in the Twentieth Century.* University of Chicago Press, 1998.

Cannan, Edwin. *The Paper Pound of 1797–1821: A Reprint of the Bullion Report with an Introduction.* P. S. King & Son, 1919.

Cantillon, Richard. *Essay on the Nature of Trade in General* (1755). Trans. from French by Henry Higgs. Macmillan, 1931. (Reprinted Augustus Kelley, 1964.)

Canzoneri, Matthew B. "Monetary Policy Games and the Role of Private Information," *American Economic Review*, December 1985, 1056–70.

Canzoneri, Matthew B. Grilli, Vittorio, and Masson, Paul R. *Establishing a Central Bank: Issues in Europe and Lessons from the U.S.* Cambridge University Press, 1992.

Capie, Forrest H., ed. *History of Banking.* Pickering, 1993.

Canzoneri, Matthew B. Goodhart, C. A. E., Fischer, Stanley, and Schnadt, Norbert, eds. *The Future of Central Banking: The Tercentenary Symposium of the Bank of England.* Cambridge University Press, 1994.

Canzoneri, Matthew B. and Webber, Alan, eds. *A Monetary History of the United Kingdom, 1870–1982.* George Allen & Unwin, 1985.

Canzoneri, Matthew B. and Wood, Geoffrey, eds. *Financial Crises and the World Banking System.* Macmillan, 1986.

Carosso, Vincent P. and Sylla, Richard. "U.S. Banks in International Finance," in Rondo Cameron and V. Borrykin, eds. *International Banking, 1870–1914.* Oxford University Press, 1991.

Catterall, R. C. H. *The Second Bank of the United States.* University of Chicago Press, 1902.

Chandler, Lester V. *Benjamin Strong, Central Banker.* Brookings Institution, 1958.
——. *American Monetary Policy, 1928–41.* Harper & Row, 1971.

Chandos, Lord (Oliver Lyttleton). *Memoirs.* Bodley Head, 1962.

Chapman, Richard A. *Decision Making: A Case Study of the Decision to Raise the Bank Rate in September 1957.* Routledge & Kegan Paul, 1968.

Chappell, Henry, Jr. and McGregor, Rob Roy. "A Long History of FOMC Voting Behavior," *Southern Economic Journal*, April 2000, 906–22.

Checkland, S. G. *Scottish Banking: A History, 1695–1973.* Collins, 1975.

Child, Josiah. *A Discourse about Trade; Wherein the Reduction of Interest in Money to 43/4 per Centum Is Recommended, etc.* A. Sowle, 1690.

Christelow, Dorothy B. "Britain's New Monetary Control System," *Federal Reserve Bank of New York Monthly Review*, January 1974, 12–24.

Church, R. A. *The Great Victorian Boom, 1850–73*. Macmillan, 1975.

Clapham, J. H. *An Economic History of Modern Britain*. Cambridge University Press, 1926–38.

——. *The Bank of England: A History*. Cambridge University Press, 1944.

Clark, Lawrence. *Central Banking under the Federal Reserve System*. Macmillan, 1935.

Clarke, M. St. Clair, and Hall, D. A., eds. *Documentary History of the Bank of the United States*. Gales and Seaton, 1832. (Reprinted Augustus Kelley, 1967.)

Clarke, Peter. *The Keynesian Revolution in the Making, 1924–36*. Clarendon Press, 1988.

Clarke, Steven V. O. *Central Bank Cooperation, 1924–31*. Federal Reserve Bank of New York, 1967.

Clay, Henry. "The Public Regulation of Wages in Great Britain," *Economic Journal*, September 1929, 323–43.

——. *Montagu Norman*. Macmillan, 1957.

Cloos, George W. "Monetary Conditions from the 1937–38 Recession to Pearl Harbor," *Financial Analysts Journal*, January-February 1966, 1–7.

Cobbett, William. *Paper against Gold and Glory against Prosperity*. J. McCreery, 1815.

Collins, Michael, ed. *Central Banking in History*. Edward Elgar, 1993.

Committee on Finance and Industry (Macmillan), *Report*, Command 3897. HMSO, 1931.

Committee on the Working of the Monetary System (Radcliffe). *Report*, Command 827. HMSO, 1959.

Corbett, Richard. *The Treaty of Maastricht*. Longman, 1993.

Cottrell, P. L. and Anderson, B. L., eds. *Money and Banking in England: The Development of the Banking System*. David & Charles, 1974.

Council of Prices, Productivity and Incomes. *Reports*. HMSO, February and August 1958.

Court, W. H. B. *British Economic History, 1870–1914: Commentary and Documents*. Cambridge University Press, 1965.

Crossman, Richard. *Diaries*, Anthony Howard, ed. Hamilton and Cape, 1979.

Crouzet, Francois. *The Victorian Economy*. Trans. from French by A. S. Forster. Methuen, 1982.

Dam, Kenneth W. *The Rules of the Game: Reform and Evolution in the International Monetary System*. University of Chicago Press, 1982.

Daugherty, Marion R. "The Banking-Currency Controversy," *Southern Economic Journal*, October 1942, 140–55, January 1943, 241–51.

de Grauwe, Paul, Janssens, Marc, and Leliaert, Hilde. *Real Exchange-Rate Variability from 1920 to 1926 and 1973 to 1982*. Princeton Studies in International Finance 56, September 1985.

de Leeuw, Frank and Gramlich, Edward. "The Federal Reserve–MIT Econometric Model," *Federal Reserve Bulletin*, January 1968, 11–40.

Dewald, William G. "The National Monetary Commission: A Look Back," *Journal of Money, Credit and Banking*, November 1972, 930–56.

Dewey, Davis R. *Financial History of the United States*, 2nd ed. Longmans, Green, 1903.

Dewey, Davis R. and Shugrue, Martin. *Banking and Credit*. Ronald Press, 1922.

Dicey, A. V. *Lectures on the Relation between Law and Public Opinion in England during the Nineteenth Century*, 2nd ed. Macmillan, 1914.

——. *Introduction to the Study of the Law of the Constitution*, 8th ed. Macmillan, 1915.

Dickson, P. G. M. *The Financial Revolution in England: A Study in the Development of Public Credit, 1688–1756*. Macmillan, 1967.

Dornbusch, Rudiger. "Comment," in Bordo and Eichengreen, eds., *Retrospective on Bretton Woods*.

Douglas, Roy. *Taxation in Britain since 1660*. Macmillan, 1999.

Dow, J. C. R. *The Management of the British Economy, 1945–60*. Cambridge University Press, 1964.

Eccles, Marriner. *Beckoning Frontiers*. Knopf, 1951.

Eichengreen, Barry. *Golden Fetters: The Gold Standard and the Great Depression, 1919–1939*. Oxford University Press, 1992.

Einzig, Paul. *Montagu Norman*. Kegan Paul, Trench, Trubner, 1932.

Eisner, Robert. "Fiscal and Monetary Policy Reconsidered," *American Economic Review*, December 1969, 897–905.

Ellis, Howard S. and Metzler, Lloyd A., eds. *Readings in the Theory of International Trade*. Blakiston, 1950.

Feavearyear, A. E. *The Pound Sterling*. Clarendon Press, 1931.

Federal Open Market Committee, *Report of the Ad Hoc Subcommittee on the Government Securities Market*, 1952. (U.S. Congress, *United States Monetary Policy*, December 1954.)

Federal Reserve Board. *Minutes of Conference of the Federal Reserve Board with the Federal Advisory Council and the Class A Directors of the Federal Reserve Banks*, May 18, 1920. Senate Doc. No. 310, 67th Cong., 4th sess., 1923.

——. *Banking and Monetary Statistics, 1914–41, 1941–70*, 1943, 1976.

——. *Historical Chart Book*. Annual.

——. "Processes and Procedure Involved in the Formulation and Executing Monetary Policy," in Commission on Money and Credit, *The Federal Reserve and the Treasury: Answers to Questions*. Prentice-Hall, 1963.

——. *The Federal Reserve System: Purposes & Functions*, 7th ed. 1984 (later editions on Federal Reserve Board Web site).

——. "Monetary Policy Report to Congress," Federal Reserve *Bulletin*, various issues.

Feinman, Joshua and Poole, William. "Federal Reserve Policymaking: An Overview and Analysis of the Policy Process: A Comment," in Brunner and Meltzer, eds., *Carnegie-Rochester Series on Public Policy* 30, Spring 1989, 63–74.

Feldstein, Martin S. "Lessons of the Bretton Woods Experience," in Bordo and Eichengreen, eds., *Retrospective on Bretton Woods*.

Fetter, Frank W. *The Irish Pound, 1797–1826*. George Allen & Unwin, 1955.

——. *Development of British Monetary Orthodoxy, 1797–1875*. Harvard University Press, 1965.

——. "Lenin, Keynes and Inflation," *Economica*, February 1977, 77–80.

Fforde, J. S. *The Federal Reserve System, 1945–49*. Clarendon Press, 1954.

——. "Setting Monetary Objectives," Bank of England *Quarterly Bulletin*, June 1983. (Reprinted Bank of England, *Development and Operation of Monetary Policy*.)

——. *The Bank of England and Public Policy, 1941–58*. Cambridge University Press, 1992.

Fisher, Irving. *Appreciation and Interest*. Macmillan, 1896.

——. *The Purchasing Power of Money*. Macmillan, 1911.

——. *Stabilizing the Dollar; a Plan to Stabilize the General Price Level without Fixing Individual Prices*. Macmillan, 1920.

——. *The Theory of Interest*. Macmillan, 1930.

——. "The Debt-Deflation Theory of Great Depressions," *Econometrica*, October 1933, 337–57.

Fleetwood, William. *Chronicon Preciosum: Or an Account of English Gold and Silver Money; the Price of Corn and Other Commodities for Six Hundred Years*. T. Osborne, 1745.

Foot, M. D. K. W., Goodhart, C. A. E., and Hotson, A. C., "Monetary Base Control," Bank of England *Quarterly Bulletin*, June 1979. (Reprinted Bank of England, *Development and Operation of Monetary Policy*.)

Fortune, Thomas. *A Concise and Authentic History of the Bank of England*. Boosey, 1797. (Reprinted Capie, *History*.)

Friedman, Milton. "The Case for Flexible Exchange Rates," in Friedman, *Essays in Positive Economics*. University of Chicago Press, 1953.

——. *A Program for Monetary Stability*. Fordham University Press, 1960.

——. *Capitalism and Freedom*. University of Chicago Press, 1962.

——. "The Monetary Theory and Policy of Henry Simons," *Journal of Law and Economics*, October 1967, 1–13. (Reprinted Friedman, *Optimum Quantity of Money and Other Essays*. Aldine, 1969.)

——. "The Federal Reserve and Monetary Instability," *Wall Street Journal*, February 1, 1982, 16.

——. "A Tale of Fed Transcripts," *Wall Street Journal,* December 20, 1993, A12.

Friedman, Milton and Roosa, Robert V. *The Balance of Payments: Free versus Fixed Exchange Rates*. American Enterprise Institute, 1967.

Friedman, Milton and Schwartz, Anna J. *A Monetary History of the United States, 1867–1960*. Princeton University Press, 1963.

Frisch, Ragnar. "Editorial," *Econometrica*, January 1933, 1–4.

Fullerton, Thomas M., Hirth, Richard A., and Smith, Mark B. "Inflationary Dynamics and the Angell–Johnson Proposals," *Atlantic Economic Journal*, March 1991, 1–14.

Furlong, Fred and Ingenito, Robert. "Commodity Prices and Inflation," *Federal Reserve Bank of San Francisco Economic Review*, 2, 1996, 27–47.

Furniss, Edgar S. *Labor Problems*. Houghton Mifflin, 1925.

Gallarotti, Giulio M. "The Scramble for Gold: Monetary Regime Transformation in the 1870s," in Michael Bordo and Forrest Capie, eds., *Monetary Regimes in Transition*. Cambridge University Press, 1993.

Gallatin, Albert. *Writings*. Henry Adams, ed. (1879). Reprinted Antiquarian Press, 1960.

——. *Considerations on the Currency and Banking System of the United States*. Carey and Lea, 1831. (*Writings*.)

——. *Suggestions on the Banks and Currency of the Several United States*. Wiley & Putnam, 1841. (*Writings*, iii.)

Gardner, Richard N. *Sterling–Dollar Diplomacy*. Oxford University Press, 1956; 2nd ed., McGraw-Hill, 1969.

Garfinkel, Michelle R. and Oh, Seonghwan. "Strategic Discipline in Monetary Policy with Private Information: Optimal Targeting Horizons," *American Economic Review*, March 1993, 99–117.

Gayer, Arthur D., Rostow, W. W., and Schwartz, Anna J. *Growth and Fluctuation of the British Economy, 1790–1850*. Clarendon Press, 1953.

George, Edward. "The New Lady of Threadneedle Street," *Bank of England Quarterly Bulletin*, May 1998, 173–77.

Gilbart, J. W. *An Inquiry into the Causes of the Pressure on the Money Market during the Year 1839*. Longman, Orme, Brown, Green, and Longmans, 1840.

——. *A Practical Treatise on Banking*, 6th ed. Longman, Brown, Green, and Longmans, 1856.

Gilbert, Martin. *Winston S. Churchill*, 8 vols. (vols. 1–2 by Randolph Churchill). Heinemann, 1966–88.

Gildea, John A. "The Regional Representation of Federal Reserve Bank Presidents," *Journal of Money, Credit and Banking*, May 1992, 215–25.

Gilman, Theodore. *A Graded Banking System*. Houghton Mifflin, 1898.

Giovannini, Alberto. "Bretton Woods and Its Precursors: Rules versus Discretion in the History of International Monetary Regimes," in Bordo and Eichengreen, eds., *Retrospective on Bretton Woods*.

Glass, Carter. *An Adventure in Constructive Finance*. Doubleday, Page, 1927.

Goldenweiser, E. A. *Federal Reserve System in Operation*. McGraw-Hill, 1925.

——. "Instruments of Federal Reserve Policy," in *Federal Reserve Board, Banking Studies*, 1941.

——. *American Monetary Policy*. McGraw-Hill, 1951.

Goodfriend, Marvin. "Monetary Mystique: Secrecy and Central Banking," *Journal of Monetary Economics* 17, January 1986, 63–92.

Goodfriend, Marvin and Lacker, Jeffrey M. "Limited Commitment and Central Bank Lending," *Federal Reserve Bank of Richmond Economic Quarterly*, Fall 1999, 1–27.

Gordon, Robert J., ed. *The American Business Cycle*. University of Chicago Press, 1986.

Gordon, Robert J. and Balke, Nathan S. "Appendix B: Historical Data," in Gordon, ed., *The American Business Cycle*.

Gorton, Gary. "Private Clearinghouses and the Origins of Central Banking," *Federal Reserve Bank of Philadelphia Business Review* January/February 1984, 3–12.

Goschen, G. J. "Speech to Leeds Incorporated Chamber of Commerce," *Times*, January 29, 1891. (Reprinted Duncan Ross, *History of Banking*. Pickering & Chatto, 1998.)

Gouge, William M. *A Short History of Paper Money and Banking in the United States*. Grigg & Elliott, 1833. (Reprinted A. M. Kelley, 1968.)

Graham, Frank D. and Whittlesey, Charles R. *Golden Avalanche*. Princeton University Press, 1939.

Greenspan, Alan. "Discussion," in Capie, ed., *Future of Central Banking*.

Gregory, T. E., ed. *Select Statutes, Documents & Reports Relating to British Banking, 1832–1928*. Oxford University Press, 1929.

Greider, William. *Secrets of the Temple: How the Federal Reserve Runs the Country*. Simon & Schuster, 1987.

Grigg, P. J. *Prejudice and Judgment*. Jonathan Cape, 1948.

Hall, Robert L. *Diaries 1947–53*. Alec Cairncross, ed. Unwin Hyman, 1989.

Hall, Robert L. and Hitch, C. J. "Price Theory and Business Behavior," *Oxford Economic Papers*, May 1939, 12–45. (Reprinted Thomas Wilson and P. W. S. Andrews, *Oxford Studies in the Price Mechanism*. Clarendon Press, 1951.)

Hall, Maximilian. *Monetary Policy since 1971*. Macmillan, 1983.

Hall, Walter. *A View of Our Late and of Our Future Currency*. J. M. Richardson, 1819.

Hamby, Alonzo L. *Man of the People: A Life of Harry S. Truman*. Oxford University Press, 1995.

Hamilton, Alexander. *Report on a National Bank*, Treasury Department, 1790. (Reprinted Krooss, *Documentary History*.)

Hammond, W. Bray. *Banks and Politics in America from the Revolution to the Civil War*. Princeton University Press, 1957.

Hankey, Thomson. *The Principles of Banking, Its Utility and Economy; with Remarks on the Working and Management of the Bank of England*. Effingham Wilson, 1867.

Hansard Parliamentary Debates. Parliament, 1803–1973.

Hansen, Alvin. "Monetary Policy," *Review of Economics and Statistics*, May 1955, 110–19.

Harding, W. P. G. *The Formative Period of the Federal Reserve System*. Houghton Mifflin, 1925.

Hargrove, Erwin C. and Morley, Samuel A. *The President and the Council of Economic Advisors: Interviews with CEA Chairmen*. Westview Press, 1984.

Harr, Luther and Harris, W. Carlton. *Banking Theory and Practice*, 2nd ed. McGraw-Hill, 1936.

Harris, Seymour E. *Twenty Years of Federal Reserve Policy*. Harvard University Press, 1933.

Harrod, R. F. *The Life of John Maynard Keynes*. Macmillan, 1951.

Havrilesky, Thomas. *The Pressures on American Monetary Policy*. Kluwer, 1993.

Havrilesky, Thomas and Gildea, John. "The Biases of Federal Reserve Bank Presidents," *Economic Inquiry*, April 1995, 274–84.

Hawtrey, R. G. *The Art of Central Banking*. Longmans, Green, 1932. (Reprinted A. M. Kelley, 1962.)

———. *A Century of Bank Rate*. Longmans, Green, 1938; 2nd ed., Frank Cass, 1962.

Hawtrey, R. G. *Currency and Credit*. Longmans, Green, 1919.

Hayek, F. A. *Prices and Production*. Kegan Paul, 1931; 2nd ed., 1935.

———. "The Fate of the Gold Standard," 1932. (Reprinted R. McCloughy, *Money, Capital and Fluctuations: Early Essays of F. A. Hayek*. Routledge & Kegan Paul, 1984.)

Hayes, Alfred. "The 1966 Credit Crunch," in David Eastburn, ed., *Essays in Honor of Karl Bopp*. Federal Reserve Bank of Philadelphia, 1970.

Healey, Denis. *The Time of My Life*. Michael Joseph, 1989.

Hennessy, Elizabeth. *A Domestic History of the Bank of England, 1930–60.* Cambridge University Press, 1992.

——. "The Governors, Directors and Management of the Bank of England," in Roberts and Kynaston, eds., *Bank of England.*

Hepburn, A. Barton. *History of Coinage and Currency in the United States and the Perennial Contest for Sound Money.* Macmillan, 1903.

Hicks, J. R. "The Theory of Monopoly," *Econometrica*, January 1935, 1–20.

Highfield, Richard A., O'Hara, Maureen, and Wood, John H. "Public Ends, Private Means: Central Banking and the Profit Motive, 1823–32," *Journal of Monetary Economics*, October 1991, 287–322.

Hilton, Boyd. *Corn, Cash, Commerce: The Economic Policies of the Tory Governments, 1815–30.* Oxford University Press, 1977.

Hirsch, Fred. "The Bagehot Problem," *Manchester School of Economic and Social Studies*, September 1977, 241–57. (Reprinted Collins, *Central Banking.*)

Holmes, Geoffrey. *The Making of a Great Power: Late Stuart and Early Georgian Britain, 1660–1722.* Longman, 1993.

Homer, Sidney and Sylla, Richard. *A History of Interest Rates*, 3rd ed. Rutgers University Press, 1991.

Hoover, Herbert C. *Memoirs: The Great Depression, 1929–41.* Macmillan, 1952.

Hoppit, Julian. "Financial Crises in Eighteenth-Century England," *Economic History Review*, February 1986, 39–58.

Horner, Francis. "Review of Thornton on the Paper Credit of Great Britain," *Edinburgh Review*, October 1802, 172–201. (Reprinted in Frank Fetter, ed., *The Economic Writings of Francis Horner in the Edinburgh Review, 1802–1806.* London School of Economics and Political Science, 1957.)

Horsefield, J. Keith. "The Duties of a Banker: The Eighteenth-Century View," *Economica*, February 1941, 37–51. (Reprinted Ashton and Sayers, *Papers.*)

——. "The Duties of a Banker: The Effects of Inconvertibility," *Economica*, May 1944, 74–85. (Reprinted Ashton and Sayers, *Papers.*)

——. "The Origins of the Bank Charter Act, 1844," *Economica*, November 1944, 180–89. (Reprinted Ashton and Sayers, *Papers.*)

——. *British Monetary Experiments, 1650–1710.* Harvard University Press, 1960.

——. "The 'Stop of the Exchequer' Revisited," *Economic History Review*, November 1982, 489–510.

Horwich, George. "Tight Money, Monetary Restraint and the Price Level," *Journal of Finance*, March 1966, 15–33.

House of Commons. *Report from the Select Committee Appointed to Take into Consideration the Present State of Commercial Credit and to Report Their Opinion and Observations Thereupon to the House*, April 29, 1793. (*British Parliamentary Papers, Monetary Policy, General, 1.*)

——. *Third Report from the Committee of Secrecy on the Outstanding Demands of the Bank of England*, April 21, 1797. (*BPP, Monetary Policy, General, 1.*)

——. *Report from the Committee on the Circulating Paper, the Specie and the Current Coin of Ireland; and Also on the Exchange between That Part of the United Kingdom and Great Britain.* May and June 1804. (Reprinted Fetter, *Irish Pound.*)

——. *Second Report from the Committee on the Public Expenditure etc. of the United Kingdom: The Bank*, August 10, 1807. (*BPP, Monetary Policy, General, 1.*)

——. *Report, Together with Minutes of Evidence, and Accounts, from the Select Committee on the High Price of Bullion*, June, 8, 1810. (*BPP, Monetary Policy, General, 1.*)

——. *Second Report from the Secret Committee on the Expediency of the Bank Resuming Cash Payments*, May 6, 1819. (*BPP, Monetary Policy, General, 2.*)

——. *Report from the Committee of Secrecy on the Bank of England Charter.* August 11, 1832. (*BPP, Monetary Policy, General, 4.*)

——. *Reports from the Select Committees on Banks of Issue*, August 7, 1840, and September 6, 1841. (*BPP, Monetary Policy, General, 5–6.*)

——. *Reports from the Secret Committee on Commercial Distress*, June 8 and August 2, 1848. (*BPP, Monetary Policy, Commercial Distress, 1–2.*)

——. *Report from the Select Committee on Bank Acts*, together with the proceedings of the Committee and minutes of evidence, July 1857.

——. *Royal Commission on Indian Currency and Finance. Minutes of Evidence.* 1926.

House of Lords. *Report of the Committee of Secrecy to Inquire into the Causes Which Produced the Order of Council of the 26th* of February 1797 and Minutes of Evidence *(BPP, Monetary Policy, General, 1.)*

——. *Report from the Secret Committee to Inquire into the Causes of the Distress Which Has for Some Time Prevailed among the Commercial Classes, and How Far It Has Been Affected by the Laws for Regulating the Issue of Bank Notes Payable on Demand*, July 29, 1848. (*BPP, Monetary Policy, Commercial Distress, 3.*)

Howson, Susan. *Domestic Monetary Management in Britain, 1919–38*. Cambridge University Press, 1975.

——. *British Monetary Policy, 1945–51*. Clarendon Press, 1993.

Hume, David. *Writings on Economics*. Eugene Rotwein, ed. University of Wisconsin Press, 1970.

Hunnings, Neville M. and Hill, Joe, M. *The Treaty of Rome Consolidated and the Treaty of Maastricht*. European Law Centre, 1992.

Huskisson, William. *The Question Concerning the Depreciation of Our Currency Stated and Examined*, 3rd ed. John Murray, 1810. (Reprinted McCulloch, *Select Collection of Scarce and Valuable Tracts and other Publications on Paper Currency and Banking*.)

Hutchison, T. W. *Economics and Economic Policy in Britain, 1946–66*. George Allen and Unwin, 1968.

James, Harold. *International Monetary Cooperation since Bretton Woods*. Oxford University Press, 1996.

James, John A. "The Conundrum of the Low Issue of National Bank Notes," *Journal of Political Economy*, April 1976, 359–67.

Jastram, Roy W. *The Golden Constant: The English and American Experience, 1560–1967*. Wiley, 1977.

Jevons, W. S. *Investigations in Currency and Finance*. Macmillan, 1884.

Johnson, G. Griffith. *The Treasury and Monetary Policy, 1933–38*. Russell & Russell, 1939.

Johnson, Harry G. "An Overview of Price Levels, Employment, and the U.S. Balance of Payments," *Journal of Business*, July 1963, 279–89.

Jones, Kit. *An Economist among Mandarins: A Biography of Robert Hall, 1901–88.* Cambridge University Press, 1994.

Joplin, Thomas. *An Essay on the General Principles and Present Practice of Banking.* Baldwin, Cradock, and Joy, 1822.

Karamouzis, Nicholas and Lombra, Raymond. "Federal Reserve Policymaking: An Overview and Analysis of the Policy Process," in Brunner and Meltzer, eds., *International Debt, Federal Reserve Operations and Other Essays.* Carnegie-Rochester Series on Public Policy 30. North-Holland, 1989.

Katz, Samuel I. *Sterling Speculation and European Convertibility, 1955–58.* Princeton Essays in International Finance 37, October 1961.

Kemmerer, E. W. *Seasonal Variations in the Relative Demand for Money and Capital in the United States* (National Monetary Commission). U.S. Government Printing Office, 1910.

Kettl, Donald F. *Leadership at the Fed.* Yale University Press, 1973.

Keynes, J. M. *Collected Writings.* D. E. Moggridge, ed. Macmillan, 1971–89.

——. *Indian Currency and Finance.* Macmillan, 1913.

——. "Memorandum on Proposals for the Establishment of a State Bank in India," Appendix to *Report of Royal Commission on Indian Currency and Finance*, 1914. (*Writings*, xv.)

——. *Economic Consequences of the Peace.* Macmillan, 1919.

——. *A Tract on Monetary Reform.* Macmillan, 1923.

——. "The Economic Consequences of Mr. Churchill," *Evening Standard*, July 22, 23, 24, 1925. (*Essays in Persuasion, Writings*, ix.)

——. *A Treatise on Money.* Macmillan, 1930.

——. *The General Theory of Employment, Interest and Money.* Macmillan, 1936.

Keynes, J. M. and Henderson, Hubert D. *Can Lloyd George Do It? – The Pledge Examined.* The Nation, 1929. (Chaps. 3, 9, 10, and 11 Reprinted in *Essays in Persuasion, Writings*, ix.)

King, W. T. C. "Should Liquidity Ratios Be Prescribed?," *The Banker*, April 1956, 186–97.

Kinley, David. *The Independent Treasury of the United States and Its Relations to the Banks of the Country* (National Monetary Commission). U.S. Government Printing Office, 1910.

Klein, Judy L. *Statistical Visions in Time: A History of Time Series Analysis, 1662–1938.* Cambridge University Press, 1997.

Kolko, Gabriel. *The Triumph of Conservatism: A Reinterpretation of American History, 1900–1916.* Macmillan, 1963.

Krooss, Herman E., ed. *Documentary History of Banking and Currency in the United States.* Chelsea House, 1969.

Kydland, Finn and Prescott, Edward. "Rules Rather Than Discretion: The Inconsistency of Optimal Plans," *Journal of Political Economy*, June 1977, 473–90.

Kynaston, David. *The City of London: A World of Its Own, 1815–90.* Pimlico, 1988.

——. "The Bank and the Government," in Roberts and Kynaston, eds., *Bank of England*.

Laidler, D. E. W. "Thomas Tooke on Monetary Reform," in Maurice Peston and Bernard Corry, eds., *Essays in Honour of Lord Robbins*. Weidenfeld and Nicolson, 1972.

Laughlin, J. Laurence. *Banking Reform*. National Citizens League for the Promotion of a Sound Banking System, 1912.

Laurent, Robert D. "Lagged Reserve Accounting and the Fed's New Operating Procedure," Federal Reserve Bank of Chicago *Economic Perspectives*, Midyear 1982, 32–43.

Lavington, F. *The Trade Cycle*. King, 1925.

Law, John. *Money and Trade Considered, with a Proposal for Supplying the Nation with Money*. Anderson, 1705.

Lawson, Nigel. *The View from No. 11: Memoirs of a Tory Radical*. Bantam, 1992.

Leffingwell, Russell C. "The Discount Policy of the Federal Reserve Banks: Discussion," *American Economic Review*, March 1921, 30–36.

Lent, George E. *The Impact of the Undistributed Profits Tax, 1936–37*. Columbia University Press, 1948.

Levin, Fred J. and Meulendyke, Ann-Marie. "Monetary Policy and Open Market Operations in 1978," Federal Reserve Bank of New York *Quarterly Review*, Spring 1979, 53–66.

Link, Arthur S. *Wilson: The New Freedom*. Princeton University Press, 1956.

Liverpool, Earl (Charles Jenkinson). *A Treatise on the Coins of the Realm, in a Letter to the King*. 1805. (Reprinted McCulloch, *A Select Collection of Scarce and Valuable Tracts and other Publications on Paper Currency and Banking*.)

Livingston, James. *Origins of the Federal Reserve System: Money, Class, and Corporate Capitalism, 1890–1913*. Cornell University Press, 1986.

Locke, John. *Some Considerations of the Consequences of the Lowering of Interest and Raising the Value of Money* (1691). 2nd ed. in *Several Papers Relating to Money, Interest and Trade*. A. and J. Churchill, 1696. (Reprinted A. M. Kelley, 1989.)

Lombra, Raymond E. "Reflections on Burns's Reflections," *Journal of Money, Credit and Banking*, February 1980, 94–105.

Loyd, Samuel Jones. *Remarks on the Management of the Circulation, and on the Condition and Conduct of the Bank of England and of the Country Issuers during the Year 1839*. Pelham Richardson, 1840. (Reprinted Loyd, *Tracts*.)

——. *Thoughts on the Separation of the Departments of the Bank of England*. Pelham Richardson, 1844. (Reprinted Capie, *History*; Loyd, *Tracts*.)

——. (Lord Overstone). *Tracts and Other Publications on Metallic and Paper Currency*. J. R. McCulloch, ed. Longman Brown, 1858.

Lucas, Robert E., Jr., and Sargent, Thomas J. "After Keynesian Macroeconomics," in Federal Reserve Bank of Boston, *After the Phillips Curve: Persistence of High Inflation and Unemployment*, 1978. (Reprinted Lucas and Sargent, eds., *Rational Expectations and Econometric Practice*. University of Minnesota Press, 1981.)

Macaulay, Thomas Babington. *The History of England from the Accession of James the Second*. Longman, Green, Longman, Roberts & Green, 1848, 1855.

MacLeod, H. D. *The Theory and Practice of Banking*, 4th ed. Longmans, Green, Reader & Dyer, 1883.

Maisel, Sherman J. *Managing the Dollar*. Norton, 1973.

Marshall, Alfred. *Principles of Economics*, 8th ed. Macmillan, 1920.

Marshall, John. *The Life of George Washington*. C. P. Wayne, 1807. (Reprinted Chelsea House, 1983.)

Matusow, Allen J. *Nixon's Economy: Booms, Busts, Dollars, and Votes*. University Press of Kansas, 1998.

Mayer, Thomas. "The Structure of Monetarism," in Mayer, ed., *Structure of Monetarism*. W.W. Norton, 1978.

McCallum, Bennett T. "Price Level Determinacy with an Interest Rate Policy Rule and Rational Expectations," *Journal of Monetary Economics*, November 1981, 319–29.

McCulloch, Hugh. *Men and Measures of Half a Century*. Charles Scribner's Sons, 1888.

McCulloch, J. R., ed. *A Select Collection of Scarce and Valuable Tracts and Other Publications on the National Debt and the Sinking Fund*. Lord Overstone, 1857. (Reprinted A. M. Kelley, 1966.)

——. *A Treatise on Metallic and Paper Money and Banks*, for *Encyclopaedia Britannica*, 8th ed. Adam and Charles Black, 1858.

——. *A Select Collection of Scarce and Valuable Tracts and Other Publications on Paper Currency and Banking*. Lord Overstone 1857. (Reprinted A. M. Kelley, 1966.)

McNeill, William H. *America, Britain, & Russia: Their Co-operation and Conflict, 1941–46*. Oxford University Press, 1953.

Meerman, Jacob P. "The Climax of the Bank War: Biddle's Contraction, 1833–34," *Journal of Political Economy*, August 1963, 378–88.

Melton, William C. *Inside the Fed: Making Monetary Policy*. Dow Jones-Irwin, 1985.

Meltzer, Allan H. "Commentary," in Federal Reserve Bank of Kansas City, *Changing Capital Markets: Implications for Monetary Policy*, 1993.

——. "Monetarism: The Issues and the Outcome," *Atlantic Economic Journal*, March 1998, 8–31.

——. *A History of the Federal Reserve, 1913–51*. University of Chicago Press, 2003.

Mikesell, Raymond F. "The Role of the International Monetary Agreements in a World of Planned Economies," *Journal of Political Economy*, December 1947, 497–512. (Reprinted Ellis and Metzler, *Readings in the Theory of International Trade*.)

——. *Foreign Exchange in the Postwar World*. Twentieth Century Fund, 1954.

Milesi-Ferreti, Gian M. "The Disadvantage of Tying Their Hands: On the Political Economy of Policy Commitments," *Economic Journal*, November 1995, 1381–402.

Mill, J. S. *Principles of Political Economy, with Some of Their Applications to Social Philosophy* (7 eds. 1848–71). W. J. Ashley, ed. Longmans, Green, 1909.

——. *Collected Works*. J. M. Robson, ed. University of Toronto Press, 1963.

Miller, Marion M., ed. *Great Debates in American History*. Current Literature, 1913.

Milward, Alan S. *The European Rescue of the Nation-State*. University of California Press, 1992.

Mints, Lloyd W. *A History of Banking Theory in Great Britain and the United States*. University of Chicago Press, 1945.

Miron, Jeffrey A. "Financial Panics, the Seasonality of the Nominal Interest Rate, and the Founding of the Fed," *American Economic Review*, March, 1986, 125–40.

Mishkin, Frederic S. and Posen, Adam S. "Inflation Targeting: Lessons from Four Countries," Federal Reserve Bank of New York *Economic Policy Review*, August 1997, 9–110.

Mitchell, B. R. *European Historical Statistics, 1750–1975*. Macmillan, 1980.

——. *British Historical Statistics*. Cambridge University Press, 1988.

Mitchell, Waldo F. *The Uses of Bank Funds*. University of Chicago Press, 1925.

Mitchell, Wesley C. *A History of the Greenbacks*. University of Chicago Press, 1903.

——. *Business Cycles and Their Causes*. University of California Press, 1913.

Moggridge, D. E. *The Return to Gold, 1925*. Cambridge University Press, 1969.

——. *British Monetary Policy, 1924–31: The Norman Conquest of $4.86*. Cambridge University Press, 1972.

Morawetz, Victor. *The Banking and Currency Problem in the United States*. North American Review Publishing Company, 1909.

Morgan, William. "On the Finances of the Bank," *Monthly Magazine and British Register*, October 1797, 248–51.

Morley, John. *The Life of William Ewart Gladstone*. Macmillan, 1903.

Mullineaux, Donald. "Competitive Monies and the Suffolk Bank System: A Contractual Perspective," *Southern Economic Journal*, April 1987, 884–98.

Mundell, Robert A. "Discussion," in Bordo and Eichengreen, eds., *Retrospective on Bretton Woods*.

Munn, Glenn G. and Garcia, F. L. *Encyclopedia of Banking and Finance*, 8th ed. Bankers Publishing Company, 1983.

Myers, Margaret G. *The New York Money Market: Origins and Development*. Columbia University Press, 1931.

——. *A Financial History of the United States*. Columbia University Press, 1970.

Neikirk, William R. *Volcker: Portrait of the Money Man*. Congdon and Weed, 1987.

Nettels, Curtin P. *The Emergence of a National Economy, 1775–1815*. Holt, Rinehart and Winston, 1962.

Nevin, Edward. *The Mechanism of Cheap Money: A Study of British Monetary Policy, 1931–39*. University of Wales Press, 1955.

Nixon, Richard M. *Memoirs*. Grosset & Dunlap, 1978.

North, Dudley. *Discourses upon Trade*. Thomas Basset, 1691.

Nurkse, Ragnar. *Conditions of International Monetary Equilibrium*. Princeton Essays in International Finance, Spring 1945. (Reprinted Ellis and Metzler, *Readings in the Theory of International Trade*.)

O'Brien, D. P., ed. *Foundations of Monetary Economics*. William Pickering, 1994.

Odell, John. *U.S. International Monetary Policy: Markets, Power and Ideas as Sources of Change*. Princeton University Press, 1982.

Ogg, David. *England in the Reigns of James II and William III*. Clarendon Press, 1955.

Ó Gráda, C. "Agricultural Decline, 1860–1914," in R. Floud and D. McCloskey, eds., *The Economic History of Britain since 1700*. Cambridge University Press, 1981.

Oliver, Michael. *Whatever Happened to Monetarism? Economic Policy-Making and Social Learning in the U.K. since 1979*. Ashgate, 1997.

Osborne, Dale K. "Ten Approaches to the Definition of Money." Federal Reserve Bank of Dallas *Economic Review*, March 1984, 1–23.

———. "What Is Money Today?," Federal Reserve Bank of Dallas *Economic Review*, January 1985, 1–15.

Page, William. *Commerce and Industry: A Historical Review of the Economic Condition of the British Empire from the Peace of Paris in 1815 to the Declaration of War in 1914 Based on the Parliamentary Debates*. Constable, 1919.

Palgrave, R. H. I. *Bank Rate and the Money Market in England, France, Germany, Holland, and Belgium, 1844–1900*. John Murray, 1903.

———. *The English Banking System* (National Monetary Commission). U.S. Government Printing Office, 1911.

Palmer, J. Horsley. *The Causes and Consequences of the Pressure upon the Money Market*. Pelham Richardson, 1837. (Reprinted Capie, *History*.)

Panić, M. *European Monetary Union: Lessons from the Gold Standard*. Macmillan, 1992.

Parker, C. S. *Sir Robert Peel from His Private Correspondence*. John Murray, 1891, 1899.

Peden, G. C. *British Economic and Social Policy: Lloyd George to Margaret Thatcher*. Philip Allan, 1985.

Pepys, Samuel. *Diary*. Robert Latham and William Matthews, eds. University of California Press, 1970–83.

Petty, William. *Quantulumcunque Concerning Money* (1682). Reprinted A. & J. Churchill, 1695. (Reprinted Charles Hull, ed. *Economic Writings*. A. M. Kelley, 1963.)

Phillips, A. W. "The Relation between Unemployment and the Rate of Change of Money Wage Rates in the United Kingdom, 1861–1957," *Economica*, November 1958, 283–99.

Phillips, Ronnie J. *The Chicago Plan and New Deal Banking Reform*. M. E. Sharpe, 1995.

Pierce, James L. "The Myth of Congressional Supervision of Monetary Policy," *Journal of Monetary Economics*, April 1978, 363–70.

Pigou, A. C. *Wealth and Welfare*. Macmillan, 1912.

———. *Industrial Fluctuations*. Macmillan, 1927.

Poole, William. "Optimal Choice of Monetary Policy Instruments in a Simple Stochastic Model," *Quarterly Journal of Economics*, May 1970, 1–20.

———. "Burnsian Monetary Policy," *Journal of Finance*, May 1979, 473–84.

Pressnell, L. S. "Gold Reserves, Banking Reserves, and the Baring Crisis of 1890," in Whittlesey, C. R. and Wilson, J. S. G., eds., *Essays in Money and Banking in Honour of R.S. Sayers*. Clarendon Press, 1968.

Price, Bonamy. *Chapters on Practical Political Economy*. Kegan Paul, 1878.

Redish, Angela. "Lender of Last Resort Policies: From Bagehot to Bailout," ms. University of British Columbia, 2001.

Redlich, Fritz. *The Molding of American Banking*. New Hafner, 1951.

Rees, Albert. "Patterns of Wages, Prices and Productivity," in Charles Myers, ed., *Wages, Prices, Profits and Productivity*. American Assembly, 1959.

Ricardo, David. *Works and Correspondence*. Piero Sraffa, ed. Cambridge University Press, 1951–73.

——. *The High Price of Bullion. A Proof of the Depreciation of Bank Notes*. John Murray, 1810; 4th ed., 1811. (*Works*, iii.)

——. *Proposals for an Economical and Secure Currency*, 2nd. ed. John Murray, 1816. (*Works*, iv.)

——. *The Principles of Political Economy and Taxation*, 3rd. ed. John Murray, 1821.

——. *Plan for the Establishment of a National Bank*. John Murray, 1824. (*Works*, iv.)

Ricardo, Samson. *Observations on the Recent Pamphlet of J. Horsley Palmer, Esq., on the Causes and Consequences of the Pressure on the Money Market*. C. Knight, 1837.

——. *A National Bank: The Remedy for the Evils Attendant upon Our Present System of Paper Currency*. Pelham Richardson, 1838. (Reprinted Capie, *History*.)

Richards, R. D. "The First Fifty Years of the Bank of England," in J. G. Van Dillen, ed., *History of the Principal Public Banks*. Martinus Nijhoff, 1934.

Riefler, Winfield W. *Money Rates and Money Markets in the United States*. Harper, 1930.

Robbins, Lionel. *The Great Depression*. Macmillan, 1934.

——. "Thoughts on the Crisis," *Lloyds Bank Review*, April 1958. (Reprinted Robbins, *Politics and Economics*. St. Martin's, 1963.)

Roberts, Richard and Kynaston, David, eds. *The Bank of England: Money, Power and Influence, 1694–1994*. Clarendon Press, 1995.

Robertson, D. H. *A Study of Industrial Fluctuation*. P. S. King, 1915.

Robertson, Ross M. *The Comptroller and Bank Supervision: A Historical Appraisal*. Comptroller of the Currency, 1968.

Robinson, Joan. "Beggar-My-Neighbour Remedies for Unemployment," *Essays in the Theory of Unemployment*. Macmillan, 1937.

Rockoff, Hugh. "Walter Bagehot and the Theory of Central Banking," in Capie and Wood, eds., *Financial Crises and the World Banking System*.

Rodgers, Peter. "The Bank of England Act," *Bank of England Quarterly Bulletin*, May 1998, 93–99.

Rogers, J. E. Thorold. *The First Nine Years of the Bank of England*. Clarendon Press, 1887.

Rolnick, Arthur J., Smith, Bruce D., and Weber, Warren E. "The Suffolk Bank and the Panic of 1837," *Federal Reserve Bank of Minneapolis Quarterly Review*, Spring 2000, 3–13.

Rose, Sanford. "The Agony of the Federal Reserve," *Fortune*, July 1974, 90–93, 180–90.

Ross, Duncan M., ed. *History of Banking*. Pickering & Chatto, 1998.

Rothbard, Murray N. *The Panic of 1819; Reactions and Policies*. Columbia University Press, 1962.

Sack, Brian and Wieland, Volcker. "Interest-Rate Smoothing and Optimal Monetary Policy: A Review of Recent Empirical Evidence," Federal Reserve Board Working Paper, August 1999.

Safire, William. *Before the Fall. An Inside View of the Pre-Watergate White House*. Doubleday, 1975.

Sampson, Anthony. *Anatomy of Britain*. Hodder & Stoughton, 1961.

Sargent, Thomas J. and Wallace, Neil. "'Rational' Expectations, the Optimal Monetary Instrument and the Optimal Money Supply Rule," *Journal of Political Economy*, April 1975, 241–54.

Saul, S. B. *The Myth of the Great Depression, 1873–1896*. Macmillan, 1969.

Sayers, R. S. *Bank of England Operations, 1890–1914*. P. S. King & Son, 1936.

——. "The Development of Central Banking after Bagehot," *Economic History Review*, No. 2, 1951, 109–116. (Reprinted Sayers, *Central Banking after Bagehot*.)

——. "Ricardo's Views on Monetary Questions," *Quarterly Journal of Economics*, February 1953, 30–49. (Reprinted Ashton and Sayers, *Papers*.)

——. "The Determination of the Volume of Bank Deposits: England 1955–56," *Quarterly Review of the Banca Nazionale del Lavore*, December 1955, 179–88.

——. *Financial Policy, 1939–45*. Longmans, Green, 1956.

——. *Central Banking after Bagehot*. Clarendon Press, 1957.

——. *The Bank of England, 1891–1944*. Cambridge University Press, 1976.

Schuettinger, Robert L. and Butler, Eamonn F. *Forty Centuries of Wage and Price Controls*. Heritage Foundation, 1979.

Schumpeter, J. A. *History of Economic Analysis*. Oxford University Press, 1954.

Schwartz, Anna J. "Why Financial Stability Depends on Price Stability," *Economic Affairs*, Autumn 1995, 21–25.

Seldon, Anthony. *Churchill's Indian Summer: The Conservative Government, 1951–55*. Hodder and Stoughton, 1981.

Senior, Nassau W. "On the Quantity and Value of Money," in *Three Lectures on the Value of Money*, B. Fellowes, 1840. (Reprinted Senior, *Selected Writings*. A. M. Kelley, 1966.)

Shaw, William A. "The 'Treasury Order Book'," *Economic Journal*, March 1906, 33–40.

Shonfield, Andrew. *British Economic Policy since the War*. Penguin, 1958.

Simons, Henry. "Rules versus Authorities in Monetary Policy," *Journal of Political Economy*, February 1936, 1–30.

Skidelsky, Robert. *Politicians and the Slump: The Labour Government of 1929–31*. Macmillan, 1967.

——. *John Maynard Keynes*. Macmillan, 1983, 1992, 2000.

Smith, Adam. *An Inquiry into the Nature and Causes of the Wealth of Nations.* Strahan and Cadell, 1776. (Reprinted Random House, 1937.)

Smith, Walter B. *Economic Aspects of the Second Bank of the United States.* Harvard University Press, 1953.

Smith, Warren L. "Are There Enough Policy Tools?," *American Economic Review*, May 1965, 208–220.

Smithies, Arthur. "Forecasting Postwar Demand: I," *Econometrica* 13, January 1945, 1–14.

Sorensen, Theodore C. *Kennedy.* Harper & Row, 1965.

Spiegel, Mark M. "Central Bank Independence and Inflation Expectations: Evidence from British Index-Linked Gilts," Federal Reserve Bank of San Francisco *Economic Review*, No. 1, 1998, 3–13.

Sprague, O. M. W. *History of Crises under the National Banking System* (National Monetary Commission). U.S. Government Printing Office, 1910.

Sproul, Allan. *Selected Papers.* L. S. Ritter, ed. Federal Reserve Bank of New York, 1980.

Sraffa, Piero. "The Ingenious Calculator," in *Ricardo, Writings*, iv, 415–18.

——. "Mr.——of the Bullion Report," in *Ricardo, Writings*, iii, 428–34.

Stein, Herbert. *The Fiscal Revolution in America.* University of Chicago Press, 1969.

——. *Presidential Economics*, 3rd. ed. American Enterprise Institute, 1994.

Stettinius, Edward R., Jr. *Lend-Lease: Weapon for Victory.* Macmillan, 1944.

Strong, Benjamin. *Interpretations of Federal Reserve Policy.* W. R. Burgess, ed. Harper & Row, 1930.

Svensson, Lars E. O. "What Is Wrong with Taylor Rules? Using Judgment in Monetary Policy through Targeting Rules," *Journal of Economic Literature*, June 2003, 426–77.

Taus, Esther R. *Central Banking Functions of the U.S. Treasury, 1789–1941.* Columbia University Press, 1943.

Taylor, John B. "Discretion versus Policy Rules in Practice," in Allen Meltzer and Charles Plosser, eds., *Carnegie-Rochester Conference Series on Public Policy* 39. North-Holland, 1993, 195–214.

Temin, Peter. *The Jacksonian Economy.* Norton, 1969.

——. *Did Monetary Forces Cause the Great Depression?* Norton, 1976.

Thatcher, Margaret. *The Downing Street Years.* Harper Collins, 1993.

Theil, Henri. "On the Theory of Economic Policy," *American Economic Review*, May 1956, 360–66.

Thomas, S. Evelyn. *The Rise and Growth of Joint Stock Banking.* Pitman, 1934.

Thornton, Daniel L. and Wheelock, David C. "A History of the Asymmetric Policy Directive," Federal Reserve Bank of St. Louis *Review*, September 2000, 1–16.

Thornton, Henry. *An Enquiry into the Nature and Effects of the Paper Credit of Great Britain.* Hatchard, 1802. (Edited with Introduction by F. A. Hayek and selected evidence and speeches. George Allen & Unwin, 1939.)

Thorp, Willard L. *Business Annals.* National Bureau of Economic Research, 1926.

Timberlake, Richard H. "The Central Banking Role of Clearinghouse Associations," *Journal of Money, Credit and Banking*, February 1984, 1–15.

——. *Monetary Policy in the United States: An Intellectual and Institutional History*. University of Chicago Press, 1993.

Tinbergen, Jan. *On the Theory of Economic Policy*. North-Holland, 1952.

Tobin, James. "Defense, Dollars, and Doctrine," *Yale Review*, March 1958, 321–34 (Reprinted Tobin. *National Economic Policy: Essays*. Yale University Press, 1966.)

Tooke, Thomas. *Thoughts and Details of the High and Low Prices of the Last Thirty Years*. John Murray, 1823.

——. *A Letter to Lord Grenville on the Effects Ascribed to the Resumption of Cash Payments on the Value of the Currency*. John Murray, 1829.

——. *An Inquiry into the Currency Principle: The Connection of the Currency with Prices, and the Expediency of a Separation of Issue from Banking*. Longman, Brown, Green, and Longmans, 1844.

——. *A History of Prices and of the State of the Circulation from 1793 to 1837*, 2 vols. Longman, Orme, Brown, Green and Longmans, 1838. Vols. 3 and 4, 1840 and 1848; with William Newmarch, vol. 5–6, 1857.

Triffin, Robert. *Gold and the Dollar Crisis*. Yale University Press, 1960.

——. *Our International Monetary System: Yesterday, Today and Tomorrow*. Random House, 1968.

Truman, Harry S. *Memoirs*. Doubleday, 1955.

Unger, Irwin. "Business Men and Specie Resumption," *Political Science Quarterly*, March 1959, 46–70.

——. *The Greenback Era: A Social and Political History of American Finance, 1865–79*. Princeton University Press, 1964.

U.S. Congress. *To Inspect the Books of the Bank of the United States to Report Whether Its Charter Has Been Violated*. House Report 460, 22nd Congr., 1st sess. April 1832.

——. *Speech by Daniel Webster on the Independent Treasury Bill*. 25th Congr., 2nd sess., appendix to *Congressional Globe*, March 12, 1838, 632–41.

——. *Report on the Introduction of the Gold-Exchange Standard into China and Other Silver-Using Countries*, Hugh Hanna, Charles Conant, and Jeremiah Jenks. House doc. 144, 58th Congr., 2nd sess., October 1903.

——. *Hearings on Banking and Currency Plans*. House Banking and Currency Committee, 62nd Congr., 3rd sess., January 1913.

——. *Senate Majority Report on the Federal Reserve Bill*. Senate report 133, 63rd Congr., 1st sess., November 22, 1913, 6002–9.

——. *Agricultural Inquiry*. Hearings before the Joint Commission of Agricultural Inquiry, 67th Congr., 1st sess., 1922.

——. *Federal Reserve Board Conference*. Senate doc. 310, 67th Congr., 4th sess., February 1923.

——. *Stabilization*. Hearing before the House Committee on Banking and Currency (Strong bill), 69th Congr., 1st sess., March–April 1926, and 70th Congr., 1st sess., March–April 1928.

——. *Operation of the National and Federal Reserve Banking Systems*. Senate Committee on Banking and Currency, 71st Congr., 1st sess., 1931.

——. *Stabilization of Commodity Prices*. Hearings before the Subcommittee of the House Committee on Banking and Currency (Goldsborough committee) on H. R. 10517. *For Increasing and Stabilizing the Price Level and for Other Purposes*, 72nd Congr., 1st sess, March 1932.

——. *Banking Act of 1935. Hearings*, House Banking and Currency Committee, 74th Congr., 1st sess., March 1935.

——. *Hearings on Extension of Reciprocal Trade Agreements Act*, House Committee on Ways and Means, 76th Congr., 1st sess., 1940.

——. *Report*. Joint Committee on the Economic Report. Subcommittee on Monetary, Credit and Financial Policies, 81st Congr., 2nd sess., 1950.

——. *Nomination of William McChesney Martin, Jr.*, Senate. Hearings. 82nd Congr., 1st sess., 1951.

——. *United States Monetary Policy. Recent Thinking and Experience*. Hearings before the Subcommittee on Economic Stabilization of the Joint Committee on the Economic Report (Flanders Committee), 83rd Congr., 2nd sess., December 1954.

——. *Nomination of Wm. McC. Martin, Jr.* Hearings, Senate Banking Committee, 84th Congr., 2nd sess., 1956.

——. *January 1957 Economic Report of the President*. Hearings, Joint Economic Committee, 85th Congr., 1st sess., 1957.

——. *Public Debt Ceiling and Interest Rate Ceiling on Bonds*. Hearings, House Committee on Ways and Means, 86th Congr., 2nd sess., 1960.

——. *The Federal Reserve after Fifty Years*. Hearings, Subcommittee on Domestic Finance of the House Committee on Banking and Currency, 88th Congr., 2nd sess., 1964.

——. *The 1971 Midyear Review of the Economy*. Hearings, Joint Economic Committee, 92nd Congr., 1st sess., 1971.

——. *The 1973 Economic Report of the President*. Hearings, Joint Economic Committee, 93rd Congr., 1st sess., 1973.

——. *Hearings on Price Stabilization Goal*. Subcommittee on Domestic Monetary Policy of the House Committee on Banking, Finance and Urban Affairs, 101st Congr., 2nd sess., February 1990.

U.S. Department of Commerce, Bureau of the Census. *Historical Statistics of the United States: Colonial Times to 1970*. U.S. Government Printing Office, 1975.

U.S. Department of Commerce, Bureau of Economic Analysis. *Long-Term Economic Growth, 1860–1970*. U.S. Government Printing Office, 1973.

——. *Business Statistics, 1963–91*. U. S. Government Printing Office, 1992.

Viner, Jacob. *Studies in the Theory of International Trade*. George Allen & Unwin, 1937.

——. "Views," in M. Shields, ed., *International Financial Stabilization: A Symposium*. Irving Trust, 1944.

Volcker, Paul A. "Discussion," in Capie, ed., *Future of Central Banking*.

Volcker, Paul A. and Gyohten, Toyoo. *Changing Fortunes*. Times Books, 1992.

Walsh, Carl. *Monetary Theory and Policy*. MIT Press, 1998.

Walters, Raymond. "The Origins of the Second Bank of the United States," *Journal of Political Economy*, June 1945, 115–31.

Warburg, Paul M. *The Federal Reserve System: Its Origin and Growth*. Macmillan, 1930.

Wechsberg, Joseph. *The Merchant Bankers*. Little, Brown, 1966.

Weintraub, Sidney. "'Monetary Policy': A Comment," *Review of Economics & Statistics*, May 1955, 292–96.

Wells, Wyatt C. *Economist in an Uncertain World: Arthur F. Burns and the Federal Reserve, 1970–78*. Columbia University Press, 1994.

West, Robert C. *Banking Reform and the Federal Reserve, 1863–1923*. Cornell University Press, 1977.

Whale, P. Barrett. "A Retrospective View of the Bank Charter Act of 1844," *Economica*, August 1944, 109–111.

Wheatley, John. *Remarks on Currency and Commerce*. Cadell and Davies, Publish 1803. (Reprinted *History of British Economic Thought*, 1st Series, 19th century Works. Thoemmes, 1991.)

Wheelock, David C. *The Strategy and Consistency of Federal Reserve Monetary Policy, 1924–1933*. Cambridge University Press, 1991.

——. "Monetary Policy in the Great Depression: What the Fed Did, and Why," Federal Reserve Bank of St. Louis *Review*, March/April 1992, 3–28.

White, Lawrence H. *Free Banking in Britain: Theory, Experience, and Debate, 1800–1845*. Cambridge University Press, 1984.

——. ed. *Free Banking*. Edward Elgar, 1993.

Wicker, Elmus. *Federal Reserve Monetary Policy, 1917–33*. Random House, 1966.

——. "Brunner and Meltzer on Federal Reserve Monetary Policy during the Great Depression," *Canadian Journal of Economics*, May 1969, 318–21.

——. "The World War II Policy of Fixing a Pattern of Interest Rates," *Journal of Finance*, June 1969, 447–58.

——. *Banking Panics of the Great Depression*. Cambridge University Press, 1996.

——. *Banking Panics of the Gilded Age*. Cambridge University Press, 2000.

Wicksell, Knut. *Interest and Prices* (1898). Trans. from German by R. F. Kahn for the Royal Economic Society, 1936.

Wilberforce, R. I. and Wilberforce, S. *The Life of William Wilberforce*. J. Murray, 1838.

Wiles, Peter. "Cost Inflation and the State of Economic Theory," *Economic Journal*, June 1973, 377–98.

Williams, John H. *Postwar Monetary Plans and Other Essays*. Alfred Knopf, 1944.

Willis, H. Parker. *The Federal Reserve System*. Ronald Press, 1923.

Wilson, Harold. *A Personal Record: The Labour Government, 1964–70*. Weidenfeld and Nicolson, 1971.

Wilson, J. S. G. "The Rise of Central Banking in India," in R. S. Sayers, ed., *Banking in the British Commonwealth*. Clarendon Press, 1952.

Wilson, Woodrow. *Congressional Government: A Study in American Politics*. Houghton Mifflin, 1885.

——. *Papers*. Arthur S. Link, ed. Princeton University Press, 1966–94.

Wood, Elmer. *English Theories of Central Banking Control, 1819–58*. Harvard University Press, 1939.

Wood, John H. "The Expectations Hypothesis, the Yield Curve, and Monetary Policy," *Quarterly Journal of Economics*, August 1964, 457–70.

——. "A Model of Federal Reserve Behavior," in George Horwich, ed., *Monetary Process and Policy*. Irwin, 1967.

———. "Bagehot's Lender of Last Resort: A Hollow Hallowed Tradition," *Independent Review*, Winter 2003, 343–51.

Wood, John H. and Wood, Norma L. *Financial Markets*. Harcourt Brace Jovanovich, 1985.

Woodford, Michael. *Interest and Prices*. Princeton University Press, 2003.

Woodward, Llewellyn. *The Age of Reform, 1815–70*. Clarendon Press, 1962.

Yonge, Charles D. *The Life and Administration of Robert Banks Jenkinson, Second Earl of Liverpool*. Macmillan, 1868.

Youngdahl, C. Richard. "Open-Market Operations," in Herbert V. Prochnow, ed., *The Federal Reserve System*. Harper & Brothers, 1960.

Zweig, Stefan. *Die Welt von Gestern*. Bermann-Fischer Verlag, 1944.

Index

425